THE JOHN GOULD FLETCHER SERIES

Lucas Carpenter, General Editor
Volume VII

SELECTED LETTERS OF JOHN GOULD FLETCHER

Edited by Leighton Rudolph,
Lucas Carpenter, and Ethel C. Simpson

The University of Arkansas Press
Fayetteville   1996

Copyright 1996 by Leighton Rudolph, Lucas Carpenter, and Ethel C. Simpson

All rights reserved
Manufactured in the United States of America

00 99 98 97 96   5 4 3 2 1

Designed by Ellen Beeler

♾ The paper used in this publication meets the minimum requirements of the American National Standard for Permanence of Paper for Printed Library Materials Z39.48-1984.

Library of Congress Cataloging-in-Publication Data

Fletcher, John Gould, 1886–1950.
    [Letters. Selections]
    Selected letters of John Gould Fletcher / edited by Leighton Rudolph, Lucas Carpenter, and Ethel C. Simpson.
        p. cm. — (John Gould Fletcher series ; v. 7)
    Includes index.
    ISBN 1-55728-329-X (c : alk. paper)
    1. Fletcher, John Gould, 1886–1950—Correspondence. 2. Poets, American—20th century—Correspondence. I. Rudolph, Leighton. II. Carpenter, Lucas. III. Simpson, Ethel C., 1937– . IV. Title. V. Series.
PS3511.L457Z48   1996
811'.52—dc20
[B]
                                                      95-39410
                                                        CIP

For Charlie May

ACKNOWLEDGMENTS

The permission to print these letters has been given by William Terry, the literary executor of the Fletcher estate, which holds title to the literary property in the correspondence. The support of the University of Arkansas Press and its director, Miller Williams, has done American literature a great service by publishing the John Gould Fletcher Series, a means whereby the most important works of Fletcher will again be available to students of American literature.

I appreciate the way my endless questions about Fletcher, his life, and his poetry have been answered with never failing courtesy and patience. Especially helpful, among my friends on the faculty and staff of the English department of the University of Arkansas, have been Charles Adams, Chad Andrews, Rhonda Benish, Robert Cochran, Keneth Kinnamon, Lyna Lee Montgomery, Peggy Moore, William A. Quinn, Nancy Saunders, Leo Van Scyoc, and Bryan Wilkie. Professional competence and patient good humor characterized the members of the staff of Mullins Library, particularly John Harrison, director of libraries, and Michael Dabrishus, head of the Special Collections; and equally understanding were Donald Batson, Andrea Cantrell, Stephen Chism, Mariah E. Juhl, Cassandra McCraw, Ellen C. Shipley, and Anthony E. Wappel. Harmon L. Remmel, a native of Little Rock but long a resident of Fayetteville, who knew the ramifications of the Fletcher family, was of great assistance in identifying friends and acquaintances of the poet.

There were several thousand of his letters in the Fletcher papers acquired by Special Collections of David Mullins Library the year after his death. Later Charlie May Fletcher, his widow, and a graduate student spent a year organizing the papers and collecting Fletcher's letters from those correspondents willing to part with them, and copies of letters or facsimiles from those who wished to retain them. As a result, there are in this collection Fletcher's own letters, typed or facsimile copies from owners, and miscellaneous letters. Although the literary executor of Fletcher's estate, which owns the literary property involved, has granted the University of Arkansas Press permission to publish his letters, an attempt has been made to secure the permission of the present owners of the letters where possible. Therefore we gratefully acknowledge the further permission to publish their holdings from the following libraries:

Brooks, Van Wyck
    Van Wyck Brooks Papers
    Special Collections
    Van Pelt Library
    University of Pennsylvania

Damon, Samuel Foster
    John Hay Library
    Brown University Library
    Providence, Rhode Island

Eliot, T. S.
    By permission of the Houghton Library, Harvard University

Fletcher, Daisy Arbuthnot
    Harry Ransom Humanities Research Center
    University of Texas at Austin

Gregory, Horace
    Horace Gregory Papers, George Arents Resource Library for Special Collections at Syracuse University

Haun, Frederic Eugene
    Haun Fletcher Collection in Special Collections at the University of Arkansas (not a part of the John Gould Fletcher Papers)

Hughes, Glenn
    Harry Ransom Humanities Research Center
    University of Texas at Austin

Lowell, Amy
    By permission of the Houghton Library, Harvard University

Miner, Earl
    Letter of October 4, 1994, on deposit in the Department of Special Collections in the Research Library of UCLA

Monroe, Harriet
    Joseph Regenstein Library
    Manuscripts and Archives
    University of Chicago

Mumford, Lewis
    Lewis Mumford Papers
    Special Collections

Van Pelt Library
University of Pennsylvania

Schevill, James
Personal letter of October 21, 1994

Teasdale, Sara
By permission of the Houghton Library, Harvard University

—L. R.

CONTENTS

General Editor's Preface   xv
Preface   xvii
Introduction   xix
Chronology   xxiii

LETTERS

TO HARRIET MONROE 2 AUG. 1913	1
TO AMY LOWELL 7 SEPT. 1913	2
TO AMY LOWELL 25 OCT. 1913	5
TO AMY LOWELL ? DEC. 1913	7
TO HARRIET MONROE 23 JAN. 1914	9
TO AMY LOWELL 7 APR. 1914	10
TO AMY LOWELL 16 APR. 1914	12
TO AMY LOWELL 29 OCT. 1914	14
TO DAISY FLETCHER 28 NOV. 1914	15
TO AMY LOWELL 16 DEC. 1914	17
TO AMY LOWELL 22 DEC. 1914	18
TO DAISY FLETCHER 4 JAN. 1915	20
TO AMY LOWELL 29 JAN. 1915	23
TO HARRIET MONROE 3 JUNE 1915	24
TO DAISY FLETCHER 4 JUNE 1915	26
TO AMY LOWELL 20 SEPT. 1915	28
TO AMY LOWELL 27 SEPT. 1915	30
TO AMY LOWELL 15 OCT. 1915	32
TO DAISY FLETCHER 17 JAN. 1916	33
TO HARRIET MONROE 28 JAN. 1916	37
TO AMY LOWELL 11 JUNE 1916	40
TO AMY LOWELL 28 JUNE 1916	42
TO AMY LOWELL 16 JULY 1916	44
TO AMY LOWELL 25 SEPT. 1916	48
TO AMY LOWELL 21 OCT. 1916	49
TO HARRIET MONROE 25 OCT. 1916	52
TO CONRAD AIKEN 1 NOV. 1916	55
TO CONRAD AIKEN 25 APR. 1917	58

TO ROBERT LINSCOTT 27 MAY 1917	60
TO CONRAD AIKEN 4 JULY 1917	62
TO CONRAD AIKEN 31 JAN. 1918	64
TO ROBERT LINSCOTT 2 APR. 1918	66
TO ROBERT LINSCOTT 11 MAY 1918	69
TO JOHN COURNOS 6 JULY 1918	71
TO HARRIET MONROE 27 SEPT. 1918	72
TO ROBERT LINSCOTT 22 OCT. 1918	74
TO ROBERT LINSCOTT 28 DEC. 1918	76
TO HARRIET MONROE 17 MAR. 1919	78
TO ROBERT LINSCOTT 2 OCT. 1919	78
TO CONRAD AIKEN 29 APR. 1920	81
TO T. S. ELIOT 16 SEPT. 1920	83
TO FRANK STEWART FLINT 23 NOV. 1920	84
TO VAN WYCK BROOKS 1 MAR. 1921	86
TO SARA TEASDALE 21 JULY 1921	86
TO JOHN COURNOS 25 SEPT. 1921	88
TO ROBERT LINSCOTT 25 DEC. 1922	90
TO CONRAD AIKEN 12 JULY 1923	92
TO VAN WYCK BROOKS 21 MAR. 1924	93
TO HARRIET MONROE 13 DEC. 1926	95
TO DONALD DAVIDSON 26 JUNE 1927	96
TO LEWIS MUMFORD 2 OCT. 1927	98
TO DONALD DAVIDSON 24 OCT. 1927	99
TO LEWIS MUMFORD 18 NOV. 1927	100
TO T. S. ELIOT 19 NOV. 1927	103
TO DONALD DAVIDSON 28 FEB. 1928	104
TO T. S. ELIOT 3 MAR. 1928	105
TO HAVELOCK ELLIS 18 AUG. 1928	105
TO GLENN HUGHES 27 SEPT. 1928	107
TO GLENN HUGHES 5 OCT. 1928	108
TO HENRY BERGEN 11 DEC. 1928	110
TO HENRY BERGEN 27 FEB. 1929	111
TO S. FOSTER DAMON 1 MAY 1929	112
TO T. S. ELIOT 11 OCT. 1929	114
TO T. S. ELIOT 13 DEC. 1929	116
TO LEWIS MUMFORD 18 JULY 1930	116
TO DONALD DAVIDSON 20 NOV. 1930	118
TO HENRY BERGEN 18 APR. 1931	120

TO CONRAD AIKEN 17 JUNE 1931	121
TO CONRAD AIKEN 26 DEC. 1931	122
TO CONRAD AIKEN 5 JAN. 1932	123
TO CONRAD AIKEN 24 FEB. 1932	125
TO CONRAD AIKEN 20 MAR. 1932	125
TO ADOLPHINE TERRY 21 MAR. 1932	126
TO CONRAD AIKEN ? DEC. 1932	128
TO HENRY BERGEN 9 MAY 1933	133
TO FRANK OWSLEY 18 JUNE 1933	135
TO LEWIS MUMFORD 5 JULY 1933	136
TO DONALD DAVIDSON 27 JULY 1933	139
TO LEWIS MUMFORD 19 AUG. 1933	140
TO HENRY BERGEN 4 NOV. 1933	142
TO HENRY BERGEN 15 NOV. 1933	144
TO THE EDITORS OF *THE NATION* ? DEC. 1933 ERNEST GRUENING, FREDA KIRCHWEY, JOSEPH WOOD KRUTCH	147
TO FRANK OWSLEY 1 DEC. 1933	149
TO HENRY BERGEN 11 DEC. 1933	151
TO FRANK OWSLEY 12 DEC. 1933	154
TO HENRY BERGEN 6 JAN. 1934	155
TO HENRY BERGEN 9 JAN. 1934	158
TO HENRY BERGEN 6 MAR. 1934	161
TO LEWIS MUMFORD 9 MAY 1934	164
TO HENRY BERGEN 13 JULY 1934	166
TO HENRY BERGEN 29 AUG. 1934	168
TO HENRY BERGEN 19 NOV. 1934	170
TO HENRY SEIDEL CANBY 12 DEC. 1934	172
TO VAN WYCK BROOKS 28 FEB. 1935	174
TO FRANK OWSLEY 2 MAR. 1935	176
TO FRANK OWSLEY 11 MAR. 1935	177
TO LOUIS UNTERMEYER 17 JUNE 1935	178
TO VAN WYCK BROOKS 2 AUG. 1935	179
TO CONRAD AIKEN 6 OCT. 1935	180
TO CONRAD AIKEN 2 APR. 1936	182
TO CONRAD AIKEN 4 APR. 1936	183
TO CONRAD AIKEN 15 MAY 1936	184
TO DONALD DAVIDSON 5 NOV. 1937	185
TO DONALD DAVIDSON 17 DEC. 1937	186

TO HENRY SEIDEL CANBY ? JAN. 1938	188
TO DONALD DAVIDSON 28 JAN. 1938	189
TO THOMAS MATTHEWS PEARCE 7 JUNE 1939	191
TO HORACE GREGORY 27 FEB. 1941	192
TO EDWIN JOHN STRINGHAM 28 NOV. 1941	194
TO GERALD SANDERS 2 FEB. 1942	195
TO GERALD SANDERS 23 OCT. 1942	198
TO JAMES FRANKLIN LEWIS 29 MAR. 1943	200
TO GERALD SANDERS 16 APR. 1943	204
TO JAMES FRANKLIN LEWIS 14 MAY 1943	205
TO FREDERIC EUGENE HAUN 20 NOV. 1943	208
TO SCOTT GREER 17 JAN. 1944	209
TO JAMES FRANKLIN LEWIS 26 APR. 1944	211
TO FREDERIC EUGENE HAUN 18 JAN. 1945	214
TO SCOTT GREER 5 MAR. 1945	216
TO SCOTT GREER 20 AUG. 1945	218
TO SCOTT GREER 11 JAN. 1946	221
TO CONRAD AIKEN 29 JAN. 1946	225
TO FREDERIC EUGENE HAUN 3 APR. 1946	227
TO RAYMOND AND SARA HENDERSON HAY HOLDEN 2 JAN. 1947	229
TO CONRAD AIKEN 3 FEB. 1947	230
TO JAMES SCHEVILL 13 FEB. 1947	232
TO SCOTT GREER 14 MAR. 1947	233
TO JAMES SCHEVILL 13 OCT. 1947	235
TO KARL SHAPIRO 10 NOV. 1948	237
TO ROBERT W. STALLMAN 4 APR. 1949	239
TO SCOTT GREER 26 APR. 1949	240
TO CHARLIE MAY FLETCHER 29 MAY 1949	242
TO KARL SHAPIRO 17 AUG. 1949	246
TO CONRAD AIKEN 23 AUG. 1949	248
TO EARL MINER 27 JAN. 1950	250
TO EARL MINER 24 FEB. 1950	251
CHARLIE MAY FLETCHER TO JERRY WALLACE 17 MAY 1950	252
Correspondents	255
People Mentioned	261
Index	273

GENERAL EDITOR'S PREFACE

John Gould Fletcher was a prolific correspondent who wrote hundreds of letters during the course of his life. These expressed his ideas and beliefs concerning a remarkably broad range of subjects, among them art, literature, music, religion, politics, economics, and philosophy. Fletcher numbered among his correspondents such literary luminaries as Harriet Monroe, T. S. Eliot, Amy Lowell, Conrad Aiken, H. D., John Crowe Ransom, Allen Tate, and Donald Davidson.

Because he was a prominent participant in both the Imagist and Fugitive-Agrarian groups, Fletcher's letters offer much insight into the many crosscurrents and personalities that characterize the Modernist movement. For example, we find Fletcher writing to Harriet Monroe, recommending that she publish a new poem, "The Love Song of J. Alfred Prufrock," by a then little-known T. S. Eliot. We also see firsthand his reasoning in advising Amy Lowell to split with Ezra Pound and found her own "Amygist" group and his suggestions to Donald Davidson on what course of political action should be pursued by the Agrarians in the face of vigorous opposition to the beliefs expressed in their controversial manifesto *I'll Take My Stand*, to which Fletcher had contributed the chapter on education.

On a more personal note, we find letters to his first wife, Daisy Arbuthnot, chronicling the course of their tempestuous relationship, and other letters, mainly to Conrad Aiken, detailing Fletcher's lifelong struggle with severe depression and the circumstances of his several critical mental breakdowns. In addition, there are many letters included here that shed light on the composition of Fletcher's own works and on his influential theories of poetry and poetics.

Editor Leighton Rudolph's selections are astute, and his introduction provides a valuable overview of Fletcher's life. As the first collection of Fletcher's correspondence ever to appear in print, *Selected Letters of John Gould Fletcher* is a highly significant contribution to literary history and scholarship.

Lucas Carpenter

PREFACE

As Fletcher usually expressed his ideas in essays or in long review-articles, his letters are a distinctly less important medium of expression. His habit of sitting down after dinner and spending the evening dashing off hasty notes created a large number of missives but most of little literary interest. Moreover, his inability to type and his lack of carefully planned writing meant that he kept no carbon copies, and very few drafts of his letters. Mostly he mailed a hasty scrawl designed to ask a question or give a brief answer, and only rarely did he discuss poetic theory, as in the letters to Amy Lowell and Harriet Monroe, or political ideas, as in the long treatises to Henry Bergen. Usually Fletcher said less in a letter than Ezra Pound typed on a postcard.

Since he could not type, although he frequently excused writing in longhand by saying his typewriter was being repaired, he kept no copies of his letters and at times forgot what he had written earlier. He scribbled rapidly in a sprawling hand on his own stationery, that from a hotel, or whatever, with underlining, interlinear corrections, and multiple exclamation marks. He was not given to pictorial illustrations or diagrams. At some times, on certain formal occasions, such as his letter to Ada Russell offering his sympathy after the death of Amy Lowell, his letter could be a textbook model of penmanship and form—unfortunately a rare occurrence.

In his hasty composition Fletcher usually ignored the inside address and often the date, although at times he wished to call attention to a religious or political event. His greetings were usually stiff—it usually required several years for him to drop a formal address for a Christian name, and he never fell to the informality of addressing Pound as Ez or T. S. Eliot as Possum. His greetings were as starched as his collars. The body of his letters was usually brief and to the point: I want to organize a boycott of *The Southern Review;* how can we organize a folklore society; or, you need to make certain changes in your last poem. There was a high seriousness at all times: his calling Amy Lowell his fairy princess could not have been tongue-in-cheek; and the scatology of Eliot's Bolo poems or Aiken's exercise in broad humor left him, like Queen Victoria, not amused. Restraints of language were ingrained. When discussing *Lady Chatterley's Lover* he said that he knew and appreciated the use of four-letter Anglo-Saxon words—but he didn't use them. And on the rare occasions in which he ventured to insert a *damn*, one is reminded of Sir Joseph Porter in *H. M. S. Pinafore*. His self-imposed limitation on subject matter may seem prim if not prudish, but Fletcher was too serious about his poetry to treat his language with less than proper respect. The complimentary close he solved usually by omitting it entirely except in his very formal efforts. His signature ranged from Don (his family's pet name) to John to John Gould Fletcher to his initials—with no perceptible degree of familiarity governing his choice. Most amazing were postscripts, some longer than the body of the letter, and often more than one. If he had no space for a postscript at the end of the letter, it might be wedged at the top of the first page or between the salutation and the body of the letter. The signs of hasty composition were probably the outstanding characterization of most of his letters.

The text of the letters represents an attempt to present Fletcher's work without improvement but at the same time unadorned by a spattering of *sics*. Obvious errors in spelling have been regularized without comment, and English forms (*-our*, etc.) have been Americanized. Interlinear corrections have been placed in the text as representing a final intention. Underlinings, which in the letters may run to five or six, have been changed to italics for indication of emphasis. Fletcher's use of the acute accent is very rare, although consistent in *Santa Fé* and *Benét;* the grave, cedilla, and tilde he almost never bothered to use. Long familiarity with Fletcher's often difficult script leaves any claim to perfect transcription open to a charge of hubris, although it is certainly safe to claim that there are fewer errors in the readings than there might have been.

Annotations, which too often are a mere parade of an editorial fondness for trivia, have been held to a minimum. In recent editions of the letters of some of Fletcher's contemporaries, the reader is solemnly informed that Chaucer, Shakespeare, and Milton are English poets; Washington, Jefferson, and Lincoln were American presidents; and Robert Penn Warren was called "Red" by his intimates because he had red hair. The appended index of names is intended to supply any necessary information on people, and other necessary information has been supplied after the text of the individual letters. In those cases in which Fletcher had some particular association or connection with a major figure, that fact is mentioned in the appendix.

Leighton Rudolph

INTRODUCTION

Any selection of Fletcher's letters presents the usual problems for an editor who must submit his volume to severe limitations of space and to a particular focus on subject. In the present case the thousands of letters surviving in dozens of repositories were screened down to some 1,800 and then reduced painfully to a mere 658. The general editor, finding nothing mere in that number, with an inexorable eye for editorial triage, reduced the number first to 199 and then finally to 137. Although the letters printed herein place Fletcher in the context of the poetry of his day, many aspects of his life are ignored—his often acerbic relations with his sisters and his mother, his interest in folklore and a folk opera to be written with Lawrence Powell, his efforts to secure murals for the state capitol, his attempts to help found a symphony—but the list is endless.

The Fletchers all seem to have the characteristics of pack rats, for the number of letters, cards, and miscellaneous papers retained is astounding. The juvenilia are just that and can be omitted without loss, although much of the adult Fletcher is evident in his adolescent notes. From his childhood no single letter has been printed, nor have any of the love letters to Lois (or Louise, Fletcher seems to use both) Rogers, who married Lyman Willett Rogers, his best friend and classmate at Harvard. The first major section of the correspondence is composed of letters to his mother and sisters, Adolphine Fletcher Terry and Mary Fletcher Drennan, after the death of the husband and father. In these letters his volcanic temper and determination to find a life of his own in Europe obscure the details of his immediate problems and interests and at the same time display a fierce intent to become a poet. Once in London in 1909, his correspondence was somewhat limited because of the frequent personal contact with the literary friends he met in Soho and elsewhere. During the years just before World War I, Ezra Pound introduced him to Amy Lowell and John Cournos. Fletcher became alienated from Pound almost at once and from Amy Lowell in 1917. The letters to Pound are of little interest, although Fletcher said that Pound was no gentleman and even called him a vampire. The exchange with Amy Lowell between 1913 and 1917 is a rich exchange of two ambitious experimenters and deserves a full reproduction to show the ferment in current poetry. At the same time Fletcher was writing daily and sometimes twice daily, to Florence Emily (Daisy) Goold Arbuthnot, whom he married in 1916. Fletcher complained that he did not know how to express affection in a letter, but he certainly labored at the task.

About the time of his marriage he began an exchange of letters with Conrad Aiken, who became a faithful friend during the final days of the marriage to Daisy; and Henry Bergen, a medieval scholar and fervent Marxist who tried for years to instill Communist orthodoxy in a difficult student. In addition, of course, there was a continuing flow of letters of submission, inquiry, and complaint that reveal his interest in contemporary literary movements, such as The New Humanism, Freudianism, and American regionalism. His association with the Vanderbilt group led to a correspondence with Davidson, Owsley, and Robert Penn Warren and his contribution of a chapter on education to the symposium *I'll Take My Stand* (1930). During the same years he was dabbling in what today would be called city planning and environmentalism while trying to persuade Foster Damon and T. S. Eliot that William Blake needed a new interpreter.

After his return to Arkansas in 1933 Fletcher became a professed regionalist and devoted much of his energy to promoting the arts and letters in Arkansas. He wrote voluminously to a number of younger men whom he regarded as promising: Louis Freund, a painter at Hendrix College, Conway, Arkansas, who illustrated several of Fletcher's war poems; James Franklin Lewis, a professor of chemistry at Arkansas College at Batesville, Arkansas; and Fray Angelico Chavez, a Dominican monk at Peña Blanca, New Mexico, who was not only a poet but a muralist who included recognizable faces in his murals. In such instances, and these are but a few, Fletcher enjoyed playing the role of guru and seer while making many strenuous efforts to assist his young friends. At the same time he supported a state symphony, a folklore society, and an art museum through letters as well as by personal solicitation.

Fletcher was anxious to have his letters and papers preserved and sometimes requested in marginalia that his letters be saved or returned. As he did not type and kept no copies of his letters, it is surprising that so many have survived. At any rate, soon after his return to Arkansas in 1933, the University of Arkansas awarded him an honorary degree (LL.D.), presumably with the understanding that his papers would be bequeathed to the University of Arkansas. A decade later Frederic Eugene Haun, a student at Hendrix College, expressed an interest in writing a doctoral dissertation on Fletcher and poetry. Fletcher almost immediately agreed to help Haun by lending him books and manuscripts, raising funds for a scholarship at Vanderbilt, and asking various friends to assist Haun by giving him access to letters. Haun submitted a master's thesis, "The Allusive Method of John Gould Fletcher" (1946), at Vanderbilt. Unfortunately, no member of the English department at Vanderbilt seemed interested in directing a student's work on Fletcher, so Haun moved on to the University of Pennsylvania, where he took his doctorate with study of another subject.

There was a serpent in Eden: Professor Norman Holmes Pearson of Yale had spent years making the Beinecke Library a great depository of the works of American poets. Pearson had befriended Fletcher in 1939 in a period of illness and remained a constant correspondent. When Pearson found that Haun and the University of Arkansas seemed destined to get Fletcher's papers, he indulged in a stratagem worthy of his wartime activity in military intelligence: first he told Fletcher that the University of Arkansas was too remote, that his papers should be found with those of the major modern American poets and that doubtless the University of Arkansas would be happily satisfied with a token bequest of books and manuscripts sufficient for a display in the library; then to forestall Haun's work, Pearson wrote Fletcher that Haun, a mere graduate student, was totally incapable of giving Fletcher's work the treatment it deserved. Overwhelmed, Fletcher withdrew his support of Haun as his authorized biographer but did not alter the bequest to the University of Arkansas, perhaps because President Lewis Webster Jones had appointed Fletcher a visiting professor in the spring of 1949. Haun, meanwhile, had amassed 217 letters to Henry Bergen, 20 letters to Walter Edwin Peck, 10 typescripts of letters to Donald Davidson, and microfilm from Harvard of letters to T. S. Eliot and Amy Lowell and from the University of Chicago of those to Harriet Monroe.

After Fletcher's death in the spring of 1950, his books and papers were acquired by the library of the University of Arkansas, where Charlie May Fletcher spent a year with a graduate student assistant arranging the papers in chronological order and supplying names and dates wherever possible. Later Thomas Ernest Douglass, a graduate student from Little Rock, undertook to make a catalogue of the correspondence and collect letters or copies from any available correspondents, a work finished in 1965. The first attempt at a formal publication of the letters was made by William M. Baker, whose work was abruptly ended by his death in 1986. Baker's project was later continued by Dr. Ethel C. Simpson, associate librarian at Mullins Library, the University of Arkansas, until Dr. Simpson decided to go to Rwanda as a member of the Peace Corps in the summer of 1989. In December of that year the Haun Collection was acquired by the University of Arkansas and is the last major addition of Fletcheriana, although small additions have been made from time to time. With these letters the Fletcher Series concludes.

These letters are certainly not intended to be biographical or to supplant or even supplement Ben F. Johnson III's truly magnificent and scholarly *Fierce Solitude: A Life of John Gould Fletcher* (1994). Even less is it intended to provide bibliographical data beyond that to be found in Bruce Morton's earlier *John Gould Fletcher: A Bibliography* (1979). The most that can be hoped for is that these letters will give the reader a fair impression of the personality, interests, and activities of their author.

CHRONOLOGY

1886　　　Born in Little Rock, Arkansas, on January 3, the second child and only son of John Gould and Adolphine Krause Fletcher.

1889　　　Family moved into Albert Pike mansion.

1891　　　Began study of Latin and German under tutors.

1896–1899　Attended private academy.

1899–1902　Attended Little Rock High School.

1902　　　After cramming during the summer, failed Harvard entrance examinations and enrolled in Phillips Academy, Andover, Mass.

1903　　　Entered Harvard in the class of 1907 but was less interested in classes than in the library, the Boston Museum of Fine Arts, and the Boston Symphony Orchestra.

1904　　　Met Lyman Willett Rogers, who wrote poetry, read Nietzsche, and introduced Fletcher to his fiancee, Louise (Lois) Howard.

1905　　　With elder sister, Adolphine, traveled to the West Coast and returned via El Paso, Arizona, Los Angeles, Portland, Yosemite, Salt Lake, and Denver. Wrote his first poetry in Los Angeles.

1906　　　The death of his father in January, 1906, having left him financially independent, moved to Boston and abandoned his studies.

1907　　　In the summer at his own expense joined a Harvard Peabody Museum field trip to western Colorado with his friend Sylvanus Griswold Morley and Alfred Kidder Peabody under the direction of Prof. Edgar L. Hewett. After about three weeks of strenuous digging, Fletcher left Mesa Verde and returned to Boston.

1908　　　In August sailed for Trieste, went to Rome in November to remain there for six months, and then settled in London in May, 1909.

1909　　　Returned to Italy for a three months' tour with younger sister, Mary.

1910　　　Became interested in the Fabian Society.

1911	Made his first trip to Paris to escape the turbulence of the coronation of George V. Started a tour of Europe with artist Horace Brodzky but a quarrel ended the venture prematurely.
1912	Met photographer Malcolm Arbuthnot, who with Steichen, Stieglitz, and others planned "The Linked Ring," a movement to promote photography as an art. Found Florence Emily (Daisy) Goold Arbuthnot attractive. Toured Sicily with Mary. Spent a month in Paris where he met artist/gallery owner Horace Holley, artist John Duncan Fergusson, and others. In London took a luxurious apartment in Adelphi Terrace and began sending out manuscripts.
1913	Published five volumes of poetry; introduced to Pound in Paris; became a member of the Egoist group; met Ford, Yeats, Hulme, Flint, Aldington, H. D., and later Amy Lowell. Persuaded by Pound to subsidize *The Egoist*. Became enamored of Daisy.
1914	Still enjoying the results of earlier publication, he moved in the Imagist circle. Left for a walking trip in the Italian Alps in time to be caught by the outbreak of World War I. Returned to join the Arbuthnots in Cornwall and make plans for marriage to Daisy. In November returned to America to wait for the divorce. Visited Boston, studied Oriental art, proceeded to Chicago to enjoy the Art Institute, and home to Little Rock for Christmas.
1915	After a visit to New Orleans, returned to Little Rock until mid-February when he went to Chicago for a week in which he studied the Japanese prints at the Art Institute and wrote haiku later published as *Japanese Prints*. After an extended visit to Boston he joined Adolphine and family in Chicago and Michigan for the summer with time out for a steamboat trip down the Mississippi to New Orleans and a western jaunt to San Antonio, El Paso, New Mexico, Arizona, and San Francisco. In the autumn back to Boston to enjoy the company of Amy Lowell and Conrad Aiken.
1916	Met Louis Untermeyer and Stark Young at Sevenels, the Lowell estate, in February. Met E. A. Robinson in March. Left for England in May. Married Daisy on July 5.
1917	Settled in Daisy's eleven-room house in Sydenham and saw much of T. S. Eliot and other writers. Not bothered by bombs dropped from Zeppelins and Gothas but found inflation and

	shortages irksome. Estranged from Amy Lowell by her failure to recommend the publication of a volume of poems.
1918	John Cournos, whom he described as his best friend, introduced him to D. H. Lawrence.
1920	May–August back in the United States.
1923	April–May brought Daisy to the United States in hopes of persuading her to migrate.
1925	Spent January in Rome, where he was impressed by the Fascists.
1926	Hospitalized two weeks in February for depression. In September brought Daisy and daughter Gwennie to New York, but they left after three months. Spent Christmas in Little Rock.
1927	Lectured under the auspices of Prof. Armstrong of Baylor in January. On a leisurely trip home he stopped at Nashville to meet the Southerners of the Centennial Club (Ransom, Davidson, et al.). After a few weeks in Greenwich Village, he was back in London by May 1.
1929	Spent six weeks in New York in early spring. Allen Tate suggested he contribute an essay on education to the anthology to be produced at Nashville.
1930	Already interested in Major Douglas's Social Credit, Fletcher joined and lectured for "New Europe," a reformed Adler Society studying the entire background of contemporary Europe. Lawrence and Lorna Hyde were among the activists. He contributed "Education—Past and Present" to *I'll Take My Stand*.
1931	Spent two months in the United States, attending a round table on regionalism at the University of Virginia on July 9. Back in London met Lorna Hyde on Oct. 16. In December, while Daisy was in a nursing home Fletcher spent the weekends with the Hydes and on Dec. 14 deserted Daisy for Lorna.
1932	Played hide-and-seek eluding Daisy all spring but then went back to Sydenham, where in July he jumped from an upper window and broke his shoulder blade. In September Daisy had him committed to Bedlam.
1933	After incarceration or hospitalization for five months, he escaped with the help of his solicitor, his physician, Conrad Aiken, Bergen, Mary, and others and by March 16 was in New York on

his way to Little Rock. He visited Natchez and Eureka Springs, and with Lawrence Powell interviewed Emma Dusenbury, the blind ballad-singer of Mena. After four months in Santa Fe, he visited the Century of Progress Exhibition in Chicago and lectured in Oklahoma and at Little Rock Junior College. By the end of the year he had become a reactionary defender of the Scottsboro trial and proposed the formation of a paramilitary organization, the Gray Jackets, to defend the ideals of the Old South.

1934   In February met Howard and Charlie May Simon at the Pike-Terry mansion, and in May visited Charlie May's Possum Trot homestead with them. The summer was spent in Santa Fe working on his poem on the history of Arkansas. In October saw Charlie May in New York.

1935   Finished the epic of Arkansas. Worked with Lawrence Powell, Adrian Brewer, Josef Rosenberg, S. C. Dellinger, C. J. Finger, and others to promote the arts and the regional character of the state. In April attended the L.S.U. Writers Conference in Baton Rouge and met Brooks, Warren, and the *Southern Review* group before being hospitalized in Memphis. In May headed east for the MacDowell Colony. After a brief sojourn at Yaddo in September, he returned to Little Rock in time to attend the Oklahoma Symposium in Norman in November.

1936   Married Charlie May Simon on January 18. Summered at the MacDowell colony. Went to Mexico City in December.

1937   In Mexico City, Taxco, Cuernavaca, and Puebla until May. Summer in the MacDowell Colony. Beginning of long friendship with Norman Holmes Pearson. Visiting lecturer at the University of Kansas City the fall semester.

1938   Awarded the Pulitzer Prize for *Selected Poems*.

1941   Built Johnswood, moved in before Christmas. Entertained soldiers from Camp Robinson through the war years.

1943   Frederic Eugene Haun began his association with Fletcher and planned to undertake a major study of life and works; long encouraged and aided by Fletcher.

1944   Visited Japanese relocation camp at Rohwer in May. Hospitalized in December in Memphis.

1945	Released from hospital in February. Participated in the University of Washington's Writers Conference in August.
1946	July–August at Mills College, Oakland. Remained in Pasadena until spring.
1947	Told Haun he preferred another biographer. Became active in support of proposed murals for Arkansas State Capitol.
1948	Summer at UCLA.
1949	Spring semester at the University of Arkansas. Active in forming the Ozark Folklore Society, of which he became the first president. Inducted into the National Institute of Arts and Letters in May. Presided over the first Ozark Folk Festival on July 11. Planned a folklore issue of *The Arkansas Historical Quarterly* and a second folk festival to be held in 1950.
1950	Died May 10.

TO HARRIET MONROE

[For a brief identification of each correspondent, see Correspondents at the end of the text.]

4, Adelphi Terrace
London, W.C.
August 2, 1913

Dear Miss Monroe,
   You certainly have never heard of me. I am glad to say that I have heard of you. From the beginning of your enterprise, I have bought each number of *Poetry*, and I have always determined to send you some of my work, if you would permit me to cooperate. For I am an American, although I have buried myself for the past five years in various places on the European continent, and for the last three years of that period in London. Also I have wished to do what I can in helping to create a national literature of my unhappy country. *Poetry* and a few other things like it have almost given me hope that this literature will come.
   Recently I had the pleasure of meeting Mr. Pound, who seems to have thought that some of my books were worth reading. He has obtained some work from me which I believe he has sent you, and which is probably in your office now. So my ambition to submit to you something has been gratified. But I would have preferred to have done it independently, than to rely on any outside aid.
   Mr. Pound, as you know, is the great apostle of vers libre and "Imagiste," and the MSS he sent you were vers libre, but not "Imagiste." I do not know in what direction your inclination may tend, but I may say that I am not exclusively a vers librist—as witness a copy of my *Dominant City*, which I enclose. I have experimented in many forms, and shall continue to seek for a more supple and less monstrous technique than that of the average cutter of verses to measure. Whether I shall ever find my own technique is questionable. I have too great a regard for independence, in my own case and in others.
   It would need a national inquiry of all American poets to discover what is the general trend of opinion in regard to vers libre. To my mind vers libre, as I understand it, can scarcely produce, in the English language, the same effects it has undoubtedly produced in the French. There is a fatal tendency on the part of the language to fall back into an essentially prose rhythm. There is also a tendency on the part of vers librists in English not to adopt a certain regularity of meter and depart from it occasionally, but to be constantly shifting the rhythm (the direct contrary of the French practice).
   I hope that vers libre will develop. But so far as it has gone, I think it is useful merely in extremely short poems, especially in descriptions of a

single brief emotion or small scene, where the play of rhyme would interfere with the full intensity of the color and the words. For long narrative poems, dramatic poems, or a mixture of narrative, descriptive, and dramatic, I am convinced—against my will—that vers libre is at present impotent, and that rhyme and regular meter are essential to give the speed and unity that are required.

With Mr. Pound's "School" of "Imagisme" I am in even greater disagreement. "Imagisme" is an attitude towards technique, pure and simple. I am unable, and I wish that everyone else were unable, to impose upon myself the pedantic yoke of any particular technique. I agree with schools only in the French sense, that a "school" represents a certain attitude toward *life* held in common by a certain group. I do not agree that a poem must be written according to certain fixed rules before it is permitted to be poetry. Poetry, so defined, would become a mere convention. I believe in unity of form with all my heart: but not in unity of technique. A good picture, for instance, must conform to certain rules of space-composition to be effective: but it need not be painted in a certain fixed style. This is also true of a poem. I have informed Mr. Pound that I do not intend to hamper myself with his techniques and his "don'ts."

I could write much more concerning my theories of poetry, but I prefer not to bore you. I merely want you not to misinterpret the accident that resulted in Mr. Pound sending in my work for your approval—an accident caused by the fact that he happened to read one of my books. I prefer to remain independent and unknown rather than permit a misunderstanding should be to my advantage. If *Irradiations* (the MSS Mr. Pound sent) do not please you, and you would like some poems of the *Dominant City* type, I shall be very pleased to send you some. In the meantime, permit me to wish you success with *Poetry*.

Yours very sincerely
John Gould Fletcher

TO AMY LOWELL

4, Adelphi Terrace
London, W.C.
Friday, September 7, 1913

Dear Miss Lowell,

I have a very important piece of news for you, which will excuse my writing thus bluntly. I want to advise you very strongly against going in Pound's proposed anthology.

The anthology is not to be edited, really, by Pound. Aldington, the author of the silly sophomoric letter in *The New Freewoman*, is really the editor. The aim and object—not avowed but secret—of the whole affair is to boom Aldington—to give him such a send-off in the United States that he and Pound will divide the country between them.

If Aldington were really any good as a poet, I would not care. But I hate to see a rigged-up game being played on the public to boom a silly cub who deserves nothing but a licking.

You see, the more names he has to act as satellites to his work, and his wife's (he has just married H. D., another "arriviste") the more likely his book is to be puffed. Therefore he wants yours. Also mine. He intends to use, of course, our weakest work, so his own will shine by comparison.

He proposed to print, as a sort of annex, *parodies of himself*, and the letter mentioned above.

You will say my letter is actuated by jealousy or spite. Not at all.

I have refused, not once but several times, to enter this anthology. And if I were starving on the streets I should continue to refuse. I will not let my name or my work stand as the support of a school with which I disapprove.

On the other hand, I believe you are sincerely trying to create great art. And there is a quality in your work—some of it—that I extremely admire, and that I rate higher than Aldington's or Pound's.

You were also very nice to me personally. I am not one of those who take favors from others, and then slip my knife in their backs. I am too proud, as Pound may or may not have told you. I honestly don't want to see you enter into the ranks of the Imagists under a misconception. If you enter, it must be with open eyes.

I am now returning the favors you did me.

My relations with Pound are at an end. In confidence, I have no objections to stating what these were.

A friend of mine [Skipwith Cannéll] in Paris—another would-be poet—met him and introduced me. Another friend of mine [Harold Brodzky]—with whom I have since quarreled for this very reason—told him about my books and about my project (which I have finally abandoned) of founding a review.

Pound then approached me and proposed that I finance *The New Freewoman*. I consented, very unwillingly, but refused to let my own work appear, and did not encourage Pound to boom me. Nevertheless, he did, with the result that I met you.

I have now withdrawn my financial support from the paper.

In return, Pound sent *Irradiations* to Miss Monroe. At the same time I sent her a letter disassociating myself from Pound and his school. She accepted some of them, provisionally, but she is at perfect liberty to change her mind if she pleases.

Pound also introduced me to you, and wrote a flattering review of me in *The Freewoman,* which I told him beforehand not to do.

He is now trying to inveigle me into giving support to Richard Aldington, a thing I won't do.

That is the "artistic" "literary" life as it is lived in London today. A lot of tradesmen puffing each other's wares would be a better name for them. I do not call such people artists. I call them dealers in self-advertisement.

It's all very well to talk about "artists have to make a living," but for myself, I can say once and for all that I never will consent to degrade myself to this level. I would prefer to starve or to steal. I will not let my name or my influence ever be used to sell anyone's work, for the simple reason that they are prepared to sell mine. If the work is good, I will admit its goodness whether the author is a friend of mine or not. If it isn't, nothing will induce me to support it.

Of all things on Earth, the most nauseating, the most abominable, is the London literary clique with its external politeness and internal petty jealousies and underground tactics.

I have known what I was up against since I came here in 1909. That was why I shunned everybody, and finally published my books without asking anyone's permission. May I add that I paid for all my books? And that I squabbled with the publishers, who of course looked askance on a person who came to them without "friends" or "backing."

To return to you. There are two things you can do. You can write Pound insisting on being given more space. Or you can withdraw altogether.

In case you withdraw, if you feel inclined to lose any money (which I strongly recommend you not to do) I will put up equal shares with you, and we will bring out in England another anthology which you will have the pleasure of seeing unsparingly condemned by Pound and his crew (if they take the trouble to notice at all).

But I shall insist on full liberty of selecting or rejecting anything I choose. You will take the same liberty with my work. And if we bring in any friends, it will have to be with full understanding who these are and what their work is to be.

All this has nothing to do with Art, and therefore I prefer not to meddle with it. I like your work well enough at least to set it beside mine. If it does ever get set beside mine is a minor consideration to me.

I am one of art's martyrs and mean to die in the last ditch. I will always recognize good work from whatever source, and if no one wants to recognize mine, then let my work perish. I prefer the low admiration of the vulgar, or the cold contempt of all, to that sort of admiration which can only be bought with favors, to the P. T. Barnum methods of advertising that are in vogue in this twentieth century of commercialized "art" and "book-markets."

If you think this letter is worth your confidence, you will say nothing about it to anyone else. I pledged myself not to say anything about my being behind *The Freewoman,* and asked Pound to make the same pledge. I would have kept mine, at least, but I wanted you to take warning by my example. Pound is far too clever ever to be honest. This has nothing to do with his poetry, which I still admire (in part).

If you do not think this letter deals honestly and uprightly with you and your friends, I hope you will send it to Pound, Aldington, Miss Monroe, or any other people you like.

Yours very sincerely,
John Gould Fletcher

TO AMY LOWELL

4, Adelphi Terrace
London, W.C.
October 25, 1913

Dear Miss Lowell,

Your letter of the 16th and the MSS arrived together today. The praise which you gave to *Irradiations* is rather overwhelming. I had hoped, for the sake of my modesty and peace of mind, that you would be able to pick them to pieces. But I must thank you again for your interested and generous appreciation.

My methods are really quite simple. In fact I have only one method, that of absolute and unquestioning devotion to poetry and incessant cultivation of its fruits. All my life I have read all the poetry I could lay my hands on; for the last eight years I have written practically nothing else; and for the last three years I have always gone about with a notebook in my pocket, and my senses on the alert for any phrase or emotion or idea that occurred to me. I have submitted myself freely to all influences trusting to my memory (which is prodigious) to harmonize them and to my individuality to choose the most favorable for itself. I don't suppose there has been a single good concert or exhibition of paintings for the last three years in London that I have not attended. Probably out of this interest in music, color, and form were born *Irradiations:* but I could not have written them had it not been that I had passed through long years of practice and experiment beforehand.

As they stand, they represent each a moment when I found my mood and the mood of nature about me absolutely akin. My aim was to express my mood in the terms of external nature by means of words which by their value as sound gave the exact musical equivalent of both mood and picture. Do I make myself clear? It is this combination of music, mood, and picture that gives them their value. The nearest thing I know to them is your "Pike": which I wish I could steal outright and plant it in their midst.

There is only one thing more that need be said and that is that what may be called "innocence of eyes" played a large part in their composition. I wrote all of them this spring and summer: almost all under the combined influences of perfect good health, liberty to go about and see as many or few people as I pleased, sunlight, Post-Impressionist pictures, the Russian Ballet, and Paris atmosphere. All these things I saw with the eyes of a child and wrote with the skill of a juggler with words. Repeated reading—aloud of them to myself—was necessary to test their verbal effect. I have read them so often that the other night I almost repeated them all by memory to some astonished friends.

The only literary influence that was at work during their composition was a book (published by the *Mercure*) called *Les Fêtes Quotidiennes*, by Guy Charles Cros. This is the book I told you to get. It has been called *"la dernière et la suprême larme Verlainienne."*

Miss Monroe has provisionally accepted Nos. IV, V, X, XV, XVII, XXI, XXII, XXIV, XXV, XXVI, XXXIV. But this is purely provisional, and I have not the least idea whether they will ever appear.

By the way, in the MS I sent you there are two versions of XXVI. The version beginning "Slowly along the lamp-emblazoned street" is the final one to my mind for the reason that the sound-quality of the words helps to build up the picture better than the one beginning "Down the street after midnight," which is earlier. Perhaps if you compare the two, you will find some key to my technique.

I am sorry that "batter with my matter" still displeases you. I admit it is naive to the point of grotesqueness. But I don't see what I could put there except perhaps "I crash with my mass against the walls of the atmosphere." Is that better?

Thanks very much for the correction of the blunder in XXVIII.

But it is high time I stopped writing about myself. I was delighted to renew my acquaintance with your things. I have already said what I think of "The Pike"—that I wish I could bag it for *Irradiations*, where it would be no inconspicuous ornament, I assure you. "The Waltz" is a gem of horror that becomes absolutely insupportable and nauseating at the last—it is magnificently unpleasant, and the way the waltz itself is worked in is very clever. But my best favorite is "The Foreigner," which I am sure you wrote with your heart's blood. I shall take "The Foreigner" as a tonic whenever I feel depressed. I literally howled with joy at the conclusion.

      For I've come here to win!
It makes the blood leap high.

I must really wait until I have cooled down a little before I look again at the others. At present I am intoxicated with that glorious "Foreigner."

Do send me some of your new things. I hope Ezra won't take "In a Garden" for his anthology. The trouble with "In a Garden"—I didn't see it at first—is that the second part (beginning "And I thought of the night and you") is not sufficiently prepared for at the outset, so the thing seems rather *two good poems* than *one good one*. At least that is my impression, which I offer for what it is worth.

If I were you I wouldn't scruple to be a little high-handed with Ezra. You ought to know what is good in your work better than anyone else. And if you have written a poem that ends on a dissonance, I can assure you that a dissonance is the very best kind of an ending (unless you want to repeat what you said at the beginning).

By the way, I have quarreled with Ezra and I am not to appear in *The Freewoman* nor in the *Anthology*. You see I cannot be as polite to people as he is: I am more at the mercy of my temperament. I found him rather antipathetic, and was obliged to break it off.

Certainly I could not put up with his picking my work to pieces, while his work was sacrosanct. Criticism in this world, if it is going to be of any use, must be mutual. But the whole squabble was probably more my fault than his.

You wrote that yours was an unconscionably long letter, but I seem to have written a perfect treatise. I hope it won't put you to sleep. Do write me as long and often as you feel inclined, and if I can do anything for you, remember that I am at your service.

With best wishes for your health and happiness, I am very sincerely your friend
John Gould Fletcher

P.S. I hope you can read this. My handwriting must be a terrible trial to others.

TO AMY LOWELL

4, Adelphi Terrace
London, W.C.
[Probably December 1913]

Dear Miss Lowell,
You must excuse me for having taken so long a time before criticizing your poems. I have not been very well, and have had a great many worries, so this is why I delayed.

I have read your two essays in the Paul Fort manner, "The Basket" and "In a Castle," several times but I cannot truthfully say that I think they are successful. I do not care for Paul Fort's work; it seems to disguise an immense deal of superficial cleverness under an affectation of bucolic simplicity. In this respect it is like Jammes, whom I also dislike (except in quite small doses). Fort's typography was undoubtedly adopted in order to persuade the reader into reading at great speed (his poetry is essentially light and flimsy in its texture, like the perpetual jet of a very small fountain). I do not share your belief that this method of writing has any particular dramatic value. In fact, the parts of your two poems which stand out in my mind are not the dramatic, but the descriptive detail, such as "Puffs of darkness sweep into the corners and keep rolling through the room behind his chair" or "Overhead hammers and clinks the rain"—both of which examples are really superb.

Whether it would or would not be possible to construct a really dramatic lyric on the Fort model, I do not know: but in the two examples you sent me, I have an uneasy feeling that the dramatic interest is kept in the background: that there is not enough action, and far too much description, for a dramatic poem. The description is excellent, I admit, but as your intention seems to have been dramatic, I must say that I look on these two poems as experiments rather than as achievements. No one will deny your priority in this medium, but I do not seem to be able to feel that you have grasped its possibilities altogether. "The Basket" is certainly the most ambitious thing you have ever done, but the climax seems to be too forced and is not sufficiently prepared for by what goes before. Why the fire? Why does the poet not simply go blind?

About the others: "Clear With Light Variable Winds" is as near perfection as anything you have done. I was not sure about 'nipples' at first and preferred 'tips' but perhaps you intended the internal rhyme with ripple. The last line seems a little weak. The gardener would hardly say, "It is uncanny to see a dead man": he would be more likely to say "I do not like to see a dead man."

"White and Green" interests me most of all. It is certainly not stale or blasé: it has exulting good spirits, which is something. For some reason I would prefer "Slim, wet, and without sandals" to your second line: and I must remark that "almond flower" is rather disturbing, since an almond flower is *pink* and not white. But the last line is magnificent especially "unsheathed" and "leaping"—this is the sort of effect I have been trying to get in a great many of my own things.

The others I do not care very much for. They seem to be tamer and more conventional. "Aubade" is poor—how an almond can become a gem I do not exactly see. "Obligation" is not so bad—in fact I rather like it after all, although it attempts the simple, which is very difficult to do.

"Epitaph" is amusing but both unfair and slight, or at least so I think. I do not know or care whether anyone else shares my opinion or not.

I enclose a few things of my own that you may have an opportunity of studying the latest developments. *The Sea Symphony* is unfinished: it lacks the last movement, which is to be called "The Calm" and bear the indication *andante tranquillo*.

The Epigrams were partly inspired by *Poetry*'s award—or lack of it—and by your "Epitaph on a Young Poet." They are merely *jeux d'esprit*.

"Procession" is an attempt to convey the rolling of drums and blowing of trumpets of a funeral march.

"Night's Dark Towers," "One Day in Versailles," and "The Noise of the Wind" are of the pre-vers libre period (near the end thereof). In fact, "One Day in Versailles" was written during the composition of *Irradiations*.

"Blake" is quite recent.

I enclose also third and final series of *Epigrams* in MS.

With best wishes for a happy Christmas, I remain,

Yours very sincerely

John Gould Fletcher

TO HARRIET MONROE

4, Adelphi Terrace
London, W.C.
Jan. 23, 1914

Dear Miss Monroe,

An editor ought never to have any personal friends. If editing a paper means promising one's friends to print their two-for-a-penny doggerel, then it is time your paper ceased to exist.

This is not a question of Olympian mind. It is a question of whether you have the courage enough to print only good work, and the sense to know good work when you get it. Ezra Pound, with whom I greatly disagree in artistic theory and practice, has the sense to know decent stuff when he sees it, and to say so. You ought to make him editor of your paper.

As regards the bunch of stuff I sent you, I purposely included some highly inferior work to see whether you could spot it. Your letter makes me despair of your even taking the trouble to look it over. You will doubtless be too busy promising people who don't matter to print their unspeakable rubbish.

If the *English Review* and *Poetry and Drama* are bad, there is no excuse for making it a case of "we three."

John Gould Fletcher

TO AMY LOWELL

37 Crystal Palace Park Road
Sydenham
London, S.E.
April 7, 1914

Dear Miss Lowell,

Your letter of March 24 has come. You are quite mistaken if you think that I was angry at you for not writing me in reply to my last. I knew you must be pretty busy, and I was about to write you myself when your letter came.

As the heading at the top of this page will tell you, I have altered my address and am now in the suburbs. I have just got settled after great difficulties. My work will keep me very busy, and you must not tax me if I, too, prove remiss in correspondence.

As you have surmised I have made up my differences with Pound and have even written an Imagist work, *The Blue Symphony*, a copy of which I am sending you. I think Pound is certainly a very fine critic, although as a poet we are still poles asunder in personality, if not in method.

The *Anthology* disappointed me. Barring Aldington, who is represented at his best, the thing has not scope enough. Pound, in order to counteract the excessive Hellenism of the Aldington faction, put in some Chinese things which give only a small idea of his powers.

About *Irradiations,* I am glad that you still like them. I agree with you that in VII "in ribbons up summits" is after all better. This is a ticklish point, which I am very glad you settled for me.

The fountain thing I am afraid I cannot change at present.

The poems printed in *The Egoist* were Pound's own selection. This is the reason for the omission of XXVII.

About *The Sea Symphony,* I am quite aware that it has its faults. All these poems were written at the same spot and have a certain connection or rather continuation in mood, therefore I called the thing a symphony. I am aware that it does not follow the technical rules of a symphony as established by Beethoven, and broken by almost every great composer since him. I merely meant the title to indicate what I have been striving for since *Irradiations*— to orchestrate my moods in words. The sea is so admirably fitted to vers libre, and has been so neglected by the poets of the greatest sea-faring nation in the world, that I thought I ought to do my best to supply the deficiency. The thing is a tour de force of meters and rhythms and colors—but the musical indications—as you point out—are inexact.

"The Gale" and "Steamers" are the best of this series. Your remarks about the rhymed funeral march are quite just. The "long wet fingers"—unconscious plagiary—were *seen* by me.

Pound agrees with you that *The Sea Symphony* does not mark any advance on *Irradiations*. I altogether agree, but I have decided to write nine more symphonies, of somewhat closer texture, to bring out what I am trying to do, viz. orchestrate the English language.

The other things I sent you are mostly juvenile and poor. I must confess that I have not yet cured myself of the habit of scribbling for my amusement, or amusing myself with exhuming such occasional verses from my notebooks. I dare say what you say about my fecundity is true. Still I think "Trianon" and "sun" is quite as good a rhyme as Hueffer's "Rue de la Paix" with "snakes" in *To All the Dead*.

Your remarks about my letters to Harriet Monroe *do* rather make me angry. From a long and bitter experience with editors I have come to think that they are the natural and inevitable enemies of the artist. I don't think youth has anything to do with this attitude. The mere fact that Harriet *means well* does not excuse her (or any other editor) from the consequences of incompetence. What would you say if your business was managed by such a person? You would insist on their resigning at once. Therefore I have every right to criticize her if I please. I expect to be criticized in turn. If my criticism means that I am barred as a contributor because of it, very well. Editors need not take my stuff unless they want to. I certainly do not propose to cajole or flatter anyone into doing so—may God preserve me from this!

If Harriet is in earnest—and I think she is—I believe what I have said to her will do her some good. If I can make *Poetry* better I am going to do it, at whatever cost to myself. And I will not print any letters as "documents" later, either!

Excuse my feelings, but I do feel very strongly on this point. Possibly I may write quite unjust things to Harriet and others. But I always intend to speak as I feel to the person who judges my MS.

Thanks very much for the offer concerning *The Atlantic [Monthly]*. I will send you what I have, but I am afraid my writing has rather suffered recently, as I have had a great many worries and anxieties.

I have seen Sadleir and he has asked me to send him *Irradiations*. They will not be published, however, as my family have been in financial difficulties all winter, and I cannot spare the money at present which Constable will desire. Many thanks all the same for your very great kindness.

I have left the topic of your own work to the last. When I wrote you last, I was in a very irritable frame of mind, and disinclined to be generous. I frequently am like that—especially in the winter. Besides Paul Fort, with his sentimental wishy-washy crapulosity of pages plucking guitars with dirty fingernails amid simpering patchouli-scented shepherdesses, seems to me to represent the weakest phase of the French character: their mania for the pretty—especially the slightly obscenely pretty—the admiration for the cocotte. Reading Paul Fort is like bathing in scented soap suds, sickening and slightly greasy. However I am ready to respect your contrary opinion, and to admit your right to experiment in any form you choose.

Of your new things (I was glad to see some of them in *The Egoist* the other day) I am most pleased with "White and Green"—I am glad to hear that there is a white almond. The last lines keep haunting my memory—and also those "flights of rose, layers of vermilion."

Please send me some of your new work. I shall doubtless criticize it severely—Pound's influence is gradually telling on me, and I feel that I am becoming a martinet of phrases. Yet my own fecundity seems to be unabated. I am dreaming of two or three big projects besides the *Symphonies,* of which you may learn more when you come over—an event I am greatly looking forward to.

I am afraid this letter will neither be as legible or as interesting or as generous as yours. However, excuse lapses and believe me that I am always aware that you are one of the most sincere and unselfish and devoted upholders of art that we have today in America.

I will certainly send anything new and unpublished I have.

Yours sincerely
John Gould Fletcher

TO AMY LOWELL

37 Crystal Palace Park Road
Sydenham
April 16, 1914

Dear Miss Lowell,

I have just seen your poems in the April number of *Poetry*. Besides the pleasure of rereading "The Cyclists" and "The Foreigner," I have had the enjoyment of four new ones. Also I have tried to read "The Forsaken," which I regret that you have printed.

Let me speak the worst first. This new attempt to follow Paul Fort seems to me to be the weakest of them all. Where his technique in French gives one the impression of a soufflé—of something light and sweet, yours in

English is like the dribble from a leaking rain-spout. Words, words, words. Rattle, rattle, jingle. You were so concerned to drag the utmost number of rhymes (not always good or effective) and the last degree of sentiment out of your subject that you did not think of the devastating effect of the whole.

This is not altogether your fault, I admit. You have convinced me that Paul Fort cannot be done in English. If you would only give up Fort and Rostand and Fiona Macleod and all pseudo-romanticism and show yourself less favorably disposed to juvenile poets simply because they are Americans (witness your review of Benét), you would be doing yourself a good service, I am convinced.

As for your other poems, I cannot choose between them. They all have a freshness, a sincerity, a simplicity about them that I like intensely. Certain lines are noteworthy. The sealed spice-jars and the last four lines of "A Lady"; "he is fat and has a bald head" in "Music" (I wish I had written that line; I would give one of my ears for it); all of "The Bungler"; the last three of "Anticipation"; and all of "The Gift," which is a very beautiful gift indeed. In these things you seem to be entering into your domain: and your position does not belong with the *voulu* Fort of *faux chansonettes* but with the naive Jammes of true "idylls."

I hope you will send me your new book when it is out. And I hope there will be sealed spice jars and sweetness of flowers and crushed grasses among what you offer to the public and less of "Let the baby not be. Only take this stigma *off of* me"—which is bad English and false sentiment and jingly meter.

In the last lines of "The Gift," "When I shall have given you the last one"—it seems to me that the *shall* is quite unnecessary.

About *The Atlantic*. I enclose the *Irradiations* which Ezra has finally decided not to use. One you like is among them. I also enclose a MS. *The Divine Tragedy* which was written between July and November—that is to say, immediately after *Irradiations* and before *The Sea Symphony*. I cannot make up my mind whether these poems are the best or the worst I have written. Some are highly rhetorical, some are sentimental, some are almost bathos. Yet for some reason I am inclined to think that there is something in them—especially perhaps the "Walk in the Garden." However this is for you to judge. You can pick out anything you think *The Atlantic* would care for and return me the rest.

My health is excellent, but I have done practically nothing in the way of poetry this year. I have been busy undergoing a thorough spiritual housecleaning: I find my early enthusiasms about dead, and my flow of crude inspiration checked. I am reassembling and doubly concentrating my forces in the hope of doing some really strong and mature work. I send you *The Blue Symphony* which is about the only thing I have done this year so far, which counts. Ezra has taken it for *Poetry*, so *The Atlantic* cannot have it.

I suppose you have heard that he is to be married. I hope it won't dry-rot his imagination.

Many thanks for your kindness about *The Atlantic*, and many thanks for the new poems and for "Music" above all. What a delicate exquisite picture you have there!

John Gould Fletcher

[Amy Lowell had praised William Rose Benét's Merchants from Cathay *in* Poetry *IV (April 1914): 32–33.]*

TO AMY LOWELL

October 29, 1914

Dear Miss Lowell,

I have booked passage on Cunard Liner *Franconia*, leaving Liverpool November 14, and will be in New York on the 21st. My present financial situation will not enable me, I am afraid, to run up to Boston and see you, though I should greatly like to do so. In any case you will know where I am, and if you want to communicate with me, the American Express, New York, will be the most convenient place to send your letters to, until further notice.

My plans for the future are quite unsettled—at present all I know is that I shall probably spend Christmas in the United States.

I read with great pleasure your poems in *Poetry and Drama* which came out, unfortunately, under the cloud of this war. However, they still kept their qualities in my eyes. "Miscast" is very good. But I like best "The Taxicab," which I rather envy you. Your article in *Poetry* (October Number) was splendid —the right thing said in the right place. I am glad someone is still fighting and telling the fools over there what they ought to have found out for themselves long ago—that there *is* an American note in poetry, and it is to be found precisely in those works which carry on and develop further the elements of the universal art-tradition, not in those who try to be "barbaric yawps" and nothing else.

About the anthology. It is too bad the Hueffer poem is not acceptable. It is a very fine thing. I don't think Hueffer will ever do better, and I dare say you will only make another enemy by publishing without it. Still, I think you are probably right. It is much more important, if the group is going to carry any weight at all, for its anthology to be published by a good firm than for it to go out looking for trouble. However, I am not at all sure that the best policy would not be to abandon the whole business. Ezra seems to have queered the pitch for good, and doubtless after publication will continue doing so. Couldn't we call ourselves the Independents or the Vitalists or the Young America Group or something like that and disassociate ourselves from any *isms* except free verse and definite treatment of a subject, in a preface?

As for myself, I object to most anthologies, but am willing to take part in *any* in which a perfectly fair field is shown. I didn't think it was in the case of the Imagist volume. I may have been mistaken. Ezra, however, rubbed me up the wrong way—likewise Aldington. I like Aldington a lot better now, and think him fair-minded. Ezra I *never* will be able to endure. As for yourself, you have put me so far into your debt that if my support is of any earthly use to you, you are quite welcome to it.

For the rest, I am heartily sick of these artistic jealousies and backbitings, and bushwhacking tactics, varied by guerrilla dictatorships of the Ezra type. It is time for artists to become a new army and to make some sort of stand against the encroaching bourgeoisie, instead of wasting time in sharpshooting among themselves. Until we show ourselves more tolerant of one another, how can we expect to make any effect upon a country like America, where toleration is the greatest of virtues? I feel most strongly about this.

I will be here at this hotel [Hotel Belmont] over tomorrow (Tuesday) and will turn up at the St. Regis about 7:30—if that isn't too early. You can communicate with me here.

Yours sincerely
J. G. Fletcher

[Amy Lowell published "Nationalism in Art" in Poetry *V (October 1914): 33–38. "Miscast" and "The Taxi" are the poems in* Poetry and Drama.*]*

TO DAISY FLETCHER

Sunday 28th November [1914]

My own dearest one,

I haven't written you a letter like this since I went away because I have been afraid they might be opened, but I am going to risk it this time. Dearest, your first sweet letter has come to me, and it was *so* precious to me. I have missed you every day since I left, and every day I have wanted you to be with me. You would enjoy it, I am sure, especially the climate, which is the most wonderful in the world, I keep saying to myself. The only trouble is that the houses are absurdly overheated and stuffy, and the air outside is so keen and rare that it makes my head almost giddy.

For the first few days since I have been here—it has seemed an age already—I came almost to the conclusion that I wanted to live here the rest of my life. It is really so fascinating, and it is all so fresh and new, and there is a lot of fine, beautiful work being done. In the six years since I have seen it last, New York is completely altered. Besides I love it. When our ship after its miserable stormy gray voyage slipped into the harbor of New York on a perfectly windless cloudless, warm sunny afternoon, and I could see in that absolutely crystalline atmosphere the great white masses of the skyscrapers rising out of the water three miles away, I burst into tears. I simply broke down and sobbed. Dear, I will always love England for your sake: but this is my country and I am proud of what it has done and ashamed of its defects.

If you ever do want to part with Malcolm Arbuthnot and to become legally mine, it would be easy enough for you to move over here and obtain a divorce. You would get it all settled inside a year—I think—though of course it would be costly. Darling, I do hope that some day your vision will be true and that we can go traveling about somehow! I am going to make some inquiries and find out, if I can, how long you have to reside in the U.S. in order to obtain a divorce.

It is extraordinary, isn't it, that when I was at home—for 37 Crystal Palace Park Road is my home—I never found time to do half the things I wanted, while here I have been on the go since I came, and yet I have plenty of time on my hands. Life is strange, and as for me since I have become parted from you, I have seen even more clearly that this life is not everything—that there is a great and beautiful life to come and that God rules the universe.

Dear, if you ever get in any perplexity about anything,—especially Malcolm—you had better consult your brother about it. You can tell him all about your love for me, if you think best.

I pray that we may soon meet. I am not happy here and I never will be happy anywhere without you. I am glad I came, and am happy to see my own country again, but if it wasn't my country, and my own people were not here, I would be going back tomorrow.

I see I will have to get a passport in order to return, which is going to be troublesome. God bless you always. Your own.

This letter ought to catch the *Franconia* on its return voyage.

[No signature]

TO AMY LOWELL

The Virginia Hotel
Chicago
Wednesday, Dec. 16, 1914

Dear Miss Lowell,

The little case arrived safely yesterday morning. Very many thanks.

It is too cold to stay here—besides I am not over-enthusiastic about this place—between us be it spoken.

Harriet has taken the article on you, but will not be able to use it for three months. I have tried to hustle her up about it as much as possible.

Harriet and I manage to get along fairly well, though I dare say I haven't made a hit. I have had to talk about nothing but Lindsay and Pound since I arrived. I am sick of these two worthies, but have been very polite and scrupulously refrained from hurting their feelings. Harriet yearned for me to pay a visit to Lindsay and behold the lion, but I rapidly extinguished her yearning

The Little Review is a *scream*. Picture a typical Vassar sophomore and you have Miss Anderson. Giggles, enthusiasm, blind confidence, utter lack of knowledge, fondness for pickles and chocolates, the delightful dilly-dallying with revolutionisms—all these are there. She loves Rupert Brooke, and Arthur Davison Ficke, and heaven knows who else. She hadn't the slightest idea who I was, but I left the *Green Symphony* with her and departed. *Later she telephoned Harriet about it to find out if it was all right! Isn't that a gem!!!*

Incidentally, *The Little Review* is not going to keep up—I am afraid. Nothing back of it but girlish enthusiasm and complete ignorance. They are changing printers for the third time and I think that three months more of it will finish them. I don't hope to see the *Symphony* in print.

I narrowly missed meeting *Sandburg* last night. Score, one to the good. Instead I met a few more *dynamic personalities*—how I love that charming American adjective!—of the Lindsay type. Number one was Masters of *Spoon River Anthology* fame. Never heard of it? My own undynamic personality was completely eclipsed by Mr. Masters. Also there were Mr. and Mrs. Henderson whom I manage—perhaps on account of Mrs. H's bohemian temperament—to endure. The husband I heartily dislike.

This is an amusing spot and I would not have missed it. Its intellectual life is completely bossed by the Middle West Female of the Chautauqua type who conspires together to exalt revivalist vaudevillians like Lindsay to the top notch and to leave servants of the Muse in the background. What I think of the same Middle-West female is best left unsaid.

I leave here tomorrow. As I said in my first paragraph, it's too cold, and a little of Chicago goes a long way with your humble servant.

As ever, yours
John Gould Fletcher

TO AMY LOWELL

December 22, 1914

Dear Miss Lowell,

I had intended writing you fully soon after my arrival, but I found I had to meet so many people that I postponed it. And now I have a letter from you to answer.

I am awfully glad the reading went off so well. I would have given anything to have heard it, but I am sure that my nervousness would have been even greater than yours and that it would nearly have wrecked me to sit still and listen. Congratulations to yourself and Engel, who has written me a nice letter which I am going to answer soon.

The polyphonic red slippers sound awfully fascinating. I have not attempted the form since I got the hammer poem off my chest. By the way, I read the hammer thing to Harriet and Alice Corbin (who is the person to "work" in that office, I think), just to cinch matters about the article. They were deeply impressed, so much so that Harriet asked me for a copy, which I have sent with *strict injunctions that she is not to print it until the article appears.* I have dedicated it to Richard as a sort of Christmas present and inducement to come to America.

About *The New Republic,* I think that you obtained everything that *you* need reasonably ask for from *them.* Doubtless the cantankerous and pseudo-libelous tendencies of certain poets—we need not name names—so well, that they hesitated. I am ashamed to send them anything—you ought to draw first blood from their columns yourself—and I hope that you are not standing aside on my account. Do send them the slipper thing, unless you are afraid they will get frightened at the outset. Meantime I will get to work and cut down my Indian [poem] to the shortest possible.

Greenslet has sent me the contract so *Irradiations* is really coming through at last, thanks first, last, and altogether to you.

It is very dull here, but I have so far got along with my sisters and have managed to raise three hundred dollars for personal expenses up to next June. I don't think I shall manage to get another penny out of them, after this. In fact, I know I shan't. I will write you again shortly, unless I hear from you in the meantime, and tell you what my plans are. At present I don't know what to do, as it seems somewhat doubtful whether this will get me up to Boston and enable me to live there until June.

When I was in Chicago, Harriet showed me a letter from Lawrence, hectically damning the War Number of *Poetry* (which was Alice Corbin's idea, I learn) and saying your bohemian glasses were frivolous, or something like that. He had enclosed a very poor (in my opinion) war poem of his own, in not very good vers libre, about a soldier who hated his own body so much that he wanted the enemy to hack it to pieces (here realistic detail) and that women were abominable for lusting after hacked bodies rather than healthy ones, and more neurasthenic detail. I tried my best to get Harriet to turn it down, largely because I think the public have got sick of war poems, and because I felt that Lawrence would not help *Poetry*'s cause any, but would merely antagonize people. I don't know if my effort in this direction will have any effect.

She also showed me another thing by Pound's latest discovery, T. S. Eliot, which was very, very Huefferish, and trailed off badly towards the conclusion. She had written EP saying that it was too much like "Henry James carried to the Nth degree" and had received the usual insulting note in reply. She got frightened and intends probably to print it. I told her that I thought it fairly good. It has an excellent beginning—a description of a London fog (Eliot is in London somewhere) and is called "The Love Song of J. Alfred Prufrock," being an attempt to put down the state of mind of a man who is so well bred as to be incapable of affirming his love for anyone on earth.

This is all the news. I expect to have a very dull, quiet Christmas. I wish you could have the same sort of one, as I really am sure you are overworking yourself in the most horrible way and that you need rest. Couldn't you let things slide for about a week or so?

I hope this will reach you before you leave Brookline. Do take good care of your health. Remember that I want to see you again, not as a wreck, but as your own self. You don't know how much it means to me—particularly since that night I relapsed and broke down—to have somebody who cares as much for poetry, and for me, as you do.

Let me wish you a merry Christmas, if Christmas be not past when this reaches you; and in any case a gloriously polyphonic New Year.

As ever, your friend
John Gould Fletcher

TO DAISY FLETCHER

January 4, 1915
9:30–12:30 A.M.

Daisy Fletcher
Do not destroy this letter. It is sacred truth, and I am not ashamed of having written it.
Dear Daisy:—

I have received from you a letter dated the 18th, and also two copies of *The Daily Mail* and *The Evening News* of the same date. Many thanks for these. At present I shall not say any more about them but shall deal with another matter, which is more important.

Since I left England, I have been thinking very long and hard about the future. I have prayed often that God might guide me in the right path. Finally, after long consideration, I have arrived at a conclusion which I hope is the correct one.

Last year about this time, or rather the time when you will receive this letter, you were recovering from your influenza, and we were on the brink of our terrible, ghastly trouble. What I really wanted then, I do not know. I was far too young, and my nerves were too unsettled to do anything else but drift. For all the troubles you were called upon to bear, I, and I alone, am responsible. I will not attempt to excuse my conduct which was wicked and unforgivable. May God be merciful to me a sinner, for the way I treated you then and may I never, with God's help, do such a thing again.

As things happened, everything turned out better than I either hoped or deserved. I had the happiness of living under the same roof with you for many months. You had the opportunity of studying my character, of learning to understand my ways, and of knowing whether or not you could live happily with me. I thank God that He has given me this priceless glimpse of a Paradise far beyond my deserts. It will never—it can never—be forgotten by me, no matter what happens, no matter how long I live.

It was this terrible, but doubtless just and righteous war which woke me from the day-dream of happiness which was mine at Holme Lea. I realized sharply that I had other parts to play in this world that the part of "your John." I realized that, though the life of this world is made up mostly of crosses, we much learn to bear our crosses as best we may, for His sake, who to save us, was nailed upon a Cross. The choice presented itself to me of joining the British Army and dying for England's sake, or returning to my own country (for which I have an even greater love) and living and writing for its sake and my own. I concluded, as you know, that I might be of greater service to my own country than to England. Which choice, I believe, was the better one. It has made no difference at all in my love for you, which today is even broader and better, I hope, than it ever was before.

Yesterday was my twenty-ninth birthday. I have now arrived at my fullest physical and mental maturity. I know I have a man's mind and a man's might to carry my plans into execution. Twelve years and nine months ago, I left this very house in which I am sitting today to go to school. That was the end of my boyhood, in September 1902. In September 1914—just twelve years later—came the end of my youth, with my departure from London. Twelve years from today, in 1928, I shall be forty-one years old. All my best work shall by that time be accomplished, or I shall be on the point of accomplishing it during the remainder of my existence. This I know, and I also know that it is my first duty to God as my Maker and my fellow-man to accomplish that which I was sent here to do.

When I left England, I thought it was possible for me to return and to take up the sort of life I had been living. Since I have been in America, I can see that it is not possible for me to do so. Even were the war to conclude shortly—and of that there is no sign—it would be impossible. It might give us a few months or even years of happiness, but it would inevitably lead to misery for us both in the end. I should be a failure as a poet and as a man. You would have to bear with my temper, and you would always feel that it had been your fault, and that I did not really want you. Rather than spoil the marvelous brief happiness that we have had together, I would prefer to face the situation like a full-grown man, and for you to face the situation as a full-grown woman. There is only one choice for us. Either you and I *must be* man and wife in the eyes of the law, or we must face a lifelong separation. Of that I am certain now; and I am prepared to face whichever you say it must be. It is for you to choose.

I have an income sufficient to meet my needs and yours to the end of my life. As I said in my last letter, I shall not be able to get this income increased, and it will lapse at my death. But my health is excellent, and I shall take the very best care of myself, so I hope, please God, to have at least ten years more of life. By that time, the works I shall write and have written will be making a stir in the world. I shall be gaining an income from my pen, and this income will not be diminishing, but increasing. That money I shall leave to you, if you survive me, and to my adopted children. Perhaps it will not work out this way; life at best is full of uncertainties; but if God will grant me ten years' time to develop my plans, and if you will help me to your utmost, as you have always done, it will come to pass. If I were not sure of this, I would not be writing you now.

As regards the children, you know that if you decide to divorce yourself from Malcolm and become my wife, we would move to the United States. That is my plan. It is necessary for me to live here, if I am to make enough money to leave you and them anything. Besides it will enable us to forget the past better and to face the future bravely without regrets for the past. Well, the children would come too, and I believe it would do them good. They would grow up in a big, progressive, modern country and would have plenty of opportunities to distinguish themselves. They would have more chances, I really believe, to make a start in life than in England, which will be saddled with debt and taxes for fifty years after this war. What I offer to you, I also offer to those dear children, who put their arms around my neck and kissed me as I was leaving your house—I offer them also a new life and a *real* father. May God help me to carry out my wishes for them.

As regards Malcolm. He will undoubtedly have to suffer. It cannot be helped. If he has any manhood left, he ought to be happier to suffer and have it over with, than to go on leading this life of lies and subterfuges. After all, he still will have his painting, his photography (in which I have given him as much a start as I could), and the opportunity of making a new fresh start. For Malcolm's misfortunes in the past, I am not responsible. I have striven harder, possibly, than many another would have striven, to do Malcolm justice. Let him have his divorce in any way he chooses—it will doubtless be bitter medicine any way—but when it is over, I feel sure that Malcolm will be all the better for it; and if he ever wants to visit America and see his children, I shall not raise any objection.

As regards your mother and sister. Here you may have trouble, not from Ella, but from your mother. This trouble cannot be helped. After all, it is a question of the value of my love and hers. If her love is so much more to you than mine, if you feel *sure* that you owe it to her never to do anything that she disagrees with, then that means that you need her more than me, and that during the last year I have given you nothing. If that is the way you feel—if God makes you feel like this—then the sooner I know it, the better. I can bear the truth, if this is the truth, and it will be better for me to know my faults, than to go on believing, as I do, that my love is more to you than your mother's disapproval. But if you are ready to make this sacrifice, then I may say that when your mother dies, I should like Ella, too, to come and live with us, if she feels she can, and if you want her.

After all, I too have sacrificed all my relations to our love. My sisters have no more interest in me, or in my affairs, or in my poetry, than they have in those of a total stranger. In fact, if a total stranger came to them and began living in their house, they would show him more politeness than they do to me. I am always on the verge of a squabble here; and once or twice already I have fallen over the verge. It is simply impossible to keep one's temper when one can see that one is not wanted and thought of as a fool. While I was writing this letter my younger sister came in and called me a fool to my face. Thank God they have shown no disposition to ask me how I spent my time in England. Whether they privately know something or whether they would get nothing out of me, or whether they are actually indifferent, I don't ask. I am glad I don't have to fight them off this topic or my temper would boil over and I would do something violent. But I would rather not write any more about my miserable life here. It is only the thought of you, and how much you, too, must endure that enables me to bear it at all.

My faith is in you, my hope is in you, my love is in you. I have written this letter slowly and with tears, but half remains to be said. As I wrote on the first page, I have prayed God for guidance, and I have decided not only to appeal to you to settle this matter once and for all by divorcing Malcolm and marrying me, but I have also decided to write Malcolm and to Ella the same appeal. Perhaps I am mistaken. Perhaps I will only bring unhappiness on my own head, which deserves it, and on your dear head which I have hoped to protect from all unhappiness. But if you think best, you need not listen to my appeal. My whole life, my future, all my hopes of success and fears of failure are absolutely in your hands. If you are brave and strong enough to help me win the success that I have striven so hard and desperately for, then God, not I, will pour a million blessings on your head. If you cannot make the necessary sacrifice, then you must not expect me to be either good to you, or successful, or happy. *I cannot do what is beyond my strength,* but if you decide not to help me now, I will still always bless you as much as I can, for you and you alone have given me first and foremost, of your own free will, most content and power of song and happiness and love.

God bless you always and may His will be done to
Your own
John

P.S. Do not destroy this letter. Keep it always. John Gould Fletcher

---

TO AMY LOWELL

January 29, 1915

Dear Miss Lowell,

I have just received yours of the twenty-fifth. I am glad to hear that Aldington, H. D. and Flint have relented and the anthology is going through after all. I did not realize that it was already in the press, or I would not have added to your difficulties by my last letter. As it is, I am glad that you are taking my permission to include me—despite my letter—for granted. If there is any fighting to be done, I may be of service later on.

Flint's recollection of the Poetry Club is absolutely correct. I remember that when I first came to London, when Flint was publishing his "Net of the Stars" in *The New Age,* and Hulme was trying to write metaphysical articles for the same paper, I met the editor, who introduced me to Hulme. This was in 1910. Hulme invited me to come to the Club, which used to hold meetings in some dirty little Italian restaurant somewhere, but I didn't go. However, shortly afterward, Hulme's "Poetic Works" appeared in *The New Age,* and these were reprinted by Ezra in his *Ripostes* with a preface, all about the *École des Images* and their successors the Imagists. This book of Ezra's is in your library and was published in 1913 or late in 1912. The whole business is just another case of Ezra's appropriating someone else's idea and acting as its entrepreneur.

I am glad after all that it is to be a fight with Ezra on the old ground. In fact, I think if I were in command of the anthology's destiny, I would call it *The Imagist Poets* instead of *Some.* But it is not a question of priority, or superiority, or any of the things on which Ezra sets so much store and which, incidentally, he has no right to claim unto himself at all. We have a perfect right to call ourselves Imagists and to snap our fingers at him—if Houghton Mifflin can stand the torrent of abuse that will follow, I think we can.

There is only one thing more to say, and that is, that I have received the proofs from Houghton Mifflin after all, and with these resting on my desk to accuse me of how much I owe you, I really don't know what to say. When you have so unselfishly and so fully rendered me a service that is as big and warm-hearted as any person can render to another, there is nothing for me to do but to gratefully and humbly accept it at your hands, and to try to deserve it as far as I can. Thank you, dear Miss Lowell.

I would like to see the operettas—I am sure they will be beautifully and fitly done. But, as you already know, I cannot. I still hope to get my financial affairs straightened out and to come and see you sometime—if for nothing else, than to thank you again in person.

Affectionately,
John Gould Fletcher

[The three volumes of the Imagist group were Some Imagist Poets, 1915; Some Imagist Poets, 1916 *and* Some Imagist Poets, 1917.*]*

TO HARRIET MONROE

June 3, 1915

Dear Miss Monroe,

I expect to start for the West in about a week, but I don't know whether I will be in Chicago until the late summer. I will be for the most part of the time in Bay View (near Petoskey), Michigan, where my sister has taken a house. My address there is c/o Mrs. D. D. Terry, Bay View, Michigan.

I don't know whether you saw or not that they put Chicago in the Imagist number of *The Egoist.*

The June number of *Poetry* I have just seen. For the love of God, and for the sake of a good poet who has ruined his own talent utterly, do put a stop to Ezra's futilities. What he said about Masters was fairly good and quite true—I saw it in *Reedy's Mirror.* But his remarks on George Moore are perfectly inane and insufferable. Not that Moore is a bad poet. But Ezra does not even stop to discuss Moore—instead of that we have—the everlasting and tedious jawing about critics, reviewers, editors, the "New York school" (which doesn't exist) etc. etc. Ezra's idea of America is so false that it is ludicrous. And his idea of his own importance in the scheme of things is merely the old, old Oscar Wilde idea—so utterly moth-eaten, so feeble, so pitifully decrepit and ancient! "I am boring my little hole in the adamantine stupidity of England," etc. etc. etc. This sort of thing will kill your paper. If I have to read any more of it I shall be sea-sick. Ezra is, in truth, "boring."

I am sorry also that you said of "polyphonic prose" that it was "artificial and scientific." What you mean by "scientific" I don't know. How a form which spurns fixed laws like "polyphonic" can be "scientific," I do not see. As for artificiality, all good poetry is artificial. Masters is artificial—Whitman was tremendously and intensely artificial in his best moments. Realism, when it is done with any sense of spiritual values at all—when it is not simply the realism of a Zola, who was a sort of inverted romanticist at bottom—realism is always artificial. "Polyphonic" may be *fantastic* if you like—it may be *imaginatively grotesque or flamboyant*—but it isn't a bit artificial, except in the sense, which as I have said above, every work of art is artificial.

What I mean is, to one artist—the realist—life may appear as a set of terrible tragic realities: to another artist (the true romanticist) life may appear as a series of curious, weird, fascinating dreams and visions. Both artists use highly artificial means (fashioned by centuries of predecessors) to get their results. But to say one is right and the other wrong is simply to blind one's eyes to one side of life.

I am afraid you will have to modify your opinion of "polyphonic" some day—I do not say that it will do everything, or always prove successful. I do say that for *certain new kinds of poetry* it is a tremendously fine new form—and that as you have always stood for new forms, you ought to be more welcoming to it.

At all events I hope you will soon print the two "polyphonics" you have of mine, or else permit me to send you something else which you can use soon. I have about $300, which will have to tide me over the next six months—and living in America is not cheap. Can't you help me out a little?

Yours,
John Gould Fletcher

P.S. I hope that you will understand that it is *not* because I feel the least personal enmity towards Ezra that I write you in this way. On the contrary, it is precisely because I have a certain admiration and respect for his achievements in the past, that I express my opinion about his present silly antics. It is purely my own opinion and you can take it for what it is worth.

By the way, I have just discovered a rather serious blunder you made in the review of *Some Imagist Poets*. You say of Lawrence that his work is not imagistic because it rhymes. But in the *first* Imagistic Anthology *two poems rhymed: Joyce's and Hueffer's*. And over and over again we have said that practice in writing the ordinary metrical forms was part of our creed. Aldington wrote a rhymed poem in the last number of *Poetry and Drama*. Pound has rhymed dozens of times. I think you had better say something about this mistake in your next number, or the rest of the school will write you angry letters.

J. G. F.

TO DAISY FLETCHER

June 4, 1915

Dear Daisy,

Your *letter of May 25* has come. I meant to write you again this week but felt so depressed that I decided to wait until I heard from you.

Things have not been going very well with your John, Daisykins. In the first place my book—of which the English publisher I told you about—bought 100 copies, was sent over to England, but *it was unloaded on the wharf at Liverpool and never moved away from there. They say the freight on the wharves there is lying in boxes still that had come five and six months ago*. There is a law that unless a book gets into the English publisher's hands within a month after being copyrighted in some other country, that book cannot be copyrighted in England. So now I will not make a penny out of England! All my effort has gone for just nothing!

I also feel terribly depressed about the war. It seems to me that the last chance England had of winning has gone by. The Russians who have fought so bravely and who have spent so many lives and so much treasure in this war are now at last beaten absolutely and finally in the biggest battle of the war. And still in England Lloyd George goes up and down the country making speeches and talking about how well the new armies will be equipped when they take the field! Well, it's too late for them to take the field now. How can they hope to win against the brutes that have crushed France and destroyed Russia?

Oh well, I don't suppose it does any good to talk about it. What will happen will happen.

I am going west next week to try to find some rest and recuperation for my nerves. There is also another bad piece of news I have to tell you. Did you notice a poet named Aldington in *The Imagist Anthology*? Also a poet named H. D.! H. D. is Aldington's wife, and she has just had a baby which did not breathe after it was born. They are awfully nice people, and it is terribly sad as this is their first child. Why is the world so sad, Daisy dear? It almost makes me lose my faith in God sometimes.

I tried writing them a letter of condolence, but I am no good at that sort of thing! Poor Aldington! He has had a hard time of it in his life. First, he was very poor; second, he fought with Pound; then he thought he would have to go to war; now his wife has a still-born baby. I wish somehow you could write them, but I don't see how you could. Their address is 7 Christ Church Place, Hampstead, NW.

I feel terribly depressed still and worried about you. I do hope the money I sent you will do you some good. You mustn't send it back by any means—not any of it. But if prices go on soaring, etc., it may be the best plan to shut up the house for awhile and go to live with your grandmother. I realize that this would be a hard blow to you, but we need every penny, dear, and the prospect ahead is *not* reassuring. You must do what your best judgment dictates. I don't think you will ever get your money back on those Mexican bonds. You will lose everything.

My own plans are to return in any case by next November—I don't believe the suit will be over by then, but a year's absence from you is enough to inflict on myself, and I am not going to be away from you another Christmas. Only, dear, if I do come back before the suit is over, you must promise to do *absolutely* as I tell you—if I tell you that you must *not* love and kiss me (you know what I mean) you must somehow refrain, for my sake. It may be hard, but you must help me all you can. It will be quite as hard on me. But I am not going to run any risks of losing the suit—if I can possibly help.

Your idea of sending me an envelope in your own handwriting is a good one. You might send me two or three addressed to you. You can fold them and put them into one of your letters.

Miss L has just been elected president of a New England Poetry Society which has just been formed. The first meeting is in September. I would like to join, but have had to refuse, for I don't know whether or not I will be in America then. I dare say this will make her angry, and it would be an honor to me to be on the committee. Daisy, dear, I have had a very hard time of it this year—worse, I think, than I ever had before in my life—in more ways than you can imagine.

I do hope this letter will not depress you terribly. I know some of my

letters do make you feel happy, but I cannot always write that way. Fancy, I don't even know *now* whether the proceedings have started or not. If they haven't, it will be nearly the last straw for your poor old
    John

P.S. Love to the children. Tell them to write me a letter—anything that comes into their heads—it will cheer me up.
Address
    c/o Mrs. D. D. Terry
    Bay View
    Emmet County
    Michigan
    U.S.A
You need not write your address on the envelope as I told you to do before.

TO AMY LOWELL

Sunday, September 20th, 1915

Dear Miss Lowell,

    Please forgive me for writing to you in such a way as I did in my last. I was really quite *dead* with fatigue—induced partly by long train journeys, partly by the change of climate and altitude, partly by my financial condition, and partly by Harriet.

    It is for this reason that I forgot to thank you in my last for what you did on my behalf with Braithwaite. It was very nice of you.

    Also I suppose I must have written something that sounded rude about my coming to Boston. I hope you understand that I would gladly come there, and it would be a great pleasure to me to renew some of the talks we had last winter. Indeed I do not know of any pleasure I could enjoy better. But beggars must not be choosers and at present I am in that position.

    Harriet has fortunately rescued me from practical starvation by bringing me out to Winnetka for a few days where she is stopping with her brother. On Monday I shall move into a room—29 E. Superior Street—for which I have one week's rent paid.

    I am doing a series of character-sketches in prose which she may take, and if *The New Republic* turns down "Red Poppies" as they almost certainly will, I shall send them on there. I shall do one or two art-criticisms as well. Meanwhile of course, poetry has gone to the wall with me before the insistent need of bread without butter.

So much for my news about myself, which if it is as dull reading, as it is for me to write, must be dull indeed.

Latest news in the *Poetry* office. Harriet's next number is pretty good. She is publishing Aldington's "Images"—likewise a review (favorable) of *Irradiations* by Alice Henderson. She has received a long and tedious poem by Pound, which will kill anybody who tries to read it, with its dullness. I dare not attempt to dissuade her from printing it.

She asked me to advise her concerning the next prize—to whom I thought it should be given. It is from October of last year to Sept. of this (inclusive)—I said it ought to be given to H. D. She said she thought of Miss Skinner (the Indian person) or *Lindsay! Toujours Lindsay!*—I muttered to myself with a groan. I think of course, that "Bombardment" is the best poem she published in that period—at any event *whichever is your best poem*, the prize belongs to you—but as far as cash is concerned, I know that H. D. needs that more, and her things are very good—far and away better than Miss Skinner's. If Harriet gives the prize to Lindsay she is making a fool of herself. Besides, it ought to be given to a woman this time. I vote for H. D. and hope you agree with me.

It appears that she wants to give it to someone who is hard up and that Lindsay is hard up!!!! *Mon Dieu!*

I have not seen Margaret Anderson. She certainly tried to make her last number brilliant. Ficke surpassed himself for once, and wrote something *almost* memorable.

Harriet is publishing next month some very amusing things by T. S. Eliot, much better than "Prufrock." This young scamp is worth watching. She is also publishing Sandburg, and a poem by Wallace Stevens which I can make nothing of. I hope you read Stevens' "Peter Quince" in the second number of *Others*—it was very good. He is thirty-five, I learn, and a lawyer in New York. He has never published. He and Eliot seem to be the only new men with anything at all to them. And both suffer from being too damnably clever—a great sin in the opinion of

Yours affectionately,
John Gould Fletcher
who thinks that both these men are worth watching, nevertheless. Eliot, however, may be swamped with the Pound influence—he is very young.

Monday

P.S. Your letter with the check has come. Twenty-eight dollars is a fabulous, an incredible sum. You are a fairy princess, an angel—I can now snap my fingers at Harriet, thank God—this is enough to keep me alive for a whole month.

J. G. F.

TO AMY LOWELL

Sept. 27 [1915]

Dear Miss Lowell,

Your letters are so interesting, I cannot refrain from answering them as they come.

As to your very generous offer to provide me with twenty-five dollars, I decided that I might as well get the hundred out of my sisters, as I would have to come to Boston. They let me have it, and I have the check now in my pocket. So you see I do not need your check, but thank you *very* much all the same.

Harriet only loaned me ten dollars, and that is all. Yes, I know she means well, but——. I suppose I will inveigle (I really have forgotten how to spell it) her into taking some poems. I proposed the *hors concours* idea to her myself, and she said she would write you. I think she will mention "Venus Transiens."

As an example of her absurdities, take the Bryant attack. Everybody knows that Bryant was a mere high-browed sham. Why, then, didn't she leave him alone? She dragged him in, and now she is writing a perfectly senseless reply—amounting to complete surrender—to *The Dial!* She simply hasn't guts enough to stand her ground.

I have something amusing for you, which you must keep a secret. Ezra has just written her a long letter in which he says that Storer was not an Imagist—being quite the antipodes to him. Also that although the movement started before he entered it, yet it was not discovered seriously. Its only aim was to get three poems of H. D. printed. That he first mentioned the school in *Ripostes*. He winds up remarking, "Since the latest manifestation, I scarcely know whether to repudiate all connection, or whether to attempt to continue the movement on the basis of the common-sense of the original program. I don't suppose that either way it will matter a tupenny d——n!"

What do you think of this? Is this not enough to make you forget those joyless translations and to laugh long and uproariously?

Harriet read me this much of his letter—of course, *not realizing*—so for goodness sake, let it go no further.

I have also learned from an outside source that *Poetry* has guaranteed Pound two appearances a year! Ezra drove a good hard bargain, didn't he?

Ezra also wrote that he preferred *Aiken* to anybody in the last issue! Then he went on to remark on the echo of Swinburne in "Eyes that have lighted so many eyes"—and on the "Vermilioned mouth" taken from "elsewhere" —methinks I could almost guess who "elsewhere" is.

So much for our ex-impresario. Now, about the next anthology.

There is a bunch of poems by Clarice Shanafelt in the *Poetry* office which Harriet let me see. Alice Henderson had called them "echoes of Emily Dickinson and of Fletcher." This judgment I considered to be somewhat unjust. I think there is more Dickinson than Fletcher, but for all that, *she is not bad*—some of the things were *distinctly good of their sort*—And she wrote Harriet a delightful letter. She might be worth considering.

Marianne Moore I have no use for and never will. If you must take one of these two, Shanafelt seems to me the best guess. I would much prefer giving one poet a large space to play about in, to giving a page apiece to two or three. However, that is how I feel, and you know that you are at liberty to do just as you like with any suggestion I may offer.

I will see you in Boston at the time you mention if not before. I have been greatly cheered by *The Egoist's* taking of "Ghosts." My western trip was absolutely unproductive of anything resembling a good poem. But I have not done badly this year. I have written five good things. "Ghosts" is one; "Poppies" is another; and "Clipper-Ships," "The Old South," and "Chicago" are the rest. That, I think, is not bad for a year. You have done lots more with your *Violin Poems* which still sticks in my head, with your "Spring-Day," with "Patterns" and "Middle-Age," and "The Windmill" (I think I shall like that better than "The Lead Soldiers"), and several others—not to mention this French book on top of all, or your lectures, or your other innumerable activities. But then you are older than I, and have gotten into what will probably be your ripest period.

I will say one thing about myself: that if "Ghosts" is *not* poetry, then by the powers, I never will know what poetry is! There are one or two poems in that series that need an occasional change—one particularly has a somewhat shopworn adjective—but take it all in all, I am content with it.

I am very, very sorry to hear about Mrs. Russell and all your other troubles. This is truly a most unreasonable planet, to put it mildly. When you finish that book, I don't expect you will ever again be able to look at another French poem—and if Richard keeps discovering "young hopefuls," I don't expect you will ever want to read another English poem, very shortly. *C'est la vie.*

Yours affectionately
John Gould Fletcher

P.S. Why worry yourself over Greenslet's ridiculous series? It is energy wasted! Faber is *awful* and Aiken is ———[sic]. If the man wants to be a damn fool, let him!   J. G. F.
P.P.S. I am not keen on the woodcut idea, but will send photo and see what a hash they make of it.

[Harriet Monroe, in Poetry *6 (July 1915): 197–200, had used the reading of "Thanatopsis" at a memorial service for a casualty of the* Lusitania *to criticize Bryant.]*

TO AMY LOWELL

Oct. 15, 1915

Dear Miss Lowell:

By God, I am so mad I could bite somebody's head off. Since I wrote you this morning I went to *Poetry*'s office to see what Harriet was up to. She was out. The proofs of the new number were on the table. I looked at them.

She has given a prize of a hundred dollars to Lindsay.

She has given a second prize of one hundred to Skinner.

She has given a third prize of fifty to H. D.

This is *hell*. I hope that H. D. refuses to take it. She mentioned, by the way, "Venus Transiens," along with people like Ajam Syrian!!!!!!!

There is worse yet. She is going to print a page of blatherskite by Pound *about us*. About Imagism. About "what I object to in *mes amis et confreres* is their looseness, their treatment of what should be a vortex as a decorative poster or fence-wash"—etc.

Now she shall not do this. We have enough to contend with without this creature coming in and stealing our thunder with the old tommyrot about his critical judgment, etc.

I am prepared to break off with her. Why *should* such people be permitted to live, anyway?

I am through, absolutely through, with her. I have endured with patience all her airs of superiority, her utter unbounded ignorance, her academic desire to hand out prizes for the deserving poor, etc. She is a fool—a Biblical fool—and worthy of nothing but my contempt.

I shall starve rather than let this mountebank Pound utter his inanities about us. If she prints this, she will never print anything more of mine. I am determined on that.

Oh it is enough to make me sick-sick-sick of life!

J. G. Fletcher

[The November 1915 issue of Poetry *announced the winners of the poetry contest as first place ($200.00) to Vachel Lindsay for "The Chinese Nightingale"; second place ($100.00) to Constance Lindsay Skinner for "Songs of the Coast-Dwellers"; and third place ($50.00) to H. D. for "Poems." Also mentioned were Ajam Syrian for "The Syrian Lover in Exile" and other poems. Fletcher seems to have thought that Lowell's "Venus Transiens" deserved better than mention.]*

TO DAISY FLETCHER

Jan. 17 [1916]

Darling,

Your dear letter of the 30th has come, in answer to mine of the sixth. I won't say anything about the dear loving part of it, because almost all of your letters are opened by the censor (thank goodness, this one wasn't) and I suppose mine are having the same fate. It is so hateful to write about love when we feel somebody else may be reading them.

My health, thank God, has picked up again in the last few weeks and my eyes are greatly improved. For a time around Christmas I suffered terribly with them. But I must tell you of something which has happened here, and ask your advice about it. It is about Miss Lowell. I hope it won't be boring to you to listen to this long story.

As you may know, I first met Miss L in the summer of 1913 shortly before I came up to Liverpool. There were some things I liked about her at the time. I did not see her again until that summer of 1914 before the war broke out. Then I saw her quite frequently as you may remember, as I was with you at the time.

At that time I had been invited by Ezra Pound to take part in the next *Imagist Anthology*. This man Pound at the time was head of the school of Imagists. I never liked him because he is shallow, very self-conceited (is that the way you spell it) and very bullying and domineering in his ways—besides being a little 'crooked.' He intended to bring out a new Imagist anthology, and to pick out for himself the poems he wanted in it—an idea I did not like.

Now at that time, Miss L had talked with him over the idea of founding a magazine—monthly—of poetry and literature. What they had written each other, I don't know. But she gave him to believe that she was going to start this magazine, and that he would be editor. When she came back to England (in June 1914) she decided after all to drop this project of a magazine. The result was that Pound became very angry and swore that he would have nothing more to do with her.

I regret to say that she pulled the wool over my eyes in this instance (as the saying goes). She has a very conniving way with her, and she can persuade people better than anyone I ever met. She persuaded me, *anyhow*, that Pound was at fault—and I had a few scores to settle with Pound myself (who had treated me badly), so I decided to come in with her and start a new *Imagist Anthology*, with Pound left out.

In November 1914 as you know I left England, and she received me in her house in Boston and was very nice to me. I only stayed there about two weeks and all during that time she treated me like a prince (she has lots of money). I went to Little Rock and did not come back to Boston until February, 1915, just before the Imagist book came out.

When I came back to Boston she was still very nice to me and the prospect of coming out in the Imagist anthology, and also of publishing *Irradiations* (she had insisted on taking the manuscript of this book, and offering it herself to the publishers) was enough to keep us still on very friendly terms. I wrote an article in *Poetry*—a magazine to which I contribute—praising her work to the skies and also one in *The Egoist*. This, by the way, was just what she wanted. She doubtless went about telling all her friends about these articles and asking them to read them. That is the sort she is.

I forgot to tell you that one of the reasons I had come into the Imagist School was because I was allowed full liberty *to pick out my own poems* and did not have her as an editor to domineer over me as to what I should put in. This is important for you to know in view of what has happened later.

Our friendship began to wane about the time I left Boston for Bay View. She began prying into my private affairs and asking questions as I have told you, and this roused my suspicions. Whether she saw a change in my manner I don't know, but when I came back to Boston last autumn, she still acted very graciously—*for a time.*

She offered to take the Manuscript of my new book *Goblins and Pagodas*—to another and a better publisher, who publishes all her things. I agreed to let her have it. The publisher refused it, and I have found out later that reason is, *that she told him that it would not sell.*

You see, by this time, she thought she had me at her mercy—I would just be a sort of *subordinate* to her—She would borrow ideas from me, get me to do most of her work, and *use* me for all I was worth. She is very vain and very conceited at bottom, and she made up her mind when she first came to London, to get *fame* and glory for herself, by fair means or foul. She had been very kind to me so long as I could be of help to her, now she decided to squelch and suppress me if possible as she did not want me to be her competitor.

I have been so long unused to the ways of this world that I did not understand what was happening at first, and I have always been generous to others as much as possible, so I said to myself, "It's just her way of doing things," and said nothing. My book was accepted promptly by another publisher, and this time she had nothing to do with its acceptance. I still thought that she was not changed, and I might have continued to do so, but my eyes have been opened by two things.

About two weeks before Christmas I wrote my poem I sent to you, "The Kaiser's Christmas Tree." This is a good poem, and she herself thought so. I told her that I was sending it to a Boston paper (to which she had contributed) and that I hoped they would put it in. The people on the paper kept it up to Christmas Eve, and then decided they didn't have room for it. I am perfectly convinced in my mind that they would have put it in, if she had telephoned them and insisted—but she didn't stir a finger on my behalf!

If this was all, I would have nothing to say. But there is worse than this.

About the same time—about two weeks before Christmas—she suddenly came to me with the idea of starting a monthly magazine in the U.S. She had persuaded someone to put up some money and was ready to put up some herself. She wanted an editor, and she decided to have Aldington for the job. She wrote him a most enthusiastic letter and asked me to write him, and urge him to accept. I did so.

Now Aldington is a young Englishman, only about twenty-five, and he would have been taken for conscription but for the fact that he is married. Both he and his wife *are very nice people*—he is not much of a poet and is rather weak, but he has been very decent and upright in every way to her and to me. He had been a good friend of Pound, and when he decided to quit Pound and to go into this new anthology idea (Miss L worked him around, as she did me), Pound acted as nasty to the poor boy as he could, and made everything very unpleasant for him. He was dreadfully poor and he and his wife have had a hard struggle. His wife is delicate, and suffers from ill-health, and he hasn't offered himself for the army because he has got to support her and because if he got killed, it would probably kill her. He doubtless is very anxious to leave England in order to escape conscription, which will probably come for *married men* some time this year. I cannot blame him, because he is not very strong himself, and the army would probably be the death of him. He replied to Miss L saying he would be delighted to become editor of the proposed paper, *if he could obtain a passport to leave England.*

Now what do you suppose has happened? *The moment* this letter arrived, she changed her mind and cabled him not to come over, *that she could not raise the money for the paper.* This is a lie. She *could* raise it if she wanted to. She hasn't made much of an attempt *so far*. No, the truth of it is, that she is not to be depended upon. She misled that poor devil Aldington into thinking that she was going to start a paper and when he took her at her word *she backed out of it.* And she misled me into writing him and urging him to accept when she never seriously intended such a thing.

Now the question arises, what am I to do about this? I have to go explain matters to Aldington somehow. Also I have got to break off friendship with her—I couldn't be friends any longer. *And here arises the difficulty.*

When she took up *The Imagist Anthology* idea, she told me that she had agreed to publish it for three years (this she is doing at her own expense, which proves she could endow the magazine if she wanted to). The second

Imagist book will be out this spring. She has already made things very disagreeable for me about this second book, and I feel sure that if I told her outright that we could not be friends any more, and that I must withdraw my support for this next Imagist volume, she would simply refuse to publish it at all—and as this book is being published by the same publishers who are publishing *my own book*, that would be the end of *that*, too. Also it would simply leave Aldington in the lurch—and all the rest of the school. *It would not be fair to them to make a squabble with her now*, so I must hold my tongue and say nothing until the next Imagist volume has appeared.

At the same time, I must somehow let Aldington understand that I do *not* think she has treated him fairly. I don't want him to think that I am supporting her in this matter. I don't want him to think I have backed down along with her. So you see my position is very difficult, and the worst of it is, I am living here in Boston where she has me under her nose so to speak, and if I tell her honestly what I think of her, she will use all the spite in her tongue to *smash me*—she won't stop at telling lies about me, I know, because I know what sort she is.

I wish to God I were in England, and that it were June. The next months are going to be *hell* for me, and I know that there will be a clean break before I have gone. I will break absolutely with her, and *never under any circumstances will I ever again take part in this anthology that she is directing*. She can say and think of me as she chooses. I am a gentleman and therefore *my* tongue is sealed. But I am not going to lend my further support to a person who has acted so shabbily as she has, in the last few months.

I suppose I shall have to write all this to Aldington, and he is such a silly well-meaning boy, that he will probably repeat it to her—he doesn't know her as I do—and then she will say I have been stabbing her in the back. My God, what a world this is! Sometimes I wonder if this is not really hell and we have not been sent here as a punishment.

Now, dear, don't tell this to anyone, but tell me honestly what you would do if you were in my case. Would you tell her outright that she was dishonest? Or would you wait until the next anthology is safely out, and then just before leaving for England, tell her *fully that there could be no hope of any further friendship?*

One or the other I must do, because this last treatment of that poor devil Aldington puts her really *beyond the pale—if she had treated me this way, I might forgive her, but she has treated a friend of mine in this way, and tried to get me to stand for it and that I cannot endure.*

I believe I will write her this very day and tell her that I hold myself at liberty henceforward to write to Aldington whatever I choose.

Last night I dreamed I was riding horseback by great red cliffs, which towered far above me in the sky. I saw there were clouds above them, very close to the top, and somebody whom I was riding with pointed them out to me, and said there was green in the clouds. I looked and there was. I wonder what the dream means. There is something about colors in that dream book in the bookcase, but what it is I can't remember.

Forgive me, darling, if I have bored you by writing all this but you are the only one I can talk these matters over with, and I wish you were here and could tell me what I am to do. Whatever I do, I hope that you will never have to be ashamed of
Your
John

[Ferris Greenslet was the first of a long series of editors whose rejections earned the enmity of the poet.]

TO HARRIET MONROE

Jan. 28 [1916]

Dear Harriet,

Miss Lowell telephoned me this morning and told me that you had refused to allow any poem in polyphonic prose to appear in your new anthology. This decision is regrettable, and you will live to regret it. I want to prove to you, if I can, that you are wrong.

I have been interested in your paper from its beginning, as a complete file (including the first number) will testify. It has always seemed to me that the paper was an achievement of which anybody could be proud. Under your hands, it has added immensely to the interest in poetry which is growing up on all sides, every day, in this country. And how has it done it? By printing everyone who was any good, without caring whether they followed the received tradition or not. You have established vers libre, by proving that poetry can be just as good if written in that form, as it can be in any form. Not only that. You have printed—and I daresay you will reprint in your anthology—certain poems of Rabindranath Tagore which are in prose— *prose pure and simple.*

Now I don't know what is your objection to this form of prose poem that Miss Lowell and myself write. Is it simply because we give it a title "polyphonic" to explain that it was prose heightened by all sorts of metrical devices till it pours over into poetry? Is it because you think the form artificial? Or is it simply because you dislike it? I don't know. It seems strange that you should have printed "polyphonic" first, just like you did so many other things first—for example, Mr. Lindsay's work which is very close to "polyphonic"—which might almost be called "polyphonic" in ragtime—and that you should now refuse to reprint the three best specimens of it so far written—Miss Lowell's "Bombardment," her "Lead Soldiers," and my "Old South"—in your anthology. Why then, if you dislike poetry that looks like prose, didn't you turn down Tagore?

About this prose argument. It doesn't make a scrap of difference how a poem—how any poem—is printed. Whether I write, for example,

>   High
>   Streaks of cottony white cloud fill the sky.
>   The sun
>   Swings his long jewelled mace
>   Before his face
>   As he plays
>   With the ripples that gurgle
>   Under the rotting cypress knees.

or whether I write the same thing as prose, the effect is exactly the same. Neither does it matter whether Miss Lowell writes

>   Slowly, without force
>   The rain drops into the city,
>   It stops a moment on the carved beard of Saint John,
>   Then glides on
>   Again
>   Slipping and trickling
>   Over his stone cloak.

or whether she too, puts the whole thing down as a line of prose.

About this verse and prose argument, I really wish you would read an article by D. S. McColl in *Essays and Studies by Members of the English Association*, Oxford, Clarendon Press, 1914. The article is called "Rhythm in English Verse, Prose, and Speech." In it the author distinguishes four kinds of verse and prose: characteristic prose, numerous prose, verse invaded by prose emphasis, and characteristic verse. Now all we claim for polyphonic is that it is a combination of verse invaded by prose emphasis (what might be called vers libre) and characteristic verse. We print it as prose—why? Merely to mark its freedom from set rules. What has printing, typography, to do with poetry? Are not *Job, The Song of Solomon*, Mr. Tagore, De Quincey's "Suspiria de Profundis," whole pages of Gibbon, etc. perfectly metrical and poetical, despite their being printed as prose?

You may say, "But polyphonic prose is artificial." Now what is artificial about a form like this? I understand that you intend to print in your anthology a sonnet by Miss Lowell? There you have an artificial form—a rhyme-pattern, absolutely rigid, octave balancing sestet, something as fixed and as stereotyped as a conventionalized design on an Oriental rug or a piece of wall paper. When the fact of the matter is, polyphonic was adopted by Miss Lowell and myself simply because it was the freest form we could find. It permits of such endless variation of rhythm that rhyme is necessary to enforce it—not only rhyme but refrain. Note the rain refrain in "The Bombardment"—or the river refrain in "The Old South." Polyphonic prose comes far nearer to the conditions of modern music—to Wagner and Richard Strauss than anything I know. There is literally endless rhythm, endless melody in this form. That is because it is so free. You cannot write this form unless you are stirred and exalted to the topmost pitch of feeling. With sonnets etc. you are hampered by rhyme scheme and meter, and nine times out of ten you produce something so artificial that it is worthless. Polyphonic is the freest, most open-air form of poetry. It is Greek dithyramb all over again.

You may say you do not like polyphonic. I wonder whether anyone ever does like a new form at first acquaintance. I wonder whether Petrarch when he first wrote sonnets did not have people shaking their heads and saying that canzoni were much better. I wonder if it isn't that many of us are *taught* to like certain forms. For example, take the sonnet again. To my mind, the Shakespearean form of sonnet is far finer than the Petrarchan as far as English goes. It may be otherwise in Italian. To achieve such climaxes as Shakespeare does in the last two lines—to lead up to them all the way—that is to be a poet and not to juggle with three rhymes at the end like Milton. Well, just such climaxes do we get out of "polyphonic" by use of certain refrains and swift metrical passages. You may or may not like it. It may take you years to see it. But the form is there, and if we do not achieve success, someone will do so after we are gone.

Poetry is not going to stop where you want it to stop, not where I and Miss Lowell want it to stop. It will go on and on. I have worked at poetry for ten years and if I work for ten years more, I shall just begin to know what this force is that made me its instrument. I know this indeed—it is the form of rhythm and not of certain stereotyped forms. It is a force therefore of *sound,* and not of typographical arrangement. It is a force of freedom and joy—it is the energy of which Blake speaks when he says energy is an eternal delight. Yes, energy is an eternal delight; whether the end be tragic or not, matters nothing. And I say to you that there is no form today in contemporary poetry that has more of this energy than this form you refuse to print in your anthology.

Very well. Have it your own way. Only remember—you already have Mr. Braithwaite's anthology in the market ahead of you and you want to outsell him. Are people going to buy your book if it is reactionary? If it is tedious? If it does not present a complete view of contemporary verse? I don't think so.

Purely for the sake of our friendship in the past I will consent to your using my "Irradiations" and "Blue Symphony," but for the future you need not expect me to show any enthusiasm. My next polyphonic piece will be sent to *The Century*. I will not trouble you with it.

I enclose the Blake volume, also a review which I fear is too long. You can use any part you like, or if useless send it back to me.

I believe you paid me $28.00 for poetry last fall. If you would rather have this money stand as payment for one of the Arizona-Chicago set, and send the others back, I don't mind.

I hope I have not offended you by speaking my mind about this matter.

John Gould Fletcher

[The first selection of poetry is the opening of Fletcher's "The Old South"; the second is Amy Lowell's "The Bombardment." The anthology, The New Poetry, *edited with Alice Corbin (Henderson), was published in 1917.]*

TO AMY LOWELL

Sunday, June 11, 1916

Dear Amy:—

Here I am in London at last, safe and well.

I only got here last Thursday, and as I have had to purchase some new clothes, I have been very busy and haven't seen much.

Everything seems almost the same on the surface, but under the surface everything is changed. The English people are taking the war better than I thought. They have been publicly warned (warnings are posted in every railway carriage) not to discuss military and naval matters in public. And so one seldom hears anything said about the war at all. The streets are simply full of soldiers. But there are quite a number of young men like myself in civilian dress. These are unmolested, as everybody concludes from the fact that conscription is now in, that they are either rejected aliens (my first business in London was to register at a police station) or else exempt for some special reason.

The Zeppelins did very little damage and no one seems to be at all frightened at the prospect of seeing more of them. They dropped bombs very near the Strand, from the Law Courts to Drury Lane Theater, without hitting a single important building! Altogether the Zeppelins are about the worst bluff Germany has made during the war.

Everybody seems quite determined to go on and end this war, however long it may take, and the only complaint that exists is against the high cost of living, which is really quite terrifying. Things are just about double what they were and it is quite as expensive now to live here as in America. Everybody is wearing old clothes and well-dressed women are rare now. In front of the lions in Trafalgar Square is now a large sign:—"To dress extravagantly in war time is worse than bad form. It is unpatriotic."

There is still a fuss going on in the papers about the Germans and naturalized Germans over here, who have by no means all been interned. The trouble is, the whole matter is in the hands of the Home Office, not the soldiery. It is a bad scandal. Everybody is saying that Lord Kitchener, who opposed himself the internment of Germans at the outset of the war, owed his death to information given the Germans by a spy.

Altogether I feel less worried about the war than I did in America. There is no doubt England is now making a tremendous effort and she is not talking about it either, but working. Tomorrow is bank holiday in normal times, but it has been given up this year in order to ensure an uninterrupted supply of shells. About half the bus conductors in London are now women. The daylight saving law has been passed, and now the streets do not have to be lighted at all, as the light lasts till nearly half past ten in the evening (the clock has been shoved an hour ahead to do this). Although I arrived in England just in time to see the last men taken, and to hear of Lord Kitchener's death (a very heavy loss) and also to hear of the heavy losses, equal on both sides, in the naval fight (which undoubtedly the Germans only fought because they had to have some sort of "victory" to buck up the people), and also to hear of the loss of Vaux fort, yet nobody seems to be discouraged, and I must say I think the English have been greatly improved by the war. This from Masefield!

I have not heard one word about us or seen yet a copy of any of our books. But as I have only been to one bookshop, I dare say I will find them somewhere.

We are having the usual rain every day and a double portion for Sundays. England is exquisite, however, but the rhododendrons are almost bloomed out.

I expect to be married before the end of this month, and so you can see I will be busy, and I expect to be away somewhere in the country during July and Aug. The address given below will always reach me, however.

Yours affectionately

J. G. F.

c/o 37 Crystal Palace Park Road

Sydenham

London, S.E.

England

[On June 5 Secretary of War Lord Kitchener was drowned when the cruiser Hampshire *was sunk by a mine in the Orkneys. On June 7 the Vaux fort fell to the Germans advancing on Verdun.]*

TO AMY LOWELL

June 28, 1916

Dear Amy,

I have received your letter of June 16, sent through Constables, also the cutting from *The Forum*, concerning the Spectrist School. The latter is distinctly amusing. I wonder why they do not call themselves the Spectral or even the Ghastly School—I have never read worse rubbish. They are beneath our notice. Somehow I have been completely out of patience with all these "school" ideas. This school business has been overdone, even in France and the best thing we can be is to be poets, not members of a school. After all, all that Imagism has stood for, is the eternal verities of all good writing in the past, and so, in that sense, we are not a school, but merely an attempt to restore the old qualities of sincerity and good taste.

I have not received Braithwaite's paper yet, and am wild to see what my poems look like, also to read Phelps' article. There is no doubt in my mind that we have, in a sense, *"arrived"* and the future activities of our group will depend not on propaganda, but on what each of us is able to contribute of fine and lasting work. I am very anxious to read your "Hummers" which I am sure, will be a fine thing. As regards my own work, I recognize in myself a change in the direction of greater breadth, simplicity of means, and also a stronger impersonal note. I am going out for "high seriousness" as you say, and I feel more sure that I am on the right track than I did six months ago when I was in the transition stage. It seems to me that I was, in *Goblins and Pagodas*, too preoccupied with style, that is to say, with the way in which I say things, rather than in the thing said. Now I am the other way about.

I have been to Harold Monro's bookshop, but did not see him. He is in anti-aircraft work at present. The New Poetry series was there, but I don't suppose Constable has seen the latest Imagist one, as they wrote me some days ago, saying they hadn't seen *Goblins and Pagodas*. I have also written a lot to Aldington and H. D., but have not seen them. Aldington joined his regiment on the 24th, I understand. He says he has decided not to do the letter for Braithwaite, so that's all right. He wants me to do it instead. I probably will send B something of the sort if I ever find them.

The wedding has been postponed to the 5th of July, when it will certainly take place. I have been very busy making arrangements. I thought my wife-to-be would probably write you, but she hasn't had the time.

Things are so frightfully expensive over here now that I find I must economize a great deal, and I would like to be able to add a few dollars to my income. I have written some poems on the present aspect of London of which I am sending you too. My typewriter is out of repair, and so I cannot type them. Would you mind doing just one more favor for me? You might get your secretary to type them, and send them to *The Century.* If you would rather not, then don't bother about it.

You can see by the poems that I am working at rhyme now. In the main, things are very interesting over here, and I am surprised that the poetry this war has produced has been so feeble, so far. But no one in England wants to think of the tragic side, everybody is trying to be as cheerful as possible. Except for the soldiers and the wounded, one sees very little of the dreadful side. Altogether the war has tightened the moral fiber of the English in the sense they have grown so accustomed to this state of affairs that any other seems to them almost incredible and untrue. It has loosened it in the sense that a lot of the old Puritan morality has been swept overboard at a stroke. The amount of immorality that goes on in munitions factories, etc., is staggering. The working classes who do not have to be called up are simply making loads of money—so much that they don't know how to spend it. The first excitement has completely subsided, and less interest than ever is now taken in the war news. The whole attitude might be summed up in two phrases one hears constantly: "We are going to win this war" and "We wish this war were over." The contrast is paradoxical, but after all there is no real contradiction between these ideas. Everyone is looking forward to a great future offensive which the Allies—particularly the British—will undertake and which they expect to settle matters. For my part, I have some doubts, but am content for the present to wait and see.

I don't know Lawrence's address but will try to get it from H. D. I think he is in want, as I see that he has another book of Italian travel sketches published through Duckworth, also he is to have some more poems published shortly under the title of "Amores." However, I will write and see.

I am very well, and my brain is simply teeming with ideas for poems, which I haven't at present time to write. I feel I must do something, as your book will put us all in the shade, completely. Those Napoleonic things will probably be the best that you have ever done.

Do you remember that I told you about Napoleon's coffin being opened, and they finding him intact? Well, I saw in a book the other day that about 1773 the grave of Edward I of England in Westminster Abbey was opened and for a moment the people saw the face of the king absolutely as it was when he died in 1307. The next moment, it crumbled to dust. More interesting still, in 1813 the grave of Charles I (who had been embalmed, however) was opened. The head was seen sewn back on the neck—features very handsome. The next minute, however, the nose fell in. This I got out of *The Red Blake* by Edwin J. Ellis—that about Charles is also mentioned in *The Encyclopedia Britannica.*

Enough of this gossip. I wonder if you could do anything with the theme of the flight of Louis XVI and his family to Varennes in a coach. The best account of this I have seen is in a recent book by Hilaire Belloc, *The Last Days of the French Monarchy*. It is tremendously dramatic as an episode in history, and you should make a fine polyphonic.

Yours affectionately
John Gould Fletcher

P.S. Have just seen Harriet's June number. The Lindsay things are "Congo-and-water." Three of Shanafelt's are good. The rest is rubbish. Ezra with his prehistoric grouch and Harriet with her petty spite. I wonder what Steven's play *is* like.

[Irked by the pretensions of the Imagists, the Vorticists, and other poetic groups, Witter Bynner and Arthur Davison Ficke founded the Spectrist school allegedly inspired by Nijinsky's performance in Le Spectre de la Rose. *Under the pseudonyms Emmanuel Morgan and Anne Knish they published* Spectra: Experiments *(1916). The hoax enjoyed great publicity for some time. The history of the Spectrists was described in William J. Smith's* The Hoax *(1961).]*

TO AMY LOWELL

July 16, 1916

Dear Amy,

Your letter of June 28 reached me on honeymoon, so please excuse my delay in answering it. Your other letter addressed to Constable has come also, and if I did not acknowledge it previously I am sorry.

I shall be very pleased to hold the job on Braithwaite's paper pro tem for Richard. I will send B an article on the present state of English poetry as soon as I can. He can take it or not as he likes. H. D. has written me asking me to do it, and I will try my best to fill the gap.

About what you write on the W. C. Williams letter and *Others*. When I was in New York, I heard that Williams was going to get out a special number of *Others* containing one page apiece from about fifteen of the best poets in America—and that I was to contribute something, and was invited to do so. Kreymborg, I heard also, had gone all to pieces as a result of a divorce case with his wife, who apparently is tired of him and loves another. It seemed to me not to matter much whether I went in or not for this special occasion, and it also seemed to me that Williams would not be so bad as Kreymborg (whom I do not like), to judge by all that you and other people had said in his favor. So when I arrived in London, I sent Williams a short and rather inferior thing—only about 12 or 14 lines—and forgot all about it. I am dreadfully sorry if this seems to you to be bad behavior on my part—it is really so difficult to remember what it is we have agreed on as regards this thing and that—and after all, I don't intend to boycott *Others* absolutely, if it shows any signs of grace. I prefer

[page missing]

gone under, and Williams and the paper will shortly follow. So I hope it won't matter much.

As regards anecdotes of my early life, I am afraid I haven't any. But here are the best I can offer.

Born Jan. 3, 1886. Father of Scotch-Irish stock, son of a pioneer, who moved to Arkansas (the wilderness) about 1815 from Tennessee. Family had lived in Tennessee from pre-Revolutionary days. Father born in a log cabin in the country in 1833. At that time Little Rock had about a dozen houses in it. Father had a backwoods education. In 1860 at the outbreak of the Civil War he volunteered to serve the Confederacy and served to 1863, being promoted out of the ranks to be captain of his company after the battle of Chickamauga, and being wounded at Murfreesboro on January 31, 1862, after being mentioned in dispatches for bravery. After war father kept a small general store in Little Rock, made enough money to be cotton buyer, rose steadily, undertook a trip to Europe in 1873 (traveled over Germany, Austria as far as Prague, Paris, London) and returning to Little Rock married in 1877 Adolphine Krause, the daughter of a Danish father (naturalized American in 1839) and a mother from Hannover (who had come to America in 1835 with her brother, at the age of 15. The brother died without children about 1850 or thereabouts. I fancy my mother's father must have been much older than his wife, as she was left a widow early—before the Civil War, with three daughters on her hands.)

Children of my father and mother were one daughter, then myself four years later, and then another daughter (three years after that). In 1890 we moved to the former home of General Albert Pike, a prominent Freemason, a poet mentioned by Poe (in his article on handwriting) and one of the first settlers of Little Rock. This house, much battered when we moved into it, is the Old House of the "Ghost" poems. After the Pikes went north (after the Civil War), it had been successively a school and a boarding house, and some of the walls had layers of wall-paper on them four and five deep. It was much too large for us, and we had little furniture, as my father about this time met with some bad financial reverses, owing to the fact that his brother at the time was sheriff (and tax collector) of Pulaski County, in which Little Rock is situated, and this brother had deposited the taxes he collected at a bank, of which the cashier defaulted and absconded. My father with his usual generosity stood for the loss and made it good. His motive was mistaken, and it was supposed that he was trying to shelter his brother, who had been in some way criminal. I think this embittered my father for the rest of his life.

My mother was musical, with leanings to art. She loved to buy books and we had quite a library. The first thing I can remember seriously reading was "The Rhyme of the Ancient Mariner," which I did not at all understand or appreciate. I liked *Tom Sawyer* very much better, and the scene in the graveyard sent shivers up and down my spine and gave me an unquenchable taste for the uncanny and weird. At the age of seven or eight, I began to be educated by private teachers, having previously been taught to read and write by my mother (out of Webster's Blue Back Spelling Book—the classic primer of my childhood). I started to learn German and Latin at about 8, and used to revel in Schiller, Uhland, and other German romantic poets. Went to school in 1897 and had a craze for Longfellow, Scott, and Tennyson. I began to write verses about this time.

My first schools were private affairs and did not flourish. I was sent to high school in 1899 and graduated in 1902. In 1900, or 1901, I had a set of Poe presented to me and this made an effect on me that was tremendous. I swallowed all of Poe's theories wholesale, and even then began to dream of an American literature such as he had dreamed of.

In 1902 I went to Phillips Academy, Andover, Mass., to prepare for Harvard. I was there one year. The system of compulsory gymnasium training at this school worked wonders for me. Before this I had been sickly and undersized—now I rapidly shot up. For a time I took a great interest in matters unconnected with literature. Chemistry greatly fascinated me at Andover—I obtained the highest grade in my class in it. Mathematics I was poor in, yet I finally mastered algebra completely, but dismally failed to grasp geometry. Languages were easy but I was too lazy to study them carefully and to remember them.

In 1903 I entered Harvard. Here for the first time I set to work on French. Previous to this I only knew Latin and German. Latin made French easy to read for me. Poe had led me on to Gautier and Baudelaire, which I first read in translations.

In the summer of 1905 I went west to California and the Yosemite, returning by Portland and Salt Lake City. This trip stirred me up to write more poetry than I had ever done before. The West fascinated me.

In January 1906 my father suddenly died of heart failure. He had not shared any of my aspirations and his one desire was to see me a banker or a lawyer. After his death I was left with means within my grasp. In one year I would be of age. I decided to devote myself to the literary life.

Accordingly next year, Feb. 1907 I abandoned college and took a flat in Boston intending vaguely to write something that would bring me immediate fame and recognition. I remember vaguely my idol at this time was Heine, whom I imitated as closely as possible. But after a while, finding no congenial companionship, and no suitable surroundings (I had shunned the "literary" set at Harvard of deliberate intent) I left America on August 20, 1908, going first to Naples and then up the Adriatic by steamer to Trieste and from there to Venice, where I stayed to November, then to Rome.

In Italy the Byron-Shelley craze struck me and I read quantities of Shelley and tried to write like him. Fortunately, I acquired a knowledge of Browning soon after and this perhaps prevented Shelley from doing too much harm.

I stayed in Rome till May of 1909 then came to London, being moved by curiosity to see what it was like. This was another tremendous impression, and after a short return to Italy I settled in London in October 1909 and had a flat in London from that time until shortly before the outbreak of the war. I moved three times and the last time to Adelphi Terrace, a place full of literary people.

It was in London in 1909 that I first really carefully read Walt Whitman and that he made an impression on me. He seems to me always the only poet who gave any sort of true impression of the typically modern city. Whitman's poems are jumbles, but so are modern cities.

I began to write vers libre at this period, of a Whitmanite cast, and only returned to meter a year later in 1910.

In this year I first saw Paris (hitherto I had passed through without stopping) and a poem by Verhaeren awakened me to the fact that other poets had written besides Baudelaire, Verlaine, and Mallarmé. I started reading modern French poetry. This gave a new impetus and the result was that two years later I found myself with a great deal of material on my hands. I decided to publish a book, but I had no instinct of selection and so I published five books in the month of May of the following year. This harebrained experiment had the usual success.

I had no friends or acquaintances in London for a long time. I spent all my time in reading and writing quantities of poetry. My first connections with the Imagists came from reading Pound's "Goodly Fere" in *The English Review* sometime in 1910. Later I met Hulme and he asked me to come to a restaurant where he was holding meetings of people interested in modern poetry. I did not go.

I was equally interested in art and music as in poetry, but poetry to me still meant, for the most part, rhyme and meter. It was the first Post-Impressionist Exhibition of pictures in London in 1912 that finally demolished my conservatism. I knew that music was free, and here painting was breaking its old bounds. Poetry, I saw finally, must follow.

Having filled my juvenile aspirations by printing not one but five books of bad verses, I went over to Paris in the spring of 1913 determined to write only to suit myself. The result was "Irradiations," which were almost all written in May of 1913. Shortly after this I met Pound. He introduced me to you.

The rest you know. There is nothing more to tell than that I was married on July 5, 1916, to Florence Emily Arbuthnot (Daisy is a pet name). Hoping this sketch will satisfy you,
 I remain
 Your old friend
 J. G. F.

P.S. Thanks for the cutting. But I have never tried to conceal the fact that I was born in Arkansas. I am proud of it!

Has *The Craftsman* come out yet? Do keep me posted all you can. And thank you ever so much for subscribing to Braithwaite's paper for me.
P.P.S. My mother died in May 1910 while I was in London.

TO AMY LOWELL

September 25, 1916

Dear Amy:—

In the last few days I have seen Richard and H. D., also Flint; in fact, it has been quite a reunion.

Richard is looking very well; in fact, you would scarcely know he is the same, so completely has the army changed him. I find him much more human than he used to be, and much more modest.

H. D. does not look very well—she is dreadfully thin, and I think this whole business of R's going into the army, etc., has had a very bad effect on her. When I saw her first I was shocked at the change; she looked so absolutely frail and wasted that I was afraid she wouldn't be long for this world. Please keep this to yourself. The strain, however, has made her produce better poetry—as witness her book. She is more cheerful now as R has been promised a job at training recruits in England—he has done very well as a soldier, so far—and unless he has to go, I suppose everything will be all right.

Flint is exactly the same as he used to be.

We had dinner together—R has been in London for a few days' leave—and we talked about the Anthology, among other things I hinted that I had heard from Linscott (it wasn't really him, but I thought I had better ascribe it so) that Houghton Mifflin were likely to abandon the New Poetry series altogether—and that there might not be any more anthology. Hilda said that she had heard from you that you didn't want any preface. We all agreed that a preface was unnecessary, and this removed from my mind at least the weight of a terrible bugbear because I don't think any of them have swallowed the last preface at all, and it seems almost impossible to get another preface done under the present conditions. I would almost rather not see another Imagist Anthology than to have to fact *that* prospect.

As regards the poems, we are all agreed to send all our stuff to H. D. and to get it into her hands by the first of November if possible. I have no idea how all this will be brought about, as so many have practically written nothing. Richard has some soldier things which he is afraid you won't like as they aren't patriotic. Hilda has one poem which is said to be a fine thing fairly long—entitled "The Tribute." Flint, I learn, has absolutely nothing. As for Lawrence, I know nothing, but Hilda says she knows him, and will jog him up:—As regards your humble servant, I have three long things on hand—I was represented by short ones last time—so I prefer to be represented by long things this time—which I am considering. One of them is the "Lincoln"—I probably will send it along with the other two and you can pick out two from the three.

I hope you will be lenient with Richard's contribution. He feels grumpy about something I am sure. He doesn't at all like the idea of having to be first in the anthology as he feels that is the reason you are so severe with his work—at least, I gathered he thought you too severe. As this is the last time the Imagists appear together—at least, I hope it is the last, as I see we are all so different in so many ways that we must go it alone in the future—I think the best thing to do is to let everyone put in whatever they like and if the kick is to be made, let the publisher do the kicking. At least, that is what I think. [I have] really quite settled down to my surroundings.

Yours affectionately,
John Gould Fletcher

P.S. I shall be here all winter and probably up to June of next year—unless they refuse to extend my passport. I wonder where you will be next winter. I hope you will go out West and rest awhile. They say the Grand Canyon is lovely in the winter. Best regards to Mrs. Russell.

J. G. F.

TO AMY LOWELL

October 21, 1916

Dear Amy:—

I send you herewith my poems for the next *Imagist Anthology* (if there is going to be such a thing, which I sincerely hope there won't be). I must add this parenthesis because I have seen the poems which the others have submitted, and I can give no hope. Aldington is in the army and hasn't either the time or the energy to do anything new. His things were passable, but left me altogether cold, with the possible exception of "Leave-taking." H. D. has sent me a long poem which makes a distinct falling off in my opinion. Flint sent in some things which were perhaps a little better than last year, but they left me altogether cold. Lawrence sent in some dreadful things. As for me, I leave you to judge for yourself and to pick out anything that is good in this selection—if anything is.

I say all this not because I consider myself in any way good, as a poet, or even better than the other Imagists, but merely because I know that whatever I am, these people are definitely and finally of no use, and had better stop writing for awhile or do something else than to try this task of poetry which is one to which they are not fitted and which is one that I know from experience only demands increasing strength and ability to accomplish as the years go on. I cannot hold with their work, nor can I hold with their theories of art. I do not believe that a poem should present an "image", I believe it should present an emotion. I do not believe in "clear, hard and definite presentation." I believe in complete, that is to say, shifting and fluid presentation. I do not believe in "absolute freedom in choice of subject." I believe that the very word "choice" means lack of freedom. If one chooses, one has certain standards whereby one chooses. I do not believe that the "exact word" is possible. I do not believe in "cadence," but in rhythm (a different thing altogether). I do not believe altogether in "externality." Therefore I do not accept Imagism. I am a Rhythmist or a Symbolist, but not an Imagist.

Pardon me if I go a step farther in my brutal frankness. You may say that Imagism has nevertheless been of great value to me because it has advertised my work. That is true, and for all the tremendous generosity you have shown me personally, I am most deeply and sincerely grateful. But nevertheless this does not blind my eyes to the fact that you are doing yourself an ill service, and the cause of literature an ill service, by publishing year after year in this Imagist volume, stuff that you know and that every other good critic must know, is second-rate. It is all very well to preach and practice personal loyalty, but we who are artists demand a higher loyalty— a loyalty to the finest and best work that can be accomplished, whether it is done by an enemy or a friend, or whether it absolutely shatters all one's own creation. I have a firm belief in the interest, vitality and beauty of what you are achieving—I do not altogether and always agree with your own work or your theories, but I believe that what you are doing is something with which posterity will have to reckon, and that the U.S. ought to put up a monument to you, by public subscription for having through precept and example done more to shake poetry out if its rut of commonplace than anyone for a century. I also happen to know that I am the only person in the entire Imagist group who supports this opinion. It seems to me that the art and craft of writing letters is calling you to a higher destiny than this of being the chief supporter of a group of "have-beens" and "might-have-beens". Let my work perish, let me perish if necessary, let loyalty perish, but let the art to which I have dedicated myself go on! You are wasting your time, your money, your energy, your loyalty in an unworthy cause. You have an unique opportunity to emerge from Imagism into something greater. Why don't you do it?

Is it because you are a woman? I cannot think so. Your work is masculine enough. Masculinity is a quality of the soul, not the body—and so is femininity. You and I have, I hope, something better to do than to tell these people their poems are bad and their theories rotten. I don't propose to criticize their stuff for them. Let them write any rubbish they like. And if you try and criticize them, they won't understand it. Better to save your breath. You can be the head of any group of poets in America you want to pick out, so why don't you end this wretched Imagist farce?

If I were in your position and circumstances, I swear I would do it. I would start a "New America" group, and run it for all it was worth. And I would simply leave England out. The program, if program is necessary, to be as follows:—

1. Nationalism in art. Independence from English standards and traditions.

2. No restriction upon anyone in regard to the form chosen. If a poem is a good one, it will be good in whatever form it is written.

3. It is necessary for every poet to grapple with and to depict contemporary life, but without rhetoric and without prejudices against the past.

4. No restriction upon religious attitude. Christianity, paganism, or agnosticism equally welcomed.

5. Opposition to all ex-parte theories on life and art and propaganda. Theories must be tested by experience.

6. Yourself as arbiter and final court of appeal. This can be done, if everyone understands that you are responsible to publishers for selection.

And the title? "New America: An Annual Anthology."

As for myself, I might as well say that, being in England, I don't expect to come in at all. So you can see that I am disinterested when I urge you to do this and *to give Imagism its decent and long delayed burial.*

Yours affectionately,
John Gould Fletcher

TO HARRIET MONROE

October 25 [1916]

Dear Harriet Monroe:—

The copies of *Poetry* have come, and also your letter. Many thanks for your good wishes.

I have read carefully Mr. Head's play and I humbly confess I am unmoved by it. This is doubtless due largely to the fact that I am unable to depict the accompanying pantomime—which must have gone far to "make" the production—altogether to myself. But it is also due to the fact that this play, like most modern productions, seems to me to approach the drama from the wrong angle and point of view.

The only two periods of the world's history in which poetry took a strong dramatic slant (if we except the early Sanskrit drama, of which I know nothing) were the Greek and the Elizabethan. And it may perhaps be useful to note that there were strong points of similarity between the two, not external, but psychological. To the Greeks the world was ruled by certain Olympian divinities. It was useless to deny this fact, and whatever doubts the dramatists may have had in those days, they always were obliged (since the drama itself was a Dionysian festival) to have the gods in their themes. Thus the drama concerned itself with human questionings, struggles, failures. The powers that stood for the absolute—that is to say, the gods—did not appear. At most only their messengers appeared. Not until Euripides did the God himself make appearance at the close, to cut the knot of the tangle and it is notorious fact that with Euripides, Greek tragedy died.

In the Elizabethan, we see the same thing at work. Shakespeare no more questioned the Christian dispensation than any Greek poet questioned the pagan one. The dispensation was there—that was all. Lear and Hamlet might stand up for a moment against it, but their efforts were silenced. The Gods remained quite the same—the entire drama was a conflict of human wills against something that did not ever appear.

Now at first sight it might appear that Mr. Head has followed the old precedent—Greek and Elizabethan—by making his "decoration" a struggle of man against a higher will. But he has not really done this. What he has done is to reverse the process and to try to depict on the stage a higher will actually at play with man. Instead of working from cause to effect, he has tried to achieve drama out of showing how effect goes back to cause. Let me illustrate. In the Greek drama, and in the Elizabethan, the cause is man's revolt against his destiny—Oedipus tries to learn what sacrifice must be made to stop the plague, Hamlet feels he must avenge his father's murder yet hesitates to do it. The effect of this revolt is destruction. In Mr. Head's play the *effect* is Capulchard, a lay figure quite inhuman and passionless—who *causes* certain other figures to be endowed with life, and the *result* is revolt. So Mr. Head has merely tried to square the circle—to write a drama of anticlimax—and it is not his fault that he has failed, but the fault of the modern intelligent mind which is not sympathetic but analytical, and hence undramatic.

The same process in a lesser degree is seen in [Wallace] Stevens' play, which I have just now read for the first time. It is static, not dramatic. The motive—the suicide of an Italian—is little more than a peg whereon is hung a wondrous analysis of certain phases of the Oriental mind. The drama has no chance at all to get along this way. Far better stuff and more truly dramatic (however spoilt by sensationalism and sentimentality) may be seen in any 'movie' show. For the drama is the one art-form in which the subject becomes of overwhelming importance, and without one strong theme strongly developed, no amount of good writing or stage-cleverness will ever atone. Hence it is a noteworthy fact that neither the Greeks nor the Elizabethans relied on their wits to invent plots. They took plots ready-made from myth, legend, and history.

It is true that we are open to do the same from the newspapers—our modern retailers of myth, legend, and history. The only difference between us and the Elizabethans is that our myths do not last us as long as theirs. But we are hampered, as I have said, above all by the fact that the drama, since Ibsen—I make only the one honorable exception of Synge—has concerned itself too much with ethical, social, religious questions. The dramatist is no longer as impersonal as Fate. He is the advocate who uses his characters as puppets and masks to speak through. Also we have been hampered by the modern craft of stage-setting. This, instead of freeing the *Word*, has enslaved it. Some artists of stage craft would do without the Word altogether—like Gordon Craig—and give us merely pantomime instead. I agree with them that there is no compromise possible. If I had my way, I would abolish stage-setting altogether—I would restore the platform stage of Elizabethan days, with the soliloquy, the aside, the exit, and the chorus—above all, the chorus. Somebody really ought to do an essay on "The Chorus in Shakespeare."

So much for Mr. Head's play and other modern dramatic attempts. I have written all this because I am interested in the possible revival of the drama, and would like to have a shot at play-writing myself when I feel more mature.

In your October number, I see you make an appeal for funds to carry on the paper. I hope you will pardon me if I write to you frankly about the possibility of this project. For I have only a desire to see *Poetry* continue to exist and to improve, as well from personal reasons as from artistic ones. And though you are sure not to agree with me, I think it necessary to say what I think.

Poetry has undoubtedly done more than any other factor to revive the interest in the art in the U.S. This I admit. But to revive an interest is not enough. To create a wholesale, quite uncritical interest and enthusiasm and to let it run unchecked is not enough. As Ezra Pound said in his last *status rerum* article, (I agree so little with Ezra that it is a pleasure to agree with him in at least one instance) the whole business may be simply a straw fire. If you look about you, you see *The Poetry Review, Contemporary Verse, Others, The Poetry Journal*—all are more or less trying to do what you set out to do five years ago—to create the great audience. Well, the great audience is created, it is expectant, all it wants to know is—where is poetry tending? Who are—not the new, but the *good* poets—the poets the future will have to reckon with?

It is up to *Poetry* to give this movement a direction. You cannot simply take one step and remain there. You cannot simply lay the foundation and never get to work on the main structure. You cannot always be merely in a state of *becoming* something—you must stop and *be* something. For nearly five years you have gone on, and you are still discovering new poets. I don't object to this being done. But what becomes of the old poets, those who have supported you from the beginning? Are they simply to sit down in a back seat and fold their hands and wait?

Have you never asked yourself the question:—"What would become of *Poetry* had I not found interesting poets to fill the pages?" Would there have been any movement, any such stirring of dry bones and fluttering of old dovecotes as goes on today? Is there nothing you owe to your authors besides their occasional check? Must people who are growing old in the service of art, have to take their chance with the rawest newcomers? Are we to expect no policy out of *Poetry*—no policy out of the foison of new papers such as Braithwaite's, etc.—except the fatal policy of "I'll print what I like" and "Devil take the hindmost!"

I will make you a sporting offer. I will personally subscribe ten dollars to your paper, and will send you, besides, my very best work to be printed (and you need not pay me for it) *provided that you and Alice Henderson sit* down and make out a list of contributors—exclusive to your paper—each guaranteed two appearances a year at least—*and also provided that you will notify the world at large that you will not accept or print any new people.* This will put the onus of discovering new people on the other papers—and as new people acquire reputations, you can add them to your list by invitation. I make you this offer without any reservations. Even if I am not on the list of prospective contributors by you and Alice, and you print none of my work, I am ready to make it. For I realize that the one thing now necessary in America is a standard of *some* sort—without it, the whole poetry movement will collapse in a very short time.

Unless you do something of this sort, I have decided to withdraw myself altogether from *Poetry*'s pages in the future. I may be an extremely bad poet, but at least I have too much self-respect for myself and the labor I have accomplished to put myself any longer on a level of equality with Gretchen Warren, Lily A. Long, Lulu W. Knight, Peter Norden, Lyman Bryson, John Regnault Ellyson, Iris Barry, etc. *to take only one single number.* If *Poetry* is going to be a "free-for-all" of this sort, then no more *Poetry* for me. I am not a "free-for-all" sort of person. I believe that "that to him that hath shall be given and to him that hath not shall be taken away even that which he hath."

I hope you will read this letter since I have taken the trouble to write it, and I hope you will also follow my advice and give *Poetry* more of a tone, more of a policy. Do stop inviting MS from the four corners of the earth. Do stop loading up that safe of yours with things you will never print. Limit yourself! If you don't stop this business of being a fairy godmother to everybody who sends you a MS, the whole "movement" will collapse very shortly. Believe me, I ask it not for myself, but for the sake of the art, and your own future. For myself, I expect the whole "revival" will come to nothing in a few years—in any case, I know my goal, and I shall go on—

Please send me the Blake article back. It's too long, and I want to get it typed. Don't fail to do this. As regards my other poems you have, I do hope someday you will print them. You've had them a year now, exactly.

Yours,
J. G. Fletcher

P.S. Thank Miss Dudley for her review of me. But tell her she's dead wrong about Blake. True he said: "*Art* consists of minute particulars. He who generalizes, is a fool." But *criticism does consist of particulars.* Blake's own criticisms are always generalizations.

TO CONRAD AIKEN

November 1 [1916]

Dear Aiken,

I was delighted to hear from you again to-night, as I had quite given you up—I didn't know whether you were going back to 11 Walnut or not. The best news of all was that you had taken to visiting the Art Museum. Do give my love, when you go there again, to all the Arbats—especially the dark gentleman who looks with such horror on the fighting dragons and the wonderful old man who sits with closed eyes in his corner while the dragon coils around him. I would give lots to see them all again—I am with them all in spirit, at least. Even the memory of such things is wonderful.

I am glad to hear you have got down to work again. "Variations" sounds interesting. Never mind about the title. About "Witches Sabbath" I am not so sure. I cannot help wishing (you will acquit me of any Puritanic intention) that you would try your hand at themes a little less artificial—after all, I am afraid, it is only the poets who can hew into granite—like Frost or Masters—who will live. The rest of us are ephemerides—your humble servant included. I have grown fearfully dissatisfied with everything I have done hitherto, which is rather a good sign. I am meditating two subjects for a possible play—Harriet's attempts in the direction of discovery of dramatic talent have been so woefully inadequate—but I find myself appalled at the amount of earth-shaking imagination necessary to get even a reasonably good "scene" assembled.

When your article came out in Brown's paper about "Illusory Freedom" in *Poetry* I felt like retorting publicly, "here is the man who says there is no freedom in form, and then goes on to demand the utmost possible freedom in subject. The subject-libertine!" But I didn't. Seriously, however, that is my objection to your poetry—admitting and even enjoying in the case of Forslin your happy mingling of audacity with conservatism of form, I could wish you exercised it on a subject less vague—with more direction. Perhaps I am growing Puritanic. Eliot's last poems struck me too as echoes—rather vague repetitions of what he had already said. But enough of this.

I quite agree with you that someone ought to slay Untermeyer and all his crowd—including the moon-faced Oppenheim. That article of his was simply spleen let loose. He seems to be cross because he is fading into the background—he and all his luminaries—before a little of the light we have somehow contrived to spread about the dark places. For instance, take Braithwaite. I am delighted with the news that he is going to cut down "books of distinction" and become severe. This is all to the good, whether we suffer by it or not. But it means good-bye to glory for Untermeyer, who will never be anything else than a talented versifier. And the absurdity of his accusation that you copied Masters is too rich—he has copied everybody in town. You really ought to write a satirical ballade on him.

I have not heard from Brown, but he seems to be enterprising and getting publicity—all to the good. I have high hopes of Brown—he at least will be an excellent advertising agent. As for *Others*, which you may become sub-editor of, I should advise you strongly not to have anything to do with it. I am disgusted with the paper. They all seem to have been imbued—Williams especially—with the desire to shock the public at any price and to proclaim their own infinite importance in the scheme of things. This is the old Ezra game, and I am too wary to be caught by such tricks. I hope you give them the cold shoulder. I have just written Harriet a letter telling her brutally what I think of her appeal for help and practically informing her that I don't intend to send any more contributions. My only hope is in Braithwaite and Brown. Braithwaite is improving slowly, thanks to you in the first instance, and Amy's perspicacity in following you in the second. If Amy is given a strong lead she will always follow. Please paste that in your hat for reference. It is necessary to have a lot of patience with William Stanley. Also tact. Brown you and I know fairly well, but I have hopes. Harriet and *Others* can perish for aught I care.

Your news about Canada is curious. Over here there isn't much fuss over young men out of khaki. There are said to be three million of them up to date. Nevertheless, I believe England means to win the war and will. It's difficult to travel around here. An "identity book" witnessed by two British householders is indispensable. Also it's important not to come laden down with addresses of people—a lady on the ship I crossed in nearly failed to pass the barrier because she had a notebook full of London addresses in her bag! I don't know whether correspondents are welcome or not. Anyway, I fancy it's rather harder to get out of England than to get in. I shall stick here for the winter, but I rather fancy that next year may see me revisiting the familiar lights of Boston.

I enclose a clipping which may interest you—it gives some interesting sidelights on London today. The streets are rather darker than they were in June when I came over. Crime of all sorts is on the increase. Likewise prices. Everybody is expecting a famine after Christmas. Eggs are now six cents apiece! Altogether it's very fascinating—one can't help speculating on how long the show will last and how soon the gods will call for another turn and ring down the curtain.

I wrote you that I had seen Eliot. I hope to call on him again some time and give him a copy of my book. I believe I told you that Constable's absolutely refused to handle it—and I have had to import a dozen copies from America to give away to my friends. But I am going to get even with Constable's some day for this.

I quite agree with you that Amy does the sort of thing like "Malmaison" and "Cross-Roads" (whatever you call 'em) ever so much better than she does verse of any kind. I hope she'll give us more and more of this sort of thing. The Imagists will probably come out next year as usual, but I can't longer recommend you to read us. Our collective work is done, and what will remain to do will be done as individuals rather than as a group.

Hoping you'll write sometime.

J. G. F.

[The previous year Aiken had taken lodgings at 11 Walnut Street, Boston, to be near Fletcher, his literary guru. Others, A Magazine of New Verse, had been founded in 1915.]

TO CONRAD AIKEN

April 25 [1917]

Dear Aiken,

Your *Dial* article arrived here some days ago, and I have since read it several times, and I think it is by far the best thing you have done. You are really beating your way out to a sane criticism of art—and may Heaven hasten the day when such a thing is obtained in America!

I find myself in such strong agreement with all you say (except possibly your ranking me as one of the greater poets of America, which I am afraid I have failed to achieve), and I find all that you say so valuable that I am glad that Braithwaite brought out his miserable anthology after all, as it has provided you with such a splendid peg to hang your thesis on.

Since I came back to England I have been so seriously dissatisfied with all my tendencies in the past and with my own writing that I have destroyed more work in these past eleven months than I ever destroyed hitherto—and I am beginning to regard the waste-basket as the most sacred and indispensable utensil of sacrifice any poet can have. The war has made me more and more suspicious of modernity—more and more determined to write nothing more but that which is so absolutely permanent in substance and eternal in effect. I am not so anxious to appear in print as I was. Incidentally, the censorship is assisting, as I got back two articles the other day—neither of them had anything to do with the war—and shortly it may be impossible to send anything but personal letters to America.

I have gone back to the classics and am trying to learn Greek. One learns to appreciate the classics—especially Homer—in the midst of this turmoil. Also I am translating from the Italian. My own work goes on, more or less spasmodically, largely owing to the fact that we are now servantless and I have to double the roles of a general servant and a poet.

I have been intending for some time past to write a review of *Forslin* for Harriet Monroe—it won't be altogether favorable and will be more analytic than laudatory. But I am sure you would prefer an intelligent treatment to a mere trumpeting.

Brown has acted very decently about that omission in my article on Braithwaite, by writing to *The Transcript* about it. I owe Brown a debt and will try to send him some poems if the censor doesn't frown on my efforts.

I have received Harriet's anthology, which is not bad considering that lady's temperament. If she could only have kept herself and Alice Henderson out of it and given her pet Sandburg a little less space, I would not object. But take it all in all, it does prove that there are signs of hope—chastened hope—in the poetical firmament. If we can only, all of us, do as you say—look upon the poet simply as a human being, liable to errors, prejudices, and failures—if we can get over our absurd and childish desire to blow our own trumpets, and to have our own trumpets blown, we may yet produce a decent body of work.

The poems I sent you, tentatively, for *Contemporary Verse*, are not very good. I felt that I had to write them in order to get out of my system something which has in a way, haunted me for years—my own childhood. There are a great many more of them than I sent you—I spent nine days over the job and wrote sixty poems—1244 lines in all—in that time! And since then I have never felt the slightest desire to return to the subject.

I have just completed, after many revisions, my book of war-poems, which has taken me a year, and which interests me far more—since I realize that in it I am getting rid of my faults of disconnected sensation and have hammered out a style which has dignity and fairly regular rhythm—there are three or four poems which I think are really good in it. These are "Lincoln," at the beginning of the book, and three poems at the close. These are on Russia (the best thing in the book and quite epic), one called "Midnight," and a third on the two flags—American and British. The complete MS contains 44 poems—1914 lines, and I think it has taught me more about how to write than anything I have ever done.

I have also in mind two short dramas—very pagan and prehistoric in subject which I dare not tackle, as they will require a style of such Homeric simplicity that I feel my modern sophistications forever standing in the way. Perhaps I will somehow manage to store up the heroic impulse necessary to carry them through.

The war book has been turned down by Houghton-Mifflin, and I dare say it will be a long day before I again appear before the public. I can't help wishing that my earlier books had been better—this includes *Irradiations* and *Goblins and Pagodas*—because now, when I really am trying hard for something more permanent and less ephemerally brilliant in effect, I have to endure the present publishing crisis. There isn't anything over here but war books now. I am so sick of seeing them that I have given up going to bookshops altogether.

At all events, I hope you are keeping your health and strength and are not too satisfied with the work you are doing, or have done. I have lost most of my illusions about myself, and I see now that it will probably take ten years more of hard struggle and work to do anything even remotely good. But I am determined to give those ten years, or die in the attempt. And I think this is what we shall all have to do, sooner or later. We shall have to all bow to the logic of the present situation, and unlearn all we have learned and learn again all we have forgotten or give up the struggle in disgust.

We are having the most horrible spring in the memory of man—trees are still lifeless and leafless—everything months behind time. I hope you are better off, but I dare say that things will get worse and worse. It's not a nice age to live in, but it will help out the survival of the fittest, that is to say, the most intelligent and far-seeing specimens of the race. And it is childish, or worse, to complain against Destiny. Keep writing and keep a sharp axe ready for fools, and let the future take care of itself, is my opinion.

I hear that Braithwaite has had a squabble with *The Transcript* and has disappeared. No flowers, by request. Dole, I hear, is his successor. Let's go after Dole's scalp—what do you say? He is a perfect Philistine. We must keep up this scrap, not for our own sakes, but for the sake of the future.

Thank you again for your article, which has encouraged me more than anything I have seen for many a long day. Please write to me whenever you can.

Yours,
John Gould Fletcher

TO ROBERT LINSCOTT

May 27, 1917

Dear Linscott,

I had, like you, sung a sort of Requiem over our friendship, and I did not suppose I would ever again hear from you; when, lo, your letter of May 4 arrived, and set me to wondering what on earth we could have ever quarreled about. The only point we ever differed about was about the war; and on that, it will interest you to know that I am absolutely of your point of view now. I agree with every word you wrote me about the victory of tyranny, and the utter futility of militarism, in any form. I need say no more, as the censor is probably overworked, like most of us.

I am quite as bitter now about the whole business as you ever were. If this business goes on for two or three years more, as everyone expects now, there will be nothing left worth either living or fighting for. That is all that need be said about it. It is this prospect that makes it so unendurable.

Your letter cheered me up in various ways. For one thing, I am very pleased to see that you recognize that, after all, *Irradiations* and the *Symphonies* were written largely with my subconscious mind, and that since then I have been working with my conscious brain.

I quite agree with you when you say you don't agree with Aiken's theory that all this subconscious also in us is the work of sex. Aiken would like to take all my poems, and prove by analysis (such as the analysis in Jung's book, for instance) how they are full of symbols of suppressed *libido sexualis*. But I don't see what good it does to prove that. Even if it is true that all art is merely a medium of sex-phantasy, does that abolish the need for art? On the contrary. But I don't believe, as you say, that Nature would have given us this creative sixth sense for so small an aim. And I dare say I never will believe it.

I am growing heartily sick of my own conscious poems—"Lincoln" is a very good example of the type—as it all seems to me to be just wandering in a desert of barren intellect that leads nowhere. What earthly good are all the philosophies of mankind—they have merely increased our conceptions but have not altered the old emotional reactions of the soul which are the same as they were at the beginning. (See on this point, an amazing book:—*Dostoevsky*, by J. M. Murry published over here by Secker). I feel a great yearning in me to go back to *Irradiations*, but I find it almost impossible to recover the fresh directness of my emotional feelings—circumstances are always preventing.

My whole life has been a blind struggle with two forces in me which are absolutely at variance, and completely dissonant. These are my self-conscious intellect, and my subconscious feeling. As regards the latter, I really do not belong to this damnable century at all, and every day I spend on earth makes me realize it more and more. I really am a primitive savage, with a twentieth-century brain grafted on. There once was a time in art when a man could write work which harmonized both with his thoughts and his feelings. For instance, Homer (I hope you know the *Odyssey* in Butcher and Lang's translation), or the old ballad-singers, or the old Russian hero-tales, or the *Mabinogion*, or the people who first thought out some of the fairy-tales. This was art which was harmonious. All art since then seems to me to be quite dissonant—there has been a steady division of function between the brain and the heart—and things have now got to such a pass that one must simply exaggerate feeling, and become incoherently hysterical, or exaggerate thinking and become dull, pompous, didactic and dry.

It rather interests me to see that you like my poem "Armies"—I wrote a whole volume of war poetry, which I thought would prove popular—and I offered it to Greenslet, through Miss Lowell, as she seemed to have so much influence on his judgment. It was refused. "Armies" was one of the poems in this book, and there were others quite as good, I think.—I am almost tempted to send the whole volume to you to see what you think about it, and whether you could get any editors to print any of the other poems. Perhaps I shall. It is, I admit, a work of transition, but if my conscious style has in it more popularity than my unconscious style, as you seem to think, it seems rather a shame that I should have had all my pains for nothing.

At all events, please write me occasionally, and keep me cheered-up. Don't let me discuss the war. I don't want to read any more about it—I never want to look at another newspaper. I will keep you posted as to what I am doing. Best regards to Mrs. Linscott and the children.

Yours ever,
John Gould Fletcher

TO CONRAD AIKEN

July 4 [1917]

Dear Aiken:

Many thanks for your news about the MS. I don't think you need bother any more about it. It is not very good.

I am very interested to hear of your depression, and I feel quite sympathetic, as I have been through the same business already. The last winter was simply hell, mental, moral, and physical. Up to the last month I have felt as weak as a kitten, and though I have tried to struggle on with work, the stuff I have turned out is enough to make the gods weep. But since June, things have been getting slowly better. I have abandoned poetry, and am plunging into prose, as something more solid and requiring less intensity of emotion—I am doing a series of articles in *The Dial* on "Contemporary English Poets," which you want to look out for, as I fear some of your pet poets will come out pretty badly in it!

I am going to try to work at this every day, and adopt an attitude of as complete disregard of the war as possible. I am just over the age for the American conscription, and if I can keep renewing my passport, I can live over here with no greater terror, than a possible Hun bomb—which isn't much—or possible starvation, which will be less pleasant to face. For the rest, I shall cultivate every possible indifference. Anything may happen, but I feel that it is up to me not to be easily beaten, and I shall hold out in my corner against [Allen] Tate as long as I can.

I am sorry that there is a chance the draft may grab you, as I consider you are too valuable to be wasted in that way, but there is no avoiding one's destiny. This war ought to do us a lot of good if we can survive it. You have done some very brilliant poetry, especially in *Forslin*, which is by far your best work. But you haven't quite stability and solidity necessary to be a great poet. No more have I. I quite admit that my *Symphonies* are my best work so far, but they are like fireworks—there isn't enough pent-up explosive force behind them to keep me driving on in that direction, through this damned world of massacre and assassination. So I am trying to get the solidity and the density out of plain stodgy prose, and when the time comes, I hope I shall have sense enough to go back to the *Symphonies* and enlarge my scope from that point onwards.

Meantime, it is hellish slow work to write at all, and sheer agony to think. But after all, the artists of the past had no better sort of life—Shakespeare and all the rest of the Elizabethans had the same business to contend with, as lack of money, foreign wars, domestic torture (we have lived without a servant since March), Puritan outbreaks, etc. etc. And we ought to be able to face the same tasks, if we have anything in us.

(I interrupt this epistle at this point in order to investigate a rumor of another air-raid in progress. Such are the amenities of our life).

To resume:—

I sincerely hope you escape the draft, and I the bombs, and can both go on with our work. It is necessary, if not for our own satisfaction, at least it is necessary for the sake of the future. And if there is to be no future, it is still necessary. I hope you will continue to live in the U.S.—you wouldn't like it over here. But we must both set our faces sternly against all art and all criticism that is not fundamental.

I quite agree with you about Amy Lowell. She has quite gone to pieces—wreckage and ruin absolute! So vanishes another illusion of my youth. And I think you must agree with me that Ezra Pound is in the same predicament, of writing on with nothing to say, and saying it badly. Eliot I have not seen, but I fear that he is now merely the new string to Ezra's bow—which is as bad as it could be. I will try to help him if I can, but I know for a fact he has written no poetry since the outbreak of the war, and I am not impressed with his prose—it seems thin.

I am sorry to see that you attacked Harriet's anthology in *The Dial*, and got the worst of it in Harriet's exchange of compliments. All anthologies are bad, and *The Imagist* for 1917 is the worst of the lot! But there is one thing you *can* say about Harriet, and that is that she has a sort of porcupine-like quality that *is* unpleasant, but does mark her off from the commonplace. She put up a much better reply to you than our defunct enemy, Braithwaite. And her anthology is an attempt to do the modern school justice, though of course it has its bad side. The worst is, that she included so much of herself and

Mrs. Henderson. But here again she shows her subtlety. You should not have attacked her so directly—she is a dangerous to attack directly, and though Harriet and I have always squabbled, she has my hearty respect for being a person who has more in her than appears on the surface.

I think I shall have to subscribe to *The Dial*, which promises to be a good thing, altogether.

As for my article on Amy L. in the last number of *Poetry*, I wrote it last September rather as a sort of squaring my debt to her, than for any other reason. And now I largely agree with you that Amy is too amateurish ever to be taken completely seriously as a poet. Even in this article I suggested that Amy's *method might* be wrong, and I think now that it is. You see, I am transforming myself from an amateur to a professional writer and am revising all my old opinions. I have squared accounts with Amy at last and I feel perfectly at liberty to say what I like about her, which is that she is at times very clever, but she lacks reality of emotional experience (hence, power is lacking) and she has simply no eye for the appropriateness of detail (witness the bad detail she drags into almost every single poem). In other words, she is an amateur—and she will never be anything else. And as you say, her humanity and generous enthusiasm may be very fine, but they are not art. And without a very clear sense of what art is, and what it can do, we are not going to make much progress under the present-day conditions.

So keep your end up, and let's prove to the next century (if there's going to be one) that there were some people able to get their heads somehow clear despite the awful fracas that went on. And if my existence *is* cut short by a bomb, I hope that you won't let Amy gush about me after death, without some kind of protest.

Yours unsentimentally
J. G. Fletcher

[In "Living History" in Poetry *10 (June 1917): 149–53, Fletcher had discussed Amy Lowell's* Men, Women, and Ghosts *and* Bronze Tablets. *Harriet Monroe's anthology,* The New Poetry *(1917), gave much emphasis to free verse.]*

TO CONRAD AIKEN

January 31 [1918]

Dear Aiken,

I received today your *Nocturne of Remembered Spring*, and I want to thank you very much for sending it to me. I have written a review of it, not altogether favorable, but representing what I really think of it—which to me is more important. As soon as I get it typed, I will send it to *The Dial*.

I wanted to enclose a copy of a review of Gibson's latest book which recently appeared in *The Times Literary Supplement*, but I seem to have lost my copy (perhaps you could look it up. It was the number for January 24). The review simply slew Gibson as one writing insufferable doggerel. You really should review Gibson's latest in your old well-known slashing style. His book is called *Whin* but should be called "Thin" and the *Times* headed its review "Light-Weight."

All the old idols have fallen in the dust. Masefield has been raked over the coals for the feeble sentimentality of his latest prose, *The Old Front Line*, which is poor stuff. The Georgians are either mostly dead or stopped writing, except Harold Monro, whom I wish would stop. The latest people are all soldier-poets, and the best of them are 1. Robert Nicholls, who is really good; 2. and 3. Manning and Aldington, whom you know; Siegfried Sassoon, who isn't bad.

Lawrence has also published a volume, which is appallingly bad. "Whitman gone to seed" I call it.

It strikes me the same thing is happening in the U.S. as here. The latest works of Masters, Lindsay, Robinson, Lowell seem to me too awful for words. Frost still keeps up his end, what I have seen of his seems to have some tang and bite in it still. It is bitterly disillusioning to see this dry-rot the war is bringing about. There isn't even any decent French poetry to read now! We are all being driven back to reading the classics, and hoping in vain for the future.

I wrote a lot last year, but I liked very little of what I did. Most of it was very bald and feeble. This year I will not write much, but what I do will be good stuff, I hope—at least it has an idea back of it, which I achieved very painfully after perpetrating hundreds of failures. The idea is as yet only in its infancy, and I find it quite hard to manage, but I believe I shall do something on quite new lines—lines which were led up to by the only decent things I did last year—some of the war poems and some of another lot I called *Elements*. I believe I shall get something good out of my new idea this year, unless either a bomb or starvation comes along.

I like Garnett's article immensely, in its suave urbanity, though I disliked the poem he quoted from Edward Thomas, who is interesting because he started to write poetry only after Frost published his—he is an English Frost—to make a bad pun. I like also your article in a recent *Dial* entitled "Confectionary and Caviar." I did not like your article in *The Chicago Post* on Amy's *Tendencies*—it seemed too much an outbreak of bad temper. Amy's book proved better than I hoped—cinematographic as usual, all surface and no depth—but less bad than her poetry now seems. But I have moved so completely out of her sphere, that I can look on with amusement.

London is now full of American troops, and the other day I directed several to places they wanted to see. It is highly amusing, this latest of invasions, it makes London more cosmopolite than ever—I have seen soldiers of I think every nationality under the sun for the past year and a half, including some Germans (prisoners of war). The place is hopelessly overcrowded—everywhere new Government offices, hotels packed to the doors, theaters going full blast with things like *Chu Chin Chow*, or band revues.

But for myself, I feel a growing weariness, and boredom with it all. It is all too much like in the third century A.D., or like the last slide of an avalanche before it collapses to the bottom. I see it now coldly, sceptically, mistrustfully.

All we do now is to keep up the game to the last—whether that comes in five minutes or in five months. I am keeping up my end of it as hard as I know how, and I hope you won't let yourself go to pieces. That's the main thing.

Your ever,
J. G. F.

[Garnett's article was not identified. "Confectionary and Caviar," a review of five contemporary poets, appeared in The Dial *63 (22 November 1917): 754 and in* Scepticisms *(1919).* Chu Chin Chow *was a current musical hit by O. Clark and F. Norton.]*

TO ROBERT LINSCOTT

April 2, 1918

Dear Linscott,

Your letter of March 11th has come, and has greatly amused me. The Lowell anecdote is priceless. And to think that this was the woman for whom I played Don Quixote (that sublime, magnificent book is absolutely me from beginning to end), and whom I defended at my own peril against reviewers, editors, and critics galore! Truly the tragic-comedy of life never held a funnier situation than this combination of Lowell and Fletcher.

I wrote you that I had received *The Buffoon*, also I have seen *The North American Review*—but thanks very much for sending me a copy. I am much obliged also for your enclosure of Mencken's article, which is, as you say, tediously clever in that superficial way of his. I am much obliged also for your opinion, as well as George Moore's on Sherman.—These crusted conventional college-professor critics are the most nauseating thing in America. I do not mind attacks, but one might at least learn to attack in good taste. The whole thing is an indecent exhibition.

Your opinion on American poetry is interesting. To me it seems from all that I have read recently, that poetry is simply dead in America. I find nothing in it but echoes—echoes of the old stuff, or echoes of the stuff that made a sensation in 1914–15. It is simply painful for me to get now a copy of any American poetry magazine. It is strange when you think about it, that America always starts a movement, and then lacks the endurance and vitality to carry it out. For instance, look at the enormous effect Poe had upon French literature, or the effect Whitman had in Germany and elsewhere. Or the effect Whistler had all over Europe. Or the effect Henry James had in England. One could go on multiplying examples by the thousand fold. The trouble with America is, that she accepts her artists without intellectual self-examination. She simply commercializes them down to her level, if they remain in America—if they don't she admires them from a distance—she does not ever trouble to set to work and *think out* the real importance they have. But on this subject I could write pages.

I quite agree with your outburst about England and Japan—the whole thing was disgraceful. Thank God, and thanks to Wilson, there is a chance that Russia will survive—Wilson, by the way, seems to me the only statesman in this present war.

Yours ever,
John Gould Fletcher

P.S. The war has made England's mask of superiority rather thin, and I have been able to understand this country as I never did before. I love England better and better and better every day, in spite of all her faults. The thing that you and many others do not understand, is that the real Englishman is the plain, common, stupid, loyal, brave, long-suffering laborer—he is the strength and the sure defense of these islands. The upper class, here have been rotten through and through since the Elizabethan period, if not before. (Much as I dislike Chesterton, I believe his interpretation of English history is largely fact. The English have had no decent statesmen—that is the great English failing. The lower classes are too easy-going to be leaders themselves, so they let themselves be led by people like Balfour and Bonar Law. These people are good for nothing, except at striking attitudes—they never see further than their own noses, they never realize how ridiculous, even to their own nation (which has some sense, after all) they are.

All this comes out clearly in the story of the English army. The private soldiers do all the fighting, and nine-tenths of the thinking. They are superb—every one of them—no words will ever express my admiration for the stand England has made and is making. But look at the leaders—they are cultivated, well-groomed dummies. They can't make a plan that sees beyond the week after next. There is no hard logic, no intellectual brilliance about the English.

The most awful thing here is the public-school and university system which is a training in self-deception, and mental inertia. The greatest lie in history is the Duke of Wellington's remark that the battle of Waterloo was won on the "playing fields of Eton." The battle of Waterloo was won by the devoted self-sacrifice of hundreds of common English soldiers who held on in a tight corner, until the Prussians came up and outnumbered and outflanked Napoleon. The selfsame troops, led by the selfsame incompetent officers (who had been to Eton, every one of them) were beaten, two years later, by a handful of American backwoodsmen at New Orleans.

This extraordinary vice of the British character—this refusal to think or to value thought for its own sake, is *also a virtue*, in another way. England gets on well with her colonies—why?—because she makes no plans for ruling them, because she simply muddles along from day to day.—"Take no thought for the morrow; sufficient unto the day is the evil thereof" is absolutely the mainspring, and the *real* motto of every Englishman. They are the most reliable nation in the world, in a crisis of battle—the most unreliable in a political crisis.

The Russian affair is a splendid example. The entire attitude of the British press—with a few honorable exceptions—was outrageous. Anybody with the least sense could have told Balfour and the rest that handing Russia over to Japan was as bad as presenting her to Germany. But things like this disturb the Oxford Mind very little. Balfour had to get his country somehow out of the mess—the only way he could think of, was to fall back on the Japanese Alliance. It was pitiable, contemptible, but it was not as you think—a villainous bargain. The English have a reputation for villainy, which is absurd. They are kindly, generous even, only they are so stupid!!! Poor things, they simply don't know what a holy show they make of themselves.

Thank goodness. America has a clear-sighted man like Wilson at the helm—I *wonder* what he thinks of British statesmanship! Otherwise, I should despair of the world.

The French make admirable officers, but bad politicians. The English make splendid common soldiers, but poor officers, and poorer statesmen. The Americans seem to have it in *them* to give the world a real statesman every now and then—Franklin, Lincoln, Wilson. If the three can only combine, they can beat anything, either diplomatic or military, that Germany can do. That is my conclusion.

This is the longest P.S. on record, but I put it all in the P.S. so the censor would not slash the letter.

Yours
J. G. F.

[The Buffoon *was a ballet for which Prokofiev had been commissioned by Diaghilev to write the music.]*

TO ROBERT LINSCOTT

Saturday, May 11 [1918]

Dear Linscott,

Your good letters of April 16 and 22 have arrived.

Many thanks for the money order. It will help me considerably. I forget how much *The Bookman* check was, but I hope you haven't increased it. It seems to me that it was less than $7.25. I am almost afraid you have added to it from your private means. I hope not.

I have been very hard up this year—thanks to the cost of living. But I shall be better off after next month. Thanks awfully for your offer to let me have your money. But I could not accept it.

Although all the odds are against me, I seem to have been doing better than I ever hoped for. I enclose herewith an announcement of a publication which may interest you. Also my art book is going to be published. Finally, do you remember the love poems which I sent to Houghton Mifflin, and which you turned down, on the advice of Amy Lowell? Well, a London firm of publishers have offered to produce them at their own expense! Please don't say anything about this to anyone.

My art book is not about Chinese painting—though I hope to do something better on that field, some day, than I have ever done before. It is about a painter of whom you have never heard, probably. Paul Gauguin—a very great decorator, with a strange life-story, and whose work is not properly appreciated as it should be. Unfortunately, I have had to collaborate, in doing it, with a chap whom you may have met or heard of—his name is Sadleir, and he used to be in Constable's; he was in America about the time the war broke out. The collaboration, really, is confined to his name appearing on the title-page. I have done all the work—this is between ourselves.

I haven't the least objection to your taking the third section of my poem, "The Poet and the War," trying it on some editor, under the title "London Midnight." I sent you another war poem a short time ago. There isn't any chance that I will do anymore. I have quite exhausted all that I have to say on the subject.

Your remarks on the subject of affirmation vs. negation in art are very interesting. In the main, I agree with you. I agree absolutely that the higher a work of art is, the greater its passion for something—beauty, truth, or even negation, as in Bosschère's case. As you say, the thing that kills art is the shrug of the shoulders, the cynical skepticism of an over-cultivated intellect, like Anatole France. For this reason, a man like Anatole France cannot be a supreme artist, though he may be very interesting, charming, delightful.

Great art, to my thinking, always has some deep undertone of passion behind it—something like the ground-bass of the sea.

I have tried to get rid of negation, personally, because the world I am living in is a world of negation. But I admit that if a man has a bitter disillusionment like Swift, or to a lesser degree, Voltaire, or Bosschère, he can make great art out of it—just as Chekhov's gray melancholy is great art.

I mention Chekhov here, because you say you have been reading him. What a pity, by the way, that there isn't any universally accepted standard for the transliteration of these Russian names. I have myself seen Dostoevsky written as Dostoeivsky, Turgenev written as Turgenieff (the *v* in both names is the same Russian letter, I believe), and as for Chekhov's name, I have seen it appear in a dozen different forms. The most amusing example of these mistaken *w's* for *v's* appears in Byron's *Don Juan* (have you ever read it?) where he rhymes the name of a celebrated Russian general, Suwarrow (which should be Suvarov) to "morrow."

I am told that "Chekhov" is the best possible reading and certainly the least confusing—of the Russian sounds.

Chekhov was very good, though of course, he hadn't in him the demoniac power of a Dostoevsky—whose books seem to me the greatest things ever done by anyone, especially *The Brothers Karamazov*, *The Idiot*, and *The Possessed*. It has been some time since I read Chekhov, but I liked excessively two short stories "Mujiks" and "Ward 113" [Ward 6] (I forgot if that is the exact number). But Chekhov's two plays, "The Sea-Gull," [sic] and "The Cherry-Tree Orchard," [sic] are really his masterpieces, as far as I can judge.

On the whole, I think Chekhov was probably better than Turgenev, who has always seemed to me monstrously overrated by English and American critics—the Russians think nothing of him at all.

I will keep James' *Tragic Muse* in mind, and read it, if I find an opportunity. But I doubt if I shall like it. I have read a deal of James recently and find very little in him I like, except perhaps *Roderick Hudson* and *The Turn of the Screw*, which is artificial, but damnably well done. The older I grow, the more I like, apart from Homer, Herodotus, the Greek tragedians, Aristophanes, *Don Quixote*, and a few other classics—apart from these, the things I like are all somewhat demoniac, somewhat queer, a little mad even. I like Dostoevsky for instance. Also Poe, also Coleridge (at his best), even Maeterlinck's early plays—all these men have a visionary side to them, a purely mystical touch with which I find something of myself in sympathy. Other people I can admire, but these are the ones I like.

Forgive this long scrappy, frivolous letter. Many thanks for the money order. I am sorry that you have a weak heart—I hope it isn't serious, for I want to meet you again some day.

Yours ever,
John Gould Fletcher

P.S. About this visionary side to poetry, art, literature, which I say I like. Has it ever occurred to you what a visionary book *Don Quixote* is—or even Gogol's *Dead Souls* (I should have included him in the list of people I like intensely) and how the same quality, applied perhaps to different objects, is to be found in the Chinese poets and painters? Believe me, for all my miscellaneous and many-sided mind, there is unity in all my work—though it may not be readily apparent unity.

J. G. F.

TO JOHN COURNOS

July 6/18 Saturday [1918]

Dear friend John:—

Your two cards arrived last night, but I did not see them until after my return from the opera—Verdi's *Otello*—incidentally, if you do see any more operas, I can most strongly recommend this one. It is the nearest thing to *Boris* I know.

I agree with you profoundly to the bottom of my soul about *The Egoist*. There is something positively horrible about E. P.—his power is like a boa-constrictor's. He has now swallowed Lewis, Joyce, and Eliot, and is swallowing rapidly other people—His power is over *younger men*, exclusively—this makes it all the more horrible. You and I escaped because we were either older, or on equal terms in years—and besides, we had already gone through a lot of experience. But we have got to fight this horrible thing.

If Eliot has any sense of decency or of shame left (which is doubtful) he ought to want to put a bullet into his brain. A year or so ago, he at least had something of his soul left. Now he has none. He is a gramophone which Ezra sets in motion. It is frightful.

I am quite sure that Shakespeare knew a creature of Ezra's type and drew him in Iago. The type is not Prussian, as you think. The Prussians are brutes, but they are clumsy in their methods, and they have the courage of their own bestiality. Ezra has not—like Iago, he spends his time poisoning others with filthy promptings of his own nature—but he lacks the courage to follow out his own convictions. If he were only a villain, I would not mind—it is because he is also a hypocrite that he is so horrible.

Caesar Borgia and the people in Webster's plays were like him. He is an Italian of the decadence—absolutely—an utter vampire without one redeeming trait. I think of Iago, of Judas Iscariot, of Smerdyakov in *The Brothers Karamazov* when I think of him.

What drives me to despair is the thought that this active power for evil exists, and that I cannot destroy it. All of my life has been devoted to love and worship of the arts, especially literature. I may have wasted my time, strength, money, thought in the process—I may be quite worthless myself as a writer, but at least I have always known that one cannot follow a profession in which so many great souls like Homer, Shakespeare, Cervantes have spent themselves unless one holds it as a sacred calling—unless one believes religiously, with Dostoevsky's *Idiot,* that "beauty will save the world."

For this reason I have always helped other writers and artists to the utmost of my power. And among those I have helped are people like Ezra—it were better for such people as he not to have been born, because they do so much evil to others—and people like Aldington—spineless cowards, yielding to their own weakness—and people like Amy Lowell, accepting my loyalty and making use of it to gain their own ends.

My God, when I think of it, it makes me sick that I should have dirtied my soul by contact with such people. And to think these people and their kind are positively writing and devoting themselves to my own calling—that makes me still more sick at heart.

But, as you say, we are veterans after all. And if these *are* devils to us, we have nothing else to do but to hold the fort—they can kill us if they like, but they can't make us surrender.

I'll see you, I expect, on Tuesday and will bring *The Seven Arts.* Meanwhile your card has done me a lot of good. Whether our day ever comes or not—and it doesn't greatly matter now, whether it ever comes or not—believe me, it is something to know that I don't have to fight this fight out utterly alone. And so I subscribe myself

Your friend

John

TO HARRIET MONROE

September 27 [1918]

Dear H. M.,

Your check for one pound twelve shillings for the review in the September number has come. Many thanks.

You want to know how I think *Poetry* is going now? Frankly, I think the last two numbers were weak—the July and August numbers. Either the war is having a very bad effect on poetry in America, or you were in need of a holiday when you got out these numbers. The effect of them was almost disastrous on my mind. They were too scrappy, too miscellaneous, too helter-skelter altogether—but, there, I am not an editor, thank goodness, and I can admit and sympathize with your difficulties.

I have not seen the September number yet. Here is the list of poems in the other numbers I think worthy of mention:

1917	Oct.	"Negro Sermon"—Lindsay
	Nov.	"Four Brothers"—Sandburg
		"Poems"—James Joyce
		"New Mexico"—Alice Corbin
	Dec.	"Pine River Bay"—Dorothy Dudley
1918	January	"Chinese Poems"—Arthur Waley
	Feb.	"Chinese Poems"— " "
	March	"The Splendid Commonplace"—E. Carnevali
		"In Barracks"—Baker Brownell
	April	"Carolina Woodcuts" by the Editor
		"On the Road"—Haniel Long
	June	"War Times"—J. C. Underwood

July—A bad number. I can find nothing to praise in it but Sandburg's poem ("Prairie"), and I think this a failure. Too verbose and diffuse.

	August	"Gardens There Were" by Leslie Nelson Jennings
		"Appuldurcombe Park" by Amy Lowell

Now, out of this list I would select as first prize—Arthur Waley's translations.—But since they are merely translations, I suppose I must pass them over.

My next choice would be Wallace Stevens, undoubtedly. "Lettres d'un Soldat" is damned good, and "Carlos Among the Candles" is also interesting.

Next to Stevens I like—among the war poets—Baker Brownell, then Sandburg, then Underwood. So if your "Carolina Woodcuts" and Mrs. Henderson's "New Mexico" are out of the competition, I think I should vote for Brownell, whoever he is.

This leaves only Haniel Long, who is good, but not quite good enough; Fenton Johnson, whom I like but whose work is not original (Leslie Nelson Jennings is another poet of an imitative order); and E. Carnevali, who is puzzling.

First prize, then, goes to Stevens.
Second, to Baker Brownell.
Third, possibly to Long.
Special honorable mention to Waley; to Mrs. Henderson; and yourself.
This is my award.

I sent you yesterday a copy of my latest book, just out in England. You may think it worth a review, perhaps.

I am quite well and hope to send you something better than "A Boy's World" soon. Do send that unfortunate MS back.
Yours,
J. G. F.

TO ROBERT LINSCOTT

Oct. 22, 1918

Dear Linscott,

Your letter of the 2nd October has come, and has greatly amused and interested me. It was good of you to write such a long letter, especially as I suppose you have plenty of other work on your hands.

This war is like a plague that begins by destroying small things and ends by attacking the very roots of existence. It began by destroying the nineteenth-century politics, laws and diplomacy; it has practically wiped out nationality, art, and science; and now like Saturn devouring his children, it has spread to sex. As I wrote you in the letter to which yours is a reply, I *am* utterly disillusioned and weary of both myself and my past and my own domesticity. These are the symptoms of the sex-conflict that is bound to come, if it is not already here. For instance:—it is generally believed that the women will swing the next general election, which will almost certainly, come this autumn. And the Women's Party will vote in a body for the reactionary politicians. Here is the making of a pretty conflict! That damned phrase—"the sanctity of womanhood"—that other phrase "the women are splendid"—that sentimental nonsense that the men are fighting for the safety of the race and for their homes their wives and children—what will become of these ideas when it dawns upon the minds of the men that the women are really prolonging this war?

I write no more, for fear that the Censor is probably a middle-aged Victorian personage, with the usual ideas about the sanctity of the marriage-tie and the uplifting influence of family life. But there is a book just published here by an anonymous writer, entitled *Women*, which I should really like you to read. If I can find the money—at present I am hard up—I will send it to you. It is an eye-opener.

All this has its bearings on my poetry at present. It is quite useless for you to assure me that I am destined to immortality as a poet. I am too old to be taken in by such talk, and I know better. The poetry of the future will shovel us and our ideas into the dustheap. Frankly, after two years hard work and thought, I have no more faith in myself. I go on writing out of sheer necessity—it is too late to turn back, and it kills time—but I don't believe in this talk that anything which either I or the rest of the present generation have done, will survive.

Recently, I have received Miss Lowell's new book. I have no quarrel at all with the lady, except that I have taken a complete dislike to her personality and her methods of advertising, ever since she played me a characteristically Lowell trick in 1917. I read her new book with interest and with amazement at its cleverness. But I ask myself, has this undoubtedly magnificent and complex art any roots in the future? Does it give any new view of life? Someone has said of Henry James' later books that instead of giving a deeper view of human psychology, they simply give a more extended one: that James' method of rendering all the aspects "of a character simply presents us with an extended surface panorama, never penetrating to the depths." Dostoevsky, on the contrary, tries to throw a sudden flashlight of understanding into the depths; and Thomas Hardy, Swift, Voltaire, and a few others have directed upon the depths a cold, hard, unpitying beam.

I ask myself if Miss Lowell has done anything more than James. She gives us an extended panorama of life's surface; but all this does not give us one new fact about life.

Oh well, I suppose I am stale and disgusted with it all—with this dirty game of blackening paper, and with this other dirty game of living. The mood will pass, I dare say, as it has passed so often before, and next week I may be closing my illusions again quite cheerfully. But don't you ever believe that I am a good poet, or that writing poetry, good or bad, is worth the price. I am a rotten bad poet; and as for writing poetry, I spend most of my time nowadays trying to kill the impulse, rather than have to endure the result.

Yours cheerfully,
John Gould Fletcher

P.S. Yes, we are having the Spanish flu here, but nothing like so bad as in the summer—in July all London was down, but escaped unscathed. The outbreak is on again, but so far not nearly so bad as in America.

J. G. F.

P.P.S. Thanks for *New Republic*.

[Miss Lowell's new book, Can Grande's Castle, *appeared in 1918.]*

TO ROBERT LINSCOTT

December 28, 1918

Dear Linscott,

 I want to thank you for your extraordinarily interesting letter dated the 2nd of December, but postmarked the 11th, and especially for having given me in full your opinion about my poetry since *Goblins and Pagodas*—

 I don't think at all that you are talking damned nonsense when you say that I am a subconscious creator. *Irradiations, Goblins and Pagodas*, and most of *The Tree of Life* were purely subconscious. That is to say, they were practically improvised, with very little rewriting, and without any definite plan. My early books were conscious, and suffered from this fact. Then, about 1913, I threw this conscious idea over, and wrote for three years subconsciously. Early in 1916, the influence of the war began to bring my conscious intellect into the ascendent over my emotional faculty. I vaguely felt that civilization was menaced, with the result that I set myself to chasten my style, subdue my passions, dominate intellectually the volcanic force of my own personality. And, as you say, the poetry resulting has been largely, a disappointment to those who soared with me into the empyrean of my *Symphonies*.

 It used to annoy me to have this said of me, but now it does so no longer. Frankly, I quite admit that the realistic poetry of *Elements*, also of *Uplands*— a manuscript I have not sent you because I myself am dissatisfied with it. It is too severely restrained, too intellectualized to appeal to those who admire my *Symphonies*. But for this fact I am not altogether responsible. The war gave me a sterner outlook on life—if it had not happened, I should have written more on the lines of *Goblins and Pagodas*. And my marriage drove my thought in the same way. In a fatal hour, I decided that it was not enough to be a great poet: one must be a great man as well. I am afraid that I was mistaken.

 All these admissions are difficult enough, in all conscience, for me to make. Not only is it galling to my pride to have to admit that I haven't succeeded in a task I set myself, but also it is very painful to think that I have spent three years in writing a type of poetry which I cannot do so well as the type of *Irradiations* and *Goblins*. It is awful to think of all that work gone for nothing. But I suppose I must resign myself to it.

 I quite agree with you that there is a nobility of purpose in many of the poems of *Elements* and also in the *War Poems*, which is non-existent in *Goblins and Pagodas*. But this does not make up for the absence of emotional stimulus. I am afraid that poetry is essentially a non-moral art, at least so far as I am concerned.

This being the case, I have decided finally to ask you to send me back *Elements* and also the war poems. I mean to destroy, or at least not to publish anything that I have written since I finished *The Tree of Life* in 1916. Of course, to do this will cost me very heavily, but in art, as in war, no one can stop to count the cost. And I mean to make a last desperate effort to return to the *Symphonies* phase, or to die in the attempt. So please send me the war poems and the *Elements* MS back, and don't get them published.

I have been so interested in what you have written me about my poetry that I haven't left much space to deal with the political side of your letter. I quite agree with you that Wilson's ideas are the only thing that will save civilization at all, that will keep the world from unmixed Bolshevism. But it seems to me rather ridiculous for you to say that England, France, and Italy are trying to destroy these ideas of Wilson. It seems to me that America is giving England, France, and Italy at least a clear lead in this respect. What backing has Wilson in his own country? It looks as plain as day that he has been utterly repudiated both by the press and the people of the United States, and that Lodge or someone like him will be the next President. This jingoism in America simply gives the European jingoes their opportunity. If America had intervened in the war earlier, on the grounds that the cause of humanity was at stake, (as I all along said she should do)—then the mischief would not have been done. But Wilson was forced by his people into an attitude first of neutrality, which I do him the credit of believing to have been utterly distasteful—and now he is being equally forced by the jingo elements in America into abandoning every motive except that of pure selfishness.

Personally, I am more pessimistic about the situation now than I ever was before. This short-sighted selfishness of America and of Europe—this return to the old game of grab and secret diplomacy—will be simply the thing to give the Bolshevists and extremists everywhere their opportunity. I look for civilization to be disrupted—as it has been already in Russia, and as it apparently will be in Germany. Then after a long period of complete intellectual and artistic darkness there will emerge a new feudalism—and the Middle Ages will be repeated. The picture is not a pleasant one, and makes one wish that one had never been born.

I quite understand that you were not able to send me a present for Christmas—you need not apologize. You don't owe me any present; on the contrary, I owe you much more for the assistance and encouragement you have given be during the past three years of difficulty and struggle.

Yours ever
John Gould Fletcher

TO HARRIET MONROE

To the Editor of *Poetry*   March 17, 1919

Dear Madam:
One does not object to critics, and their amusing assumptions that they know precisely what everybody sets out to write, but one does at least wish that critics would learn to write sense. For instance, take Mrs. Henderson's remarks on my *Japanese Prints* and *The Tree of Life* in your March issue. Mrs. Henderson objects to the former because it is an empty mask—in other words, void of emotion. And she objects to the latter because it is too much a welter of emotion! In short, she flatly contradicts herself. One can forgive an artist for contradicting himself, but surely critics should have some common basis for the judgments they pass on artists.

It seems to me that if critics want to write about my work at all, they should at least attempt to learn what it is I am trying to do. My work, with all its "unevenness" (of which my critics make so much) has a perfectly clear and logical reason for every word and every syllable. When I began writing, I took up the task of exploring the unknown, which to me was personality (my own, above all, since I am more acquainted with it). Hence every book I have written is different in tone and content from every other.

My critics, on the other hand, seem to think I can only express my personality by endlessly repeating myself, always following the same track. And thereby they land themselves in an awkward dilemma. For if personality must always be the same thing, immutable and invariable, then there can be no intercommunion of ideas between one man and another, and consequently no art. But if, on the other hand, as I believe, personality is capable of endless changes and transformations, the art has the function I have given it; viz., the complete exploration of personality. I remain
   Yours sincerely,
   John Gould Fletcher

TO ROBERT LINSCOTT

Thursday, October 2, 1919
Sixth day of the Great Strike

Dear Linscott,
I am always delighted to hear from you and your letter of the thirteenth of September, which arrived this morning, was doubly welcome because I

had given up all hope of hearing from America for some time to come. Even this letter, which I am writing in response, has the quality of a proclamation launched forth into the unknown. For day by day, the vestiges of the old world are crumbling, day by day we reach nearer to the portals of a new world where hope bids us enter, but fear, mightier than hope, holds us back.

There is no doubt that a mighty transformation of the world is in progress. When the curtain was rolled up before the first act of the play in 1914, few suspected and none knew that the guns opening this awful slaughter were, in sober reality, the voice of God proclaiming to a deaf world that whole epoch of man's long and weary achievement was ended. Well, the first act of the drama came to an end on November 11th last, but the play has not ended there. It has only begun.

We are now in the midst of the second act of this world-drama, and though none of us has any reason to pose as a prophet (I as little as any) yet we can at least calculate what the forces are that are leading us, and what may be the end. It has been pointed out by historians how each of the great movements of mind and spirit have accomplished much good and some evil. When Christianity conquered the Roman Empire, it was enabled to do so because of the corruption, the bureaucratic tyranny, the chattel slavery, the break-down of original thought, art, literature. Christianity promised a "better world"; at all events it provided a different world. But even this world, the world of the Middle Ages, had its serious defects. It gave more freedom to the individual than Rome ever possessed, but not to the *mind* of the individual. Its narrow ethics, its inherent Puritanism, its theocratic doctrine, destroyed every vestige of independent judgment that lay in its way.

Then came the Renaissance, again promising "a better world." The promise again was kept—but again there were the same seeds of evil, seeds of decay. Minds were liberated, but bodies were only more enslaved. The scientific ardor, the craze for discovery, exploration, knowledge, power, of the Renaissance culminated in 19th century capitalistic Industrialism, with its appalling transformation of man to a machine for work.

Now again the old world is destroying itself to make room for a better world. The Kaiser, who thought himself an instrument of God, was perfectly right. He was but a tool in God's hands to begin the breakdown of the whole structure of Industrialism which had been preparing during the fifteenth, sixteenth, and seventeenth centuries, to culminate in the eighteenth and nineteenth. This culmination had reached its apex in England after the definite adoption of Free Trade in 1845, in America after the Civil War, when the last vestiges of the old paternalistic feudalism of the South were swept away, in Germany and on the continent of Europe generally after 1870.

What we are witnessing now in England, in Russia, in Europe generally, and even in the United States is the birth of a new Epoch! Capitalistic Industrialism has doomed itself: it has brought about a war in which some eight or nine millions have been directly killed, numberless myriads either killed outright, indirectly, or crushed, or injured, and the whole fabric of civilization set shaking from the top to the bottom. As a result, the workingman has been enabled to see for the first time, that the whole structure not only of industrialism, but of society, has rested directly, as a pyramid on its base, upon him—and he has set about to transform his role in the maintenance of existence from that of a passive agent to that of an active creator.

We are now in the midst of the greatest struggle between Capital and Labor the world has ever seen. It is too early to judge what the result will be—the conflict is all about us—but certain facts emerge clearly. One is that capital in itself is valueless. This has been worked out in Russia. There the workmen, by simply refusing to work the machine, by ignoring utterly the great resources of their own country, by passively resisting the march of Industrialism, have definitely destroyed Industrialism. Armed only with weapons of the spirit, lacking in food, clothing, machinery, they have kept the victorious allies at bay—they have not been wiped out, because it was the will of Providence that this lesson should be taught to the world, that no amount of money, no overwhelming resources in munitions, capital, organization, can avail anything against the human will (which is, taken in the aggregate, the Divine Will).

So Capitalism has failed finally in Russia—and the lesson is that it must transform itself everywhere else in the world.

The second fact that is emerging from this struggle is that each member of the community is dependent on every one else, and so with each section of the community. That lesson is being taught here today in England. We must be interdependent, we must work together, not for our own good, but for the common good of all. The Railway strike which is now going on as I write, has taught us that no one section of the community can move without the support of every other section. When the railwaymen stopped work, instantly thousands and millions more tacitly agreed to endure the blow at every industry, and to carry on without faltering. That is not because people believed the railwaymen to have been in the wrong, and Lloyd George and his government in the right. Personally, I think the railwaymen have been perfectly in the right; as regards the point of view of the whole community they have been absolutely in the wrong. This crisis has proven that the community at large is perfectly determined neither to be held to ransom. It is determined to make the use of the goods and commodities of the community for the public benefit.

Thus we are launched on the new Age of Co-operation. The future lies between complete Marxian Communism (the Russian view) which has ended by wrecking the whole industrial machine, and cooperative exchange of work and commodities (the English view, deriving from Robert Owen) which aims at running the industrial machine, not for the benefit of any one class, but in the interests of the whole community. Both movements are equally antagonistic to capitalism.

In short, what we have to do is not so much to "make the world safe for the democracy" as to make democracy safe for the world. That we will succeed in our task, I have no doubt some force mightier than man is at work. However much we may suffer as individuals, the purposes of Heaven will be fulfilled. The New Age will be born, is being born today. Individualism is finished. The future is in the hands of the whole community, not in the hands of the capitalist class. There is no turning back of the clock of progress, short of the destruction of the world—which means absolute destruction of God himself.

J. G. Fletcher

TO CONRAD AIKEN

April 29 [1920]

Dear Conrad:—

This is to welcome you to London. I have always called you "Aiken" heretofore, but I must admit that I feel towards you a special tenderness, owing to the thankless task you have undertaken of championing my work— and even in London, of all places! I want you to know that I do feel a special tenderness—for you have been extraordinarily decent to me in many ways, and the number of people who have been decent to me is so small that I can afford to remember and call them by their Christian names. Hence this letter-heading.

You will find that I am not a popular man in London. Ezra is still my pet abomination. Eliot I respect as a critic, but I have not seen him for two years. I do not run with any of the cliques, nor am I a lion of any literary circle. With the Athenaeum bunch—Huxley, Murry, Pound et al.—I have little in common. Nor with the Squirearchy on the *Mercury*. And the Boar's Hill, Oxford, crew—Masefield, Graves, Nichols, Blunden—disgust me. Masefield by the way has declared that Lindsay is "the great American poet." My God! See Nichols' preface to *Booth* if you don't believe this.

I have fought a lone hand for four years—and the upshot of it all is that I am several years older, much poorer, and even more unknown than when I began. And yet I shall go on somehow—though God or the Devil alone knows how, as the cost of living gets worse and worse. So if you find opportunity to say a word in my favor, I hope you will say it. You will at least have the pleasure of knowing that you are backing an independent writer—which is something in this world.

The number of friends I have in London is very small. First among them stands John Cournos—take him all round, he is the best, the bravest, the most independent man I know. And I think he has at least one quality that makes a writer great—the ability to say something—the passion for ideas. At present he is at Hastings finishing the sequel to *The Mask* (which will be a greater book than that novel, if it doesn't kill him to do it). His address:

>Market Cottage
>Fish Market
>Hastings

Another man whom I like, not so well as Cournos, because he is not so much of a born writer—but still an interesting chap, knowing much about the dodges of publishers, and perfectly independent of mind is Douglas Golding. Address:

>c/o Clarke
>5 York Buildings
>Adelphi
>W.C. 2

These two are about all I can offer you in the way of friends. Lawrence is at Taormina in Sicily. F. S. Flint is at 65 Highbury New Park, London. He is rather shy and *difficile*, but at bottom a good fellow. I am not on terms with Aldington or H. D. Jean de Bosschère is or was at 3 Hampstead Square, Hampstead, N.W.—he is a genius *pur sang* but entirely self-centered and self-poised—as almost all geniuses have to be. No doubt you know Monro's address. Earp and Green are at 32 Burleigh Mansions, Charing Cross Road.

I wish this list were longer, but I have inveterately acquired the habit of avoiding people. My aloofness from the London literary world has undoubtedly cost me dear, but it has been the only condition in which I have been able to work at all. And whatever the value of my work, I know profoundly that it is at least mine—not another man's. If I have paid a heavy price for this knowledge, I do not greatly care—it has been worth it.

My own special hatreds are Amy Lowell (that adroit pasticheur who once took me in—never again!), Lindsay (I have just read his last book—oh, God, oh Montreal!) and among English writers, the Squire branch (Nichols, Sassoon, Turner, etc., etc., etc.). So anything you can say to damage this crowd will be grateful music to my ears.

Welcome to London—I had almost said, welcome to the Inferno of
Yours
John Gould Fletcher

American Address:　c/o Mrs. Leonard Drennan
　　　　3 Gracewood Park
　　　　Cambridge, Mass.

P.S. I forgot to add that I have found Geoffrey Whitworth of Chatto & Windus to be a decent fellow. He has been very kind, and I like him personally. He has recently been very ill, however. J. G. F.
P.P.S. Very important. In case you are doing any articles for the American press, I think you ought to write an exposure of the quackery and charlatanism of the London literary world in general—of how its cliques engineer each other's fame, of how they are out to kill originality that comes to them from abroad, of how they form a closed corporation of interests to spoof the public. Do this, and you will earn my eternal gratitude.

TO T. S. ELIOT

September 16, 1920

Dear Eliot,
　I do not know if our acquaintance has ripened sufficiently to permit this form of address. But, in any case, I am much obliged for your card. I have discovered a copy of *The Athenaeum* of June 9, which contains the first part of your essay, which seems to me far less interesting than the second part. My article is finished and is devoted, as all such articles must be, rather to a complete exposition of your ideas, than to my own. I will quote only its last paragraph.
　"I have dwelt on this last point (the point that the critic and the creator are usually the same person) because it seems to me supremely important. It is not only true that we can never have, either in England or America, good creative work done unless we also have good criticism; it is even more true that such criticism must be impartial, thorough-going, and constructive; must, in other words, be equally prepared to destroy the bad and to patiently analyze the merits of the good, so as to derive from the contemplation of both, new applications of its own fundamental laws. The fault with the poetry as well as the criticism of today is that it is partial in one way or another. It is too much occupied with personal prejudice, with a desire to shock or to startle, or with lip service to some incomplete or enfeebled tradition. It has not yet acquired, in one single instance, that impersonal breadth of judgment which it is necessary for many men to strive after before there can be created the unquestioned and unquestionable masterpiece."

So much for the article. Personally, I have a bone to pluck with you on one or two points. For instance, you seem to deny to emotion any value either in creation or in criticism. I quite agree with you as regards criticism —certainly one should never let one's emotions stand in the way of one's critical faculty! Let us not spare our friends—there is enough and more than enough of that already. But as regards creation, I am not sure you are right. To me creation is impossible without emotion. There is a creative act, whereby the intelligence (perfectly conscious of what it is doing, and of the necessity and logic of its procedure) fastens upon the crude emotion, and through some medium (such as words) fixes it in a form wherein it is no longer mutable into sentiment or hysterics of So-and-So's war poetry. Plato, who was really a lyrical poet and not a philosopher at all, knew what he was talking about when he spoke of things existing as "pure ideas." The work of art is a "pure idea" of its emotion. Without that emotion, it could never have come into being.

You may argue that possibly what I mean by "emotion" you mean by "sensibility" in your *Athenaeum* essay, and it is of course quite possible that we may be arguing about that same thing under different names.

Another point I felt inclined to argue with you was about history, philosophy, etc. not being criticism. This, of course, is a minor point. The critic is naturally interested in an idea for its own sake apart from whether it would agree or disagree with Kant's digestive apparatus, or whether it has any perspective in history or not. But at the same time, it seems to me next to impossible to put forward an idea without referring in some way to other people's ideas or to history in general. In other words, a critic has to use this paraphernalia when he comes to making a public pronouncement. It is like your distinction in *Chapbook* between writing poetry and publishing it.

Yours sincerely
John Gould Fletcher

TO FRANK STEWART FLINT

37 Crystal Palace Park Road
Sydenham
November 23, 1920

Dear Flint,

I have just read with considerable interest and some amusement your chapbook of Dada. It is a very sound, capable piece of work. May I say that your identification of Picabia the poet with Picabia the well-known Cubist painter is correct?

In 1913 the post-impressionists, the cubists, and futurists gave a combined exhibition of their work in New York, which exhibition is famous in American art annals under the title of The Armory Show (it was held in a large drill-hall, or armory, belonging to one of the New York state militia regiments). For some reason that I have never been able to fathom, the cubists made a great sensation at this show, and people like Marcel Duchamp, Gleizes, Metzinger, Picasso, and Picabia became immediately famous. Shortly after the war broke out, several of these cubist painters visited America. Gleizes I think was there, and also Metzinger and probably Picabia, for the next important fact is that a periodical was started, to which Picabia contributed, entitled *291*. I saw the first number of this magazine myself in New York in December 1914. It think it began coming out in August or September of that year.

The title of this periodical is quite easy to explain. It was published at 291 Fifth Avenue, then the headquarters of Alfred Stieglitz, an eccentric Jewish photographer who had become interested in advanced modern art, and who had fitted up a small art gallery for the exhibition of modern works on the premises. At first the paper consisted only of reproductions of pictures and of *ideogrammes* a la Apollinaire. Picabia may have written in this style—I rather fancy he did, though I have only my memory to go on.

After America entered the war, I fancy *291* died a natural death—at all events, when I was last in New York I could find no one who could tell me what had become of Stieglitz, and on the site of his picture gallery a new building was being erected. Apparently from the information you give, Picabia went back to Barcelona, which I imagine is his birthplace. (No; I am wrong. An old catalogue of Les Artistes Independentes gives his birthplace as Paris.)

I thought you might be pleased to know that your assumption that Picabia is no longer a young man is correct. The exact date of his birth I cannot find. But it may possibly be somewhere in Gleizes and Metzinger's *Cubisme*, or in Apollinaire's *Les Peintres Cubistes*, or in *Les Soirees de Paris*. Your assumption that this Dadaism is only the latest phase of a middle-aged, and extremely bad painter (whose pictorial work was a *méleange adultère de toute l'oeuvre de Mainethi et Picasso*) is hence correct.

I remain
John Gould Fletcher

[*The International Exhibition of Modern Art presented by the Association of American Painters and Sculptors from February 15 to March 15, 1913, so-called because it took place at the 69th Infantry Regiment Armory in New York City, was a landmark in the introduction of America to modern art. 291 was a monthly published from March 1915 to February 1916; the building housing the gallery was razed in 1917. Picabia and Duchamp came to the United States, the former remaining and becoming naturalized. Picabia was born in 1879.*]

TO VAN WYCK BROOKS

March 1, 1921

Dear Van Wyck Brooks,
I noticed in your columns recently that T. S. Eliot's book had made its appearance in America; as this book is very important, I enclose a note I have written of it. Eliot is a bold searcher for truth, but like most of the minds of this generation, he is disoriented by the war and the resultant anarchy of thought. I thought you'd like to see my opinion of him.
I remain
Yours sincerely
John Gould Fletcher

[Eliot's first important volume of criticism was The Sacred Wood *(1920). Fletcher enclosed a copy of his review.]*

TO SARA TEASDALE

Holme Lea
Crystal Palace Park Road
Sydenham, S.E., England
July 21, 1921

Dear Sara Teasdale—
Your letter of July 4 has arrived, and I want to thank you for it. During my stay in New York last summer, the talks we had together were among the few real pleasures I experienced, and since I have returned, I have been suffering from real homesickness—I mean that I have been wanting to come back and live in America. London is a dead-alive place, and has never been more so than this spring and summer. There are no signs of revival here in literature, or in art, or in life. Unfortunately it seems impossible for economic and other reasons to make the move from London just now.

But every bit of news I can get from America interests me. I believe in the country and its future. Your news about Amy Lowell and Leonora Speyer interested me. I quite agree with you that Amy's latest was her worst. I did not succeed in reading it through—and the stunts worked by the various cities on its behalf seemed very forced. I happened to see a copy of Speyer's book in London, and such awful rubbish I have never read. I am glad that it has been overboomed and overpraised because all this sort of paid-with-a-dinner criticism will fall into more disrepute, the more often it is worked. At least, I hope so.

Your remarks about Charlotte Mew's poetry interested me very much. When her book first came out, during the war, I remember reading it and rather liking it—but owing to the pressure of other matters, forgetting entirely its existence. This year I saw the new edition and fell under the spell. She is certainly an amazing poet, and when I think how good she is, I wish I had never tried writing at all. Harold Monro, who knows her, says that in real life she is a little gray-haired woman, with a tragic look, who sits in a corner of the room and says nothing, but if spoken to, seems almost ignorant, and totally uneducated. She is also said to have destroyed dozens of poems because the papers won't print them.—I would like to write something about her work in America; has her book been published there? The ones I like the best of hers are those terrible poems "In Nunhead Cemetery" (Nunhead, by the way, is quite near here in the dismalest suburb of South London, and the train to the Crystal Palace runs just alongside, as the poem says), "Ken" and those last two astounding "I Have Been Through the Gates" and "The Cenotaph" (the last three lines of that poem are really unforgettable). And of course there are also "Madeleine in Church," and "The Road Down to the Sea."

As regards the proposed anthology for children I quite agree with you that it ought to consist of something else besides verses written *for* children. Here are a few suggestions:—

1. Matthew Arnold's "Forsaken Merman"
2. Christina Rossetti's "Goblin Market"—or is this too mature for children?
3. William Blake's "Infant Joy"
    "Nurse's Song"
    "Spring"
    "The Lamb"
    (all from *The Songs of Innocence*—I would be tempted to include lots of these.)
4. Lots of Shakespeare lyrics. Ariel's song from *The Tempest*, of course. And also "Crabbed Age & Youth."
5. Some of the old ballads. I remember liking in youth such bloodthirsty things as "The Twa Corbies," "Edward, Edward," and "Sir Patrick Spens." But if I were to choose, I would select now "The Lass of Lochroyan" and add "A Fig of Morality."

After this last suggestion, perhaps I had better stop corrupting youth with my suggestions. You probably know more about what children will stand than I do. I fear I grew up as a very old child, nor have I altogether outgrown my childhood. I remain
    Yours sincerely
    John Gould Fletcher

P.S. I am very glad to hear that your husband does not write poetry. Someone in New York last summer told me that he did, and knowing as I do that authors feel very sensitive if not asked about their work, I have often had it on my mind that I never asked about his.

J. G. F.

[In 1921 Amy Lowell published Legends *and Leonora Speyer,* Canopic Jar.*]*

TO JOHN COURNOS

P.S. Above all, don't get discouraged. You are doing a big job, and one well worth doing—that is the main point. Let *The Dial* yap, if it pleases.

Sept. 25/21 [1921]

My dear John,

Your extremely interesting letter about Ford Madox Hueffer arrived yesterday. You have made it quite clear that he opposes you, and have also made clear the reason. My opinion about the controversy is as follows:

There are two schools of opinion in literature today (apart from those who simply repeat the past, and who don't matter). The first school lays its stress on technique, exclusively. Ezra is the extreme example of this tendency; the same tendency is to be found in Joyce, in Dorothy Richardson, May Sinclair (probably), Eliot, and a good many others. This school is always talking about the French writers, and about the beauty of form. They incline to rate Conrad higher than Hardy, and probably James higher than Conrad. They are all for objectivity, detail, the clear "image" (the Imagist business derived from them), etc. etc. They favor experiment in form, but argue that subject-matter is unimportant.

The second group lays less stress on technique than on covering new ground, acquiring new subject-matter. Dostoevsky was the great precursor of this school—his subject matter was profoundly original (and abstract, because it was an attempt to show the real souls of people working under their skins). This school aims at getting behind realism to something that I can only call dynamism (the exposure of the generalized springs of action and conduct—I hope I make myself clear). You belong to this school, at bottom. So, by the way, does Anderson (Ezra to him is an "empty writer," and this crowd hates empty writers). Wasserman's book is an interesting attempt in the same direction—despite its obvious sensationalism. Faure has written the philosophy of this movement—a philosophy which is a compound of Nietzsche and Dostoevsky—a sort of creative pessimism. The tendency of this whole group (if you can call it a group when it is still loose, floating, and vague) is to exalt "expression" over "description," to be, if you will, anarchic—to conquer chaos not through form, but through perpetual passionate application of new means of expression.

As regards myself, as you know well, I began largely with the first group of writers (I held that technique was everything)—and you converted me to the opposite point of view. But I see as immense, the overwhelming difficulties of the "expressionist" point of view. I am not sure that I agree entirely with either side, now. I am merely stating a case, impersonally.

It seems to me that Hueffer is largely mistaken in supposing that a knowledge of French is essential to the writer of English. I have studied French for years, and have come to the conclusion that the two languages are so different in their structure that it is next to impossible to learn anything about English by studying French. French is terse, concise, clear, just where English is often more involved, vague, and shadowy, and when English is most simple, French is most idiomatic and complex. In translating French into English one has to paraphrase continually; a literal rendering usually sounds awkward, bald, abrupt. (Pound, by the way, translates French better than Flint just for this reason; where Flint is literal, Pound has an uncanny ability for finding an approximate equivalent). French is a poor language for poetry, tragedy, epic—a fine language for the essay, for the short story, for satire; English is just the reverse. Most French poets envy English poets like Keats, Shelley, or Poe for their very vagueness and magical quality of suggestion. To suggest anything, to leave a statement imprecise, is almost impossible in French. In short the difference seems to me to be the difference between music for a string quartet or a piano, and music for a full orchestra, with organ thrown in.

I also disagree totally with Hueffer's idea that there is such a thing as "style." This is where I part company absolutely with Ezra & Co. Every writer to me has his own style, and he learns it by mastering his material, never by imitating others' ways of expression. "Style is thought itself" was said by Rémy de Gourmont, and it completely knocks in the head the idea that style can be taught or acquired by following any model.

Finally the idea about Teutonic words is nothing but sheer prejudice. There is nothing easier to abuse in English than Latinisms. The very best and most direct words in English are Anglo-Saxon.

That is all I can say against Hueffer's contentions. As for the rest, the future must settle. It is quite obvious that the one idea of Ezra now is to transplant Paris to New York or New York to Paris (it doesn't matter which so long as *The Dial* is made Parisian). But I disagree. America will never become exclusively French, and *The Dial* is merely spreading a thin veneer of cosmopolitanism over an enormous barbaric continent—most Americans regard *The Dial* as a huge joke, I am quite certain. So Hueffer is wrong on one point. And as for the novel, whether it follows the road of the new form or makes experiments in new subject-matter, I don't mind. I am quite sure your new novel will appeal to me (at all events), and I think there are plenty of others who will prefer it to anything by James Joyce. I don't see why we should quarrel with Hueffer, but I see no reason for agreeing with him.

    Yours
    John
Please turn over.

P.P.S. Monday. Your other letter has come—forgive my not answering it—I am frightfully busy. Don't come to town unless you can afford it. Don't worry about the future. I am quite sure that your work will be recognized and appreciated by the people who matter—
    J. G. F.

[Neither Fletcher nor Cournos made clear which of Jakop Wasserman's novels was interesting. Fletcher only mentioned later that he had not read The Mauritius Case, *as if it were the only one he had not.]*

TO ROBERT LINSCOTT

37 Crystal Palace Park Road
Sydenham
Dec. 25, 1922

Dear Linscott,

Your letter refusing the MS I sent you arrived this morning, in time for Christmas. Thank you for it.

I have nothing to say about your firm's decision, but about your own, I have to say a great deal. If your firm does not want to publish me, well and good. I do not consider it so great an honor to be published by the firm that is willing to print such rubbish as "A Critical Fable." If *that* is the sort of thing the public wants, so much the worse not for the public, but for your firm, for pandering to the public taste. "It must needs be that offenses shall come, but woe unto him through whom they come."

Hitherto, however, I have held you to be a good man in a bad position. Because you once had me at your house over Xmas, when I was lonely, wretched, and practically friendless in Boston, I have forgiven you many a word that I might have considered a deliberate insult to my intelligence if another had spoken it. But forgiveness has its limits. You have written me saying not only that you fail to understand *The Parables*, but that you are still so much under the spell of my earlier work as to be unable to follow me into my new development. In other words, you hint that I am a complete fool in your opinion.

My dear sir, your brain is static. You have degenerated from being a radical to an apostle of normalcy. You are in the exact position of Warren Harding, Georges Clemenceau, and all the other old fogies who want the world never to change. You have persuaded yourself to the belief that *Symphonies* are wonderful poetry—and that therefore nothing else can or should be done by me but to repeat them. You might say that Clemenceau is equally right when he says that France of 1785 was wonderful, therefore France must be the same today. This is exactly *your* attitude. Not only do you fail to understand; you do not even want to make the effort: You have "conquered thought" to such an extent that you cannot even see that nothing can be more inevitable as a development from the *Symphonies* than these *Parables*. I assure you, on my conscience as a man and an artist, that I would never have written them if I had not cherished the idea long, long ago: they are as much, as essentially *me* as the *Symphonies*. I have merely carried the idea further, into the realm of philosophic thought—if you object to thought, why read at all? That you cannot see this proves to me one thing: that you are in danger of losing, if you have not already lost, your soul.

Aiken tells me that you are a great admirer of James Joyce. I agree with you that *Ulysses* is a wonderful book, but no one can say that it does not depict this world as sheer hell. Do you like, positively *like*, to live in hell? If you don't, can't you find in my *Parables* one word, one sentence that makes this world a little less so? You may say that I am arguing that art has a moral purpose. That is exactly what I do argue—I agree that *art alone* has any moral purpose. James Joyce has a moral purpose—to show this world up as the shithouse (if I may use the term) that it largely is. And I have a moral purpose which goes further that Joyce dares to go. I propose to show how this world might cease being what it is, and how man alone might make it almost a paradise. And the result is, you say "I cannot follow you." You *cannot* follow me!

But it is no use arguing with a fool. You prefer—positively prefer—to live in a James Joyce world. I say to you soberly, seriously, and in full knowledge of the responsibility I am taking on myself, that I'll be damned if I live in a James Joyce world—damned here and hereafter. And I say further that you need not write to me ever again to inform me that you like my *Symphonies*. Faulty as they are, their inner meaning is far, far beyond your comprehension. You have learned to read them with the outward eye only. When you learn to read them with the eye that looks inward as well as outward, you will discover too late the reason why I have written this letter, which as far as I am concerned makes an end of our friendship.

    I remain

    John Gould Fletcher

P.S. Dec. 28. William Blake, whom you say you would not have understood if you had been his contemporary (are you sure you understand him today?), said:

> In Heaven the chief art of living
> Is forgetting and forgiving,
> But if on earth you do forgive
> You shall not find where to live.

Since you are one of the five people I have known who have tried to be unmercenary in their friendship, and have tried to understand my character (however thankless a task it may appear), I may say that I now forgive you. But I shall never again send a manuscript to your firm, not even if you and all the rest of that firm approach me on bended knees. And I doubt if I shall ever see you on this planet. I leave you to the enjoyment of things that you do understand—viz.: Prohibition, Christian Science, and the Ku Klux Klan—the Father, Son and Holy Ghost of American worship (to me the blasphemous Black Mass of Antichrist).

    I remain yours

    J. G. F.

[The Blake quotation is found in Jerusalem, Plate 81, in the advice given in mirror-writing by Gwendolen to Cambel.]

TO CONRAD AIKEN

37 Crystal Palace Park Road
Sydenham
[12 July 1923]

Dear Aiken,

    Yes, I quite agree with you. I am not so terribly enthusiastic of "The Waste Land," but it is in any case a serious piece of work, and a good poem—Edna Millay is neither to be taken seriously nor is she particularly poetic—her work is mere jingle of the worst order. If a better poet than that could not be found, the prize should have been withheld. Wilbur Cross and Greenslet ought to be old enough to know better. I think the committee is permanent, as Amy told me that Greenslet had been on the committee that picked Robinson.

I saw Firuski yesterday and he told me that the prize had been given to Edna for "Second April." Sara Teasdale, who is in town with her husband, tells me that "Second April" is an old piece of work (I thought it came out in 1921). She tells me that the prize was won by the sonnets (second-rate) and by *A Few Figs from Thistles* and *The Ballad of the Harp-Weaver*, etc. This is almost too horrible to believe—I'll send you both books, and you may tell me what you think of them, if you want. Why, great God, that book I lent you—*The Undertaker's Garland*—is ten thousand times better. I understand *The Century* has published an article by Carl Van Doren praising Millay up to the skies for her courage in daring to do the things in life others only talk about, etc. Are we a nation of imbeciles, or what? As if it has anything to do with poetic ability whether one has slept with one woman or man or a hundred! I don't care whether Edna is Cleopatra's peer when it comes to ensnaring men, or not. What I insist upon is that she is a bad poet, a *very* bad poet. She is simply Ella Wheeler Wilcox *a l'envers*. She has no style, no grasp, no intelligence. Surely that is sufficient to disqualify her forever.

I think we might sign a joint letter and send it to *The New Republic* or somewhere. I am going to try to interest Robinson, when I next see him. It won't do to let the matter rest.

J. G. F.

[*Teasdale was correct about the works for which Millay had been awarded the Pulitzer Prize.*]

TO VAN WYCK BROOKS

37 Crystal Palace Park Road
Sydenham
March 21st, 1924

Dear Brooks,

It is very hard for me to find words to answer your letter. There is a strange bond of sympathy between us, of the sort of which men do not usually speak. I can still see you as you stood in *The Freeman* office in your green-gray Norfolk jacket coat, with a watchchain looped into the upper lapel, and your eyes twinkling—also I can see your room at the Chelsea, with the crucifix on the wall. And this is more precious to me than your words of praise—undeserved as those probably are.

One thing I may say, however. The articles you mentioned as having pleased you—the Bali, Unamuno, Faure, Van Gogh—struck the religious note intentionally. I cannot get away from that note, in my life, or in my work. For all my effort has been to find God in man—as correspondence and complement to the God I know is in nature. I do not say that I did those articles deliberately—I work by intuition, and I cannot stand the cold-blooded deliberation of barren "aesthetic" or "scientific" minds—but I know what my message is, although I may lack strength or opportunity to convey it in any articulate form. To me, the close of the eighteenth century marked the end of the Medieval Cycle of Christianity. From that time on began the Modern Cycle—in which Christ is to appear not as God becoming Man, but as Man becoming God. And the prophets of that the new development are Ibsen, Tolstoy, Whitman, Nietzsche—possibly also Heine with his irony and arrogance. Blake at the very outset of the movement got a confused and disordered vision of what it was all about. And intellectuals like Henry Adams, Henry James, and now Unamuno and Faure (who are nearer the source than Adams and James) see that it necessitates a new spiritual communism, in the Medieval place, but on an altogether different scale, adapted to modern conditions. Where that new communism is coming from, I don't know. Not from Russia, which is merely the triumph and the failure of the old materialist communism.

Now everything is being done to hamper that development which is necessary. Everything. We have false science, aestheticism, ignorance, hypocrisy, smut, the vested interests of a million institutions to fight at every turn. And most of the people who understand at all what is coming, are uprooted from the soil (like myself) struggling to keep alive, fighting ill health and worry day and night. Look for instance at D. H. Lawrence. Here is a fine artist, a rare intuitive genius—and not one of the thousands who read him begin to grasp what he is driving at, and how much the effort has embittered him and made him feel an outcast.

No doubt you know all this as well as I, dear Brooks. I merely write it because you are a friend and I sense a certain sympathy in our natures. Someday I know—whether anyone will ever listen to me or not—someday there must be reconstruction of the religious impulse inherent in human life for every one of us, or else there will be a disaster to which the last war will appear child's play. Thomas Hardy recently uttered the following remark: "Civilization is not progressing backward. *It is progressing in the wrong direction.*"

Those who know that have their choice either to turn back or to find out if there isn't a new direction somewhere. Nothing will be gained by standing still. And the whole of America is simply standing still, marking time—the paralysis of though which descended the day America entered the war had never, in reality, lifted. Everybody is afraid of themselves.

Perhaps this overlong letter will give you some idea of what it is I am trying to do. And if you find any ideas suggestive of work or thought in it, I hope you will use them as if they were entirely your own.

I remain
Yours sincerely
John Gould Fletcher

P.S. I could not get the Renaissance article to *The Freeman* in time—and now it has gone to another paper. If you would still care to see it, and could give it a berth, I will surely send it in.

TO HARRIET MONROE

Address: 411 East 7th Street
Little Rock, Arkansas
December 13 [1926]

Dear H. M.

Your letter received. I won't be able to visit Chicago before Xmas after all, to my deep regret. At the end of this week, I leave for the South, and I expect to travel via Washington. I will be down there until January 25 or thereabouts lecturing: after that my movements are quite uncertain. Perhaps you will write me if you can obtain a lecture in Chicago for February? My fee is one hundred and fifty dollars, but I might accept less if the lecture could be clinched.

I am glad to hear that the Graves attack leaves you unmoved. You have done enough for poetry to be above such manifestations of pure personal vanity or spite. I knew Graves fairly well in Oxford in 1922 and regret that the attack should come from him. Unfortunately, he is a man who is likely to rush to conclusions on little—or no evidence at all. See for example his book on English poetry. Critically he doesn't matter at all, but as a poet he has shown a degree of fantastic imagination not too common. But I think his talent is likely to go to pieces, if it hasn't already done so—due either to some concealed jealousy or desire to startle the world at any cost which he does not seem to be able to rid himself of. As he is regarded highly in certain quarters in England, I am glad to see his remarks have provoked Benét to a public reply.

Wishing you and *Poetry* a merry Xmas and a most happy New Year.
I remain
Yours
John Gould Fletcher

[Two days earlier Monroe had written to Fletcher that she had seen an article in the public library in which Graves had been bitterly critical in an almost libelous fashion. Although Benét and another writer planned a reply, she had no plans to do so.]

TO DONALD DAVIDSON

37 Crystal Palace Park Road
Sydenham
London, SE 26
June 26, 1927

Dear Davidson,

It was a great pleasure to me to hear from you again; I feared that you might perhaps have been offended by something I said or prevented by illness from replying. Your letter is very interesting, and I could wish that you would write oftener. You and the few others who in the South are trying to keep some spark of the human spirit alive in this mechanical age are, in the only real sense, my nearest kinsmen. Unfortunately I am not able to live amongst you; to explain why this is so would be to tell you the whole story of my life, which would be painful in many respects for me to narrate and not of great interest for you to learn. But I have always believed, that the South would some day awaken, and always hoped to take some part (however small) in that consummation. My own isolation (which I feel every day and hour with a keenness that is almost unbearable) would be a small price to pay if I could feel that the South were preparing to take steps towards the recovery of its own best intellectual and cultural heritage.

The anthology scheme you have sent me is very typical of the sort of thing any conscientious poet of the present day, in almost any part of the United States, has to contend against. Our age has all sorts of commercial and industrial standards, but simply has no cultural standards: no conception whatever of values. I agree with Tate that the majority of these poets have no place in any anthology—they have neither the technical intelligence, nor the emotional range, nor the persistent grip on reality that is necessary before anyone can claim to be a poet. But I suppose they satisfy the public's taste for what Whitman called "piano-tunes," or they have a meretricious facility—and as you say, what is one to do about this aimless spawning of bad verse-writers? One is practically helpless before the ubiquitous anthologist. I am very glad to hear that the Fugitives are bringing out their anthology. There are one or two American papers that occasionally take an article from me; I would like to review a book that has so interesting a flavor of its own, besides being in some sense a landmark.

As regards my *Branches of Adam* I am glad it has interested you. I know its faults only too well, and realize how far I fell short of my aim. But I know also that it is a unit in conception; a thing very rare nowadays. And I think it is good enough to escape the fate it has had: of neither being published or noticed in America. I was unable to obtain a publisher for it in New York—my public in England is too limited to count, nor do I value very deeply *their* acclaim. As you say, the chief merit my work has, is that it sincerely aims at the "Grand Style"—I will never believe that aim to be impossible (though the whole tendency of today seems utterly opposed to it). I feel that major poetry is still possible and desirable. However, it may be that I am entirely on a wrong track; only time will tell.

You say you are tired of Frost and Robinson. Frost has always been a puzzle to me—he so definitely limits himself spiritually that I have never been able to appreciate him perhaps as much as he deserves. I am much more drawn to Robinson. His new *Tristram* is, in psychological character drawing, at least, a first-rate piece of work (though his blank verse has obvious limitations of movement and color). I sometimes feel a very perceptible irritation at his *New England correctness*. But when all is said, he has written two major poems: "The Man Against the Sky" and "Ben Jonson"—I am glad that I have been, in some measure, his contemporary.

I am even more interested in the Lindsay-Masters question. If these two could have been fused: if you could combine the lyric fire of the one with the stern uncompromising realism of the other, the result would have been a very great poet. Unfortunately, there was no fusion; and the crass vulgarity of the Middle West arrested the development of both. But I won't feel that we are altogether finished and done for yet. The South can still provide a few examples of what the future may logically aspire towards: or failing that, some critical principle enabling the next generation to do better.

This epistle grows too long. I would be very glad to be able to see you again, and if I ever get so far as Nashville, I hope to make a longer stay. If I can be of any assistance, I hope you will always count upon my most friendly attitude. I cannot say more.

Yours sincerely
John Gould Fletcher

TO LEWIS MUMFORD

37 Crystal Palace Park Road
Sydenham
London SE
Oct. 2, 1927

Dear Lewis Mumford,

Your letter of August 25 has been lying on my desk for weeks past while I have been striving to inject a little Italian sunlight into my veins as preparation for the coming winter. I only got back here two days ago; hence the delay in answering.

Thanks for the check and also for the news about *The Caravan*, which has reached me. I haven't had time to look at the book yet, but I am sure to find it interesting. As soon as I make up arrears in correspondence, I will give it closer attention.

I am very glad to hear that Brooks is better. His loss—fortunately, I hope, not total—was to me the most poignant and tragic thing that has occurred for years. I admire deeply the truth-seeking integrity of his criticism, his devotion to his task, and his character as a man. I owe him a great debt, and so does everyone in America who cared for the tradition of great literature. Thank you for sending the news.

You have probably seen in *The New Republic* of Sept. 14 some remarks of mine condemning your views in general, which may have caused you some pain. I trust you will feel that I do not attack you because of any personal malice or jealousy. As a result of long thinking and experience, I have come to the conclusion that you, like all writers who still believe in democracy today, are profoundly mistaken. Democracy means nothing but government by mobs and Menckens—such a government as you have in America today, which hounds men like Sacco and Vanzetti to the electric chair, and complacently accepts the worst corruptions of oligarchic government. Aristocracy—though its perfect form does not exist outside the pages of Plato's Republic—at least has produced decent conditions of living in the past, it has shaped gentlemen like Lee and Lincoln, it has given us all our best standards of life and conduct. I am frankly an aristocrat, not a reactionary, but a radical aristocrat. I cannot join you and Rosenfeld and Kreymborg in paeans to the democratic future—they seem to me sentimental, and any future that is won only by destroying the best of the past seems to me not worth winning. Such a future seems to me only too clearly foreshadowed by the dementia praecox chatter of Gertrude Stein, by the bludgeonings of Mencken, by the judicial assassination in which the great abolition state of Massachusetts showed it was possessed of a worse mob-fever than has ever burned in the South.

I do not expect you to agree with me on this point, but I want you to clearly understand that if I do oppose you, it is because I have thought this problem out to the final issue, and not because I have any personal feelings about the matter. I am glad to hear that *The Caravan* is to have another issue; and if I have anything to send, will let you know.

Yours sincerely
John Gould Fletcher

[The American Caravan (1927–1936) was an annual volume edited first by Van Wyck Brooks, and later by Lewis Mumford and others.]

TO DONALD DAVIDSON

37 Crystal Palace Park Road
Sydenham
October 24, 1927

Dear Donald Davidson,

Your letter and your book of poems has come. I say "book of poems," but having read your book once, and meaning to read it again, I realize that it is all one poem. You have written something that has life in it; that to me is the main thing. And it has an immense bearing on the problem of the present day precisely because it does not cut its roots away from the past, but tries to live and be the fulfillment of that past. I don't suppose anybody will pay any attention to the book; that is the fate of most good books in these times. But if I get a chance, I would like to write an article about it, and publicly say what I think of its significance to its place and period. And meanwhile, I intend to read it again.

As regards your letter, I must first of all acknowledge your overgenerous praise of my work. I wish to God that I had my life—or the last ten years of it—to live over again. I would have made a different thing altogether of my poetry. But there is no use wishing, and I agree with you that *Branches of Adam* suffers from too much imagism and phrase-making. I am all for the intellectual type of poetry now, but my early training and technique stand in the way. Still, I think this book has got a technical interest, and I will either do my best to write major poetry or nothing.

Your remarks about Ransom are shrewdly penetrating. (Incidentally I have never seen my essay since it was printed. The editor didn't send me a copy. That is how America behaves to its authors). I agree with you that there is a romantic irony at the bottom of Ransom—a sort of dandified disillusionment which I do not altogether like. I prefer your work with its harsher and raggeder outlines to his. Ransom has done his job very perfectly and very finely—he is an artist—whereas Miss Millay, whom you mention, is neither a poet nor an artist, but a fake from first to last. But Ransom's work has a sort of self-imposed limitation of slightly bored superiority which I mistrust (this in confidence). I prefer work that is not always so polished, so brittle. I believe it is possible to be intellectual without being a sort of Laforgue super-ironist about life. Life is too serious a business and commands too large issues to be met with a faint mockery. The best poet has to be dissatisfied with himself as well as with the world, and has to fuse his own dissatisfaction with that of the world. That is why I pointed out Dante as the supreme type of intellectualist. But no doubt you realize this better than I.

I am afraid that I won't be coming to the States after all this winter. It is not an easy decision to make, to give up coming. But here I can go on working after a fashion and I seem not to have even a foothold in the States any longer. If I do get the chance to come over, it will be in the spring.

Good luck to you. And if I can help you in any way, I will do so. I would like to review your book somewhere. But where? I haven't a single editor left in America whom I can rely on.

Yours
John Gould Fletcher

P.S. Have you ever read Irving Babbitt's *Democracy and Leadership*? If not, you ought to do so. It is a first-rate critical survey of what really is the matter with the modern world.

[Davidson's book mentioned by Fletcher was The Tall Men. *Fletcher had reviewed Ransom's* Two Gentlemen in Bonds *and other books in* Criterion *6 (August 1927): 168–72.]*

TO LEWIS MUMFORD

37 Crystal Palace Park Road
Sydenham
SE 26 England
November 18, 1927

Dear Lewis Mumford,

You do not owe me any apology for delay in writing; your letter (now it has come) is so interesting that I feel indebted to your for sending it to me.

Let me attempt to answer you in some detail, and in the same spirit of impartial investigation you have shown.

My chief objection to *The Golden Day* was that while it admitted that the best qualities of the American spirit had been practically destroyed in the industrial expansion and the complete loss of standards that followed the Civil War, it yet strove to minimize this tragedy (a tragedy for the North no less than for the South) and to optimistically accept the situation, even to suppose that some way out would be found. Now it is my misfortune that I cannot accept the situation. Long experience of American life and the advantages—such as they are—of exile abroad, have taught me that neither America, nor any other country, can be saved by its own undirected energy. There must be values, there must be cultural standards, there must be an ordered society with some other aim than "getting rich quick" and spending wastefully, before any intellectual development is possible. The idea that America can on laissez-faire principles, or rather lack of principles, produce a race of supermen, is a notion picked up by the Middle West about fifteen years ago from Whitman, and carried to its climax by writers such as Dreiser and Anderson. I fear it was Whitman's worst blunder; and your work seems to me now to be infected with it. I quite agree with you and Brooks—and incidentally with Taine—that art is an expression of social values, but I add that social values are impossible without a social structure to uphold them. And the Middle West particularly seems to me to lack such a structure; its real superman, its *homo Americanus,* is Babbitt or Big Bill Thompson—the democratic opportunist par excellence.

Secondly, I dispute with you that the South and the North grew out of the same social order. There seems to me to have been a shade of difference from the beginning. But waiving this point, there is no doubt that the North lost its social order, thanks to the decline of agriculture and the growth of the mercantile class, rather earlier than the South. The South was a planter aristocracy up to 1860; the North was at best a mercantile aristocracy from 1820 on. And this seems to me an important difference.

Third, you say of the South "Its achievements of the mind were feeble" and you go on to cite the poverty of Southern literary achievement! I hold that the greatest achievement of the mind in any culture is first *statesmanship;* second, *synthetic science* (such things as town planning, roads, conservation of resources, eugenics, etc. come under this); third the *plastic arts;* fourth and least, *literature*. In fact, literature is usually the voice of a minority protesting against the standards of the majority (this accounts for the ridiculous over-estimate placed on literature nowadays, and its ridiculous overproduction). For instance, Emerson, Thoreau, Whitman, Melville were all more or less rebels to the business standards of living that the North was adopting. That they were so is the reason I respect them; I admire them precisely because they opposed the direction the North was taking (that they were abolitionists, and consequently also opposed to the South I regard as subsidiary to their main drift). The South, on the other hand, excelled precisely where the North failed: in statesmanship. Jefferson, Calhoun, and Clay represent the full height of our genius. In science we had Maury and Shaler; in architecture (to take a recent example) Richardson; and with these at my back, it would not worry me in the least if the South had produced no literature at all. That a literature is now at last emerging is due to the fact that we too have had to protest somehow vocally against this industrial age which we fought and died from 1860 to 1865 to prevent. Above all, I would stress the South's really great contribution: statesmanship and the will to an ordered scheme of life. One finds remains of this Southern point of view in Woodrow Wilson, who as statesman was immensely superior to the politicians of his day. One finds it, intellectually, in the best of all the New England historians: Henry Adams. His *Education* is unthinkable without reference to the fact that he also wrote *Democracy* as a plea for the Southern point of view—and that he spent a good part of his life in Washington, essentially a Southern town.

You will see by this, that it was not because you failed to discuss Southern architecture in your *Sticks and Stones* that I attacked you: but because in your book on American culture as a whole, you failed to see that there were two Americas from the beginning, and because you related everything to the standard of literature, which to me is the least important standard of the level of cultural life. I prefer a life where at least people live under decent conditions, and are fed and housed carefully, and not choked with coal-fumes or deafened with machinery, to a life such as we have today. To obtain such a life I would cheerfully sacrifice most of the literature in existence, including my own. As regards aristocracy, I dare say our ideals coincide. Mine is Plato's *Republic;* but I am ready to accept even a hereditary caste system, with all its drawbacks, rather than the chaos of today.

So much for the points of difference between us. For the rest, I am glad to hear you are at work on Melville. You are certainly right in supposing that there is a parallel with Shakespeare. There is—and it is far stronger than most people suspect.

If you see Brooks, please give him my warmest regards.

Yours sincerely

John Gould Fletcher

[Not Irving Babbitt but George F. Babbitt in the novel of Sinclair Lewis. Thompson was the Republican boss of Chicago. Mumford's Herman Melville *was not published until 1929.]*

TO T. S. ELIOT

37 Crystal Palace Park Road
Sydenham
Nov. 19, 1927

Dear Eliot,

    Robinson Jeffers is probably the most-talked-about poet now in America. About two or three years ago, he brought out a book, *Roan Stallion, Tamar, and Other Poems*, which was certainly a work of great power and imaginative fury (though he should have cut two or three poems out of it) and in its combination of nature feeling absolutely Greek, together with a psychological interest in all sorts of queer backwoods types gone wrong (such as haunt the remote settlements almost everywhere in the U.S.), created a great sensation. His latest book, *The Women at Point Sur*, I have not seen, but I understand it has the same qualities. He is certainly worth publishing, and I hope your firm will do him. I would be glad to do anything I could for him (write an introduction, or advise concerning specific poems) in this matter as I may count myself among the earlier admirers of his work. I do not know him personally, nor have we ever had any correspondence of any sort, but I feel sure he is a major American poet.

    I am sorry to hear that you have to do so much traveling about. I am still here, but for the moment am suffering extensively from rheumatism, lumbago, and all the other ills that American flesh is heir to in this climate. In consequence, I haven't been able to tackle [René] Gulnon's book [*La crise du monde moderne*, 1927] at all, and as I have a biographical work in hand, don't know when I should be able to read it. Faber & Gwyer have decided to take my book of poems, but it is too long (208 pages of print) and they and I have agreed to submit it to you for shortening. It ought to be reduced down to 176 pages, in my opinion, and I feel sure you could point out the weak spots. If you can't do this, I shall have to go over the whole thing myself, which I almost dread doing.

    Hoping we can have a meeting when you return. If it is not too far for you, you might come out here to my home sometime. Sunday is usually the day we entertain, but Friday night in the week is also possible. Or we could have a meeting in town. You really must let me stand you the dinner on this occasion. I shudder to think of the number of meals I have already eaten at your expense.

    John Gould Fletcher

TO DONALD DAVIDSON

c/o Andrew H. Dakers
4 Adam Street
Adelphi, Strand
London W. C.
February 28 [1928]

Dear Donald Davidson,

    It was good to hear from you again, and I am very delighted to know that you liked my review of your book. I have been ill this winter, and am going away to the country for a few days. I have received the copy of the Fugitive book from Harcourt. It is very interesting. To my mind, the three outstanding men of the collection are Ransom, Moore, and yourself. Tate is a possible fourth, but he has to decide whether to be critical mainly or mainly creative, and I fear his decision will be against creative acceptance. He has tremendous gifts, especially of mind, but is unfortunately inhibited by the age—which is bad enough to inhibit anybody. The rest do not matter much. I doubt if Warren will develop—and as for Laura R, there isn't anything there but ugly showing off—such is my opinion. It may be valuable for you to have this opinion, as I stand more or less outside the movement—thought God knows I am all for its "Southernism" and all for its insistence on a kind of intellectual responsibility very rare nowadays—especially rare in mere barren rebels against everything, such as Laura R.

    I hope some day to see you again, and Ransom, and Tate, and some others of your group. It is good to know that the South is producing a few poets who have some cause for pride in what the South really was, and who do not snivel or over-sentimentalize about it. Long life to you all!

    Yours
    John Gould Fletcher

[Fletcher liked the style and subject of Davidson's The Tall Men: Portrait of a Tennessean *in a review in* The Nation *126 (18 January 1928): 71. Laura R is Laura Riding.]*

TO T. S. ELIOT

Hotel Victoria
Lyme Regis, Dorset
Saturday, March 3 [1928]

Dear Eliot,

You have not fulfilled your promise to write me, so I am writing you. Your lecture on Whitman and Tennyson was admirable: far from saying the obvious thing, you said something that was unobvious (I doubt if any of the company had thought of the matter in that light before) and something that really illustrated the whole question of what poetry is and what poets can do with it.

I hope you will take these remarks as possibly foolish but undoubtedly sincere, when I tell you that sometimes I hope that I am not inferior as a poet to you, but always I know myself to be inferior as a critic. You really should embody the substance of your remarks in an essay: possibly the first essay of a whole new book, to be set beside *The Sacred Wood* on the shelves of "the happy few." "The Laureate Type"—what a title!

Please forgive me if this suggestion offends you. I will venture another suggestion. If you feel nervous in addressing an audience, there is one thing that may help you to overcome it. Learn a mantra, and repeat it to yourself for several minutes before beginning. It always cools you down. "One old Oxford ox eating oysters" is a very good mantra.

I am here a week trying to recuperate from the last three months in London—and wrestling with typescript to boot.

Yours
J. G. F.

TO HAVELOCK ELLIS

37 Crystal Palace Park Road
August 18, 1928

Dear Havelock Ellis:

I have not answered your interesting letter of July 30 partly because I have been very busy myself in a study of American civilization from a novel point of view, and partly because I have not seen the article by Fosdick to which you refer. I am not a subscriber to the *Virginia Quarterly Review*, but if you still have the article, I should be glad to see it (it was in the third issue).

I feel somewhat that it is trespassing on your good nature not to leave you the last word in this friendly exchange of letters on the subject of civilization, religion and the machines. But I have just seen Charles A. Beard's article in the August *Harper's* on this subject, and I disagree with it so violently that I would like to make my position, if possible, clear.

In the first place, it seems to me that we have no business to discuss God as "abstract metaphysical will" (to quote your letter) at all. Such a thing is beyond our duty and limitation as human beings. That "God" does exist in this sense, I do not doubt; but it is none of our affair! I object and always have objected to the attempts of theologians to fix "God" to this or that concept: and I equally object to the attempts of the scientists to say that God's aim is "Reproduction" or anything else. We simply do not know what God is in this sense, we cannot make any definition, we do not transcend our limitations by thinking in this direction at all. The only way we can conceive of God is on some purely human plane of understanding and sympathy which is ethical and aesthetic, and not metaphysical at all. (I may add that I myself have made some attempts to formulate God in the metaphysical sense—in some poems I wrote years ago—but have given up the task.)

The great failing of our age is in the lack of any intelligent and reasonable ethic, to counterbalance the mad drift into materialism, power-cults (of which the cult of the machine is the latest), utilitarian pragmatism, and the chaos of values in which we are at present. Unfortunately—alas—Nietzsche did his work only too thoroughly. He hated the democratic, leveling tendency of his day honestly, and because of it felt he had to attack the ethics of Christianity. But all he accomplished was to upset *all ethics*—Plato's no less than Jesus'—and to put a barren power-cult in their place. And the apostles of mechanical civilization are just as bad in this respect as Nietzsche. They are utterly lacking in understanding that ethics must come first, that conduct is not three-quarters as Matthew Arnold said, but *all* of life, and they fail completely therefore to relate this mechanistic age to any scheme of either social, religious or aesthetic values.

Take Beard's article (inasmuch as it is to appear in a book to which you contribute, I suppose you have read it). He says that "technological civilization rests fundamentally on power-driven machinery which transcends the physical limits of its human directors, multiplying indefinitely the capacity for the production of goods." Yet later on, on the same page, he speaks of this civilization as *an "order."* Now how can anything be *an order* that transcends human capacity to control it? Surely the human will is morally master of the human order as the divine will is master (metaphysically) of the universe, but the two things as I have already said, are separate, not together. Beard would have us make an order out of what lies beyond our capacities to order; and it is perfectly obvious that no such order can be made. When I read such muddled and hopelessly befogged thinking as this, I feel that all the scholastics, from Scotus *Erigena* to St. Thomas Aquinas, were right—I prefer the most reactionary Catholic of the Eric Gill type to this sort of "modernism," because Catholicism does not beg the question, does not confuse man's sphere with God's.

Later on Beard again asserts that "Machinery and science are the basis of present Western civilization." I may add that this is a direct lie. The basis of present day Western civilization is Christianity (even for those who don't happen to believe in it). Machinery may be a means of conveying civilization, of speeding it up, or improving its technique, but the basis of all civilizations has rested elsewhere, in the "human critter" as Whitman said. How anyone presumably equipped with a brain could speak of machinery being the basis of civilization is a question I cannot answer. One might point out the bombs thrown down on London during the war by flying machines (we were reminded again of them this week) and say "these are the basis of present day civilization."

Then he goes on to art and literature. "Granted that we have no Shakespeare, or Goethe, we may reasonably answer that literature of their manner has little meaning for a civilization founded on a different basis." I leave this phrase without comment. Obviously the answer is that the daily paper has meaning—since Shakespeare has none. I wonder what Matthew Arnold would have said of this, or Ruskin, or Carlyle, or William Morris or anyone of the great Englishmen of the nineteenth century. Let us have literature fitted to our basis then—vulgarity and sentimentality a la Hollywood, or James Joyce and surrealism. Which is it to be?

Yours,
John Gould Fletcher

[The article was Charles A. Beard's "Democracy Holds Its Ground: a European Survey" in Harper's *157 (August 1928): 680–691.]*

TO GLENN HUGHES

Holme Lea
Crystal Palace Park Road
Sydenham, S. E.
Sept. 27, 1928

Dear Hughes,

I greatly enjoyed our talk yesterday. If you want to borrow any of my books before I sail (I hope to get away before the end of next month) please let me know. I see I have two copies of *New Voices* (including the enlarged edn), also somewhere I have a copy of Amy's *Tendencies* I don't mind parting with. I will look it up. Also *The Egoist*—I have a great many numbers stowed away for reference.

Our talk brought out very clearly what I had previously suspected: viz., that there were two sides of the Imagist movement, a Franco-Oriental influence and a Greek-Latin-Provencal influence. Amy, Flint, and myself were on one side of the fence, and H. D. and Aldington on the other. Pound, after belonging to the latter group, tried to straddle both sides of the fence and failed. That, it seems to me, is the real thesis you have to present.

I was glad you said a good word about my *Tree of Life*. This book, appearing at the end of the war, had no sales and no acclaim—all the reviewers simply tore it to pieces! But it contains much work of my *full imagist period*. The first section was written in the fall of 1913 (that is, between *Irradiations* and the *Symphonies*), the second in the spring and summer of 1914, when I was at work on the *Symphonies*, the third (inferior) in the winter of 1914–15, and the fourth (which I think has some good things in it) and fifth (inferior again) in the summer and autumn of 1915. The epilogue, which Sara Teasdale plagiarized for the subject of one of her most celebrated lyrics, was written early in 1916. This book thus bridges the whole period of my development from *Irradiations* to "Lincoln"—my entire imagist period properly speaking (1913–16). I kept it by me, and delayed publication, as the subject seemed so intensely personal and mystical, but that is not to say it is bad. Conrad Aiken once told me—and his was an independent judgment—that it contained some of my very finest work.

It's very hard for me still to speak about this particular book, because of the outrageous reception it had here in England. And in America it was ignored by everybody.

Hoping to hear from you soon, I remain
Yours
J. G. Fletcher

P.S. Have just found Amy's *Tendencies*—which I shall be glad to lend to you. I couldn't lend you her *Six French Poets*—as my copy is a presentation one.

TO GLENN HUGHES

37 Crystal Palace Park Road
Oct. 5, 1928

Dear Hughes,

I posted on to you today a file (unfortunately fragmentary) of *The Egoist*, as I understand you to say that you had not seen the paper. The copies I sent you are all I possess of the paper (except a few duplicates) and it seems to me that some note on the paper's founding and aims might be of interest.

The Egoist started as *The Freewoman* about June 1913. Its founders were two ladies, Miss Harriet Shaw Weaver and Miss Dora Marsden, who were imbued with the idea of helping out the feminist movement. This was the year of militant suffragism in England; the agitators for female suffrage were going very strong, and their paper (*Votes for Women*, run by Mrs. Pankhurst) was very prominent. Miss Weaver and Miss Marsden were not especially interested in votes merely; Miss Weaver was inclined to philosophic anarchism, and was opposed to political action, and Miss Marsden was a student of philosophy, very strongly imbued with Berkeleyan metaphysics. Miss Weaver had some money and was supporting Miss Marsden, and she put up the money for the paper in order to give Miss Marsden a chance to preach her philosophy. I myself heard of the paper through Ezra (shortly after my first meeting with him) and decided to contribute. But as I remember I did not send in anything except a few verses (not imagistic in cast) until 1914.

Some time in 1914 the paper changed its name to *The Egoist*. I don't know the reasons for the change of title, but *The Freewoman* identified the paper too strongly with the suffrage movement, which I personally did not care much about at the time. Ezra collected some funds for the literary side of the paper, and I remember subscribing a few pounds. The paper accordingly became highly imagistic on the literary side, and Aldington was taken on as sub-editor. Why Ezra did not edit it himself, I don't understand, but Miss Weaver stipulated that Miss Marsden must in any case occupy the first page, and this rule was held to (except once or twice, when Miss Marsden was ill). After 1915 the paper became a monthly, and when Aldington was in France, in the army, Eliot became sub-editor. The title of *The Egoist* persisted, and after the paper died (some time in 1919) Miss Weaver subsidized the Egoist Press, which published several books (including Eliot's *Prufrock*, Joyce's *Portrait of the Artist as a Young Man*, and a series of poetical translations under Aldington's editorship).

I thought you would like to have the paper as it was really the only Imagist paper published (the review Pound hoped to found, and the later review Aldington discussed with Miss Lowell were to be much more ambitious monthly papers, but came to nothing). The file I have sent you begins in February 1914 and goes through to November of that year (when I left England, not to return until June 1916). I have therefore only part of 1915 and I also lack some numbers during the winter of 1916—whether the paper actually suspended for a time, owing to a shortage of paper (due to the war) I can't remember. Aldington could perhaps give you fuller details as he was sub-editor.

The publication of the paper brought me one interesting contact. A man named Pender, civilian prisoner of war and publisher in Germany, wrote me and asked for my books. I sent them, and the article on my poetry which appeared in one of these numbers I sent you was the result. After the war, I believe I met him once or twice. The paper had considerable circulation in out-of-the-way quarters, and was very useful as an advertisement for our movement.

If these papers are useful to you, please keep them—if not perhaps your university would like to have them. I don't want them any more. I think you might write a chapter about *The Egoist* in your study. The translation incidentally of the "Song of Maldon" that Aldington printed in this paper was done from a copy of the book which I lent him, and which he kept some time. It is still in my possession.

I have sent you also the Lowell and the Untermeyer book. I can't let you have the other Lowell books unless you will send them back to me before the 20th of Oct. when I shall probably leave England.

With all good wishes, I remain,
Yours
John Gould Fletcher

[The repatriated R. Herdman Pender published "John Gould Fletcher" in The Egoist *3 (November 1916): 173–174, praising Fletcher's innovative rhythms rather than his Imagism.]*

TO HENRY BERGEN

Tuesday Morning, Dec. 11, [19]28

Dear Bergen,

I enclose herewith my essay on the scholastic theory of art—Maritain and Gill—for your consideration and comment. If you would like to make notes, please do so, but in pencil, in the margin. You will probably disagree, though much of the material emerged from our talks last spring.

I intend to tackle you on the subject of the machine, as soon as I possibly can.

I am glad you like Hemingway's book. But I wonder what Tolstoy would have made of it. It seems to me to have no moral bias whatever—its only "lesson" is that nothing can be done, that everything is pretty much "vanity of vanities", that the situation is hopeless. I am afraid that this sort of thing won't do in the long run. But undoubtedly Hemingway has narrative genius—though God knows whether that sort of genius, or any sort, is of much use in the present state of the world.

I remain
yours
John G. F.

[Hemingway's The Sun Also Rises *(1926).]*

TO HENRY BERGEN

Holme Lea
Crystal Palace Park Road
Sydenham, S.E.
February 27 [1929]

Dear Bergen,

I am just now reading Lawrence's *Lady Chatterley's Lover*, which Henderson let me have (incidentally I sold him my Dove's Press Bible for one hundred and twenty pounds, which enabled me to obtain the book and which will help me a good deal later on in my financial adjustments with the income tax people). I quite agree with you that the book is a sincere, brave, and honest one in every way: it gives a very fine picture (Lawrence describes Nature with a painter's eyes) of the true state of affairs in post-war England. The main tendency of the book, its anti-intellectualism, also interests me; but it seems to me that somehow Lawrence does not altogether give a fair account of the state of affairs between the two lovers: Mellors and Lady Chatterley.

I don't know whether you are able to recall much of the book. You may have read it too fast. But to me it seems that there is an artistic defect inherent in Lawrence keeping the love between this man and woman so long on the physical plane. I don't mind his use of words like "cunt" and "fuck," which are really good English. But it seems to me that an affair of this sort would have blown over very shortly without some mental contact which he nowhere posits. My own experience of life (which is all that I have to go by) is that physical love becomes a ghastly mistake unless it is kept alive and enfolded in the real living power of a mental companionship. I don't by that mean that love is an *intellectual* quality. But unless you are interested and moved by some real community of mind and interest, in the person to whom you are physically bound, all the pleasure of the physical bond rapidly passes away. It seems to me Lawrence *falsifies* the central situation of his book (probably he does it unconsciously, but that does not matter) by making the whole bond between his lovers only a physical one. In that way he gains an opportunity for writing a great deal of lyrical and erotic prose, but he does not make the bond between these two convincing and compelling for the purposes of his story.

If you'd like to see the book when I am finished with it, I'll lend it to you. It has a great deal of power in the subsidiary details: it seems to me the central focus is warped. It almost reminds me of another book I once read in which a Norwegian woman falls in love with a young English traveler, without either party understanding a word of each other's language! No doubt that can possibly happen in life. But not for long—it is only a passing episode. Lawrence seems to think that these two would really always want to stay and live together. He is mistaken.

However, this is perhaps captious criticism of a book that is on the right side sentimentally—

Yours
John Gould Fletcher

P.S. I am sitting up. And will be all right next week, but am going away. Will let you know about it.

TO S. FOSTER DAMON

Hotel Latham
24th Street and Fifth Avenue
New York
May 1, 1929

Dear Foster Damon,

You must think me the worst of all correspondents. As a matter of fact I have been so busy here trying to find a publisher for an apparently unsaleable prose book I have written that I haven't had time even for a line. I possess a considerable packet of Amy's letters (all typewritten) running from May 1916 to the time of her death and can let you see them—will probably post them on.

The letters are interesting because they cover the period of my quarrel with her. In the autumn of 1916 I submitted to Houghton-Mifflin the manuscript of some love poems then called *Love's Tragedy* (later published under the title of *Tree of Life* by Macmillan's). Ferris Greenslet turned them over to Amy to read—and she sent in an unfavorable opinion. I did not consider this altogether fair; she should have refused to read anything by me so close to her as I was then, or else have backed me up. The result was that we quarreled, and never came again to a clear understanding, though I hoped we would, and made every effort to reach one. The letters I have cover the grounds of this quarrel, and I don't know whether Mrs. Russell has released them to you or not.

I first met Amy in June 1913 at the Berkeley Hotel, Piccadilly, London. A few days before our meeting, a friend who was in the office of Constable's, the publisher (which had published one of my books) told me that an "extraordinary woman" had driven up to the office, and had demanded what had become of her book of poems, just published in America, and of which Constable had taken copies: the book unfortunately could not be found; the copies had just arrived, and apparently had not been unpacked yet; they were still on the premises. My friend went on the say that the author of this book had refused to stir from the office, and had gone on sitting there until the copies were found. He seemed very upset by the whole incident, and wondered whether "all Americans are like that." This I remember distinctly.

A few days later, I happened to call on Ezra Pound (whom I knew very well), and I told this story, together with some remarks my English friend had passed on Amy's physical appearance. To my surprise, Ezra was annoyed. He said that he had just met this "extraordinary woman," and that she was very generous, interested in modern poetry, etc. He said he was going to see her a few nights following, and invited me along.

I went and liked Amy, as was natural. She had the art of bringing out the best side of her audience. Ezra did most of the talking, and read I remember his poem "The Seafarer." Amy may have read some of her things then—some of them in the book referred to above, which was *A Dome of Many-Colored Glass*. I believe she said she had only written one free verse poem, "In a Garden," but she was very interested in the Symbolist School of the French poets, which already claimed my allegiance.

A few nights later, I called alone on her and read then "Irradiations," which was already complete, having been written a few months previously. Amy was greatly impressed. She discovered one of my ambitions, to write a poem about a great modern city, and asked me how to set about it. I said that above all one had to sit and look at things, not to think about them in relation to result, but to "grasp" them as detached objects. This excited her, and it was not long after that that she wrote her "London Thoroughfare: 2 A.M.," which was the view from her hotel window. I believe she got her "externalization" from our talks—and also much of her own color technique.

The thing that strikes me now about all this was her extraordinary receptiveness to suggestion. It was almost as if her poetic development had been arrested in some way, and she was still young in spirit and immensely eager to improve. I did not care much for her *Dome*, and said so. I advised her to go on with the French poets. She had read Henri de Regnier, and I think Jammes, but had not read my favorites—Verhaeren, Rimbaud, Baudelaire, Gerard de Nerval, Corbiere, etc. She caught up quickly.

I was unaware of her passion for Keats then, and did not become aware till the next summer, when she again came over. She went away in September, and we continued corresponding. She agreed sometime I think during the following spring to bring out the Imagists again (the early anthology *Des Imagistes* did not go well, but my absence from it was entirely due to the fact that I had begun to mistrust Ezra) with Houghton-Mifflin. Meantime, she also agreed to try and find me a publisher for *Irradiations*. It was with these two objects in mind that she came back in June 1914, bringing Mrs. Russell with her (Mrs. Russell was not on the earlier trip).

I was then writing the *Symphonies*. The *Blue, Green, Golden,* and *White* were already finished. And I was tremendously interested in Imagism, as I conceived its possibilities. Unfortunately Ezra and Amy then quarreled—Ezra insisted that if a new anthology were to appear that he should be sole editor. Amy wanted every poet to select himself. In the split, I sided with Amy (Ezra's dictatorial tactics were not to my liking), and decided to go into the movement on her side. She had also persuaded Greenslet to do the Modern Poetry series and that is how I happened to get *Irradiations* published.

As regards her characteristics, I have always found her very likable, very affable, but as she grew older, she became less and less open to suggestion: she was determined on pursuing her own way, and no one had any influence over her for long. I used to get irritated at the "business side" of her personality: she simply could or would not look at life idealistically; though her own acute business sense contained much generosity to others. She was still struggling when I first met her to free herself from convention and experiment, and I think it was the experiments of such people, Ezra, H. D., and myself that finally made her champion the cause of the radicals. In politics she was never radical, and strangely enough she cared very little for ultra-modern painting, but preferred ultra-modern music. She was a strange blend of the conservative and the innovator.

I don't know whether this is of use to you, but in case there is anything else you would like to know, please notify me: I shall probably be going back to England on the 15th of this month.

Yours
John Gould Fletcher

Will write you about Blake sometime. Meantime this epistle is long enough.
J. G. F.

TO T. S. ELIOT

Holme Lea
Crystal Palace Park Road
Sydenham, S.E.
Oct. 11, 1929

Dear Eliot,

I was sorry not to have seen you at the Grove yesterday. Your new project, The Poets by the Poets, interests me extremely and I would like to discuss with you an idea that has come to me in regard to it. On reading your Dante, it seemed to me that your idea was to decide the range and value of a particular poet's mind and individual achievement as it appeared to a poet born under different conditions, in another age and possibly with very different problems to face. I think this idea a very valuable one, and I should regret it if your example, in the numbers that follow, is not taken up. You discussed Dante from the background of your personal experience of his mind by yourself. I should like to see other poets treated the same way— equally remote from all mere academic blame or reproach.

In fact, I should like to attempt a poet in the same way. That is the point I am coming to. The poet that interests me in this particular instance is William Blake. It seems to me that no one has said exactly what he intended, and why he failed in the major part of his work, which is the Prophetic Books. I regard these as an attempt to build up a philosophic myth on the basis of the French Revolution. *The Apocalypse of St. John* is an example of the same sort of thing. As the author of the Apocalypse used the background, the fall of Jerusalem, the destruction of the Temple, the dispersal of the Jews, as a sort of frame of reference to describe the struggle of the Messiah and the Roman Empire, so Blake (with less skill) used the background of the French Revolution to describe the struggle of instinct and reason in mankind. This idea does not seem to have been brought out by any of Blake's numerous commentators, and it has important corollaries— notably in the practice of Shelley (who I understand has already been assigned in this series), who took a Greek myth as the basis for his own attempt at the same thing.

If you are at all interested in this, I should be very glad to do the Blake for the series. The books, I understand, are about thirty thousand words long. I could let you have the material by Xmas, and you could publish in the spring. I have thought and worked on Blake off and on for about fifteen years, and I should be glad of this opportunity to say exactly how he strikes me, as an individual of an entirely different social background.

Will you please let me know about this? And while you are about it, there is another question I want to ask. I understand that there is a magazine called *Contemporanios* published in Mexico City, about the size of the *Nouvelle Revue Française*, which devotes itself to articles on modern authors with quotations from their works. Your permission is sought for certain quotations, I don't know how many, by one of the editors, a Mexican in the consulate here. I don't think the paper pays anything—Mexico is not rich in literary rewards. I have promised to find out your attitude in regard to the matter. Perhaps you can let me know. I think I can vouch for the editor in question as being personally honest (not a Roth). That is all.

All good wishes. Hoping I will see you sometime, but I seem less and less disposed to come into town. Regards to Mrs. Eliot.

I remain
Yours sincerely
John Gould Fletcher

[The Grove was a restaurant at which Fletcher met friends. Contemporaneos (1928–31) was the leading Mexican literary journal. The Poets by the Poets was a proposed series of studies of earlier poets done by modern ones, a project that failed. The Prophetic Books are symbolic and prophetic poems by William Blake, expressing his complete mythology of humanity's past, present, and future, a variation on the biblical presentation of the Creation, Fall, and Redemption in which historical revolution is accompanied by a change within the mind and imagination of the individual. The major poems are The Four Zoas, Milton, *and* Jerusalem.*]*

TO T. S. ELIOT

37 Crystal Palace Pk. Road
Dec. 13 [1929]

Dear Eliot,

I gathered from our conversation of yesterday that you were short of about twenty-five pounds for the January number *[The Criterion]*. I am therefore enclosing check for this amount.

Will try to come Thursday if possible.
Yours
John Gould Fletcher

P.S. Please do not inform anyone as to the source whence this came.
J. G. F.

TO LEWIS MUMFORD

37 Crystal Palace Park Road
Sydenham
July 18, 1930

Dear Mumford,

I was beginning to wonder whether I owed you a letter; and now here comes yours, full of a budget of news—most of it none too favorable. My life here has run on much the same lines since I last wrote you. I have revised my "Apology for Solitude" which is nine essays—pretty stiff and metaphysical—intended as sort of introduction to that book on aesthetics which I ought to write. I may perhaps send one or two of them to Scribner's, but Dashiell writes me that they are taking articles of about two thousand words, on immediate problems—and heaven knows my problems are too big to be immediate! They turned down a pretty good essay on Nietzsche I did last spring.

Your news about the financial situation in the U.S. is pretty doleful. I haven't earned any money at all from that source this year, and my private income seems to be sinking steadily. I may come over this winter and try and retrieve the situation slightly, but I hate lecturing, and what I write seems to lack that snappy, immediate touch that is so necessary to a population of morons. The news you give about the dollar books is very bad—I feel it will be a death-blow to about three-quarters of the young talent and will help nobody but the bestsellers. But what can we do about it—I hope *The Caravan* will not cease, but have a deadly feeling that it may.

Meantime, the Wall-Street crash has had its repercussions over here, as you can see by reading the papers. Unemployment nearly two million. The industrial machine seems to have struck a big snag somewhere, and the wheels are held up. If it will help a little towards clear-headed thinking and planning, well and good. But the politicians—English and American—are hopeless. One wishes that the Age of the Despots were back again when one sees how badly the industrial epoch functions under eighteenth century "democracy," whether it be that of McDonald or of Hoover.

About the only thing that has happened here in a constructive way is that a man named Clough Williams Ellis has launched a society called the District Improvement Association showing how "England's green and pleasant land" is being literally butchered to death by the apostles of devil-take-the-hindmost competition and urban development. They have issued some good pamphlets, which I may send you—also they seem to be planning a resurvey of about twenty or thirty towns. Ellis (whom I don't know) seems a very good man.

In literature, there has been a slight awakening in interest in poetry (long overdue) thanks to one or two good volumes. One by Richard Eberhart, an American studying at Cambridge, called *A Bravery of Earth* interested me considerably. Eliot's new volume is pretty depressing but finely done. Roy Campbell has some interest. There are one or two others, but none excited me so much as Hart Crane's *Bridge* and MacLeish's *New Found Land*, published in Paris this spring.

In novels, William Faulkner of Mississippi has produced a minor sensation with *Soldiers' Pay*. I read it and think it the work of a very fine talent—

a superior Hemingway. *Look Homeward Angel* has just come out here also and I am half through it at the moment. It seems to me inferior to Faulkner in every way—vast, inchoate, over-written in spots, with one or two flashes of genius but utterly disordered at bottom, and not really spiritually-centered.

Except for a few Americans and Colonials and a rebel like Ellis, England is more torpid than ever. Everybody is worrying about India, whether they can hold it, or must let go. But things at home here go from bad to worse—and they were already pretty bad. The row about Empire Free Trade is a symptom. I see no future myself in this country unless they get tariffs or give preference in some way to the Dominions.

The Humanism row hasn't moved anyone here—except away from the "Humanism" of Babbitt and his crowd. Schaefer [Shafer] and Foerster are going to be the nemesis of the Movement—their cheapjack vulgarity is beyond belief. It seems to me that all the whole thing will produce will be a swing back to a naturalism of the Zola type, but still more realistic and more mystical. And this may be, in a way, no better—but it will be at least alive—whereas the Unitarian Orthodoxy and Fundamentalism of Babbitt and More is dead.

That's about all my news except that I am doing an article on Americans touring Europe, which I pray Scribner's may accept. For I don't know how I'll pay my bills this winter unless I make some money.

I'll keep *The Caravan* in mind, and if it weathers through the winter, I'll try and send it something really good next spring.

J. G. F.

Thanks for the Cologne exhibition. It looks wonderful on paper—but I fear will be whittled down considerably in practice.

[Irving Babbitt, Paul Elmer More, Norman Foerster, and Robert Shafer were leading proponents of the New Humanism, a movement Fletcher did not find congenial.]

TO DONALD DAVIDSON

37 Crystal Palace Park Road
Nov. 20, 1930

Dear Davidson,

Harper's have just sent me a copy of *I'll Take My Stand* and I sat up nearly all last night reading it. And I am again reading it this morning. The book seems to me to be a very powerful argument for what it stands for, a clear definition of the fundamental issues that really divide human beings (and not in America only, but in England) today. It is much better than the Humanist symposium because it does not suffer so much from mere empty theorizing and personal ill-will. It gets down to the ground, to the roots. And that is good.

But this is not all. I cannot let this occasion pass without telling you how much I admire your essay. It is the most honest piece of writing in the volume. It is not so profound as Lanier's completely destructive analysis of Dewey's philosophy, but it is more tonic, more bracing and stimulating, more courageous and more thoroughgoing than anything in the book except perhaps Lytle's essay. But where Lytle makes a brilliant cavalry raid in the style of Forrest, you maneuver your forces like Jackson. And you write a parable that has its meaning for every one of us, when you point out that we have nowadays to be political agents first, and artists afterwards, if we are to do our part. I don't know what I admire most of all in your essay—whether it is your defense of Romanticism, your attack on the Humanists, your condemnation of museum-culture (I have spent most of my days in museums, and I admire anyone who dares tell the truth about those pernicious institutions), or your thesis on provincialism. You have really covered the field of modern art, and have said what needed saying. I haven't read Josephson's book, but I almost think I must, after what you say about it.

But what I like best of all is your habit of calling a spade a spade. You don't scruple in the least to mention by name such things as McFadden's publications, Hollywood, book-of-the-month clubs, or Carl Van Doren! I know how much courage it requires to do this sort of thing, and I personally doubt whether I would have displayed your courage under such circumstances. I know the New York scene too well, and it has scarred me so deeply that I always hesitate before drawing the sword on it. But you draw the sword and throw away the scabbard. It is wonderful.

I feel I have to tell you this—though possibly you may know much of it yourself. Not only does the book owe nearly everything to your organizing ability and constant hard work, but you go and write an essay that puts the rest of us to shame for sheer downright courage. It has always been a cause of regret to me personally that I saw so little of you during my short stay in Nashville four years ago; if I ever get back there, I do not intend to depart until I know you really well.

I remain   Yours
   [signature clipped]

[The humanist symposium, Humanism and America, Essays on the Outlook of American Civilization *(1930), had been edited by Norman Foerster.* I'll Take My Stand: The South and the Agrarian Tradition, by Twelve Southerners *(1930), included Donald Davidson's "A Mirror*

for Artists" and Lyle H. Lanier's *"A Critique of the Philosophy of Progress,"* as well as Fletcher's *"Education, Past and Present." Matthew Josephson's* Portrait of the Artist as an American *(1930) Fletcher seems to have ignored. Bernarr McFadden was a physical culture faddist and the founder of* True Story *magazine. Carl Van Doren, the biographer of Benjamin Franklin, literary editor of* The Nation, *and editor of* The Literary Guild, *advocated the addition of American literature to the curriculum in American universities.]*

TO HENRY BERGEN

April 18, 1931

Dear Bergen,

I wrote you only yesterday but must write you again today because I have been reading more deeply into Murry's book on Lawrence and have come to its really central core—with which I totally and finally and absolutely disagree. If you will read Chapter entitled "Spirit and Flesh," p.93–104, you will find very clearly set forth what Lawrence's main doctrine was and you will find Murry's reaction to it stated. (I hope the theological symbolism of this chapter will not put you off; it is, I am afraid, impossible to state truths of this sort—truths that apply to individual self-development and self-knowledge in any other way than through use of the Christian symbols.) You need only to read the chapter to understand what Lawrence meant and to know what is wrong with Murry.

With every word that Murry *here quotes* from Lawrence, I agree—these words are precious to me, I admire their bravery, their beauty, their integrity. There is nothing new in this teaching about the Holy Ghost—You can find it also in Blake, something like it in Shelley, and it goes back to the Middle Ages via Giordano Bruno and Joachim of Flora. The passage at the foot of p. 85–6 is a complete statement of this creed—"One law for the lion and the ox is oppression."

And all that Murry has to say to it (middle of p. 96) is to attempt a false division between sexuality and sensuality. "The consciousness of guilt makes sensuality of sexuality"—just consider *that* for a moment. As if it were possible to have a deep relation to a person of the opposite sex without such a consciousness. In other words, a man who takes a dozen women on, and succeeds in deceiving his wife about them is in Murry's eyes innocent; he has no consciousness of guilt. A man who consents to live with a woman whom he knows to be a prostitute is also innocent by this doctrine; he has no consciousness of guilt. In other words, Murry says that nothing matters so long as you don't admit it to yourself. But a man who is occasionally ashamed of his own sensuality is of course damnable to Murry—why? Because Murry is the sensual egotist par excellence!

Turn now to p. 97 where Murry puts down *his* gospel to set beside Lawrence's. Can you abide such bosh? It is all nonsense and all camouflage. "When true spirit is born in a man (and it cannot be born in him except *through a death*) then he becomes nothing but true flesh and true spirit." What does this mean? Absolutely nothing. And what does "a death" mean—a death of whom or what? Not a death of the spirit, nor of the flesh, but a death of *someone else*? A death of Katherine Mansfield???

Page 100—criticizing Lawrence's Holy Ghost conception. Line 11—"he himself is, in a sense, the unity of these conflicting desires. He embodies them in a single body." You will note that Murry never mentions the *mind*—he simply says *body*. Instead of admitting that Lawrence meant *mind-body*, he denies that! "The total behavior of any other man, be he Christ or cretin, is his Holy Ghost"—yes, this is precisely what Lawrence did mean, and Murry simply cannot answer it! Instead he puts up a smoke-screen and runs away from this great and fundamental truth to me the absolute basis of all religion.

Now read the long passage from Lawrence at p. 101–104 (surely the most beautiful, the most moving, the bravest words in all of Lawrence's work) and then read Murry's flat assertion that the "doctrine is false and deathly"—without any attempt on his part to substitute anything for it! What Lawrence is here describing is Blake's "Road of excess that leads to the palace of wisdom" and this ass, this brave Murry calls it a division of self. It is not—it is perfecting of self. But it is really useless to argue with fools. If you can say you agree with Murry here—you are doomed! Better Lawrence's sufferings and death, better anything, than such an absolute ignorance and spiritual blindness as this!

Yours,
Fletcher

[J. Middleton Murry's Son of Woman: The Story of D. H. Lawrence *appeared in 1931.]*

TO CONRAD AIKEN

June 17, 1931

Dear CA,

Thanks for your letters and your information about the Richards-Leonard affair. I'm rather glad it wasn't William Ellery but another Leonard, though I suppose W. E. is a pretty well worn-out old man these days, with nothing but memories to look forward to, and I dare say haunted by the wish to die as rapidly and decently as possible.

I was interested in your remarks about *Sanctuary*. I don't altogether agree with you that the book is a failure, though Temple's character gets incredible long before the close (if indeed it isn't nearly incredible all through). But Popeye seems to me a character that owes nothing to anybody—the only thing that comes close are certain figures in Dostoevsky—and he is a masterpiece of sheer horror. I quite agree with you that the book is the product of a poisoned mind—that corncob business simply finished me for days and weeks with its sheer ghastliness—but also that the man has genius, of the horrific sort. I don't think he will ever do better, unless he gets right out of his *milieu*, or gives up drinking.

Incidentally, I thought I spotted two references to your works: one in description of the lawyer's feelings seeing the sun (or was it the moon) rise, and the other, the last scene of all.

I am trying to make up my mind to catch the *Aquitania*, sailing on June 26. I have been asked to talk at the University of Virginia Conference on Regionalism on July 9 and feel that I ought to go—I need a break somehow —besides I have MS at my publishers in America, which I'd like to discuss with them. Lord knows, it needs some nerve to go anywhere at this juncture— I have managed to save about one hundred pounds to cover the trip, but probably will lose it all! If I go (which is likely) I won't see you till the fall, unless you decide to come here for a day or two.

Hope you get Nash to find you a publisher for *Osiris*—publishers in these days, except for trash, are perfectly impossible.

Yours,
J. G. F.

[The Coming Forth by Day of Osiris Jones was published by Scribner's in 1931.]

TO CONRAD AIKEN

33 Gower Street
Boxing Day
Dec. 26, 1931

Dear Conrad,

I have meant to write you for some days past but have kept putting it off until I could get my mind a little clearer. As you probably have surmised from my letters to you, I am decidedly in a mess—being simply mad with love and having absolutely deserted my wife and family twelve days ago. The lady whom I shall call L [Lorna Hyde] and I have had a few days and nights together and the delicious joy *that* caused about drove me off my senses; I have never been so completely in love before in my life. I have not revealed my address to my wife but have written her refusing to return and giving her another address to communicate; she has been begging me to come back. Meantime, the husband of L, being perfectly aware of what was going on (for we made no concealment whatsoever), has stepped aside and agrees that we should live together indefinitely (he objects to a divorce, and so do I, as the divorce would have to be double and would involve a scandal of first-class magnitude).

So much for the mess I am in. L has gone back to her country home to try and move out, and I am supposed to be looking for a flat that two people could share under different names, but really dreaming and seething with poetry. I don't know what will happen next, I am as usual pessimistic (having had so many hard knocks of recent years), but I know I love L and I have had a few brief days of deep joy. I am glad I have had them, for otherwise I think I should take to drink, or cut my throat.

As I told you something about this, I would like to know what you now think—you have been through the mill yourself and know what to do—you have practical sense, as well as poetic understanding. I want terribly to live in retirement with L with a few friends who can understand and sympathize to come and visit us—and simply to work for a year or two, I have so much now that I could write, and it would be better than what I have written of recent years. My marriage to Daisy was a frightful mistake, the sort of mistake a generous fool like me always makes and has to pay for. My life with L will be a real physical and spiritual union—I doubt if I can ever have it for long—as everything seems to be against it. Anyhow, this is the situation. Please let me know what you think. And destroy this letter, please.

Yours
J. G. F.

TO CONRAD AIKEN

1a Epsom Lane
Tadworth, Surrey
January 5, 1932

Dear Conrad,

I quite agreed with your note, which I received up in London yesterday, and I was touched by your card, which arrived this morning. I am in a situation more complex than a Henry James or a Dostoevsky novel. As I believe I informed you, the husband of my lady has stood aside, perfectly aware of the situation, and his attitude (my lady unfortunately agrees) is that there should not be a divorce, but that I and L[orna Hyde] should live together for as long as we like; as far as I am concerned I should like to live with her forever. But D[aisy], whom I saw yesterday (and who has been told nothing of where I am, and who has never met L at all) wants me to come back and resume life with her. After the miseries I have undergone (for the sake of D's children) I cannot do so. At the same time, it is going to be frightfully difficult, on my slender resources, to find a place in which Lorna and I can live; as the place will have to be taken in her name, and as I can only appear as a lodger. I feel almost sure that D will find out, and make trouble. However, I am going to stick with L for as long as I can.

I am going into town today to look up a reasonable lodging. L and I have canvassed Rye as a possibility, but D knows that I sometimes visit you there, and she might turn up. Still if you know of a reasonable place (about four rooms) somewhere in the neighborhood of Rye, you could help me a great deal if you would let me know. I don't want to pay more than about a hundred pounds a year. I hate to bother you, but I feel sure that you will help all you can, as you are a fellow-sufferer from a situation not dissimilar.

I told D yesterday that I had been visiting you, and I would be much obliged if you will post the enclosed letter to her.

I am sorry to hear that Clarissa is not well, and that things are not going well with you. It will be a long time before I can get out of the woods, but my best hope for happiness lies, as you say, in building up a beautiful and harmonious relationship with Lwhich satisfies my nature more completely: I can't accept any more martyrdom.

I met the other day in London that appalling fraud, Edward O'Brien: he told me he had seen Lowry and was greatly impressed by his novel, which he compared to *Moby Dick*. He said that Lowry referred to you as his guardian and was very affectionate to you for your help.

I am off to London today to canvass the possibility of living in Highgate, where rents are cheap, and where I shall not be likely to cross the trail of D. I haven't done any work except some poems I wrote for L since coming back from America this summer. If I can only get settled, I mean to work hard.

Let me know how you are faring. I have read over *The Preludes* again, and with ever-increasing admiration. They are simply superb, and I fear you will be tempted to think me a plagiarist when you see my new poems: for the direction that you and Rilke have taken seems to me to be the direction that I am faring now—I must dedicate something to you as a tribute to your poetical skill and acumen, not to mention your friendship.

Yours
J. G. F.

[*Malcom Lowry's first novel was* Ultramarine *(1933). His second novel,* Under the Volcano, *was not published until 1947.*]

TO CONRAD AIKEN

Wednesday 24th [February 1932]

Dear Conrad,

Your telegram arrived this morning. I want you to come with me to Sydenham, on Friday, and help me get some books away. That is, if you can. I am in a very bad physical, mental, and nervous state. This has been brought on altogether by my wife's attitude. I offered her a greater part of my money, all my furniture, everything in short except my books and clothes, which are all at the house. She refused to let me have them, and then agreed in the end, on condition I come to the house myself to fetch them. I attempted to do so, simply could not go in—was overcome with nostalgia of associations—and she tried to cajole me into breaking with Lorna. I simply fled. And this, if you please, is the woman who, when I first married her, locked me out of the house when I was late, refused to have any of my friends at the house, drove me to keep running away to America to seek refuge from her intolerable jealousy and bad temper, and made life in general a perfect hell for me, so that in the end I was forced to break with her, or I would have shot myself. When I left Sydenham, it was not apparent that Lorna would actually leave her position, and come and live with me. She did so, and I owe everything to her for that alone. But I am a sick man, almost broken with the miseries of the past 15 years. And I feel I cannot go to Sydenham, and fetch away those books unless you come with me. I haven't the strength to go alone—if you do not come, I shall lose everything but the clothes on my back. I hope you will. My mind is so distracted that I simply cannot type this morning.
    Yours
    John

TO CONRAD AIKEN

March 20, 1932

Dear Conrad,

I am here in a London nursing home trying to recover sleep and sanity after the awful strain of the last few weeks (am at 30 Porchester Square).

I don't suppose I shall go to America after all, nor anywhere else unless it be to the very devil. I suppose I shall have to go back to Sydenham. Daisy still wants me to go back.

Lorna has of course gone back to her husband. She decided to go back over a week ago as a matter of fact. I never told you that because I hoped she wouldn't up to the last minute, but she absolutely refused to change her mind. Please say nothing about this to anyone.

Such is life.

Poor Harold [Monro]. He had one of the most miserable lives on record, all because no one would give him affection. No one cared enough for him enough in life. I suppose his first wife was a sheer horror, and his second was a cold-blooded fish, so he drank himself to death and indulged in periodic bouts of homosexuality. Poor devil—and that's all one fellow creature gets out of life! It makes one fully admire those with courage enough to put the pistols to their brains and fire. Personally I want to start a society for the propagation of suicide: that is the right thing for these days. The millionaires who have been trying it out are really on the right path.

I am all right now but could not have gone to the U.S. with so little money, and without any sleep whatever for the past week. I shall move from here in a few days. I may go back to Sydenham (for a time, only, I expect) or I may try and find somewhere to live (preferably in the country). Meantime I am sorry I could not come down and see you. But none can really solve another's problem.

John

TO ADOLPHINE TERRY

c/o Curtis Brown, Ltd.
6 Henrietta Street
Covent Garden, W.C.
London, England
March 21, 1932

Dear Adolphine,

I am horribly sorry that I have given you so much trouble in the past few weeks; I am in a desperate situation, and I need all the help you or anyone else can give me. The trouble with myself and Daisy is not at an end; and I do not see how it is to be ended. During the past twelve years or so we have constantly quarreled; first, because she refused to go to America and stay there with me. Twice I have tried bringing her to America, and each time she refused to stop there. Then there has been the trouble with her children. I fear the constant bickerings have made trouble with them; they have had difficult lives in consequence. I have loyally tried to do my utmost for them, but in each case my wishes have not been respected. I adopted them, and let them take my name out of my generosity; it gave me some satisfaction, not having children of my own to think they were mine; but I cannot go on, it has worn me down mentally and physically, and my doctor, Doctor Crookshank, of 57a Wimpole Street, London, one of the best in England, thinks definitely that I ought to part with Daisy, and continue to live apart from her. In addition to any other miseries, last fall I found myself falling in love with another married woman—unhappily married. We thought we might perhaps have a divorce all around and then thought better of it. I have lost so much sleep recently that I am in a nursing home trying to recover. I simply am at my wits' end what to do; hence my letters and telegrams of the past few weeks.

The only times I have been really happy with Daisy have been when I was away on holiday with her and the children were not present, or when I came to America myself. Last summer I felt happier because I was away from her. It has been simply impossible to try and settle the destiny of two children who were 10 years old and 8 years old when I married Daisy. I have worried myself sick over the problems they present; I have had my own literary work to carry on as well; I have honestly and loyally tried to continue loving Daisy, and I have given her every form of consideration and sympathy. I know you also have had a very hard life and have made plenty of mistakes, but I know you are fair towards me, and I ask you to try and judge my case. I am here in another country, and but for one or two friends, I do not know what would have become of me long ago. I am always afraid that I might be tempted to commit suicide. I don't know what I shall do, but it seems to me that the best thing I can do, is to try and find some very cheap lodging here in London and go on living apart from Daisy. If I return to her now, I fear my health will completely break under the strain.

Please, Adolphine, remember that I have been through a frightful time, and I have been unable to get any advice. I should have asked you in 1914 about Daisy, about whether I ought to marry her; I was in love with her then when she was getting a divorce from her husband. I made one great mistake and have had to carry on, and I may be driven down to the very lowest depths of poverty as a consequence—at least for a time. If you feel you want to send me money, do so; *but please send to the above address.* The other address is not good; hence my cable of the other day. Dear Adolphine, if I do not see you again, try and remember that I have been fond of you in the past and that I tried to help you occasionally in your own very hard life. We have been unfortunate as a family, thanks to the miserable life which Mama and Papa led together. This made us all erratic and very unreasonable in our thought and actions. I hope you are better and that life still holds something for us.

Yours
John

TO CONRAD AIKEN

> Royal Bethlehem Hospital
> Otherwise known as "Bedlam"
> Eden Park, Kent
> [Dec. ? 1932]

[P.S.] Please inform any of my friends you may be in touch with. It is terrible to think of the hundreds of friends I had in the U.S. and in England whom I shall never again see—but in London I could not have seen them. I was beyond help—this is not a lie, but the truth.

Dear Conrad,

I do not know whether this letter will ever reach you, and in any case I know I shall receive no reply. My silence which is due to a great many reasons needs this much explanation—that I am in a madhouse, patient in Room Number 4, with maniacs in padded cells nearby, and nothing in prospect but a living grave. I shall never of course get away from these walls—nor do I have any desire to do so. As you are my oldest friend living in England—if you are still in England—I confide this to you. Such is the end of my horrible existence—and the person who is responsible for my being here is actually my wife—truth is a million times stranger than fiction, and my history will only be written in terms of contempt and infamy.

Let me detail a few facts in my case. When I saw you last autumn and announced the beginning of my love-affair with Lorna Hyde, I was already toppling on the brink of insanity. My wife, who had done her feeble best by me for fifteen years, had completely broken under the strain—her health, which she had maintained only by keeping up on thyroid gland [medication] for five years or so, was crumbling, and she was drifting fast and far into imbecility. Her two children were also feeble-minded—they had never seen eye to eye with me and had suffered from my instability for years. I had but recently come from America, which I left in the midst of terrific heat which had burned a lot out of me—and was deeply engaged in a desperate attempt to make my name better known in England through the medium of a group of people known as the "New Europe," who were full of vague mystical talk about the "crisis"—this being brought on by the collapse of the gold standard.

At this group—on Oct. 16 last—I met Lorna Hyde, who was a woman about the same age as myself—that is to say, arriving at the menopause. I was attracted to her through the fact that there seemed to be a sort of mystic link between us. She was also very intelligent, but not intelligent enough to control me. At first I was equally attracted to her husband—a cold-blooded little fish, with an equally ingratiating and insulting manner. He knew of our clandestine love from the first, and naturally, opposed it. Tadworth, where they lived, is a few miles from Sydenham. I went out there for week-ends while my wife lay in a nursing home in Sydenham, and there we concocted the crazy scheme that I should elope from my house, carrying only a suitcase—a thing I did, leaving behind only a note to inform my wife of my intention to depart. This news had the not astonishing effect of utterly breaking down whatever reason my wife may have previously had. Also my stepdaughter's and son's feeble reason likewise departed. We escaped as I say to that flat on Muswell Hill where we lived from January 18 to March 19 exactly this year. The flat was actually leased for three years and I was expected to pay for the full amount. Then my own reason gave way, I utterly broke down on March 19th, and was taken to a nursing home on Porchester Square.

When I arrived there I already had no mind of any description. The doctor in my case—an old English friend, valued and honorable, and a great psychologist as well—told me *not* to return to Sydenham: nevertheless I did return for a reason you will read later in this letter. I assure you on my solemn oath—though you will not believe this—that I literally had no sleep at all, *at either nursing home, or at my wife's home,* though kept on drugs—that I could not then walk about London, that I traveled only by bus or by cab—*that I could not distinguish north from south or east from west or left from right.*

In this situation, you came into London as you will remember, met me in the lobby of the Regent Palace Hotel, took me to Nash's flat and so on to Rye, I only got away by another ruse—out of a house of incredible horror and utter vacuity.

In Rye, I appeared as sane, but as a matter of fact, I was not. I could not have walked alone from Rye to Winchelsea, I was already blundering and faltering at the simplest things—I recall that every time I walked down Mermaid Street I dreaded lest I should fall on the cobblestones. And my doctor and lawyer remained impassive. So did my wife's doctor, who had been seeing her for months—he is still unpaid, I suppose.

Once arrived at the Underwoods I fell into the last state of vacuous horror. The only honest thing I could have then done would have been to have taken the first boat for America, as you bravely and sanely advised. I actually could not, I could not have packed up my trunks, walked down the pier—not knowing the direct way about the streets, traveling only by bus or tube, and becoming extremely dirty and disheveled in my outward appearance. Also my brain thought only disconnectedly. I could not have gone into a theater, or seen a play. I tried going to films, and discovered to my horror that everything was out of focus. I could not read a line of a book, or anything but a page of a newspaper. I could not write anything—my brain would not function. My doctor, who continued with me, gave me sane advice—to take long walks, to dismiss my wife from my mind, not worry. Every time he saw me, he supposed I was curable—but really I was not. My mind had already staggered to doom. I had letters of invitation to come out to the country, from other English friends, but could not have kept an appointment. I could not have caught a train. I could not have gone alone by train anywhere. I cannot tell you what it is all like—this last stage of driveling idiocy. I lay on the bed and beslobbered the bed clothes and ate meals—that was all. The Underwoods were also cretinous idiots, and they only put up with me for that reason. I rapidly acquired their very foul habits. If you had come then to London, I *probably could not even have faced you.*

I went on till it became so bad that I could not have taken a bus from the West End to the Strand. I who knew and loved London—could not find a bus stop. In this condition, about the end of June, Lorna came, rushed me back to my doctor's office, and literally threw me into another nursing home—28th of June, with my American passport running out on the 14th of July! The doctor, to whom I was already in debt under mountain loads, took me on again, prescribed calomel and aperta water for my awful condition of perpetual constipation, and as he had tried every drug, ordered me to rest without drugs of any description. I stayed there exactly four days—till the fourth July, then literally sneaked out and took the next taxi—in full indifference to possible police pursuit—as I knew it was useless. If I had stayed, *I would have been still there to this day,* living on credit, I suppose. I assure you, though you will not believe me, that I could not have found my way out of that place in the West End of London down Oxford Street, without someone to bring me along. Lorna had done this. But the trunks and other things I had brought out from Sydenham—I had been only able to get out there once—did not follow. The Underwoods were tired of my company, and sent them back to Sydenham. After four days in a nursing home, with a single pair of pajamas and a dirty suit of clothes, between me and the devil, I sneaked out and took a taxi to Sydenham.

I escaped without a word of explanation to doctor, lawyer, or nurse—I performed an action that is incomprehensible in its sheer folly and horror, and returned to a house full of driveling idiots, left behind.

Knowing then that the game was hopeless, *I threw myself from an upstairs window at my house (37 Crystal Palace Park Road) on 10th July.* I did not kill myself, though I fell fully thirty feet to the ground. I was taken in a common ambulance to a common hospital at Lewisham—where I remained from mid July to the end of August. Then my wife brought me here, via various doctors of her own. I know this is the end, and that I shall stay on. I seem to be unkillable, but am no longer classifiable as a human being. But when I saw you last April, it was but an interval of lucidity between two gulfs of yawning madness. I was not classifiable as human then. I reflected your mind as a mirror reflects the spectator—then I had not mind of my own—the only thing I thought about was nothing.

I do not suppose my wife has money enough to buy food now! And yet the house I lived in for fifteen years is full of all the valuable books I abandoned, all the things I once cared about—and later lacked the mind or the courage or the manhood to recover. They are all there guarded by two specters, my wife and stepdaughter. After I tried to commit suicide, my wife cabled my sister, who came from the U.S. all the way, and left without knowing the worst of my ignominy. I shall never again tell a living soul that I know. I shall never again have a human being as a friend.

There is no one with any authority to move me from here but my wife, and she will not be able to exercise her authority. All the debt has fallen back on her, and she is a complete imbecile like myself. We are both past the vampiric stage of human existence—the stage of ghouls.

You may say that I should have done better—true, I should! But my attempt was lunatic from the first. My own sexual state has been curiously morbid and abnormal all my life, and when I last saw you in Rye I was fully impotent—not only physically but mentally. And I stayed impotent. Arrived at the Underwoods the first thing that happened was that my teeth began breaking away in my own face—a thing that puzzled even my doctor. When Bergen (honest fellow) arrived back from Cornwall in June, I could not have faced him—*I could not have gone into a public eating place and sat down with him*—I made some excuse or other, and waited for the inevitable doom.

It is terribly weird, my form of insanity, and I hope is equally rare. The world to me at Rye looked perfectly without perspective—everything cut out of cardboard—the only walk I took alone was up Mermaid Street to the Gun Battery and back. There at the Gun Battery, I nearly sat down on a seat that was newly painted without taking notice of the fact—I did even worse at 12 Girdler's Road. I never there took a bath or got my hair cut—or sent out trousers to be pressed.

The only description I know of my form of madness is in Eliot's "Waste Land"—the lines beginning "Unreal City." Eliot felt the same thing, but only for a moment of time. With me it traveled from Muswell Hill into nursing home, back to Sydenham and on to Rye—without stoppage or pause. It would—if I had taken ship—have accompanied me across the Atlantic. Once arrived at the Underwoods' house, I perpetually took the wrong train on the tube, the wrong bus, the wrong turning in the street. I could not have entered anyone's house, sat down, talked rationally for five minutes on anything. Meanwhile my wife was even worse in Sydenham.

I heard Underwood, in the end, say to his wife "He is not a human being.

He is a monster. He wishes to reduce you to the same state of chaos that he has already reduced Sydenham." I knew that was true but could not stop it. I could not have walked to the nearest lunatic asylum and begged to be let in.

I shall drift on to my doom, now, I suppose it will come in some way or other. There is nothing else left to do.

This is the last letter I shall write you or anyone else. I have destroyed my wife's reason, my two stepchildren, the Underwoods and their three children (all began to be affected before I left) and Lorna and Lawrence Hyde's as well. Lorna, the last day I saw her was lapsing into the same state (the state of waking coma, of chronic imbecility, of being without the earth under one's feet). And I have lost all chance now. I knew my chance was gone before I saw you at Rye. The doctor in my case, as you may remember, moved me from a nursing home to a hotel nearby, where I could have stayed, but could not face the horror of a single night alone in an ordinary hotel room. Now I must face worse, because utterly helpless and because no one had authority to move me, and I am completely bedridden.

There are manuscripts of mine at Curtis Brown's in London, and New York, royalties waiting to be collected, debts unpaid and every book and paper is in wild disorder at Sydenham, and I cannot reach them.

Fantastic! But real—one gets bored even with horror in the end.

Who or what will kill me now?

There is a state known as hell on earth—I knew that at Rye—and a state of limbo beyond—and a state even beyond that in which I am and must remain—

Excuse handwriting but I cannot write any better now.

And thanks to you for your kindness. The last free kindness I ever received. The Underwoods made me pay.

Yours, a wreck beyond memory or hope, time and space.

J. G. F.

P.S. At the Underwoods I failed to post letters, made out my income tax return wrongly.

P.S. Having nothing else to do, I add a few details. When I stood on the platform at Cannon Street, waiting for you to turn up, I knew absolutely that it would be my last trip to Rye, that unless you came and fetched me away, I would be incapable of catching the train; I knew this, and I could do nothing in the matter; even then the doctors and the lawyers on both sides had been unpaid.

Each time that I walked down Mermaid Street, I feared lest I should slip on the cobblestone. All this time my wife was writing me letters full of hope and encouragement. Yet I mistook your towel for mine in the bathroom, and dared not take that room at Winchelsea for fear of being alone at night.

On my arrival at the Underwoods, I literally did not know my way about the streets. Though I had hoped constantly for an improvement, none came. My mind automatically recorded the telephone number of my wife, of my doctor, and my lawyer, I only reached any destination by taking cabs. Once at the Underwoods I cut my face repeatedly with a safety razor. I never took a bath, or sent out trousers to be pressed. Yet in this situation I received encouraging letters from Leach and from Bergen. And I could not find my way about, I did not know right from left or east from west.

Also I could not shit. I went into an editor's office, and was offered a film chronicle. I only succeeded in doing one article, and that about a film I had already seen. Every other attempt failed—even after I had sat through a film twice, I could not recall the details.

The only description I know of my state is that the major axis of my brain was utterly destroyed. And though Daisy's was destroyed as well, I kept on thinking about her, if that can be called thinking which is an aimless reaching back and forth among shaking fragments of thought.

I could do nothing else, I had nothing else I could do. I knew I was entirely wrong in the head, but nothing that the doctor said or the lawyer either made the least impression.

TO HENRY BERGEN

411 East 7th Street
Little Rock, Arkansas
May 9, 1933

Dear H. B.

Many thanks for your letter of April 26 which arrived only yesterday. I am glad to get your news, though you say it doesn't come to much. I've been in Arkansas now ever since the end of March and have had a very good time—one of the best of my life. I haven't been down here for the spring since I was a boy, and it is surely very lovely. I arrived with the redbud and dogwood—it had been a long late winter—and have gone through all stages in the process, writing now with the magnolias blooming outside and the roses in full shower over the trellis-work my sister has put up. The temperature is about 80. I have been extremely busy. Have given three lectures on Contemp. English Lit, English and American Poetry, and World Trends in Literature to appreciative audiences here. Am going to give another this week on the European Situation. I don't want to do this last, but I have to make money somehow.

Arkansas was hard hit by the crisis—all America was in far worse plight than anyone imagined—the whole structure of organized society was crumbling visibly when Roosevelt took office. It has now been stayed, but this next year or so will show whether the disintegration has been permanently stopped, or whether it will go in to the point that Bolshevism will have to come in. I don't venture any predictions. Down here, thanks to the fact that we are largely agricultural, no one seems worrying badly. Food prices are dirt cheap—cheaper than I ever saw them in America. Everyone seems to have enough to eat, though there are some cases of sheer distress—nothing however so bad as the bread lines of New York, Chicago, Boston, and most of the Eastern cities. But no one has any money. Of the four banks that normally do business here, only one opened its doors just after Easter, and that is because its owners were public-spirited enough to put into it every penny they had. The other three opened only on May 1st after negotiating loans from the government. We are still a dry state, and so we are getting no revenue from beer. The present governor, elected to enforce strict economy has been obliged practically to repudiate some of the state bonds, raised by the spendthrift governments of the boom years to finance highway construction. Our state budget has been balanced—a good many states are struggling under large deficits, notably Michigan, which seems the worst off of all—except possibly Illinois. Altogether I think the crisis has done us good down here, if it doesn't go on too much longer. With cotton going up, we ought to be well on our feet again by the end of the year.

The people who are doing the best are the small dirt farmers—fruit growers, market gardeners, of the Ozark region, in the N.W. of this state. They don't even seem to realize there has been a depression, though most of their banks are closed. They are interesting people. Few Negroes among them—pure Protestant White Nordics. That word "Nordics" reminds me of Hitler. I am damned glad to be out of Europe, so long as that madman is loose on the premises. And I mean not to come back, unless I have to, until things get better over there.

I miss intellectual society very much, but my sister is quite an exceptional woman, with plenty of brains. Only one building of all the property we own down here rents at a reasonable profit, so my sister has taken to writing in order to pick up some money, having successfully reared her family of five children. My other sister in Maryland is doing very badly on her farm. This is the "Bible belt" and no books sell, except that volume. No one has money to buy any. The solution is, I think, better public libraries—the one here is being well run, but absolutely out of funds to buy books. A great deal of money has been spent in the last 20 years on education, in both white and

Negro schools the State ranks high. We have two Negroes on the premises, one a cook who has been with my sister since 1912 or thereabouts—Katie Washington, a very capable person—the other an amusing but very stupid gardener and chauffeur named Jeff, who was a recent acquisition. Life down here has a quality of leisure denied to the North and East and I have plenty of time for working and dreaming. I miss England occasionally, but after all most of my English friends are now either scattered or gone away from London.

Regards to Leach. I wonder whether you saw the Hughes-Stanton show at the Zwemmer Gallery, for which I did a preface—it struck me as being good. I heard from Aiken just before he went to Spain—not a word since. Haven't bought any books myself, though a few good new ones are coming out here, notably a life of Andrew Jackson by Marquis James, and also one on Cleveland by Allen Nevins. Frank Lloyd Wright's autobiography is first-rate, Ludwig Lewisohn's *Expression in America* is a fairly good book though shaky in spots. So is Van Wyck Brook's *Sketches in Criticism*. Eliot is lecturing at Harvard and being lionized by the North and the East—he had his picture the other day in the *New York Times Rotogravure Supplement*. Nat Harris is still at Dedham and seems to have survived the downfall of Lee, Higginson and Co. I am hoping to see Sylvanus Griswold Morley when he returns north from Chichenitza this spring—next week I go to Nashville to look up some of the Southern regionalists and agrarians there at Vanderbilt. Am busy getting together a new book of poems, also doing prose—am thinking I may possibly do a novel, but not sure. That's about all the news, except that I'm sorry I can't see that show at the Burlington—it probably would interest me a good deal.

J. G. F.

TO FRANK OWSLEY

924 Canyon Road
Santa Fé, New Mexico
June 18, 1933

Dear Owsley,

It really is very kind of you to send me your own copy of *King Cotton*—I shall take good care of it, and see that it returns to you. Meantime, I have been reading your *States Rights*, and I am convinced that what you say there is correct. The war could have been won, and should have been won in 1862—before the damned Yankees could outnumber us—and that it *ought* then to have been won, I have never questioned. Only Lincoln, and our own mistakes, saved the North then. After '63 it was hopeless—the Gods do not permit such mistakes and follies as we committed in the early stages to go unpunished. The fault lay not with the generals (no fighting body of men ever had better) nor with the heroic rank and file of the soldiery, but with the damned wire-pulling politicians, from first to last.

At the same time, I cannot feel disheartened. Though the North won the victory, they paid for it in the loss of their true independence. Not only Lincoln's life, but the entire life of New England was the toll. We kept some of our independence, and I hope and believe much of our real life—and now is the time, more and more so, for us to assert both—if we fail to do so, not only Lee and Jackson and Forrest, but such misguided but perhaps not altogether mistaken souls as Brown of Georgia and Stephens will have lived and died in vain.

Again, thanking you,
I remain
Yours sincerely
John Gould Fletcher

TO LEWIS MUMFORD

924 Canyon Road
Santa Fé, New Mexico
July 5, 1933

Dear Lewis,

The last time I heard from you, you promised me a long letter in case you weren't seeing me this summer. Well, you are not seeing me; I am stuck here—it is pleasant enough to be so—for the next month at least. And after that—I don't know. But your letter is present only by default.

I have come here, and I like it well enough—particularly the vestiges of Indian life—all likely to be ironed out in the next twenty years. One enjoys such things even though they don't obviously belong to the present. But I never was altogether sold on the theory that the present would, like a miraculous bird, hatch out a glorious future—as you people in the East seem to think.

My motto tends increasingly to be that line of Thomas Hardy: "If a better there be, it demands a full look at the worst." And my four months sojourn in America makes me feel that things have sunk very low in the domain of the creative spirit. Now that the novelty has worn off, I begin to see the situation in that respect clearly. One can, it seems to me, belong to one of several groups:—*The Hound-and-Horn* Eliotites, with a good deal of right-wing prancings and an occasional slip-over to the left, or the *Modern Monthly* radicals with their fiendish manners and fierce diatribes on personal themes (why is it that the usual communist loses his temper worse when any personal attack is made on his ideas than any so-called bourgeois? Is it that the property sense is exasperated in his case, and merely dormant in the other?), or the dull and ponderous New Republicans, or the slipshod but likable Nationites, or the what-have-you New Yorkers? Or one can grow dodderingly infantile, and join—alas—*The Mercury.* I omit *The Yale Review* because it bores me, or *The Virginia Quarterly,* which is one shade worse, or *Fortune,* which is by far the vulgarest display of America's essential and self-satisfied vulgarness. That is about the list, and I am not sure I belong to any of them. All are, it seems to me, slick, standardized articles, like Listerine for the breath, or Chevrolet motor-cars.

You see, I am out of pocketbook, or out of temper. I suppose it is out of pocketbook. At present I have exactly two cents in my pocket. Never mind, I have in the bank a check for a hundred dollars, but the banking collapse seems to have made American banks more snotty than ever, and the other day the bank here refused to let me draw on this check to the extent of ten dollars before they went through the long-winded machinery of collecting it. Oh, for a decent law just to show American banks their place! I really believe they think they made this country's prosperity, and that their coming-back into business saved the country all over again. And I fear a good many of my misguided fellow-countrymen think this too.

Meanwhile I have been turned down with good poems by two papers: one did it politely and one insultingly. The insulting offender was *The Nation*—which I fail to understand under Hazlitt's editorship. They kept my poems four months and then H's secretary wrote and said that they were returning them as H was off on vacation! Can you beat that? They'll never get another chance from me.

Well, nothing succeeds like failure. My final book of verse, bearing the gorgeous title of *Winged Victory* has gone to Macmillan. It's dollars to doughnuts they will turn it down. After they do, I may try Harcourt or I may give up commercial publishing altogether and respond to a suggestion of an unknown man of Jewish nomenclature who writes from N.Y. that he wants to publish me in a limited way.

I am now writing some short prose pieces trying to get into practice for a novel I have in mind—with a very shadowy and fantastic idea for a plot—I don't want to do any more criticism, or if I do it will be in the pages of *The American Monthly* which is more or less open to my pen, and where I may earn a few dollars supporting agrarianism—or what is left of that cause!

Meanwhile, I have been conferencing here at Las Vegas and had the pleasure of meeting Botkin—not a bad sort, at all—who tells me that *Folk-Say* is dead. Another casualty. And I generally find the Santa Fé art and literary crowd pretty dull as well as combining Greenwich Village artiness with feeble provinciality (not that I mind the latter). And I am studying Indians this summer hard.

I have just been reading over your final article in *Books*—Feb. 8, 1931—entitled "The Birth of Order." I wonder whether you still think it's the birth of order. It seems to me we have got down to such a point that one opinion is as good as another provided it be nonsensical enough, and not seriously meant or stated. Our chaos, however, does not seem to be of the type likely to give birth to a dancing star; there is a hollow center to all our confusion. And heaven knows what will fill that hollow center. Roosevelt may for a time. But I am afraid the utter moral collapse in private and public life that has gone on ever since 1919 has left most Americans without a backbone. And hence the popularity of such a figure as Eliot—who has great talents, but essentially no backbone, and so has to find one ready-made for himself—always and invariably.

I wonder whether your private diagnosis does not agree with mine, whatever you may publicly say. One thing I am sure of: *that modern science is not going to help us preserve our regionalism, as you seem to think*. It *might* perhaps do so, but it won't. Because our regionalism depends on the individual and the community, whereas modern science depends on mass-technique (and there are plenty of first-rate individuals who have no technique in the modern sense at all)—and mass-emotion. I cannot see how you are ever going to reconcile the two.

That's why I want to see your new book on *Form in Modern Civilization*. Form is not a thing to be applied from without. It grows from within. Jung knows more about form than any modern psychologist, and his technique in psycho-analysis is the least important thing about him for just this reason. For *form* cannot be made up of already given components—not even glass or steel, though Frank Lloyd Wright may say so—his book is an honest, a great book, but I was sorry to see that he thought the Imperial Hotel a romantic by-product and that awful St. Mark's tower the real thing—I disagree there. Form is not manufactured in any sense, or fabricated. The Chicago World's Fair is just as good form as Wright, if you accept that form can be made up, stuck on—it never can be. And the same applies to science in its dealings with local color and regional attitude.

This is my thesis, which I wanted to write you about two years ago, but didn't. Now I challenge you to answer it.

Yours
John Gould Fletcher

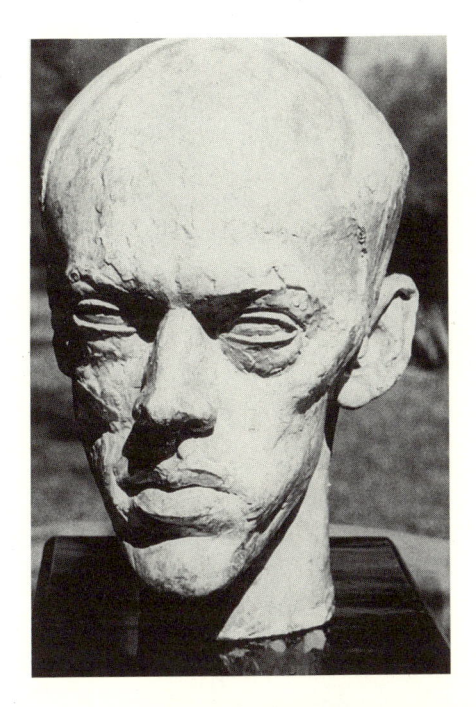

Head of John Gould Fletcher by Leon Underwood. Fletcher lived with the Underwood family in Kensington in 1932, during a period of great emotional disturbance.

From the Leslie Edwards Photographs, Special Collections, University of Arkansas Libraries.

Mask by Henry Moore, from the collection of John Gould Fletcher. It was shown in an exhibition of Moore's works that traveled to San Francisco, Chicago, and New York in the 1940s.

From the Leslie Edwards Photographs, Special Collections, University of Arkansas Libraries.

Pike-Fletcher-Terry mansion in Little Rock, Fletcher's childhood home. It was the setting of the poem sequence *Ghosts of an Old House*.

From the Leslie Edwards Photographs, Special Collections, University of Arkansas Libraries.

Library in the Pike-Fletcher-Terry mansion.
From the Leslie Edwards Photographs, Special Collections, University of Arkansas Libraries.

Portrait of a young John Gould Fletcher.
From the Historic Arkansas Project, Central Arkansas Library System, Little Rock.

Portrait of a mature John Gould Fletcher.
From the Picture Collection, Special Collections Division, University of Arkansas Libraries.

"Johnswood," the home of John Gould Fletcher and Charlie May Simon, overlooking the Arkansas River in Little Rock. *From the Historic Arkansas Project, Central Arkansas Library System, Little Rock.*

> 1.
> Please inform any of my
> friends you may be in touch with.
> It is terrible for me to think
> of the hundreds of friends I had in
> the U.S. and in England whom I shall
> never again see — but in truth I could not have
> seen them. I was beyond help — this is not a
> lie, but the truth.

Royal Bethlehem Hospital
Otherwise known as "Bedlam"
Eden Park
Kent [Sept.? 1932]

Dear Conrad,

I do not know whether this letter will ever reach you, and in any case I know I shall receive no reply. My silence which is due to a great many reasons needs this much explanation — that I am in a madhouse, patient in Room number 4, with maniacs in padded cells nearby, and nothing in prospect but a living grave. I shall never of course get away from these walls — nor do I have any desire to do so. As you are my oldest friend living in England — if you are still in England — I confide this to you. Such is the end of my horrible existence — and the person who is responsible for my being here is actually my wife — truth is a million

Excerpt from Fletcher's letter to Conrad Aiken describing his marital and mental crisis in 1932.

times stranger than fiction, and my history will only be written in times of contempt and infamy.

Let me detail a few facts in my case.

When I saw you last autumn and announced the beginning of my love-affair with Iona Hyde, I was already toppling on the brink of insanity. My wife, who had done her feeble best by me for fifteen years, had completely broken under the strain — her health which she had sustained only by keeping up on thyroid gland for five years or so, was crumbling, and she was drifting but not fast into imbecility. Her two children were also feeble minded — they had never and had suffered from an instability for years seen eye to eye with me. I had but recently come from America, which I left in the midst of terrific heat which had burned a lot out of me, — and was deeply engaged in a desperate attempt to make my name better known in England through

18

Fantastic! But real — one gets bored even with horror in the end.

Who or what will kill me now?

There is a state known as hell on earth — I knew that at Rye — and a state of limbo beyond — And a state even beyond that in which I am and must remain —

Excuse handwriting but I cannot write any better now.

~~And forgive~~ And thanks to you for your kindness. The last free kindness I ever received. The Underwoods made me pay.

Yours, a wreck beyond time and space, memory or hope,
J. U. F.

P.S.
At the Underwoods I failed to post letters, made out my income tax return wrong ~~but~~ died utterly disgraced and incredible things —

Johnswood
Route 5   Box 435
Little Rock, Ark.

January 18, 1945.

Dear Gene Haun,

You must be wondering when — if ever — you are going to hear from me. I heard through Charlie May as well as through Elsie Freund — that you were here around Christmas, when I was in a Memphis sanitorium, trying my dandest to get cured of a bad nervous breakdown which came on me in full force in New York. I am now perfectly all right again, and I hope you discounted the letter I wrote you, and which must have been absurd, that I would rather have you write about Rowan!

I am really extremely glad and proud

Letter to Frederic Eugene Haun, a student, with a chronology of Fletcher's writings.

that you decided to do your thesis on J. G. F. rather than on Imagism in general. And I can lend you all sorts of material on J. G. F. I have run to earth — after a long, fruitless search — a copy of "Japanese Prints," which I am sending on in a day or so. I also have a lot of other published work dealing with the Imagist movement and my own association with it. In sending these to you, I shall state what books I want returned. Have you Hughes' book, as well as Hulme's?

As regards early drafts and poems worked out in manuscript, I do not lend private notebooks. They probably would not be legible anyway and I do not now possess any early notebooks. You will have to formulate your conclusions concerning me from printed material, solely

Taupin's thesis that I borrowed right and left from Fontainas is all wrong. I never read one word of Fontainas till and 1918 — I first heard of him through an enthusiastic notice he gave me in the "New Republic" about that time, and the pamphlet I did on him (I have a copy of this and will send it) was written after that. The chief French poets who influenced me in the direction of Imagism were Baudelaire, Mallarmé, Rimbaud, Verlaine, and Verhaeren. By the way, I believe Taupin is now at Duke or maybe that strange place, Black mountain (Olson). Anyway, he is wrong about me.

The principal dates to recall in regard to my poetic careers are these:

1904–1913 — the five early volumes.
1913. Spring. Irradiations.
1913. Fall. Sand and Spray.
1914–1915. The Symphonies.
1913 Fall–Spring 1916. "The Tree of Life." I have an extra copy of this now to give you.
1919. Fall–1920. "Breakers and Granite." — I believe the pieces in the original book are all dated.
1922–1923. "Parables."
1923–4. "Branches of Adam". A failure, because of too much Blake.
1914–1934. XXIV Elegies. Can send you a

copy with dates to every poem added on, if you want it.
1934 – 5. "The Story of Achsavia" in "South Star". "My Father's Watch" in this book, must have been written in England, in 1924. "In mount Holly" was written 1926-7, on a return visit to Arkansas. Ditto "magnolia," a sort-of answer to Amy Lowell's "Lilacs". The "Christmas Tree", the "Scythe", the "Journey", "Big Old River" all come from that period. So does "An Unfamiliar House" which refers to the Pike mansion. The Pioneers was written at Batesville, early in 1927. "Lost Comer" was written in London in 1930 – "On my Father's Birthday" also. "Grandfather's Grave" comes from 1933 – the fall of that year, when I had definitely returned. "Conversation with an Important Ghost (Pike himself) and Arkansas Red Haw col-

from 1934-5, as does "The Three Oaks," but "The Farewell" was written as early as 1927, when I thought I was not going to return.

This covers the whole period, except for "The Black Rock". I am sending you my private copy, and if you fail to return it, I shall skin you alive. It contains the dates of these poems. All the books are out of print.

My new book, probably not out till 1946, consists of poems written since 1933. The last section of "Selected Poems" was written to Charlie May in 1935-6.

Today is the ninth anniversary of our wedding — and I hope the 18th, if I live that long, will be as happy as this is.

I am sorry if my nervous breakdown has made it hard for you to go on with your thesis. All I heard weeks ago from Harold Stebbins that enough money had been raised for you. He asked you to thank the donors — I hope you did. Am quite broke at present — thanks to doctors' bills.

Regards to Donald Davidson — if you still live — and to Frederick Cloud.

Yours,
John Gould Fletcher

P.S. Am sending you not only "Japanese Prints," but "Parables," "Black Rock," "Breakers and Granite." These must be returned to me by Easter. Also "The Tree of Life" and "XXIV Elegies." I can spare. If you don't want to keep them, please give them to Vanderbilt.

TO DONALD DAVIDSON

>924 Canyon Road
>Santa Fé, New Mexico
>July 27, 1933

Dear Davidson,

    I was glad to get your letter, for I feared you had fallen ill again. I am also glad to hear that you are out of the heat. Here on this 7000-foot plateau it is very pleasant, the sun is hot but the air is dry and the breeze cool. At night I frequently have to light a fire for comfort. It is magnificent country, with the austerity and sweep characteristic of the desert, and with strong Indian characteristics. The only trouble with it is that it makes one lazy, slows one down, makes work seem unimportant. I have done practically nothing since I came here except a meager handful of poems.

    You ask me about Ransom. I have only seen him once, and that was at Las Vegas some weeks ago. He is at Albuquerque, 65 miles away, and so far has refused to come up here and see me, though I invited him—he promises however to come this week-end. I hope he will, for I want to go thoroughly into the question of the book with him. My own idea is that we repeat largely the same topics, but this time we do not cast any longing glances at the past, but assume the present state of affairs, and ask ourselves what we can do with it to make it more Southern and more an expression of ourselves. It will be a different book, with an emphasis on the future. I quite agree with you, that if you don't want to do the same topics you did, you ought to pick out another; but that the future holds huge possibilities for good or evil should now be obvious, and I think we ought to tackle the question. For example, someone (not I) should do something on the question of the Tennessee Valley Development—which I have been watching closely from the public press, and which seems to me *might* be a great good, but probably will be a great evil. And there are other items in Roosevelt's plan that can be handled in the same way. In short, we must be now up to date, or nothing.

    I quite agree with you that we ought to say more about politics, women, and the Negro—the former especially, for unless we can create a more responsible political mindedness than I see at present in this country, all Roosevelt's well-meant efforts at reform will go for nothing. The Negro is indeed a difficult topic. Perhaps Owsley is the best man to handle it. I liked his Scottsboro essay very much indeed. The woman question is very thorny, and will require a brave man.

    I won't know how far the project has gone till I see Ransom, and all I know is that Allen is apparently champing the bit to get work started so we can have the book ready next spring. By that time, undoubtedly, the Roosevelt program will be beginning to show results of some importance in all sections of the country, and we might count on a reasonable measure of success. I propose to tackle education again, and really spread myself—it will take some time to get material together, and I hope to write a longer and better essay.

I am sorry indeed that you are having so much trouble with Collins—I merely gave you the benefit of my personal impression, in telling you that it was unfavorable. I fear he is one of those metropolitan figures, so common in New York, that have to have every bit of thinking done for them because they have no stability anywhere at all. His last number, apart from Owsley's essay, was so prevailingly Catholic in tone that I should not be surprised in the lease to see him fall into the hands of the Jesuits and achieve a "conversion" akin to T. S. Eliot's. If so, then our ammunition had better be spared; we won't get anywhere fighting on that side! Either Communism or Catholicism seems the one way out for these citified and industrialized souls—personally, I cannot accept either. I believe there is a case for Protestantism, despite Allen, whose essay made me feel really ill—Catholicism might have something to say for itself, had the present church as strong a policy as in the Middle Ages—but present-day Catholicism has no policy, and so is no whit better than Protestantism! However, this digression has nothing to do with Collins. Unless he reforms his ways by the fall, I think we might easily withdraw in a body. After all, it is our brains he is using, not his own. That being the case, he should be made to pay.

I'll let you know, as soon as I see Ransom, what he really proposes to do—meanwhile, good luck.

Yours,
John Gould Fletcher

TO LEWIS MUMFORD

924 Canyon Road
Santa Fé, New Mexico
August 19, 1933

Dear Lewis,

I am returning your MS with some annotations, which I hope you will be able to read. I went through the chapter twice, and on the whole, find little to complain about, except that I think that your argument might in some cases be simplified, and in other cases more clearly stated. I don't know what you are going to say about the value of the machine-product itself when you come to that part; but I think you ought to take notice of the fact that its chief defect is that it hampers human creativity. Strictly speaking, the original design for a motor-car body is a work of art; but the innumerable repetitions of that design are not. The reason why art, or perhaps I had better say craft, is so fascinating is that there isn't any repetition possible. One has always to vary, however slightly—and the balance of human faculties depends on such slight variation.

I note, to return to the chapter you sent me, that you put Shakespeare among the Romantics. I quite agree that he is Romantic, in the sense implied by the late (and so far as I am concerned, unlamented) Irving Babbitt and his school. But really the term has almost no meaning when applied to Shakespeare or the Renaissance, and I am beginning to think it would be better to confine it to the period which began with Gray and Walpole in England, and which began to make way before realism in 1848. The present age, in my view, is almost altogether an age of critical reaction, or of fatalistic realism (Hemingway, Faulkner, even Dos Passos belong here) or of highly experimental efforts in technique. But it is high time somebody said *what* precisely the age is going to end up at; and personally I am inclined to think that the best thing it could end up at would be a new type of symbolical realism, which could be as documented as the old, but which would use its material in order to create eternal types rather than merely temporary characters. (O'Neill, though he has gone all to pieces, started to show the way, and there is the same tendency in Thomas Mann, Wassermann, possibly Gide and Proust, and also in D. H. Lawrence—though Lawrence was inhibited by his own personal lyricism from making his characters truly typical. The attempt was made—very badly—in poetry by Hart Crane, and S. V. Benét, and one or two others. It will have to be tackled again.) I feel like I'd like to work out this idea in a long essay, or series of essays, but heaven knows what magazine would take them. If *The Caravan* was going, it would be good stuff for them.

I am enclosing some poems, if you have time to bother with them. My new book, which apparently Macmillan will not take, is a contrast to the old—*The Black Rock*. This is called provisionally *Unwinged Victory* and is all fairly long poems. It starts with a series of versified narratives of history—blank verse, loose, and perhaps less concentrated in essence than anything I've done: a sort of *Légende des Siècles*, in fact. Then a series of "Elegies," some of which I enclose—the "Tintern Abbey" one appeared in an insignificant paper in England and was admired by Patrick Geddes. Then a series of more personal poems called "Echoes from Arkansas," mostly about my own life—and to wind up, the long poem "The Western Dawn" which I wrote for *The Caravan,* and *The Caravan* died before I could print it! The poems I send you are all from the "Elegies" section except the "Lenin" and the "Wilson" which are taken from the first section called provisionally "Children of Men." I would like these copies returned please, if possible.

Don't bother about the poems, if you find they distract you from your work, but send them back unread. I remain,
    Yours,
    John

[Victor Hugo's La Lègende des Siécles *is a three-volume series of poems dealing with man, Western man, and France. Mumford's* Technics and Civilization *(1934) is the first of a projected four-volume work on the development of the modern scientific world and man's need to utilize his infinite resources. Fletcher reviewed it in "Dewey's Latest Disciple" in* American Review *3 (June 1934): 392–98.]*

TO HENRY BERGEN

411 East 7th Street
Little Rock
Nov. 4, 1933

Dear H. B.

Many thanks for your letter of October 21st. I am always glad to hear from you whenever you want to write and don't find your letters uninteresting. I don't think we disagree about essentials, and if we don't see always eye to eye on every point, that is only to be expected. I am grateful for your friendship and regard it as a happy fact in my life.

I have been very busy myself and working hard, so I have delayed answering your letter. I have a lot of work to do because I have to make money as the British Income Tax people are still after me, though I don't think it's likely that I'll come back to England for a long time, if ever. Things are better now down here than last spring, but whether Roosevelt's recovery effort will go far enough to turn the corner only time can tell. About one person in every three in this state is still on relief—either private or public. What a commentary that is on the insane "prosperity" of Harding, Coolidge, Hoover—and their allies:—Mellon, Ford, the Chase National Bank, Insull, etc. etc. etc.!

Herbert Read's book *[Art Now]* on art sounds interesting and I would be glad to have it but have no money to buy books. If you'd like to send it to me for a Xmas present, I would be very pleased. I quite agree with you that Read makes a colossal mistake in supposing that art can be analyzed from the point of view of painting only. You have to take into consideration all the crafts as well—architecture, furniture, pottery, weaving. This point of view is implied by Gill but always neglected by Read—Unfortunately this age is the first wherein art cut itself loose from a craft tradition, and it has resulted in many works which are sophisticated rubbish of the Miro sort—works which are, as you say, so uninteresting and unpleasant that they almost justify the mossbacked academicism of the Academy. I think it's almost time we stopped talking about *modern art* altogether and began discussing *art* (Gill here is a real master: he knows what *art is*), because if *modern art* is going to give us a world full of Miros and Massons (another bad egg) I don't see any justification for its existence. Personally, I like the artists you mention: Cezanne, Gaugin, Van Gogh, Seurat (not so good as these three, in my opinion, but still interesting), Lautrec, Matisse, Derain, Rouault, Modigliani, Henri Rousseau (very well represented at the Chicago Show, and at his best, very good), Robert Henri (a very fine and sensitive painter, died 1929), George Luks (just died the other day), John Marin (perhaps the best in America), Arthur Davies (also well represented at the Chicago Show, akin to Ryder), Eakins (possibly the greatest American painter of the older generation), Twachtman (better than Monet at his best), some of Bellows (but not all), and two of the Taos group: Bertram Higgins (a very fine artist) and Emil Bisstram (more experimental, but on the right lines). I also like Hopper, and Burchfield (though they are not so big as those I have mentioned), a Kansas painter named Curry, and the Mexicans—Rivera, Orozco, and Gostein (I think that's the way his name is spelt: see *Idols Behind Altars* by Anita Brenner for reproductions). I think Thomas Benton is our best muralist (though unequal) and I also like in the main Vlaminck, Marie Laurencin, Kandinsky, Lanz Marc, and some of the Russians (notably Roerich and one or two others who worked for the Old Russian Ballet). I dislike intensely Picabia, all the Surrealists without exception, all the Germans (Klee, Hofer, Kokoschka, Bukmann, etc.), who seem to me to be very crude and sensational. The only German I can stand is George Grosz, who is ugly but *ugly with a purpose:* a man akin to Goya in his furious satire on the respectable bourgeois. I don't care much for Pascin (who seems to me to have ruined a great talent and I regard Picasso as the real question-mark of "modern" art: he was great in his early phase, had nearly everything, and then went and threw it all away in a vain pursuit after notoriety and abstractionism: I agree with you there is no such thing as abstract art! I like Gill, am doubtful about Epstein, and like Moore in spots, but I believe Gaudier would have beaten them all had he lived and been given a chance. Milles is sometimes good, and so is Mestrovic, but both are overrated. I don't know Bailach's later work: his earlier was very fine. Lehmbruck had in him the power of being a first-rate sculptor; he was another war loss. Kolbe and Maillol seem to me only *fair*. I seem to have covered the ground pretty completely, except for the English painters: they don't seem to me to matter much, except possibly Gordon Craig (as a theatrical designer), Max Beerbohm (caricaturist), Stanley Spencer, and possibly Paul Nash. Sichert is fair, but not a patch on Degas or Renoir; and John seems to me to be now a total loss (thanks to whisky and the Academy).

The farmers' strike looks rather serious—anyway, I think it's likely to give more trouble than Ford's ridiculous antics over the NRA [National Recovery Administration]. The farmers down here would be in it, if it weren't for the fact that the U.S. govt. had given them money to plow up their cotton. I have a lot of sympathy for the farmers—no doubt they have been bled white by the manufacturers, and mortgaged up to the hilt by the bankers (who have been the worst of all) and I think they are perfectly entitled to kick about the way they are made the goats. Their quarrel seems to be with Secy. of Agriculture Wallace, who is an able man but possibly thinks too much in the terms of large-scale industry. If the farmers could combine better, they'd be a great force.

More anon—my paper is at an end.

J. G. F.

TO HENRY BERGEN

411 East 7th Street
Nov. 15, 1933

Dear Bergen,

The copy of Charques' book *[Contemporary Literature and Social Revolution]*, which you ordered for me has come—at least I suppose you ordered it for me, as I did not write Wilson for it, though it arrived here with a Bill enclosed. It is an interesting book, yet it somehow fails to carry complete conviction to my mind. The point that Charques makes about the modern poets, that they have turned their backs on the public and write purely of private and obscure intellectual experience, is not true of all of them. For instance, I have recently read Stephen Spender with considerable interest and find his meaning perfectly clear. The charge that the poet is no longer interested in class strife but has chosen to support a moribund bourgeois society rather than a fighting proletariat is more difficult to meet. The modern poet might well answer that there is no guarantee that the proletariat will be intelligent enough to do the right thing, or be just when it comes into power. Hitler's movement is if anything a proletarian movement: it is supported by the mob, and Hitler is a demagogue of the worst description; yet

I defy you or anyone to say that Hitler is desirable for the World or for Germany. As a matter of fact, his chief opponents are not the Communists (I have read an article by Trotsky on Hitler which is not altogether condemnatory) but if you don't mind, his opponents are the liberals, the intelligentsia, the Thomas Manns and the other authors whose books he has burnt. And further, I have heard a speech here in America made by Edgar Ansel Mowrer, who declared positively that the sole result of Hitler would be—in case he fails, as he probably will—to *immensely increase Communism in Germany.*

In view of the increasing possibility that an uprising in England would only lead to some such upshot as Hitlerism in Germany—with a Winston Churchill or a Beaverbrook playing the role of the deliverer of England from the horrors of Marxism—in view of that possibility, why does Charques kick so hard at the fact that the modern poet has stopped being interested in the social idea and has taken to exploring his private ego? It seems to me that Charques is rather naive at asking for more social faith on the part of the English poet. That may have been still possible before the world became ruled by the mob and by mob standards—that is to say, back in Shelley's time it was still possible for a first-class poet like Shelley to be a first-class revolutionist but when you get what Nietzsche called "mob at the top—mob below," the exact condition of today, then it isn't any more possible. All the first-class German poets (men like Werfel, Toller, etc. etc.) after the War protested like fury against exactly what has happened in Germany, and which every damned German in the U.S. now thinks of as the "Godlike miracle of Hitler." You even hear Americans defending him—yes, we have got down to that level.

About the novel. Charques is better. He really respects Lawrence's integrity: how it flames against the drabness of these dreamy post-war years! (By the way, I hear that Frieda has written her reminiscences; but will not publish them with any commercial publisher, as Martin Secker cheated Lawrence, nor did he have any luck with Seltzer, the only American who took him up.) He is quite correct about Huxley's cleverness, and also about his horrible look on life. He is good on Virginia Woolf, a belated aristocrat. And he is right about Forster. Charques is also good about the drama—that realm of desiccated death. But he doesn't convince me that if the poet or writer sank his individuality completely into the social urge of class-war, things would be any better. Propaganda is not art; the writings of Upton Sinclair for example, are dreary rubbish—though Sinclair may be quite sincere in writing them.

Over here things are different from England. The reading public are far more capricious, less easily classified, much more sporadic and scattered than in England. There is a dearth of respectably good bookshops, and the magazine habit (*Saturday Evening Post*, etc. etc.) still holds the American mind. A few of the magazines—*Scribner's, The Atlantic,* have broadened out and improved, but the publishing business, despite the spate of dollar books, is shot to pieces, and probably will have to be reconstructed, bit by bit. There is a large public that reads sentimental tripe of the Harold Bell Wright order, and a small public that goes to the opposite extreme and reads the hard-boiled stuff of Hemingway, Erskine Caldwell, Faulkner, George Milburn, etc. Nobody reads Mencken any longer—he has worn thin, thank God (excuse my mentioning the Deity; it was unconscious). The smart-alecks of New York are beginning also to lose their grip and this year the public has read Pearl Buck's studies of Chinese life, which I believe are not bad; also Nora Waln's book *[The House of Exile]* on China (it is excellent, superbly done) also Marjorie Kinnan Rawling's delightful *South Moon Under* (on the Florida swamp-country people) also Gladys Hasty Carroll's *As the Earth Turns* (about a farm in Maine) and the usual biographies. Poetry has suffered a bad setback (there has been too much imitation of Eliot), but Sandburg, Masters, Robinson, Jeffers, Aiken and one or two others are still writing—and have publics. I seem to have completely lost mine, and have been busy trying to get it back. O'Neill seems to be losing his importance, but there isn't another dramatist who even remotely measures up to him. Dos Passos is the white hope of the Communists—and I admit, he is very good, but a little Hemingwayish (I am afraid the public is beginning to be a little tired of Hemingway). Altogether, American literature has ten times the vitality that English literature has.

No, you cannot persuade me that Charques is right. The English simply haven't the guts enough to be anything but what they are: a bunch of sentimentalists, ringing feeble changes on feeble material—if they were men of spirit, there would be kick somewhere left in them, but even the Labor party is coming back because of pacifism (that feeblest of all attitudes) rather than on account of determination to get justice. Over here, it looks like Roosevelt is too radical for the Capitalists who run this country. First, he is made a fool of by Ford, and then the whole bunch jump on him and now seem likely to swing him back to the right. But believe me, I feel sure it won't do for them to go too far! They've been shown up in the most damaging light in connection with the Senate Banking Investigation and other unsavory details—I believe that Roosevelt is simply biding his time and will open up a real frontal attack next spring, and if he does, the people will be with him. I don't believe the Capitalist bunch has him quite tamed and entirely ready to eat out of their hands. He has courage, and I believe he knows what is now plain: that the profit-taking orgy of 1919–1929 is done for: at least I hope so—I hope he gets that agreement with Russia signed, so Japan can go into fits, and try hara-kiri by starting another war if she wants it. Then I hope and pray that Roosevelt will cut the combs of some of the big cocks of capitalism: some of the Morgans, Fords, Mellons, etc. ought to be made to *pay* for the N.R.A.—they made it necessary, with their damned profits. The farmer's strike is evaporating, for Wallace is a sensible man and has given them a straight talk—the real article. I enclose a report of it.

With all good wishes to you for a Merry Xmas,
Yours J. G. F.

TO THE EDITORS OF *THE NATION*

An Open Letter
To the Editor of *The Nation*
[December 1933]

Sir,

I wish to address you publicly on a matter which immediately concerns many thousands of peaceable citizens living today under the flag of the United States; and I do so, because though I am aware of your affiliations with various radical groups, I believe you to be honest and fair-minded enough to wish to hear both sides of a debatable issue. I believe this because last spring, when the British engineers were on trial in Moscow, you urged in their behalf a fair trial. It is because of another trial and its possible consequences among our people, that I wish now to speak.

The Scottsboro case, as I now write, seems likely to go against all the defendants. Whether the matter will be carried into the Supreme Court, I do not know. But I can envisage your comments on the case even before I read them. You will equate the Scottsboro trial with that of Sacco and Vanzetti in Massachusetts, as horrid examples of American class-legislation, and then proceed to a blanket condemnation of the whole course of Southern justice. It is against this attitude that I, as a Southerner by birth and upbringing, wish to protest.

We in the South do not legislate against the Negro as a class. Whether he is a rich man, or a poor field-laborer, his status is the same. Unlike Massachusetts, which did Sacco and Vanzetti to death not because they were guilty (they were not) but because they had agitated for better conditions of life among the industrial proletariat, we do no Negro to death because of his political affiliations. But we are determined, whether rightly or wrongly, to treat him as a race largely dependent upon us, and inferior to ours. Unquestionably certain Negro intellectuals, such as James Weldon Johnson, suffer from such discrimination. For them we have of recent years encouraged the building of great schools and universities. We believe that under our system, the great majority of the race are leading happy and contented lives. But our system, we admit, has one defect. If a white woman is prepared to swear that a Negro either raped or attempted to rape her, we see to it that the Negro is executed.

It is this feature in our attitude which has moved you, along with other papers published in the North, to indignation. You are ready to assert over and over again that no justice is ever done the Negro in the South. I would urge upon you to pause and reconsider this matter ere you pursue that course, which can only lead to a much worse situation. Suppose, for example, that the Supreme Court decided to destroy President Roosevelt's National Recovery Act, by declaring it unconstitutional. You would be the first to protest, in the name of outraged public sentiment. Cannot you see that it is precisely the same public sentiment that is dictating the present policy of the South towards the Negro, and that if you, from the vantage-ground of the North, attempt to violently alter the public sentiment of the South, you will only stiffen Southern resistance?

Into the merits or demerits of the Scottsboro case, I have no desire to enter. Whether the defendants have been given, or could have been given, a fair trial under the circumstances, I do not know. But the conduct of Mr. Leibowitz, the attorney brought down from the north for the defense, has, it seems to me, now definitely turned the scales of justice against the defendants. They will, it appears now, be convicted and executed. You are entitled to say, if you like, that this seems to you an act of injustice. But justice is in itself an abstract matter, and as every great lawyer knows, has always to yield to the morals, the usages, the customs and conveniences of a living and functioning community.

That the South is such a community was proven this summer. With the Scottsboro case still in doubt, the people of Tuscaloosa County turned out and lynched four other Negroes. Three of them were quite probably innocent, and in the case of the fourth there is considerable doubt. But the fact of the matter is that Mr. Leibowitz' conduct, as well as the taunts of the metropolitan press, have unstrung that section of the South which adjoins Scottsboro. We will not suffer further dictation from the North as to what we are to do about the Negro. All that we built up again out of the ruins of the Civil War and of Reconstruction is again at stake. Rather than permit our own peculiar conception of justice to be questioned, we will take the law into our own hands, by a resort to violence.

If, therefore, you sincerely wish good to every citizen of America, black or white, I beg of you, before you and other Northern editors proceed to condemn the South en masse, to pause and reflect on our situation. By ranking the South alongside Massachusetts, and still more, alongside of California, you are yourself supplying the ferment of irritation which has gone on now to the point where the patience of the South is rapidly breaking down. More, you are tacitly encouraging the official Communist propaganda which, as everyone knows, has gone on down here since the Russian Revolution. That propaganda counsels a new Civil War between the whites and the blacks. You are forgetting that the experience of post-war Chicago and other Northern places has shown that the people of the North are just as ready, the moment they see the Negro in large numbers, to adopt an even more hostile attitude than that of the people of the South. Further, you are demonstrating that you are unwilling or unable to see that the Negro is peculiarly not your, but our, problem. We in the South alone can find the solution to that problem. We will never accept any solution that comes to us from the North. Rather than that, we will again take up arms in our cause.

Therefore I ask you to pause and reflect before you proceed to fresh moral denunciation of Scottsboro. I believe that the Scottsboro defendants will now be executed. I believe that this decision, fair or unfair, has been forced on the people of Alabama by the way in which the defense in this cased has been conducted. I believe that further trouble is to be expected down here between the blacks and the whites, unless the Northern States rapidly show more disposition to listen to the South's case, and to cease their interferences and interventions in behalf of the Negro. And I believe I am speaking not only on behalf of Alabama alone but of the overwhelming majority of the Southern people today.

I remain
Yours sincerely
John Gould Fletcher

[The editors of The Nation *were Ernest Gruening, Freda Kirchwey, and Joseph Wood Krutch. In 1933, before December 4,* The Nation *published eleven articles defending the Scottsboro defendants. The Scottsboro case was the most publicized racial incident of the decade. On March 25, 1931, nine black youths were arrested for rape of two white women. They were tried immediately and eight of the nine sentenced to death. The second trial after an appellate court overturned the verdicts lasted five years in the state and Federal courts, when four were freed and the others given long prison terms, the last not emerging from prison until 1950. This letter appeared in* The Nation *137 (27 December 1933): 734–35 under the title "Is This the Voice of the South?"]*

TO FRANK OWSLEY

411 East 7th Street
Little Rock, Arkansas
Dec. 1, 1933

Dear Owsley,

When I left Nashville, I went straight to Tate. We had a long and interesting talk, and here are the results.

The Agrarian Symposium won't have any effect unless it is backed up with a definite political movement. This should take the form of an organization of young men and women, to be called provisionally the Gray Jackets. They should be encouraged to wear Confederate uniforms, to fly the Stars and Bars, and to march on stated days. You spoke at Ransom's house of the necessity for this sort of thing, at this juncture. I agree with you—it is very necessary. And so does Tate.

The movement should begin not by declaring any bold political program, but only with the ostensible object of keeping alive the memory of the Battles and Leaders of the Civil War. Certain days—for example, the firing on Ft. Sumter, the First Bull Run, Gettysburg Day (not on the field of Gettysburg however, for all that has been taken over and turned into handshaking)—and Lee's birthday, also Jackson's birthday, also local heroes who deserve this honor, should be commemorated by parades, speeches, unfurling of flags, and a wreath. The movement may get itself laughed at, or may be attacked in the press. If it is attacked, all the better. We can then proceed to the next step: this is the destruction of all monuments that try to persuade the South that the Civil War never took place. There is one in Nashville that ought to be blown up. The refusal of the Daughters of the Confederacy to allow a monument at Appomattox should be commended and followed up. Cyrus McCormick, the Virginian who sold to the North the means (the reaper and binder) which enabled the North to draw on the man-power of the west, and so win the war, has a monument (according to Allen) in Kentucky. It should be destroyed. It must be destroyed.

Next, the Gray Jackets can be used to threaten all Chambers of Commerce who try to industrialize us further, by encouraging Northern capital to build factories down here. They can also celebrate harvest festivals and other agrarian feasts. The possibilities of the movement are enormous.

What is needed is a good organizer, a man of action. You seem to both Allen and myself to be the fit person for the task. You might do it—we cannot. I have been asked by Allen to approach you; and here is the scheme.

We ought to get started at once, to celebrate the fall of Sumter by April next.

There is just one danger. The young people who come in may take to rowdyism and shooting up of Negroes. The movement must not, in my opinion, degenerate in this way. We have no quarrel with the black man—so long as he keeps his proper place. Personally, I should be myself in favor of a movement to bring to a close the status of country Negroes as mere tenant farmers, and to work towards Negro freeholders in a small way. You may see the problem differently—but I think you will agree with me that we want no more race riots.

I expect the Scottsboro case will probably go against the defendants, just because Leibowitz and that bunch horned in. Well, let us show them that we are ready to give the Negro a fair chance of survival. Give them freedom to use their own land—if they are intelligent enough to do so. I see no reason why there shouldn't even be Negro Gray Jackets in time! What we want to do is not to keep the Negro down, but to *throw the North out*. I write feelingly about this, because the North is very strongly entrenched in my state at the present moment.

Write me how this strikes you, and merry Xmas to you and family.

Yours sincerely

John Gould Fletcher

TO HENRY BERGEN

411 East 7th Street
Little Rock, Arkansas
December 11, 1933

P.S. Your letter of the 30th has just come—I agree in the main with what you say in it. Sorry but I am too busy to write more just now. Also got your postcard—glad to hear you are sending me Read's book—also and that Charques was a present.

Dear H. B.

I have had your letters of Nov. 10 and 12 here for a long time waiting to answer them. I have now a favorable moment, so I am writing this for Christmas. As I teach here now two evenings a week, and have critical articles to do as well, you may see that I am very busy.

About Marx (whom you wrote to me about). I think you misinterpreted my letter. I did not criticize Marx (in fact, I am reading him just now, carefully, and find I simply can't agree with his first concept of "value")—I only criticized what Hook tried to make out of him: a sort of appendage to John Dewey, who is Hook's master. Here in America, Marx has had a curious fate. A small number of fanatics have believed in him for years, but they got nowhere till, about the time of the great war, a certain number of intellectuals decided that nothing good could come from this country and that the only hope lay in Russia. Most of these intellectuals simply have no brains at all. For example, Dreiser. Dreiser knows his stuff all right when it comes to America, and he is perfectly honest, but I dare say he saw just what he wanted to see when he went to Russia, and his activities here are not very edifying. About two or three years ago he went down to look up the West Virginia Coalfield Strike (a very bad business; the miners there practically serfs of the owners) and, of course, got into trouble, not because he was on the side of the miners but because he was lugging along with him about two women—he has made love to every damn typist in New York, and his whole career is pretty notorious in that direction! Now I can't for the life of me see any connection between Communism and the morals of Casanova—I don't say that Casanova was not an interesting sort of fellow—but he didn't pose as the champion of the working class!

Everybody I believe that is in the labor movement here realizes now that it has been done to death by a bunch of bohemians—would-be left wingers, some of them nothing but literary racketeers like Calverton. The whole thing has become a mess. For one honest revolutionist like Jack Reed or Bill Haywood there have been twenty frauds who got the Jews of New York to stump up for them because they were smart. It seems to me that on the whole the American public have put up pretty well with that sort of thing. Now, at the last moment, the really intelligent radicals have been driven to doing some thinking on their own, and the result is a book like Hook's. It really tries to salvage Marx by making Marxism over into something different. That is my reason why I don't agree with it. You can't make Marxism anything different from a dictatorship—and it will be a long day before we get that sort of thing here. Even Roosevelt, who has now got dictatorial powers, holds them, as he knows well, only at the mercy of Congress and the people—and he is in for a stiff fight this next spring.

I object to being told that Marxism is going to save the world until we know more about what it can do to the world in such a place as Russia. For this reason, I prefer Maurice Hindus to all the Hooks. His latest book is very good—*The Great Offensive*—and it certainly does not paint too rosy a picture of what Marxism can do.

However I fear you won't agree at all, so let's say no more about it. Incidentally, I may say there is out here a book by Granville Hicks called *The Great Tradition* which argues Marxism very ably as regards American literature. Literature has certainly swung more and more to the left over here ever since the depression, and reactionaries like Eliot are becoming rather *vieux jeu* at present. The trouble with the left-wingers, men like Erskine Caldwell for instance, is that they are more concerned with being sexy than with writing honestly, for the most part.

I quite agree with you that this is a decadent age in the arts. For one thing, the total effect of the war was simply to increase the general atmosphere of defeat and despair—it certainly did in my case, and I dare say in millions of others. Only Russia came out with a chance to try anything new, and the chance was a bare fighting one, and has run up against all sorts of difficulties. I am in favor of letting the Russians try out what they are doing up to the limit though I don't agree with it—nor do I think it even remotely possible here: but on the whole, *it is a hope*, and that is a good thing where so much else is hopeless. Here, we also have a hope; this winter will not be so hard as the last, and there is a real democracy about this country—a frank give and take—which is a relief after Europe, also a good temper and on the whole, a finer popular tone than a lot of people give us credit for. Of course, one has to make enormous sacrifices if one wants to be an artist here, but the same applies anywhere else, and after all, the real artists ought to and must disassociate themselves more and more from the smart imitation bohemians of Greenwich Village and the like. We have a good chance (better I think now than Russia) of producing a really great literature. In painting we may not be up to the French, but could easily beat the English. In architecture, we will probably improve if we can ever break the control of big business. In music, we probably never will have a great composer, but we have very fine orchestras, and lots of executive talent. And I really hope that Roosevelt will ride the political storm through to some sort of success because I believe the great mass of the people are behind him. That is our hope, at least.

Unfortunately the publishing business and most of the publicity now centers in New York, which is a Jewish city, and the hinterland—which seems to me to have more possibilities—is neglected. There are a few interesting people in Little Rock: one or two writers, one good musician, two tolerable painters, and one or two minor talents, but I have to live on my own brain-resources all the time, and if I stay down here will go rusty in time. However, I prefer it to New York, which is commercialized up to the hilt and bad-mannered to boot. I don't want ever to see New York again. There they still want a new thrill, and the latest thing from Europe (however bad it may be) charms them far more than the best thing that the hinterland can offer. They like to be half-baked Europeans of the Mencken type in New York City, and I am long since done with that sort of thing because to me Europe at best is pretty decadent (I prefer Russia) and is not likely to produce anything now. The Hitler regime will kill German literature, just as Mussolini killed Italian; the French are still fighting over Catholicism, the Spanish are in turmoil, and in England you must choose between Eliot and Squire! Honestly, I prefer Eliot (though I disagree with him completely) because I know he is honest and not a loathsome *prig* and a hypocrite, which Squire is.

I am glad to hear that H. Ellis is coming to see you. If he hasn't come yet, give him my best regards. I still value his work, which is very free and independent, though I realize that he is now too old to say much that is new or striking, and that he is becoming too timid about conclusions. I am reading now Inge's *God and the Astronomers*—also an old man's book, but pretty keen on the weaknesses of Eddington and Co.—although Inge is a Tory, I respect him and enjoy his Neo-Platonism. I like Whitehead's last book very much—read last summer. After all, a lot of the old fellows had more sense than we—though they knew nothing of our worst problems.

Yes, for Europe this is a decadent age, but I really believe that it is going to be *our best:* also I hope it will be best for Russia, too, and China, and South America. The rest of the world can go hang, so far as I care. Let Nazis and the Schweinhunde fight it out.

Wishing you a Merry Xmas, and hoping I may someday see you again.
Yours
J. G. F.

Am sending you a small Christmas present, and would much appreciate it if you could send me Read's new book.

TO FRANK OWSLEY

411 East 7th St.
Little Rock
Dec. 12, 1933

Dear Owsley,

Thanks for your letter. I am glad you approved of my action in the Scottsboro affair. And I am glad that you and Davidson are going to combine to do something to reconsecrate Franklin battlefield (where the best soldier from my state, Cleburne, laid down his life, along with all the other unknowns—and Cleburne previously had vainly memorialized Davis to free the slaves, and arm them *against the North*—which I wish to God had been done!). I don't know Davidson very well, but I like him extremely, and I honestly hope you will get something done. Here, in this damn Chamber-of-Commerce-ridden State, nobody gives a damn any longer (they've all joined Couch and Charlie McCain in upholding things like the Chase National Bank and the unspeakable Wiggins).

I am sorry to hear that your health forbids you to do more of the fighting that will be necessary. I am rather in bad crock myself, having gone through two bad breakdowns, in 1926 and 1932—but I realize I have got to die sometime, and the only damn thing I want to die for is the South, so it matters to me very little when that event happens. I have a long personal score I would like to see settled at least in part with the Northerners—including of course the New York Jews—before I do pass out. And I frankly am in with your crowd because I have that score to settle. I want to see some action—some really definite defiance, not the Nixon "belly-dragging" as you call it, nor the Chamber-of-Commerce lickspittle toadying, nor the Y.M.C.A. slop.

I am sending you herewith a document that may interest you. It really caused my letter to *The Nation*—damn it all, can't find it now. It was a pamphlet issued by the Society for the Prevention of Lynching about the Tuscaloosa business. My own sister (who is very conscientious, had a hard life, is an excellent woman, but a liberal) is on their council, and it was through her that I came to know that this Southern Anti-Lynching Society exists. I read their pamphlet (wish I could find it and send it to you) agree with most of what they said, but then suddenly realized there was quite another side to the matter—and it was this side I tried to put in my letter to *The Nation*. And I am not ashamed of having written it.

Allen writes me that *Harper's* have refused the new Symposium. I expect all the New York publishers will try and dodge it—but I believe we must and will get our way in the end. It's either that or total extinction now.

So good luck to you and Davidson, and forgive me for writing in longhand—I never could do much with machinery, even so simple an appliance as a typewriter still stumps me completely.

Yours
Fletcher

[Fletcher refers to his older sister, Adolphine. Harvey Couch, the founder of the Arkansas power utilities network, and Charles McCain, a banker, were nationally known native sons. Archibald L. M. Wiggins was a banker and a director of the Reconstruction Finance Corporation. Herman Clarence Nixon was a reactionary historian at Tulane and Vanderbilt who attracted Fletcher and some of the other Agrarians.]

TO HENRY BERGEN

411 East 7th Street
Jan. 6, 1934

Dear Bergen,

I have been intending to write you, but have been working doubly hard over Christmas. I am teaching a course here in Romantic English Literature 1750–1832 and have arrived at the point where I must discuss Blake (I mean to give at least four lectures on him alone), Wordsworth, Byron, Keats, Coleridge, and all the big men. Blake alone is very difficult to present—I don't think many people in Little Rock have even heard of him, and there was no copy of his works to be found in the Public Library here when I arrived (I gave them a copy of the Nonesuch Edition). I have just received Murry's latest book on Blake but doubt if I can read it in time. Anyway, I dislike Murry—he writes so emotionally, he was such a bad friend to Lawrence, so selfish to Katherine Mansfield all her life (and then cashed in after her death), he talks glibly of destroying "selfhood" when his own exhibitionism (to call it by no worse name) is so manifest—I do not like the man, nor his style of writing: though he may be right on some things, he has borrowed most of his ideas from others without acknowledgment. He is what we call a racketeer, even in his Communism. So I think I will try and make up my mind about Blake without reading his book—I value Blake just as highly as he does, and have studied him just as long. In fact, I asked Eliot over three years ago to let me do a short book of Blake (I did not want to undertake the effort implied without a pre-contract) but Eliot refused, on behalf of his firm. So that's that.

I have been reading the book by Read on *Art Now* and am amazed at its superficiality. It is obviously only a piece of hurried journalism, slung together because Read wanted money, and full of statements that are very superficial and highly questionable. Read has read widely and largely, but he constantly writes nonsense himself. Thus p. 100—"Regarding the object merely as a point of departure, he (the artist) can create a number of variations, exactly as a musician takes a simple theme as a point of departure," etc. The answer to that is that a musical theme is not a natural visual object—Read confuses two arts (or justifies their confusion, which is worse). P. 103 discussing Thomas Aquinas—"This is not the theory of beauty put forward by Plato and Philebus; Plato does not commit himself to anything so definite, to anything so mathematical and rational"—now it seems to me that Plato's theory is much more akin to abstract mathematics (the bane of all cubism) than Aquinas' theory. P. 105. "Cézanne was interested in the dynamic contrast of some forms as opposed to others—the principle of his composition was that—he always balances horizontals and verticals." Read is really very superficial about the dynamic harmony of Cézanne's landscapes. He seems to think him nothing but a cubist. P. 109. "No one would ever confuse a work by Braque with a work by Léger. Far from emptying a work of the artist's personality, this process of abstraction, by *removing the mask of sentimental actuality*, leaves that personality free to shine out clearly. Landscapes and portraits have to speak their own personalities, and it is easy for the reproductive painter to mask his own lack of personality in the personality of things." That is not only nonsense, but utterly false. The interaction of the personality and the object, the perceiver and the perceived, is fundamental to art. You can't get away from it. It is just as easy to paint abstractions as it is to do the worst academic rubbish—in fact it may be easier—nine tenths of the pictures between Chaps. III and IV of Read's book are really all alike—it doesn't matter in the least who did them. There is nothing to them. Whether they are modern or not, they are simply incompetent evasions—cubism promotes incompetent evasion, and surrealism, despite its love for monstrosity, is actually a little better, in my opinion, for at least it does paint *something*, rather than a Taüber-Art or a Hélion (No. 76 or 77).

However, I haven't time or patience to go into this matter further. It seems to me the Communists are right saying that what art needs is a social concept. All over Read's book is the trail of individualism run mad, and getting more and more decadent, more and more fragmentary, less and less capable of dealing with important things in an important way.

I have just been reading Eliot's book on *The Use of Poetry* also. He talks as much nonsense about poetry as Read does about art. I reviewed the book severely but haven't found anyone to take the review. The Eliot cult is still too strong.

I am now about to read *A Glastonbury Romance*. Read the first chapter yesterday. It is good—exceptionally good. He may go to pieces at the end but he makes a very brave start.

Roosevelt has now got Congress together again (with my brother-in-law as one of its members: D. D. Terry, Mary Louise's brother). The deficit that has to be budgeted for, may, of course, lead to a revolt against him. But he seemingly is quite calm, and I think the temper of the people is still with him in the main. The South is certainly much better off than it was last spring. Literally, everyone was broke then, without an exception. There is still about one out of three drawing relief—but the CWA is going strong now, and another 6 months may see the Roosevelt drive triumphant on all fronts. He certainly has courage—it depends of course on his lieutenants. Wallace is a good man, Frances Perkins is excellent, so is Johnson, Douglas, and one or two others, but Woodin (now resigned) was a bad appointment, and there is some doubt about Ickes (he is honest, but a conservative and timid). Anyway, I genuinely like Roosevelt more and more—he has got a really great human quality about him.

I am afraid this is a very scrappy letter—but I have to write in a hurry now. Probably you won't hear from me again for another month. Had a note from Aiken for Xmas—he is at Cambridge.

Yours
J. G. F.

[*A Glastonbury Romance is by the Welsh novelist John Cowper Powys. The CWA (Civil Works Administration) was one of the earliest economic recovery programs of Roosevelt's New Deal. Henry A. Wallace was the secretary of agriculture and later vice president; Frances Perkins was secretary of labor; Gen. Hugh Johnson was a member of*

Roosevelt's staff; Helen Gahagan Douglas was a Democratic congresswoman from California later defeated by Richard Nixon; William H. Woodin was a Republican business tycoon who served as secretary of the treasury for a year; and Harold Ickes, neither conservative nor shy, held many positions in Roosevelt's administrations.]

TO HENRY BERGEN

411 East 7th Street
Little Rock, Arkansas
Jan. 9, 1934

Dear Bergen,

I wrote you only the other day a letter achieved while my mind was on something else and under the pressure of much work I have to do; but yesterday your exceptionally interesting letter of December 22 arrived, and I want to answer it. I am sending you in a day or so a copy of Granville Hicks' *Great Tradition*, which to my mind is the best-written, most intelligent and far-reaching book on American literature that has been done from *your* point of view—from the point of view of communism. You will find in it a very good discussion of the question you raise, "How far was Whitman a Socialist?" And will find in it much beside—an intelligent appreciation of Howells, whom I regret to say I have never read because I thought him unimportant, a very good summary of Henry James (about which I entirely agree) and a fairly good (though not altogether adequate, to my mind) discussion of the "New Poetry Movement" of 1913–25, in which I played my part.

I am sending you this book because you tell me you are sending me MacMurray on Communism and because I think you ought to see it. I have met MacMurray, by the way, and I liked him very much.

I don't want to dispute your ideas about Marx. You probably know more about the matter than I do. My mind literally flounders when it comes to economics—I don't seem to be able to master them at all. Incidentally, I may remark that I am going—apparently—to have to pay income tax in the same way as you are, for 1931–32, though I have given up residing in England. Where I shall find the money, God—or the Devil—only knows.

Your remarks on your impressions of the European War interested me very much. Although in my early years (1910–14) in London, I had attended Fabian Society meetings, had heard Shaw speak, had read Wells and William Morris and Oscar Wilde and others on Socialism (as well as dipping into the Anarchist arguments of Steiner, Tucker, Nietzsche, Kropotkin, et al.) yet I did not class myself as a socialist in 1914—I suppose because of my Southern ancestry, or because of my individualism. When the war came on, I was pro-Ally at the start, though I had little use for Edward Grey (Shaw had shown him up), yet I believed in Asquith (who had a real streak of rustic British honesty in him) and the ordinary English petty bourgeois seemed to me to be rather fine (I never felt for them the contempt you describe) and on the whole, pretty decent. My own philosophy had already become—under the influence of Blake—a very heterodox sort of Christian mysticism, which could admire equally Shelley, Nietzsche, Ruskin, and a lot of other outlaws. Of course, I was what you call a mere ideologist; but I can't get out of my system a sort of obstinate religiosity which Leach (a man of my sort) seems to share. The war drove me back to America in 1914 as I did not want to stay in England in a false position, but America, which I hadn't seen since I left Harvard in 1908, disgusted me utterly with its bumptiousness, its sheer undiluted money-greed, its complete and perfectly self-satisfied atheism, its sheer Philistinism in art and morals. I stayed here for two years and then fled back to England intending to offer myself for the British Army (America was still neutral) and seek death. But I found that my English friends had all changed; the really intelligent ones were already disillusioned. They had no quarrel with the German people, and they knew it. Shaw had already spoken his mind against the war; Ireland was seething with revolt; England had become "Heartbreak House."

I had to make a fresh adjustment to this situation. As I had committed myself to England, I did not want to go back to America, and to try to make things easier for myself, I married. That was a bad decision and merely made things worse, as you know. I don't want to say that my marriage and various other matters—including poor health—did keep me out of the trenches, though I was perfectly willing to go and be sacrificed (I don't believe I could have come out alive or sane; because my mind is very finely balanced, and I have a danger of insanity). I was glad and happy when Russia went into revolution under Kerensky, but sorry—*profoundly*—when it turned out that there was no other choice for her but that between Lenin and anarchy. I realized that Europe would not make the same choice; the Christian tradition (whatever you may say against it) is at all events stronger rooted in Europe than in Russia; and of course the churches were all against Lenin, though I had long since lost my respect for them, owing to their supineness during the war. I came out of the war as I said scarred, bruised, and profoundly embittered: any faith I had once had in mankind was practically shattered, and had to be very painfully built up again. Possibly it would have been better for me, and for the world at large, if I could have taken the other side, and died a heroic death like Jack Reed's. He and a few conscientious objectors were about the only people I then respected, and still do respect. I did not think much of myself for having believed that the allies really stood for justice and the Germans for oppression. It was impossible to believe that after the Treaty of Versailles.

It is for these reasons that I find myself often more in sympathy with disillusioned reactionaries like Eliot than with open revolutionists like yourself. The revolutionist per se—say a man like Stalin—has to go out and destroy and destroy and destroy; the fine things along with the bad things—before he can build anything. Now I am only interested in saving the fine things. Even Lenin, who was exceptionally honest, said that the music of Beethoven made him feel like stroking people's heads rather than breaking them, and that he had to break people's heads first—in which, by the way, Hitler entirely agrees with him. Violence has, unfortunately, two sides to it: it may be violence for a good end, and may yet bring out violence on the very opposite side (Look at Germany, my friend, if you doubt this). I realize that perhaps more than you are aware that there are persons of exceptional sensitivity and intelligence in the Communist ranks; not time-servers not lickspittles nor cowards, but people who command my respect. But I still believe (perhaps wrongly) that it is their *individuality* that matters rather than their Communism: I loathe and detest all mob-demagogues and mob heroes (the only thing a mob is ever good for is to take some probably innocent Negro out and lynch him, and *I don't believe in that* any more than I believe in German mobs beating up Jews, or Italian ones giving castor-oil to Socialists). It seems to me that orthodox, official Communism is largely a mob-movement. I am not, however, a reactionary of the Eliot sort—because he hasn't anything to offer but the decadent, twice and thrice over-worked, weary, bored, tired and tiresome gesture of fatigue and despair.

It is for these reasons—or something like them—that I find myself unable to go the whole hog on Communism, though I am tending in that way, and if Roosevelt fails to travel further to the left, or if there is a reaction here towards Hooverism, I shall probably find myself in the Revolutionary ranks after all—despite my Confederate, slave-owning ancestors. In the meantime, I am glad you like the books I sent you for Christmas. *Three Lives* is a good book whatever you may think of the others. There is a good article on her, by the way, in the January *Atlantic Monthly*. I must sent it to you—

Yours

J. G. F.

[Gertrude Stein's Three Lives *(1909).]*

TO HENRY BERGEN

411 East 7th Street
Little Rock, Arkansas
March 6, 1934

Dear HB,

    Your letter of Feb. 17–21 has just come, and it has interested me so much that I am going to answer it right away. I have not seen the lectures of Eliot at the University of Virginia you refer to; indeed I did not know he had delivered any there; his Harvard lectures I have read, and they are pretty thin. If you could either send me, or lend me, the Virginia lectures I would be glad to have them as the bookstores down here are hopeless—perhaps the book has not appeared in the U.S. yet; I have not seen it noticed anywhere, and usually Eliot enjoys a good press in this country.

    I quite agree with your criticism on the man. I first met him in the darkest days of the war in 1917, and he was kind to me—and I honestly felt sorry for him because I could see then and see now that though he writes well and has a genuine talent, his character is totally negative—so much so that there is no explaining his manifest late-Victorianism (in his Harvard lectures he even praises the "art for art's sake" aesthetes of the Pater period, as if that were not totally dead, thank God!) except by supposing that he simply lacks guts or backbone enough to be a full-grown man! Those who knew him in the Harvard days (e.g. Aiken) tell me that even then he combined extreme subtlety and sophistication with great timidity—and his moral cowardice, his refusal to face up to the hard facts, is obvious in his whole being. His mental attitude becomes a complete pose for lack of any driving purpose, and his best poem ("The Waste Land") has no center, is nothing but a brilliant series of fragmentary poems. When that poem appeared (12 years ago!) I was amazed at the furor it caused among the young intelligentsia; I could understand the discussion about Joyce (a bigger and much more integrated type) and the interest in Gertrude Stein (amusing, if superficial), but Eliot's vogue puzzled me, and still does to some extent! There never has been, as you point out, a great writer lacking in moral integrity or moral conviction, and yet *this* is precisely what Eliot lacks. If we accept what the young people say about him, and agree that he is a master, then for the first time in the history of all human literature we have to accept someone as a master who has no moral backbone—he is a timeserver, a snob, and a moral coward. I could understand his pessimism and disillusionment if it were strong and sprang out a great sympathy, like the pessimism of Thomas Hardy or James Thomson (B. V.) but Eliot's pessimism makes you really sick at the stomach because it comes from a weak, wishywashy character—one without either skepticism or animal faith (to paraphrase Santyana).

And of course, just for that reason, he has done and is still doing an enormous damage to literature! He belief that Pound is the best poet of today is an example of this—everybody who knows Pound (myself among the number) can testify that Pound has *simply nothing to say himself, his work is a mere string of quotations from others, that his only value has been that he has encouraged others*—among them Eliot, Hemingway, Joyce, and myself. Pound can discover and help other talent but can't write himself but should have been a teacher in some university instead of a writer. As for Eliot, I quite agree, he should have been a priest. As for his remarks on Lawrence, they really make me angry. Lawrence may have lacked what Eliot calls morality, but he had *personal moral courage to a supreme degree* (every line of his letters and novels proves that) and if he behaved sometimes over-egotistically it was because he was ill with tuberculosis, knew it, and knew also that a miner's son as he was, he would have to fight hard to get any recognition from a land of snobs. As for Eliot's own snobbery I can say nothing because it really is a disgusting thing, done with less justification or excuse than the similar snobbery of Henry James. Such things make me feel humbly thankful to God for taking me out of England and putting me back in a land where *some democracy* is still possible.

I have dwelt very long on this point because I feel it perhaps with more intensity than I should—I have tried even to see Eliot's own point of view, but I cannot—I, to a certain extent, share his general feeling of disappointment with this age (rich in science, possibly, but poor and feeble in art) and also his desire (which I believe to be sincere) for a real honest-to-goodness religion (not the sham and pap of the churches). But to accept his Victorian substitute of "Anglo-Catholic" Toryism; *non possumus!*

The rest of your letter is almost equally interesting as your commentary on Eliot. I was interested in what you say about Max Eastman. I never met the man, and know nothing about his general character, but he recently sent to *The New Republic* a perfectly idiotic article attacking Marx of all people, which another man quietly made hash of the very next week. Now although I may be lacking in wits somewhere, I never said what Eastman said in that article (I am sending it to you) that both Hegel and Marx were fools! Hegel, whatever you may think of him, was a very *great thinker* and Marx, though I dislike myself his eternal harping on purely competitive economic causes—I prefer to look on history and life as being guided by other interests as well as purely economic ones—yet even to overexaggerate that side of life was perfectly good tactics for Marx, considering the position he was in. Whether it is equally good tactics for Stalin and Russia I do not know.

I was also interested in what you said about yourself. To have believed in 1895 that the U.S. was "God's own country" is nothing to your discredit. I remember myself that I believed in 1898 (being 12 at the time) that we had a perfectly good reason for fighting Spain, and that Spain was far worse than we (in the epoch of Mark Hanna!) and it was only the "muck-rakers" of a later day (1900–1908) that caused me to open my eyes. As for America now, there is so much to be thankful for in Roosevelt's first year (his recognition of Russia especially) that I would not like to indulge in carping criticism. But this year with their congressional elections will provide a test just how far he intends to go—and though he has, undoubtedly and to his eternal honor, lifted this country and the presidential office out of the Harding-Coolidge-Hoover rut, he may be (very likely is) too much of a political tactician to embark on the far seeing Socialistic strategy that will be necessary in my opinion to produce permanent change in our competitive system. We must wait and see, in short, what this year brings forth. Still, I am glad he is there in the White House—it must make the Republicans feel sick to see him.

About Arkansas: I quite agree with you that bond business is pretty bad! But I hope you will understand that this state never knew anything but a very moderate prosperity from the days of the end of Reconstruction (1876) till about the time of the European War. This was due in part to the overproduction of cotton, the general backwardness of most of the farming element, in part to cheapjack politicians, in part to the fact that the Indian Territory was not open to white settlement till 1889 (and then was swamped by the worst kind of land-exploiters!). About the time of the Great War, real boom times came down here, and it was discovered that we had great mineral wealth, also that the Ozark region (up to that time very backward) was wonderful for growing fruit (apples, strawberries, peaches, and grapes) and that there was money to be made also in rice culture and forestry. Of course this prosperity coming to a state where few (except my father and one or two others) had ever done more than moderately well, went to everybody's heads, and everybody began spending money like water by about 1920 and has gone on doing so up to the time there was nothing left *(we are Southerners, and consequently not so thrifty as the New Englanders)*. So now we are paying the piper, and of course we will have a pretty bill to face for no worse crime than that we (in the simplicity of our hearts) trailed Northern prosperity, and tried to cash in on the one boom we ever had! I know my family have lost practically everything but our land (which won't either sell or rent) and whatever talents we may have (mine mostly of the non-negotiable variety). But I can't understand why *The New Republic* should pick Arkansas as a bad example. After all, the North did things far worse than that.

I like *The Nation*, by the way, better as a paper than *The New Republic*,

which used to be much better ten years ago than it is now. The March number of *The Nation* has very good editorials and remarks on Roosevelt! Also a good review of Powys, whose book I have just finished—I agree that there is much power in it, but also *too much* unreality and falsity (an insane streak somewhere in all the Powys family). I must stop now, or instead of a letter I'll be writing a volume.
    Yours
    J. G. F.

P.S. *Lecturing on Shelley this week:* I don't know the book you mention—must see it!

[Eliot's Page-Barbour lectures at the University of Virginia were published as After Strange Gods: A Primer of Modern Heresy *(1934). The "bond business" presumably refers to the so-called Holford bonds issued by the real estate bank in 1841 and illegally sold, burdening the state with a huge debt it had not incurred.]*

TO LEWIS MUMFORD

411 East 7th Street
Little Rock, Arkansas
May 9, 1934

Dear Lewis,

I was very glad to get your letter with the discussion of first principles it contained. I think you put the difference between us very fairly as regards the machine; you optimistically think it can be integrated into the forms of a living society, and present all the evidence you can to support this point of view (and do it very ably; far better than Stuart Chase, who in his machine book as well as in his other books begs the entire question, to my mind). I, on the other hand, tend to think historically as to this question, I try to find out what the basis was of living societies in the past: Greece, for instance, or Renaissance Italy, or Medieval France (which was a great thing), or Elizabethan England—and as I do not find in them the stress placed on machinery, I reject machinery. As you say, we may both be wrong—but anyway I have written a review of your book and sent it on to *The American Review*, which is about the only magazine that might take it—and in this review I frankly try to cut you up, from my own point of view.

About my *Nation* letter. I don't honestly think that you or anyone else outside of the South has the remotest understanding of the Negro problem, and just for this reason all the denunciations of the injustices inflicted by such matters as the Scottsboro case leave me cold—just as *Uncle Tom's Cabin* left me cold when I read it as a boy. I could never understand the degree of indignation the North could work up over the way the Negroes were being treated (when the poor whites are treated here still worse; I agree with Norman Thomas) on any other supposition than that the North needed some scapegoat to distract attention from the way *it* treated Italians, Hungarians, and Jews, and so found it in the Negro. I don't believe in finding scapegoats, but I don't believe that such a thing as abstract and final justice is possible. All we can do is to adjust matters to suit local conditions. (If this be, as you say, Fascism or Hitlerism, then make the most of that poor argument: I don't care what it is so long as every concept in life responds to my regional orientation. My philosophy is an expansion of regionalism to cover all walks of life). This is not, as you say, a yielding to the voice of the mob. If you will read Basso's article in the last *New Republic* you will find that no one hates the Negro worse than the poor white worker; my class, if I may say so, were slaveowners, I played in my childhood with the descendants of the slaves of my family—we were like one family. I have never hated a Negro in my life; and my sister, who has lived all her life in this house, is well-known all over this state as a friend of the Negro: she is a member of the Association of Southern Women for the Prevention of Lynching, to which Odum also belongs (Odum is, I think, a very good man). But the nature of the Scottsboro defense, and the way it was conducted, made it not only impossible to release these Negroes (I am sincerely sorry they are in jail, and I fear they may be someday hanged, which would bring everlasting disgrace to us, for though they are not as valuable to the community as Sacco and Vanzetti, they probably never had a fair trial), but it also made other innocent Negroes suffer, brought on the Tuscaloosa business last summer. That is why I wrote my letter—I did not expect *The Nation* to print it, for I do not believe that we in this part of America have ever been allowed even a fair hearing by the North (hence our "don't-give-a-darn" attitude).

So much for this difficult question. I was, if I may say so, rather shocked myself on discovering last winter some remarks of yours in *The New Yorker* on a Regional Art Show, to the effect, as I remember them, that regionalism did not help artists much here—it may be quite true that artists who stick to their regions are starving—I know of three good painters in Arkansas who are having a hard struggle, and no support whatever—but I deny absolutely that they could ever be improved or helped by going to New York! I also saw some other remarks of yours praising an utterly worthless painter, Joan Miro, who has nothing to offer, nothing to say, and who conceals the fact behind a sham facade of surrealism. It seems to me—to be frank with you—that you still suffer from a great deal of the Paul Rosenberg–Alfred Stieglitz attitude— what is "up to the minute" is necessarily good art, what is "out of date," not "sophisticated" to suit the vicious taste of the New York intelligentsia, is of course poor! I cannot accept such an attitude—it is my business precisely to fight it, and fight it I shall.

    Yours
    John

P.S. I should be very grateful to you if you could persuade Norton to let me do the Blake book. I have some excellent material in the shape of notes, and would be delighted to write it. I think you would not object to my point of view, in this case, either!

TO HENRY BERGEN

545 Canyon Road
Santa Fé, New Mexico
July 13, 1934

Dear Bergen,

    I sent you today five recent copies of *The New Masses*. So you can see for yourself the level at which Communist mentality stands in this country. So far as I know, *The New Masses* is the most intelligent Communist paper in this country. Their daily paper, *The Daily Worker,* is pretty feeble. I hope the postal authorities will not confiscate the *package*.

    There is nothing much in these papers that I think worth reading except possibly Ilya Ehrenberg's very moving and fine account of the Vienna uprising. The rest seems to me just another "Hymn of Hate" of the capitalist.

    I have gone very thoroughly into the Communist position and arguments —having met several of them recently—from my own standpoint as an American of no party (but with democratic sympathies) who is not satisfied with the existing disorder in America, not altogether satisfied with President Roosevelt's efforts to mend it. And I must say, once and for all, that I do not think the Communists have any solution that is valid for this country. Their criticism of NRA and AAA [Agricultural Adjustment Administration] I largely accept; it is quite obvious that neither of these institutions have entirely done what everyone hoped of them. But when the Communists are asked (as I have asked them) what they would do *in place of the bungling efforts of Roosevelt*, the only answer they offer is that they would go on increasing strikes, (with fighting between the National Guard and the strikers), increasing agitation, etc. Even such a harmless piece of "reformism" as President Roosevelt's taking of millions of homeless and workless youths and putting them into Civilian Conservation Camps under army officers is denounced by them as being nothing but—Fascism! Well, if Fascism does come into this country (which God prevent), it will be because Communism, by such sabotaging tactics, has put it in power!

The only future for us, short of a blind Republican reaction, or short of a continuance of such well-meaning but essentially sporadic and not too well organized efforts as President Roosevelt has tried to mend the bad system under which we live, *is some sort of socializing of the farmer as well as the industrial worker* so that both will see eye to eye. And instead of that—which I believe to be the real solution here (it was not tried in Russia except by force)—we have the Communists prating about helping the trade unions to strike! They ought to propagandize the farmers instead because if there is an exploited class in this country, it is the farmer! And unless the farmer brings about the classless society and the proletarian state, *it will never be brought about on this continent.*

This was the point of all my recent letters to you, but like all Communists you have either missed or evaded that point completely. The technique successfully adopted in Russia could not begin to work here except to destroy what little civilization, what little wealth, there is. 78 per cent of our national income is derived from wages; about 75 or 80 per cent of the people are, I fancy, where I am: in the distinctly lower middle class. And it is these people who have to be converted here, not the industrial proletariat. All efforts to stir up the proletariat will only leave this lower middle class more and more open to Fascism.

In the meantime, what seems most likely to happen is that Republican reaction, masking itself under a few catch-phrases about democracy, will undo the little good that the Roosevelt regime has attempted. This is the hope of *The Saturday Evening Post,* the Chamber of Commerce, all the big financial and industrial "interests," as well as the *New York Herald-Tribune* and the *Chicago Tribune.* I send you a cartoon from the latter paper—"the world's greatest newspaper" as it calls itself. Perhaps such a regime would suit the Communists better here; it would give them more chances to agitate and more chances to promote death and disorder. But for my part, such a regime would be the end of any hopes I ever once felt for this country.

I do not intend to carry the question further because, like yourself, I have to work, but I have to work purely in order to earn money. I am down to my last five dollars as I write, and I see nothing facing me in the future but complete starvation. Which reminds me of your old remark about "eating one's cake and having it too."

Yours
John Gould Fletcher

P.S. August 18. I never sent this letter—because I thought I might offend you. But I have decided to send it after all. Roosevelt is now back and has reaffirmed (at Green Lake, Wisconsin) his conviction that further inroads into capitalism will have to be made. This is precisely the sort of news that all the reactionaries do not want to hear, and unless Roosevelt eats his own words, I don't see how he is going to get out of further reforms. Meanwhile, the Communist *New Masses* which I sent you goes from bad to worse. It is now attacking Upton Sinclair for being—a Fascist! Really, these gentry see Fascism everywhere except where it existed—in themselves. I am a little better off than I was last month, but I fear it is borrowed money which I will have to return that I am now living on. I saw S. G. Morley yesterday and he again invited me most cordially to come to Yucatan. I wish I could go.
J. G. F.

TO HENRY BERGEN

Taos, New Mexico
Aug. 29, 1934

Dear Bergen,

Here I am, stopping at Mabel Luhan's. I have been here a week, but owing to some work I had to finish, I have been unable to write anybody. In another week, I shall be in Little Rock, at the old address.

It is very pleasant up here, now that the fall has come, after heavy rains which broke the drought but were too late to do any good. I have a large room to myself and am not interrupted in any way; I frequently do not see Mabel until lunch time. Tony is away, visiting the Snake Dance, which I missed this year as I did last. The ordinary tourist agencies which take tourists out to it are very expensive (the Hopi Reservation is still very inaccessible) and do not permit of seeing it under the best conditions. It was owing to Mabel that D. H. Lawrence saw it in 1924, and wrote his very fine description, published in "Mornings in Mexico." She has not seen it herself since then.

Mabel herself is, I think, between 50 and 60. She has obviously grown much fatter during the last ten years, and is quite easy to get along with. She has the reputation of being eccentric and temperamental, but personally I find her very pleasant, and less temperamental than Mary Austin, who died early this month in Santa Fé and who was the best woman writer dealing with this country (her *Land of Little Rain* and *Land of Journey's Ending* are excellent books, if you have not read them). Mabel is not very highly educated—she is not an intellectual in the ordinary sense of the word. She likes company, likes to be entertained, and likes people about her who will talk on intellectual topics. Her chief interests are in mysticism and in psychology. In her library are many books on both subjects, and like most American mystics, she felt the theosophical current, has been interested in Madame Blavatsky, and is at present much interested in Rudolph Steiner. There is living near here a young American painter who spent much time at Dornach with Steiner during the last years of his life, and who comes over and talks in the evenings. Much of his talk I cannot follow, but it is interesting to hear of Steiner from first hand (I find Steiner's books almost unreadable, and it is obvious that his influence and his personality were more important than his written words).

I have not seen Frieda nor Brett yet. Both live up at the Lawrence ranch several miles away, up on the mountain. We were to go up there last Sunday, but it poured so hard that the mountains roads were impassable. I shall get up there before I go, I expect.

I had an interesting talk with Mabel about Lawrence. According to her, Lawrence and Frieda practically broke with each other after Lawrence went to Mexico in 1925 (just after they had been to Taos). Frieda wanted to go back to England and Lawrence let her go alone. After a while he followed, and then occurred that famous last scene with Murry in the Cafe Royal which has been so differently described. They went on to Germany and to Italy, where they settled near Florence, but apparently the reconciliation between them was half-hearted, for according to Mabel, it was then, some three years before Lawrence's death, that Frieda met the Italian officer (Angelino) with whom she is now at present living. According to Mabel *Lady Chatterley's Lover* is really the story of Frieda and this Italian officer, which Lawrence divined without Frieda's admitting it (he had very strong intuitions, particularly about women). He is the crippled husband of the story. Anyway, whether this opinion of Mabel's is true or not, Lawrence desperately wanted to leave Italy and come back here to an atmosphere which was more favorable, but Frieda refused to quit Italy, and Lawrence felt a dying man from that time on. The Italian officer was very nice to Lawrence and made Frieda look after him (I am quoting Mabel here), though she was willing to desert him. He also (this too is Mabel's opinion) persuaded Frieda to write her book—practically forced her to do so. He came down here one day—I saw him—he is nice looking, gray haired, just a good tempered well-built Italian. He can only stay here 6 months at a time—he has a wife and 3 children in Italy and has to go back frequently. Frieda will have to spend this winter alone.

I give you what Mabel has told me, without any comment of my own, because I thought it would interest you. Of course, it is true that Mabel became furiously jealous of Frieda when she saw that Frieda was not going to let her have Lawrence (her own book admits as much). And that jealousy probably still persists. But on the whole, I have always felt myself that Frieda's taking up with this Italian right after Lawrence died shows that she and Lawrence had practically broken with each other before the end (Frieda's own book admits this, though she never mentions the Italian officer). Mabel's assertion that Angelino (I cannot remember his last name [Angelo Ravagli]) came into Frieda's life as early as Florence is worth thinking about.

That is about all my news. There are two Chinese paintings here, both very good. Mabel says that she bought them from a Paris collection before the war, and that they were passed on by Roger Fry. One is a standing Kwannon, on a gold ground, with beautiful blue robe, and the usual tall headdress. It is Ming, I think, but probably harks back to an earlier original. The other, in the dining room, is of a man's figure standing in a stream and apparently sharpening a sword on a rock. His clothes, rather scanty, are all much windblown, and so is his hair; the pose is very free, with lots of life and movement. Mabel says it is the Chinese war-god, but I am doubtful. Probably some storm-spirit, or Buddhist arhat. It is much faded, and is probably Sung—a very fine thing indeed.

Mabel has done 8 vols. of her Memoirs (one volume has been published) but none of these are to be published until after her death. She is now attempting a novel, and also has in mind a book describing the seasons in Taos (prose purely, with a lot of Indian color; the pueblo is about 5 miles away from the town and gives it a special quality). She has black hair (turning gray), blue eyes, wears generally loose-bodied dresses (rather likes wrappers), is moderately but not offensively Bohemian, and firmly believes that white civilization will somehow collapse in this country and that the Mexicans & the Indians will carry on. Anyhow, she likes it out here, and has fulfilled something in her destiny by staying (she came in 1922) and accepting Tony and the Indians completely.

Yours
J. G. F.

TO HENRY BERGEN

411 East 7th
Little Rock
Nov. 19 [1934]

Dear Bergen,
Your letter of the 25th of October received. I have been away lecturing the last two weeks and will be very busy the next month.

It seems to me the Lawrence affair boils down to this. He was asked to the house by Frieda's husband and fell in love with her on the spot. She was older, with two children, but ready to have an affair with him. He was serious, told the husband, insisted on marriage. Now unless you are prepared to say outright that he should have let her have her way and simply stop at a transitory erotic experience, it seems to me he was right in demanding marriage. She reacts by being jealous of all other women—insanely so in the case of Mabel and poor harmless Brett. He gets tired of her rages, fits of jealousy, etc. and lets her go to Europe alone. He finally thinks better of it and comes after her. They go off to Florence. Then Angelino appears and she has an affair with him.

It seems to me she was an uninteresting nymphomaniac. He was fundamentally, I suppose, a Puritan—which is better at least than being a nymphomaniac.

She has gone off, I hear, to Mexico for the winter, along with Bynner (a pure horror) and a lot of other Santa Fé frauds.

The election is over and the New York papers are already predicting that the Republicans will never come back—that the party is utterly finished. The Democrats will now become the conservatives, and a new Farmer-Labor-Progressive combination, headed by young LaFollette, will take up radicalism in its new form. It is too bad Sinclair lost (Herbert Read, *New English Weekly*, Nov. 8, says he won—please tell him not to be a fool). Cutting, in New Mexico, an interesting progressive, almost lost too. You should watch LaFollette very closely—also a governor of Wisconsin named Olson—even more radical than Sinclair! and Norris in the Senate.

We won't go Fascist yet, but Europe almost certainly will, and that very soon.

I think your idea of doing ethics in dialogue form (a la Plato) is good. Why not a round table, with one character hedonist, another stoic, a third Laodicean, a fourth Marxist? It would be interesting to read.

Orage, I see, is dead, I am very sorry—he was the finest journalist and one of the best writers, when all is said and done, of my time.

I haven't a penny to send you anything for Christmas. There are a lot of books I might care for, which have not as yet come out here. There are, for instance, Pound's *Make It New*, I. A. Richard's *On Imagination*, and Waley's book on Taoism. Belloc's *Short History of England* is good, I believe, and probably his book on Cromwell might interest, but also irritate me. Aiken's *Landscape West of Eden* is good—he showed me it in MS some years ago. I haven't enough to buy anything now.

All good wishes. G. Stein is now here—the New York papers emitting tons of gush over her.

J. G. F.

TO HENRY SEIDEL CANBY

Little Rock, Arkansas
[December 12, 1934]

To the Editor
The Saturday Review of Literature

Sir,

The question you put in your editorial of December 1st, "Why is it so difficult to interest this immense reading public of ours in really good books?" is a question that can only be answered by pointing to certain dominant factors in American history which do not carry out the optimistic picture of American life portrayed by the schoolbooks of my youth. Perhaps you will permit me to say what these, in any opinion, are.

1. Before the Civil War, there was a reading public in this country. It may have been a small one, but it was definitely determined to read good books, and not trash, and it may have comprised a larger percentage of the people than the reading public of today. Emerson, Longfellow, Lowell all had respectably large followings in New England and the Middle West. Even Melville began as a success. The South had its own local writers, possibly not quite so well supported, but unquestionably prominent in their day.

2. The Civil War, coming as it did, only 12 years after the discovery of gold in California, spread over the face of the land a single type of American mind, to take the place of the older pioneer; the mind of the business pioneer, the hard-headed inventor type (Edison, Ford) who had reduced life to a practical, pragmatic equation. It was the prevalence of this type that led such men as Henry Adams to take refuge in sardonic silence; that drove Henry James abroad; that made of Mark Twain a humorous (too humorous) defeatist, and that silenced Whitman. For good literature may co-exist with great science (in the abstract sense) but it cannot flourish in an atmosphere where materialist science has big business, industrial and financial, for its armed ally.

3. Literature from abroad began to trickle in, slowly, throughout the nineties. But along with it came the idea, perfectly acceptable to the typical middle-class Protestant mentality—the poor ailing mentality of these States—that to be "literary" it was necessary to be "bohemian," in other words both intoxicated and immoral. Witness the extraordinary vogue of such a book as Max Nordau's *Degeneration,* and even later attempts to have cut a form of "neurotic escape," on the part of many Freudians.

4. At about the same time that art began to be considered highly "bohemian" and naughty, the colleges broke out in an epidemic of athletics which has no parallel and which is scarcely yet at an end. To produce the best football team or to break the track record became the ideal of our educational system, not to acquire wisdom or perspective on life.

These four causes, the Civil War and the consequent ignoring of local and regional attitudes under the drive of successful mass-industrialism, the reprise of the one-track type of mind—inventor, financier, industrial pioneer—as the ideal American human being, the wide-spread belief (suitable to the Protestant mentality) that the literary artist was a "bohemian" and a bad citizen, and the substitution of athletics for learning in the colleges did the trick of making the American public book-shy. Nor has the belated attempt of the last twenty years to change this state of affairs improved matters much. For though the American people have been offered a great range of the most varied reading matter during that period, the pace of life has become all too swift for it to be at all properly assimilated and digested.

The remedy for this state of things rests not on any single class, but on the whole American people at large—writers, publishers, reviewers, and readers. Let me suggest what can be done:

1. The reviewer and the publishers must both learn that no book can be made popular by merely ballyhooing it into popularity. The reading public itself, insofar as it exists, in this country, is already showing signs of impatience, of no longer wishing to regard the latest piece of sensational trash that same publisher "puts over" as being another masterpiece.

2. The desire to read must be stimulated in the American people, not from metropolitan centers such as New York and Chicago, but slowly and painstakingly from within the country itself. It must proceed from the backwoods towards New York and not vice versa.

3. Local and regional cultures must be fostered and protected. It would be a good thing if every American University had its chair of American folklore and folk-literature. (I owe this excellent suggestion to Miss Constance Mayfield Rourke).

4. There is reason to think that Europe is *not* likely to give us many more masterpieces in the future. Why import trash then? We have enough of that sort of thing already on our own hands over here.

5. If these suggestions are followed, it is quite probable that we will someday have a reading public [that] will demand good books. But let us not be in a hurry about it. To create such a thing will take at least fifty years. And we will have to train our writers as well in a matter few American writers have even faced: the matter of respect for the tradition and the possibilities of their craft.

I remain
Yours respectfully
John Gould Fletcher
Little Rock, Arkansas
Dec. 12, 1934

[The editorial to which Fletcher refers is "What the Proletariat Reads" by Louis Adamic.]

TO VAN WYCK BROOKS

411 East 7th Street
Little Rock, Arkansas
Feb. 28, 1935

Dear Van Wyck,

Your letter of February 25 arrived here today and was welcome as a shower of rain in the desert. As you doubtless know, isolation—which seems to be the lot of the genuine creative talents in this country (even Whitman and Mark Twain undoubtedly felt it)—has its dangers. One goes on doing one's work as best as one may, but with a constant sinking feeling in one's stomach that there is no use in it all—especially if one works in such an unpopular medium as poetry. Therefore to know of such a friendship as you now offer is a great privilege. It takes some of the edge off one's loneliness.

You ask me what I am now doing. I decided in 1929 for the regional movement in the South as I understood it, and contributed to *I'll Take My Stand* accordingly: probably this move shocked and horrified many of my Socialist friends, but I do not regret it. I might have done more, then, but I was unfortunately tied to England; but I did publish *The Two Frontiers* that year; a cultural study of America *and* Russia, based on an idea entirely stolen from you, and not a good book, though I worked hard on it. It had no success at all. In 1931 I burnt another bridge by taking part in the Round Table at Charlottesville, Virginia, on *Regionalism;* I had men like Mumford, Burton McKaye, and Clarence Stein to oppose me, and tried opposing them all by using the very radical viewpoint that *the machine-age has no right to exist so long as it fails to contribute anything to human culture.* Mumford was disturbed by this line of attack; he has tried since to prove that the machine-age has a culture of sorts, but, honestly, I am not satisfied by the proofs he offers. I then decided, after that, to return to the U.S. and give the rest of my life to the cause of regionalism. This decision cost me more than anything else in my life. It cost me a separation from my wife and family (still in England, and never likely to come over here), it meant remaking my entire career (if I *could* do so), it lost me all contacts with England, it was my last adventure into the unknown, and just before I came over, in 1932, I had a horrible accident which broke several bones in my body and nearly killed me once and for all. (Lewis Mumford, then in London, saw me in hospital). However, I came over in March 1933, and have been in the South or the Southwest ever since.

I am still flying the same flag, but it is a very disheartening task, and entails great strain. The inroads of the mass-industrial system backed by the financial system into every human value, have been great even here, where agrarianism is still powerful. But personally, I feel a great measure of hope. Despite everything, the New Deal is better than the Coolidge prosperity of the *Freeman* years; it is far better than the horrible Hooverism I saw in 1931. I think it is up to us to support it, not blindly, but sensibly; nay more, to *reinforce it* by creating within its framework a sense of regional necessity and regional need and regional value. The task is a gigantic one, and demands thousands of workers, where it has only a paltry handful. Whatever power I may have is henceforth dedicated to a new decentralization of American effort—economically, culturally, and politically we are going to have to become regionally and sectionally conscious. And unless the South and West take the lead, no one else will. New England is finished, and New York is a nightmare monstrosity where nothing has value except pure and simple Marxism of a sort that the rest of this country *cannot* and *should not* adopt.

The next two years will, I feel sure, witness the crisis in this stage of America's growth. Either we shall become more and more conscious not only of ourselves as Americans, but of ourselves as Southerners, New Englanders, Middle Westerners, Far Westerners, etc., or we shall be driven into some blind reaction of Fascism or Communism which will leave us stranded at the bottom of the Gulf. I, for one, only hope and pray that the momentum engendered by the New Deal, which seems to me absolutely miraculous, will not lose its force. We are becoming self-conscious and self-aware of ourselves in a strange and complete way. And the only way we will ever face our diversity (was ever a nation so diverse as ours?) is to regionalize it!

That, briefly, defines what I am aiming at. As for the financial side, I am now a poor man, but so long as I have a roof over my head and food to eat, I am going on working. I am interested in *The New Mexico Quarterly*, in *The Southwest Review*, in *Space*, the little paper edited at Norman, Oklahoma; in *The Westminster Quarterly* edited in Georgia; I am interested in all of these, and write when I can for them, and do my work without one cent of payment. I believe that my country—*this country, not Russia*—will be only saved, if at all, by some such effort as I am making, and I only wish I were a younger man, I only wish I had some fire to give to this effort and to this movement. But I do not regret anything. Maybe someday some of the younger people will after all understand what it means.

I write this to you because it was your criticism that set me on the right track. I might have gone the way of Eliot or Joyce or anyone of the tired, unrooted aesthetes, but something in your criticism as far back as 1915 stopped me and made me question my background, and made me want to find a background. Well, I have found it, after many years. It is one that I dare say I shall never do justice to; for it contains strange hints and is very inarticulate (the formlessness of American life compared to the formed sense of European life—one always has that to contend against), but it is, after all, my own life, and it is the thing that my own people *had* to create. And I hope I shall believe in its possibilities to the last day of my life.

Yours
John Gould Fletcher

TO FRANK OWSLEY

411 East 7th St.
Little Rock, Arkansas
March 2, 1935

Dear Owsley,

I have just received *The American Review* for March, containing your magnificent article, "The Five Pillars of Agrarianism." I cannot thank you too much for that article. When I reflect that *The Virginia Quarterly* can publish and pay for the sour beer-belchings of a man like Mencken, and that you, who are a first-class historian, and an economist of head and heart, have to publish this splendid article in an obscure magazine run by such a scatterbrain as Collins, then I very nearly despair. But courage, old man! We are going to get the West on our side, unless I am much mistaken. We must just hammer, hammer away—give them Rhett and Calhoun brought up to date! That is what you are doing.

Your idea of regional congresses! That is just what we want, and the sooner we come to it, the better. The rotten, impotent Legislature here—which has tried, year after year, to suppress the State History Commission—is now engaged in an effort to pass a sedition bill, because Commonwealth College had the courage to stand up and defend some share-croppers thrown out to starve by the roadside by the absentee landlords of Poinsett County! By heaven, I would rather destroy the Arkansas legislature than see them playing the game that the same landlords want them to play! I am making a stand here for free speech—yes, even for *Communist free speech*—rather than see the sharecroppers' perfectly just grievances go unventilated.

I have just been to L.S.U. where I saw Pipkin and Warren. Pipkin is a man we would do well to win to our side, and keep there. He has powerful force, and much direct ability at organizing. Warren seems very happy in his new job. They are going to have a conference April 10–12, on Southern Reading at which all sorts of people will be invited: it may develop into a fight—I shall go there primed up to the hilt with all the Agrarian ammunition I can to cover this program. I am sending him your article: it will make him sit up and take notice.

Give my regards to Davidson, whose spade-work in *The American Review* is going to bear fruit: I really owe him a letter, but cannot write it (snowed up with other work). And don't lose courage, don't think such an article as yours is falling on barren soil. It isn't. I am sending you under separate cover, a copy of the last *New Mexico Quarterly*. Read, mark, learn, and inwardly digest the article by Wynn about the *Southwest Straddling the Agrarian Issue!* We are going to make some converts yet!

Meanwhile, I say, in the spirit of Lee and Jackson, long live Agrarianism! And hooray for Frank Owsley!

John Gould Fletcher

[Commonwealth College was a socialist community, allegedly Communist, near Mena, Arkansas, locally famous for its radicalism, its support of the Southern Tenant Farmers Union, and for the brief attendance of Orval Faubus. Fletcher delivered three lectures there in 1935.]

TO FRANK OWSLEY

411 East 7th St.
Little Rock, Arkansas
March 11, 1935

Dear Owsley,

I have received a letter today from Davidson that fairly staggers me. He tells me that both Barr and Davis have *refused to allow him to reply to Mencken in their Anniversary Number of the Virginia Quarterly Review.*

I understand that Ransom, Tate, Wade, possibly Warren, are going to appear in the Anniversary Number of this magazine. I have written them all, explaining that if they do so, my connection with the Agrarian movement is ended as far as they are concerned. I will not fight with a pack of cowards. If they are not men enough to withdraw from *The Virginia Quarterly* in protest, then I am not going to fight this battle with them. I am rid of them, now and forever. I shall have no truck of any sort, henceforward, with anyone who straddles this issue: who feeds with the lambs of Barr, he is my enemy—I don't care *what he calls himself.*

I demand therefore that everyone associated with our group who is going to write for any future issue of *The Virginia Quarterly,* immediately withdraw his contribution! I have a right to demand this!

Please show this letter to Ransom and to whoever is concerned.

Yours,

John Gould Fletcher

TO LOUIS UNTERMEYER

411 East 7th Street
Little Rock, Arkansas
June 17, 1935

Dear Untermeyer,

Your letter of the 12th has just come. I returned to the U.S. on March 16th, 1933, and have lived in this country ever since. Permanent address as above. The last two summers I was in Santa Fé, New Mexico—this summer I expect to be after August 1st at Yaddo, Saratoga Springs—perhaps that is somewhere near your address. Will return here after September.

My remark about Davidson's finest passage and your possibly not reading it was meant more or less as a joke. Sorry you felt hurt about it. But, as a matter of fact, the only thing that stands in the way of modern poetry is the attitude of the public (including the critics) that it is neither worth reading nor writing about. However, I must admit you *have* done a good deal of reading in your day.

This summer (July) I expect to publish a new book, entitled *XXIV Elegies* (please keep Roman numerals) through "Writers' Editions," Box 750, Santa Fé, New Mexico. You might list the book in your bibliography. As it will be published only in a limited edition of 400 copies, it will probably cost you $2.50 to own it.

Personally, I don't mind your using "The Lofty House" for your anthology —though I have written better poems than that recently. But I shall have to charge you for the privilege. I believe that, years ago, you were one of the two anthologists to whom I gave my work for nothing (the other was Harriet Monroe). In both cases, but in yours on the whole the least, I regretted doing so later. In the first place, I haven't a penny to bless myself with. In the second, about a thousand people, more or less, have made names and reputations out of what they could lift from my work. It will now have to stop.

You may quote from my essay without paying me anything—provided you give me due acknowledgment. But I really should charge you now, and feel strongly disposed to do so, for every poem you use of mine. Considering I have to publish them now at my own expense, largely, I see no reason why I should grant to an anthologist the privilege of taking them free.

It is amusing to see that Frost is going to introduce Robinson's last volume to the world. I remember Robinson telling me years ago that he considered Frost a megalomaniac and absolutely insane; I am not saying either that he was not right. I have letters from both of them, and can testify that the Frost letters are so egoistic as to be pathological. The complete silence that surrounded Robinson's death and funeral just shows you what a real poet is worth!

> Das Glück ist eine leichte Dirne
> Und weilt nicht gern am selben Ort;
> Sie streicht das Haar dir von der Stirne
> Und küsst dich rasch und flattert fort.
>
> Frau Unglück hat, im Gegenteile,
> Dich liebefest ans Herz gedrückt;
> Sie sagt, sie habe keine Eile—
> [Setzt sich zu dir ans Bett und strickt].
>   John Gould Fletcher

[Untermeyer had long been familiar with this poem. In 1917 he had published a translation of the poetry of Heine which included the following version of "Das Glück":

> Good Fortune is a giddy maid,
> Fickle and restless as a fawn;
> She smoothes your hair; and then the jade
> Kisses you quickly and is gone.
>
> But Madam Sorrow scorns all this,
> She shows no eagerness for flitting;
> But with a long and fervent kiss
> Sits by your bed—and brings her knitting.*]*

TO VAN WYCK BROOKS

Yaddo
Saratoga Springs
August 2, 1935

Dear Van Wyck,

    I arrived here only yesterday, after a very hot and exhausting journey, and have yet to get fully settled. As I lost your letter with the address on it somewhere en route, I hope this will reach you. The first news I had of George Russell's (AE's) death was your letter. I did not know him personally, and never had any correspondence with him. Apart from a rather unfavorable notice that he once wrote of one of my books of poetry in *The Irish Statesman*, I did not have any links with his life. But I always valued his view of life, especially as expressed in that really remarkable book *The Interpreters*. His mysticism made a very strong impression on me, and I have known several people who have met him, and who realized to the full his unworldliness and his saintly quality. He is a loss to Ireland and to the world, I feel, and I am sorry he has gone. I suspect that Yeats (whom I have met) will be next to go, as I always understood that he and Russell were such good friends that when they met each other, they seemed several years younger. It seems terrible to think that in a few years there will be no great literary figures left in Europe, but such seems to be the trend of our age, with its stress on some insane and rigidly deterministic dogma of "science." If one looks back to 1900 one sees quite a number of first class men! Tolstoy, Shaw, Hauptmann (then with something to say), Strindberg, Verhaeren, Hamsun, and so on. Now there is scarcely a figure of first rank under sixty unless it be Thomas Mann. Quite recently *Books Abroad*, a magazine published by the University of Oklahoma, asked me whom I would nominate for the Nobel Prize. I would not answer the question—the list of great European writers seems steadily to grow less, and I have not much faith that any of the Americans are big enough.

Yours
John

TO CONRAD AIKEN

411 East 7th Street
Little Rock, Arkansas
October 6, 1935

Dear Conrad,

I have not heard from you for many moons, but the other day I got a letter from Bergen, who told me that you were still very hard up and were playing with the idea of turning your house into a shop for the sale of pottery and other handicraft. I do not know whether you will do it, but I would imagine that you might save some money that way, especially in the summer months. I don't suppose Rye has enough visitors in the winter to make it profitable.

I was in New York last month, and saw Max Perkins, who gave me a copy of your book *[King Coal]*, telling me that he did not suppose it would sell, as people in general have lost interest in psychological subtlety and are now interested mostly in something economic—the publishers, however, in New York have done better since last spring and are all embarking on ambitious programs for this next winter and spring. I have read your book and I think it is an excellent piece of work—stylistically it sustains a very high level of writing, without too many divagations into the fantastic, and it holds its interest from beginning to end. It also has a richer sense of humanity than anything that you have done; this is due to the character of Jones, who is made to appeal very strongly! I almost wish you could have somehow given more of him; he is perfectly fascinating. Ammen is, of course, more in your own line and is, I think, also quite life-like and astoundingly real. The interplay of these two characters on each other is very skillfully handled. I liked what *The New York Times Literary Supplement* said about the book, and about your literary position in general: the lack of popularity your work suffers from is due to no fault of your writing, or of your mind. You are a born writer, if there ever was one, and a fine artist, in an age when there is no room for such—less room than there ever was. It simply is your misfortune—perhaps I share it also.

I also liked your article in *The New Republic*, "A Plea for Anonymity," to which Cowley made such a poor reply. His theory that it is well that writers should have politicians recognize the importance of literature—is simply arrant nonsense, and his notion that human nature is so much putty to be pulled and prodded about, lacking any fundamental values, is even worse—Cowley is a lost soul, if indeed he ever had much soul to lose. I am glad you said in that article something I have had it in mind to say—indeed, I have written to *The New Republic* protesting about Cowley's nonsense, several times—ever since I came back here two years ago. The crowd in New York now has all turned Communist as that happens to be the latest fashion; and the publishers are all following them, raving about "proletarian" novels—as if these could not be as bad as the worst *Saturday Evening Post* short story, unless handled by someone with sensitivity and intelligence! It is really sickening, but I don't know how it can be broken down, unless by such articles as yours. I have just read *Europa* by Robert Briffault—a particularly vicious example of bad writing, poor characterization, and cheap brothel-house detail—but admired by Cowley because it is "proletarian" and points a Soviet moral.

I am now engaged in a novel myself, at last—after several false starts, I plunged in this summer, and have written 356 pages of what will be a five-hundred-page work. I am working hard against time to get it finished by 1st November, when the publishers want to see it. It is good fun but very exhausting, and I believe it is readable—more I cannot say. I may have to go to New York later on, in December, to see the publishers about it, though two of them are already interested. It certainly takes all my time, and I scarcely have any leisure for letters.

I suppose that if the Italian-Ethiopian business leads to a general European war (heaven only knows), you will close Jeake's House and come back. I hope then to see you. As soon as I can get together some money—my wife still takes every cent of what I have—I intend to move out of the

South, and come North again, somewhere near New York, where I hope to be able to support myself by reviewing, if nothing else offers, or by teaching. I may come up this winter. Let me know where you are likely to be, and I will look you up. It's been years now since we last met.

Yours
John

TO CONRAD AIKEN

1801 Gaines Street
Little Rock, Arkansas
April 2, 1936

Dear Conrad,

I have not written you, or heard from you, for many months. Early this year, I divorced my wife, who is still in London. And a little later on, on January 18 of this year, I married Charlie May Simon, with whom I now am living a life that is certainly, compared to anything that I ever had in my past, a life of great happiness.

I am writing you now confidentially concerning a personal matter which I would like you to help me about. As you know, during a brief period late in 1931 and early in 1932 I lived apart from my wife, with a married woman. Later as you also know, I returned to my wife, lived with her for some three or four months, and then had a breakdown, which led to my wife's putting me in Bethlem, before I returned here to America. Now the thing I want to write you about is this. The woman I lived with during the brief episode when I was away from my wife has certain letters of mine, which I am now ashamed of having written and which I do not wish to come to light later in my life. I want you to give me the name of a reliable lawyer (your own for preference) in London, whom I can employ to recover these letters. I am exceedingly anxious to do this, as I believe this woman might later on bring out or sell these letters to my detriment. I would be glad to employ you as agent for obtaining these letters, but I do not believe you would care to undertake the job. I have no lawyer now in London, and do not wish to re-employ the lawyer whom I employed in my abortive attempt to get a separation from my wife, back in 1931.

If you could please put me into touch with a reliable lawyer to act as my agent, to buy these letters back, or to obtain them in some way from this woman, I would be very much indebted to you. I am very much ashamed of this episode in my life, and I don't know what nonsense I may have put on paper during or after the brief course of this sordid affair I had with this woman—her name is Lorna Hyde, and she lives with her husband somewhere in Tadworth, Surrey—I don't remember the exact address, but no doubt your lawyer could find out where these people are. I wish you could help me in this, so your lawyer could write her, and find out what she is willing to take in return for these letters. Please let me know as soon as possible.

I shall probably be coming to New York later on this summer, and wonder whether I can get a chance of seeing you. I hope you are better in health and spirits than when I last wrote. I remain,

Yours
John

TO CONRAD AIKEN

1801 Gaines Street
Little Rock, Arkansas
April 4, 1936

Dear Conrad,

I am writing you again because I feel that my letters of yesterday and of the day before are open to misinterpretation. I want you to understand very clearly that in writing to you as I did in both these letters, I meant every word I said—that I am sickened and ashamed beyond measure that I ever had any relations with Mrs. Hyde, and that I feel disgusted at the thought that she has any letters of mine. As I wrote you yesterday, I have discussed the matter fully with my wife before I wrote you, asking for the name of your lawyer, so that I could negotiate through him for the return of these letters. We both jointly agreed on writing to you, asking you to do this favor, and I am very sorry if anything in my letter of yesterday gave you a different impression.

I am therefore renewing my request, that you send me at once the name of your lawyer, and I should be very much obliged to you if you will also let it be known among any old friends of mine who may still be in England, that I am sickened and ashamed of my former association with Mrs. Hyde, and I want also to request that you tell all my friends that I am now so very happily married that I feel sure that the marriage will last for life. My wife and I have everything in common and keep no secrets from each other. She is, by the way, a writer of decided merit, so I am not suffering from any of the lack of understanding and appreciation that I suffered from in my previous marriage. Professor Sanders of the University of Michigan, writing me recently about his new edition of his anthology, told me that you had revealed to him something concerning the unhappy years I spent in England. I do not know what you said, but I do not wish it ever said that I cared for or valued in any way my association with Mrs. Hyde. That sordid and disgusting and vulgar affair was of no importance to me whatsoever, and I want every trace of it blotted out now and forever. So please send along the name of your lawyer, and believe me, you will be doing me a friendly service.

Yours
John Gould

TO CONRAD AIKEN

The MacDowell Colony
Peterborough, New Hampshire
May 15, 1936

Dear Conrad,

Your letter reached me as we were traveling north from Little Rock to the MacDowell Colony at Peterborough, New Hampshire, where we expect to arrive on June 1st, and where we will stay over June and July. You can reach me by writing to that address, in case you feel like it.

Your remarks about the Hyde affair astonished me. As I recall, you have not seen me since then, nor for some time before that affair took place. Yet this Hyde woman has, according to your own account, written you a "considerable correspondence," dealing no doubt with her side in this sordid and disgusting business. I don't know what she said, but apparently she has persuaded you into believing that I was in love with her and that her behavior was beyond reproach. Both statements are falsehoods. The fact of the matter is that she indulged herself in a last fling apart from her husband, and that I would never for a moment have taken the business seriously but for the fact that before I met her, I was practically on the brink of a breakdown in nerves which had been pending for a long time before.

I don't know, as I repeat, her side of this story; but I do know that I ran the risk of a serious disease in taking up with her, and it was the thought of how awful the whole business had been that drove me back to Daisy as I did. I felt that Daisy, whatever her faults, had been preferable to this woman. And I stayed with Daisy four months before my attempt at suicide, so this woman had nothing to do with that.

I mention these facts merely to show you that the case has another angle than that you have already heard. And I mention them also because from the time I returned to America (how this woman heard of it I do not know) I have been pestered with persistent letters from her, which I was foolish enough to answer at first, telling me probably the same sort of nonsense she told you. No doubt the woman is insane; I came to that conclusion even before I heard that she had been writing you.

I now want to stop discussing this affair, and can only hope that you have not been the medium of spreading any false rumors and that you were telling me the truth when you said nothing to Sanders about it except that my marriage had been unhappy. I hope you will stick to that. I ask only that this other business be over and done with and that it does not pursue me in later life with any false notions.

I am glad to hear that you are all right and that Jerry is well. My own literary and financial position is pretty bad at the moment, but I have a chance of doing a prose book which may put me back on the map. I intend to work on it this summer. Hoping to see you sometime, I am

Yours
John Gould

TO DONALD DAVIDSON

4127 Locust Street
Kansas City, Missouri
November 5, 1937

Dear Donald Davidson,

The spirit moves me to write to you again. As you may or may not have heard, I am here now, teaching at the University of Kansas City, and going on with my writing (am contemplating a novel, if I can get enough time away from my teaching schedule).

Your excellent essays in *The Southern Review* seem to me to have made you the chief spokesman of the Southern Agrarians—and I am extremely glad and delighted that, in them, you adopt a more liberal tone than was envisaged by some of the other agrarians. Now that Ransom has definitely gone to Ohio, I feel that you and Owsley (who also seems to feel that Liberalism can be a genuine thing) and possibly Nixon are rapidly becoming the leading spokesmen of the group who want to preserve the best features of the Old South without recourse to such outrageous and bad economic and moral conditions as prevail, for example, in eastern Arkansas. I personally espoused the side of the Tenant Farmers Union in that struggle, and I am still on their side.

As regards my own philosophy, I think you will find it pretty clearly stated in my autobiography, *Life Is My Song*, which Farrar & Rinehart published in New York last month. The book has been damned without mercy by Lewis Gannet of *The Herald Tribune*, and has been ignored utterly by all the other reviewers. It states fully and honestly what I think—on politics, religion, and all other matters. I don't suppose Stokes and Stockell have even bought one copy—because I am being boycotted by the New York gang—though if the book doesn't sell, it is going to make it doubly hard for me to exist in the future. However, I had to be honest with myself in writing it. If the book fails, it just shows how completely "American literature" is controlled from New York.

I shall be teaching here up to the spring; but next April, I am going to Blue Mountain College, Mississippi, where the Dean [Charles Johnson] is a friend of mine, for one lecture, and perhaps some others. I would like to come back to Nashville again, and see you—but cannot do so on my present slender budget, unless I can get a lecture in your city, to cover the expense of making the trip.

Yours sincerely
John Gould Fletcher

Regards to Owsley and to any friends I may have left in Nashville.

TO DONALD DAVIDSON

4127 Locust Street
Kansas City, Missouri
December 17, 1937

Dear Davidson,

It was very nice of you to write me, and I want to thank you for your excellent letter. There were in it so many points I wanted to discuss with you, but heaven alone knows whether I shall ever see Nashville again, and in the meantime, I can only hope we won't lose sight of each other. I am just on the verge of going down, with my wife, to Little Rock, for the Christmas holidays. My teaching here has left me very tired; I have discovered that if I do it well, I cannot do much of anything else, and for my part, I shall be glad when the one term I was asked for, comes to an end at the close of January, and I can go back to my writing with a clear conscience.

I shall probably live on here till the spring, when I expect I shall go South again—have some tentative dates for lectures in Mississippi in April. Where I shall be next I don't know; I am yearning for a place to live in all the year around, and to get my roots in. I have wandered all over the map these last two years.

Your regret that the Agrarians are now dispersed is not altogether shared by me. As I see the situation, the group always contained elements that would tend, inevitably, to divide into a left wing and a right wing. I frankly am of the left wing element, and had decided that such was my place before the Baton Rouge conference of 1935, which I wish you had attended. Ransom and Allen are, it seems to me, on the right-wing side. Ransom I continue to like and respect; though I know nothing of the reasons which motivated him to quit Vanderbilt. I have seen his *Selected Poems* and his *Reactionary Essays*, and I agree as little now with his ideas about his own poetry, as his ideas what poetry should be. He seems to me merely one more tragic case of waste and futility, proceeding from false premises, and from a standpoint lacking in both intellectual breadth and in spiritual dignity. These may seem to you harsh words, but I can only repeat them and regret that I wasted so much time and effort in an effort to comprehend his mind, and to give him some encouragement. He is the kind of person who spoils everything he takes up—because of some lack of tolerance, magnanimity, humaneness, in himself. I have said what I think of him in my autobiography, and I must leave it at that.

I do hope that the writing of your essays will not interfere with your poetry—and that you will get out a new volume, and with it, take the place you deserve. About two weeks ago, I went on a lecture trip to Iowa City, where I met—at the State University there—a group of very interesting and vital young writers who are working under Norman Foerster. One of them was a Southerner—a Tennessean named Abbot, who remembered clearly and still believed in the Agrarian gospel—and he said that he thought it a pity you had given up poetry for polemics. With which I agreed; but maybe you haven't given it up!

I myself haven't written anything at all this year, except a dozen short poems, dealing with Mexico, which I did last winter, and sent off to *The Southern Review* (they were not accepted as Warren told me the subject was unsuitable) and fifteen better ones written this fall, which deal with the Middle-West. They went off to *The Southern Review* a month ago, and I have not heard anything—but I don't think *The Southern Review* will take them, as Warren seems to have no particular interest in anything I write—this is the third lot of poems I have sent them, and all but this bunch have come back. I don't want to impugn Warren's judgment, for I really, on the whole, like him, and like him still; but I am quite sure that I am a better poet than Howard Baker or Randall Jarrell!

Well, this is a long letter, and, as usual, all about myself. Maybe it would have been otherwise could I have had a good talk with you. I believe we at bottom would agree on most things—certainly my feeling that you on the whole, are most sympathetic of the Agrarians—which I tried to express in my autobiography—has not waned. My best wishes to you for a happy Christmas and a joyous New Year.

Yours

John Gould Fletcher

TO HENRY SEIDEL CANBY

4127 Locust Street
Kansas City, Missouri
[January ? 1938]

To the Editors
Saturday Review of Literature

Sir,

No one need possibly cavil at Mr. Bernard De Voto's admiration for the poetry of Mr. Robert Frost. It is both fine and generous. But when that admiration leads Mr. De Voto to proclaim that Mr. Frost's poetry is the "highest achievement" of its period, and that Mr. Frost is the "finest American poet, living or dead," those with some interest in American poetic achievement over the space of the last quarter-century, and some respect for critical perspective, may well call a halt.

On what basis does Mr. De Voto formulate this judgment? In his article, he brings forward the following points. First, Mr. Frost writes with authority. Second, "His is the only body of poetry of this age which originates in the experience of humble people, treated with the profound respect of identification and used as the sole measure of the reality and value of all experience." Third, he is akin to Thoreau in spirit. These are the three main points Mr. De Voto makes. I shall deal with each of them in turn.

1. As regards writing with authority. Mr. Jeffers—whose range of ideas and of experience is even more limited than that of Mr. Frost—writes with even more authority. "He dominates both his materials and his methods 'til they are inseparable from each other and from his will." Yet Mr. Jeffers does not say, as Mr. Frost does, that : "Whether in tragedy or in fulfillment, life *counts*, is worthy, can be trusted, has dignity." This, however, has nothing whatever to do with the question of "authority." As regards the authority of a great, articulated, complex, and unmistakable style, Mr. Jeffers is as superior to Mr. Frost as Mr. Frost is—to Edgar Guest.

2. "His is the only body of poetry of this age which originates in the

experience of the humble people" etc. Has Mr. De Voto forgotten Carl Sandburg? Mr. Sandburg is more uneven as a writer than Mr. Frost: granted. But what about him, Mr. De Voto? Or about Mr. Masters, either?

3. Mr. Frost is akin to Thoreau in spirit. I grant this virtue—which, in fact, is a limitation. It places Mr. Frost just where he always has been—well inside New England, but outside the whole of the other United States. Long ago, Mr. De Voto praised Mr. Gilbert Seldes for saying that the great American arts could come from somewhere near to the Mississippi. What has this to do with Mr. Frost? Everything—he lacks precisely that *Further Range*—he lacks precisely what Mr. Sandburg or Mr. Masters have shown us can be done with the midwestern material.

Not only is this true, but it is true that Mr. Frost lacks his fellow New Englander's, Mr. Robinson's, insight into humanity. Mr. Frost writes well enough about Robert Frost. But Mr. Robinson's mind went, deeper.—And it serves neither American poetry, nor honesty, for Mr. De Voto to ignore this fact.

I am in agreement with Mr. De Voto's attempt to persuade the younger American poets to leave off writing like Eliot and Pound. I do not think they will gain anything by writing like Eliot or Pound, but this does not make of Mr. Frost the major poet Mr. De Voto thinks he is. Robert Frost remains a minor poet, minor by any standards we have. It may be that his work is the more perfect precisely because of that fact. If Mr. De Voto had been honest as a critic, he might as well have said so.

Yours
John Gould Fletcher

[Bernard De Voto's was a review-article, "The Critics and Robert Frost," largely a review of Richard Thornton's The Recognition of Robert Frost. *The concluding paragraph sums up De Voto's opinion that of the three greatest American poets—Whitman, Eliot, and Frost—Frost is his choice. There is no survey of major poets. Saturday Review, Jan. 1, 1938.]*

TO DONALD DAVIDSON

411 East 7th Street
Little Rock, Arkansas
Jan. 28, 1938
Written at Kansas City

Dear Davidson,

My course here is finished, and I leave about February 7 for Little Rock—my address there will be as above. I am glad to say that in my lecture on the Fugitives, I gave your work as poet the prominence it deserved;

I said, in effect, that *The Tall Men* was the *best* single long poem on American History published by *anyone of the whole American group;* and my interest in it caused several of my class (of 34, the largest class in the whole English department) to take out the copy I loaned to the Library here, and read it at length. I reread it for my course, and liked it better than ever.

I only hope that the day will someday come, when my opinion of your poetical ability will be vindicated. That day still seems a long way off. The miserable little "intellectualist" cliques that rule our critical journals hold the whip hand; and there isn't a hope in the world for an honest conception of American poetry (either Southern or Northern) as long as they have their way.

The latest, and by far the most pernicious, group of these gentry is to be found in the pages of *The Southern Review*. I believe I wrote you that I had sent Warren a group of some 16 poems which I valued highly. It has just come back with a note from Brooks which is a complete rejection.

Here is the record of what I have done for *The Southern Review*.

1. I was in Baton Rouge in the Spring of 1935, when the magazine was first started. *I was not asked to contribute,* but I circulated copies among my Arkansas friends, and tried to push the enterprise in every way I could.

2. A book was sent me for review in the second issue. I sent a review of it.

3. Late in the summer of 1935, I sent Warren a poem I valued highly. It was returned by Warren himself after three months wait. He then proposed an article on Damon's life of Amy Lowell—I did the article.

4. Throughout 1936, I kept writing Warren for further reviews. No answer. I also subscribed to the magazine.

5. Early this year, I sent ten poems—on Mexico—to Warren. He wrote that he did not like the subject.

6. This summer I sent an essay on regionalism to Warren—an essay I valued. It was returned with the remark that they had already published enough on regionalism.

7. This last fall I sent the 19 poems mentioned. All have been rejected!

My opinion of such conduct I have just expressed, in a letter to Pipkin, to which he has just replied that he can do nothing!!

I would not complain, but my name is known from one end of this country to another as one of the best American poets. Instead of taking my work, *The Southern Review* prefers the rubbish that they print—Dorothy Van Ghent—Howard Baker—Lincoln Fitzell! They are a small clique, having nothing in connection with the South that they traduce, engaged in proving only that Eliot—the New Englander—is superior to us all. Personally, this idea is not only nauseating—it doesn't even have the merit of being anything else but a cheap falsehood.

I apparently have no recourse but to accept *their* opinion. Nevertheless, my work is in every anthology of American poetry—and the work of these people is likely to molder in the pages of *The Southern Review* till doomsday!

John Gould Fletcher

[Fletcher taught at the University of Kansas City the fall semester of 1937.]

TO THOMAS MATTHEWS PEARCE

Remembrance Farm
Route 1
Roland, Arkansas
June 7, 1939

Dear Pearce,

Your letter of May 27 has taken all this time to reach me. I do not know whether you put the right address on it; anyway, the above is now my address.

Thank you very much for your congratulations on my winning the Pulitzer. It certainly has put a different aspect on life since I got it—and I don't think I could have gone on much further as I was. The prize was given me for my *Selected Poems* published last year by Farrar & Rinehart—it is never given for individual poems, but only for books. The Associated Press made me gratuitously the author of a poem I did not write, by stating publicly that I won the prize for a poem entitled *T. Fester Cohen;* which, I suppose was their way of stating that my book was called *Selected Poems*.

I hope you will win your fight to be made head of the department—and I also hope you will feel disposed to print the poems I gave you—or some of them. The summer number should be about due, now.

Charlie May likes *The Yearling* too well to appreciate your remarks, which I suppose were meant as a compliment. She has started a novel herself, today. My own effort in this direction was refused by 3 publishers this spring; it is now on the retired list, among a host of other things.

If I can get down to Pine Bluff (it's already too hot here to travel), I'll look up those names.

Yours
John Gould Fletcher

TO HORACE GREGORY

>1922 Arch Street
>Little Rock, Arkansas
>February 27, 1941

Dear Horace,

    I have been intending to write you ever since my return from Chicago ten days ago. *Hélas! les jours volent et ne retournaient jamais!* I had a good time in Chicago, and at the home of an old friend in Michigan, but the whole trip took only five days. What I am most sorry for is that I failed to see Morton Zabel. I did not know his Chicago address but looked it up in the telephone book on the day of my arrival. He was busy teaching and was unable to get in touch with me, though we had a brief telephone conversation.

    My book on Arkansas has progressed steadily and I have not time to think of anything else. I am now tackling the theme of the Years of Reconstruction following on the Civil War. What people outside the South fail to understand about it is the fact that the South is still paying, and will never cease to pay, for the course it took when it went out of the union. The thesis that the South is backward (the Nation's Number One Economic Problem) is correct, of course. But everything was done to make the South backward, and to make life difficult, for fully thirty years after 1865. Since then we have never been able to catch up, partly because we are agricultural and conservative rather than mechanical and ingenious in our outlook; partly because we were left with no practical solution to our worst problems.

    I do not agree with the thesis, recently presented again by W. J. Cash—a thesis owing its origin to H. L. Mencken and others—that the South has failed because of its religion, which is Puritanic and literal, and its temperament, which is Romantic and hedonistic! This thesis is clever but just doesn't cover all the facts. In regard to religion, this is still the "Bible Belt"; but no one thinks the Mormons are an inferior people because Joseph Smith was charlatan of genius, or dislikes the Catholics because they still endure Father Coughlin. The Southern religion—intensely evangelical and apocalyptic—was bound to be Baptist or Methodist, naturally, because the Baptists and Methodists were better at penetrating the backwoods than the more ritualistic sects. But the same thing happened elsewhere and did apparently less damage—because the South remained a backwoods region during my own boyhood, thanks to political and economic causes! And it is these I am trying to stress, in my book.

    I have sent a subscription to *Decision* as I understand their second number is out. I am wondering whether you, or Marya, have any copies of the first number of *Accent*—the little quarterly edited by Kerker Quinn, at Urbana, Illinois, (I think) that I saw in your apartment last fall. I still want to read Marya's poem in it and have lost their address and don't know where to send for a copy. Could you get me one—and also later issues? I would gladly repay you.

I finished reading Auden's "Letter to Elizabeth Mayer" with a feeling that no one quite so clever in handling octosyllabics had been seen in English verse since Butler wrote *Hudibras*. But his knowledge of the U.S. is still largely theoretical and literary, not actual. And the poem took up too much space for what it actually had to say. It could all have been said in one-third the number of pages it covered.

What is going on in New York? Someone—I don't know who—sent me a catalogue of the superb Indian show now going on at the Museum of Modern Art. Maybe it was Marya who sent it to me—I don't know. I was very glad to get it.

In Chicago, I got downtown and saw the Goyas at the Art Institute despite a blizzard raging. I came away with my early impression largely confirmed—that Goya's painting is chiefly interesting because he anticipated so many technical devices and effects that were later taken up and developed through the Impressionists and even up to Cézanne (there was one late picture there, that might have been by Cézanne!). In black-and-white he really let himself go; and the result is overwhelming. In that field, there isn't another artist like him: and it is the Goya of the *Caprichos*, the *Desastres de Guerra*, the *Tauromachia* lithographs, the *Disparates* (which are pure surrealism) who is one of the most amazing artists the world has ever seen. Had he been merely a painter and done no black-and-white work, he would not have been of the first rank.

How are you both? Do you ever hear from England now—from Bryher or any of the others? And when do your books come out?

We have some friends from the East coming down to Arkansas to visit—they arrive today—and Charlie May is out marketing for them just now. But I am sure she wants to be remembered to you both, just the same.

John

P.S. I see Norman Pearson has married. Who is the girl? I believe he was married before? Please tell me something about her.

[On February 11, 1941, Pearson had married Susan Silliman Bennett, who had two daughters by an earlier marriage.]

TO EDWIN JOHN STRINGHAM

2024 State Street
Little Rock, Arkansas
November 28, 1941

Dear Ed Stringham,

Your letter gave me great delight, inadequately expressed by this answer. In the first place, I have been needing for a long time past someone (not a writer, for writers necessarily have their own axes to grind) who is well versed in the arts, and equipped with some knowledge of form, to tell me just how to proceed with my poetry nowadays; and in the second, you have not only agreed to act as a sympathetic critic but have said some things to give me courage and more confidence in myself. For both of these I thank you.

You are quite right in saying that I am now in the third period of my poetic development. The first was the "imagist" work of *Irradiations* and *Symphonies*—represented by the first 100 pages of my *Selected Poems*. This was extremely free in form, rather lush, tropical, and romantic. This ended with the Lincoln poem written in 1916. The second period was an attempt to get greater breadth and depth—and it went on till about 1935. The Columbus poem which Gregory once told me he thought good, is about at the center of this—it was written in 1924 and some of the *South Star* material also comes from that date, or little later. In a lot of these poems I was trying for a philosophy of my own—something I think I got hints for out of Blake and Whitman and Thomas Hardy—the Columbus poem has a lot of this philosophy, and so has "In Mount Holly" (written at the end of 1926) which is now in *South Star* (but is probably less good).

After my first visit to the Colony, 1936, and with my prose autobiography out of the way, I felt sure I would have to evolve along some new track—or stop writing poetry altogether. Nothing for an artist is worse than stagnation, and inability to go further in his field. At that time (1936) every page in my *South Star* book was already written, and the book itself was only waiting for someone to publish it. When *that* was off my chest, I began to develop again. My new idea is this:—to write poems in four, five, or six contrasted movements, in the style of the *Symphonies*, but to write them as thought-pictures, rather than as mood-pictures. And "August 1940" is as far as I know, the first moderately good attempt in this direction I have made so far.

This poem, which you have now written me about—having read it in *Furioso*—is, as you say, uneven:—but when I wrote it, I was so rusty from lack of practice, I scarcely thought I could recover any sense of form at all.

In 1937, practically nothing at all. It makes me very happy that you have said that this poem of six sections, written in August, 1940, is a work of merit. I agree with you that the sections numbered I, III, V are the best. Section II is very weak; and IV is an afterthought based on VI, and in the same form, which is bad. I realize these are defects—formal and structural—and you as a musician, are just the man I wanted to point them out to me. I needed just such criticism from you as you have now given, and I am grateful to you for giving it.

Unfortunately, I could not reciprocate and take any of your compositions (or those of any other composer) and offer such valuable structural suggestions. In the meantime, this year—despite the fact that I have been engaged the whole first part of it in writing a prose book (now finished) and since August, busy in planning and building a new and permanent home, I have made two or three other attempts to fulfill the same intention I tried to fulfill in "August 1940." If, after I move to my new address (around Dec. 10th), any of these new attempts seem worth saving, I may even inflict these on you, as I did "August 1940." For what I am trying to do, seems so new and untried (to me at least) that I often think I shall never be able to accomplish anything at all in this field. I was not a philosophic or a metaphysical poet at all twenty years ago; and now I apparently have to be, if I am to be anything!

You need not therefore apologize for sending me any criticism you may care to make. Such criticism can only help me—for in your own field of music, structural weaknesses, such as you have noted on this attempt of mine, are far more easy to detect than in poetry, probably; and you have a good ear for them. My gratitude is much more deep; and I will always be grateful to you—who have worked in another field, and probably know it better than I do mine—for what you have said.

Mrs. Fletcher sends her kind regards to Mrs. Stringham.

John Gould Fletcher

TO GERALD SANDERS

Route 5, Box 435
Little Rock, Arkansas
February 2, 1942

Dear Gerald Sanders,

At last I can answer your letter of January 23rd, now that yours of the 30th has arrived! Thanks a thousand times for excellent pointers about writing for permissions on the poets Mrs. Fletcher and I are thinking about including. It was especially good of you to mention the outrageous difficulty that confronts the anthologist in the case of Emily Dickinson. I had heard before that between Little, Brown and that Bianchi woman the case was desperate. Now we are thinking of putting in Emerson instead, as you suggest. I shall also follow out your idea about Edgar Lee [Masters?]. Many thanks.

To revert to your earlier letter. It is good news to hear your anthology is finished. I am sorry, however, to learn it is hung up. It seems to me that poetry is needed now, as never before—even if it is only an escape (such as much of De la Mare, nevertheless an excellent poet) from the day-to-day grim realities of this war. I believe I wrote you that my Arkansas book, which is not poetry, is also hung up. I don't know just yet what I will do this coming year. But I mean, every chance I can get, to get back into writing poetry—even if there is no market. I have let myself get rusty in the last 5 years. I won't criticize your English inclusions. I quite agree with you that Elinor Wylie should be in, on the American side. Although you gathered, from reading my review of Benét's poem, that I despise *the woman* Elinor Wylie, I admire the poet. Despite its chill artifice, I think her poetry may outlast that of Millay, who to my mind, is much overrated. Elinor Wylie (the woman) led a thoroughly dishonest kind of a life (so did Villon, and other good poets), but Elinor Wylie the poet was a fine craftswoman, full of brilliant and extraordinary qualities. I never met her in life—but this is my judgment.

I also like John Crowe Ransom best among the present-day Southerners (would have liked Donald Davidson still better, if he had persisted, but he—alas!—did not). I have known Ransom, Tate, Davidson, Warren all personally (indeed, I stopped several days in Ransom's home—also in Tate's—some years back). Ransom's quality of humor—an ironical sort of humor—has saved him, over and over, from the metaphysical kinks that Tate is now tied up to, completely. I wish that Ransom would give us less criticism and more poetry of his best sort: "Captain Carpenter" (almost our friend, Jesus) or "Judith of Bethulia." There is an undertone of revolt in his best work, carefully concealed, that seems to me very good, if quite sardonic.

Hart Crane of course should be included, and Horace Gregory is one of the very few modern poets (he is nearly unique in this) who can write with spiritual insight and illumination about present-day problems. His M'Phail poems are marvelous—I never can have done envying the man who wrote them—they really *continue* what Eliot only *began* (but did not go on with) in his early poems. I know Gregory, too, and shall be dining with him shortly (see end of this letter). He is a remarkable person in a hundred different ways.

But best of all, I am glad you fought Nelson to a standstill, and put in E. E. Cummings—that *enfant terrible* whom I hold to be one of our very finest and most beautiful and tender poets, whenever he wants to be! Three cheers over that! I suppose Fearing, too, is necessary—though I think of him as spawned out of a tabloid by the depression. Wallace Stevens (I forget whether you included him before) seems to me better. I still sit on the fence, considerably, in regard to William Carlos Williams, and Marianne Moore—both seem only good in occasional spots, like that egg of the Anglican curate you doubtless wot of.

Here in Little Rock nothing spectacular as the insurgence of Henry the First Ford into the airplane field has taken place. We have a camp nearby, large enough for 30,000 draftees. The first bunch, after maneuvers in Louisiana last summer, moved on to the Pacific coast after Pearl Harbor. Now another large bunch is here—nice youths from northern cities—to wonder, as one of them said to me the other day, why palm trees are not growing in Arkansas as they supposed before setting out in this direction. Also, there is a shell-case works started in Jacksonville, northeast; a picric acid plant at West Marche (north-west of Little Rock), a bomb-making plant at Pine Bluff (southeast), another big army camp at Fort Smith. I have been asked to become head observer for one of a chain of aircraft observation posts to be established along the Arkansas River—which my home overlooks. I have accepted, tentatively. It appears we are going to have practice tests later on—just in case some hostile aircraft embarks on a suicidal mission of destruction from somewhere in the Gulf of Mexico and destroys the whole defense setup in these parts!

Meanwhile, I leave here (I believe I didn't write this before) by train next Friday from Memphis, to fulfill 6 lectures at Miami, Florida, and one at New Haven, Connecticut (in the midst of the Miami engagement). On the way north, I stop off in New York around 24 hours—and there will meet Horace Gregory, among others (see earlier part of letter). I hope to make enough out of this to cover those back income taxes at any rate—but I won't be here again, till the end of February. Then this correspondence can be resumed.

I quite agree with Mrs. Sanders about knitting socks and aircraft productions.

Yours
John Gould Fletcher

TO GERALD SANDERS

> Route 5 Box 435
> Little Rock, Ark.
> October 23, 1942

Dear Gerald Sanders,

    I am going to warn you at the onset that there may be something that you will dislike about this letter. It is one of those things that you as editor of an important anthology are likely to receive, and probably have received, from your contributors to this anthology: it is a complaint. You must read it as you doubtless have read the others. Having now delivered my preliminary warning, I proceed.

    I am quite seriously annoyed that you have dropped "The Wedding Ring" from representation. This poem (incidentally it is reprinted in my *Selected Poems*, which won the Pulitzer) you tell me, is too personal! Well, "The Caged Eagle," which you still include, is also personal; it is exactly how I felt back in 1911–12. And the third section of "The Grand Canyon of the Colorado," which you also include, is intensely personal, personal to the Fletcher of 1915 who wrote it. And so, too, is "The Blue Symphony."

    It is none of my business to quarrel with an editor's task. But I have wondered, for a long time past, just on what basis you included some of my poems and excluded others. Since we are personal friends, and since I value your friendship, I have never before raised this question. But this is what I think: you use several of the pages devoted to me, to poems I consider inferior. If another edition of the anthology is ever asked for, I want to be well represented in it. Here is what I think of your present selection.

    "The Caged Eagle" is representative, all right, of my early desperation which lasted from 1907 (when I left Harvard) to early 1913. But you pass by *Irradiations* without including anything but seven lines (and these not the best), and then include two fairly good poems from *Sand and Spray*, which are good enough but cover far more space. *The Blue Symphony* and *The White Symphony* follow—this is all to the good, though possibly *The White Symphony* is too long. After that, no less than seven poems from *Japanese Prints*, when one or two could have done. You have told me, personally, that *you* like these poems: to me they are simply amusing trifles, work of secondary intensity. I don't think you should have included so many, and I don't think you should have laid so much stress on this side of my work.

    There follow three poems from *The Tree of Life:*—"Faith," "In the Open Air," and "Ebb-Tide." Of these, I like "Ebb Tide" the least. It is dreadfully sentimental and altogether maundering—like your friend Masters at his worst. I should say it is the weakest poem in my whole selection, and you might well have substituted for it some of the better things in *The Tree of Life*, to advantage. For instance, "Autumnal Clouds" (which Aiken has often admired), or "The Walk in the Garden." You really should reconsider your grounds carefully, before admitting any of these poems to another edition.

Then in "Skyscrapers," "Down the Mississippi," "The Grand Canyon," "Mexican Quarter," and "Lincoln" you get back to poems I am proud to have written! However, this is followed by a hiatus which you have admitted to me more than once, in our correspondence. Not one of the "Elegies" is here, and several of them are among my best poems. What about "Elegy on An Empty Skyscraper," or "Elegy on the Building of the Washington Bridge," or "Elegy on Tintern Abbey" (which that damned ass, Untermeyer, took for an imitation of Wordsworth, whereas it is an ironic commentary on the whole Romantic movement)—or even "Elegy in a Civil War Cemetery"? Surely these poems would not have been passed over as if they didn't exist! Or what about the last Elegy of all—which reads to me like a prophecy of today!

"Lost Corner," representative of my best mood in *South Star* follows—it is a good poem, and I thank you for including it. But I still protest about the dropping of "The Wedding Ring," when other poems, inferior to it, stand, untouched, in your pages!

There, I have done; and this clears the air between us. Please keep this much in mind: that if ever, in 1950 or at any other time, another edition of your anthology appears, I will, if living, vigorously object. I have written poetry long enough to know when I am reasonably successful in accomplishing my aim. You should reconsider the entire problem, and sift each individual author, in my own case no less than in the others!

This brings me (at last) to the pleasanter part of my letter. You speak of Hodgson, and of those dreadfully bad pamphlets he has recently issued (I have seen them). The man—I have met, and talked with him—is really a tragic case. He had his moment, and it was a good moment: you have included every poem that belongs to it, every poem of his I want to ever read, or re-read, in your book. I have been told, by those who knew him better than I ever did, that for years following on his *good* period, he wrote things and destroyed them, refused to publish anything! Now, in his old age (he is 70 according to the dates in your book) he gets out these feeble pamphlets, just as bad as the worst things in *Last Blackbird*, and with even less excuse. It won't do anything but make people realize how long some poets have to survive their creative years—I suspect that Hodgson, like many others, owes his best work less to himself than to outward circumstances. Certainly these new pamphlets are utterly empty of anything worth while. They aren't worth the paper they are printed upon.

My lectures here are *not* about American poetry but about American literature as a whole, from 1776 to 1942. These 165 years have to be handled in *eight* lectures exactly: it demands a terrific amount of generalization. I might work up the notes for them into a solid volume, later; I do not know. Meanwhile, as is usually the case, these lectures have sidetracked my mind from poetry, so that the new book of poems (on which I have been working intermittently since last fall) still remains suspended, like Mahomet's coffin, between heaven and earth.

Yours,
John Gould Fletcher

[The Last Blackbird and Other Poems (1907) was Hodgson's first book.]

TO JAMES FRANKLIN LEWIS

Johnswood
Route 5, Box 435
Little Rock, Arkansas
March 29, 1943

Dear Frank Lewis,

I am dropping now the "Mr." from your name, for I have now come into closer contact with you indirectly. On the 19th of March, Mrs. Fletcher and I left for Memphis, and we stayed there a week, meeting among others Virginia Sledge (whom you mention in your letter, which I found waiting for me on my return) and Quincy Wolf, whom I have known off and on since 1927. Both of them gave me descriptions of you, which were invaluable. Also they reassured me on one point. It had worried me from the start of our correspondence that you taught chemistry and were so interested in science. Science is a subject I much respect, but it has very little to do with poetry as such (someday you and I must get together and argue this out; it's too long for a letter). Take for instance, Shelley. At the time I wrote *Irradiations,* 1913, I believed Shelley to be the greatest poet among the Romantics. But about 1916–17, *I tended increasingly to forget Shelley and to admire Wordsworth.* Now it is true that Shelley's interest in science was intense (*Prometheus Unbound* has been supposed, in one of the best books on Shelley, to be a play symbolic of the discovery of electrical power). But Wordsworth seems to me to be (at his best) a greater poet, with a richer human quality. And he was not interested in science at all.

Both Quincy Wolf and Virginia Sledge told me that your literary and poetical interests stand foremost in your life; that science to you is only secondary—a means to making a living. That is as it should be, so far as I am concerned. I am now more deeply interested than before. I also hear you had come to Arkansas College because, in the college you were at before, your attitude had been considered dangerously radical; which also interests me extremely as there *was* a time—long, long ago—when I believed that I was the only Socialist ever to spring from Arkansas. (Incidentally, I think you will find K.C.U. to be very liberal as regards political opinions.) Your left-wing sympathies no doubt are the reason why Greer is attracted to you; he is a *Socialist at heart (I prefer the older term to the more modern "Communist"),* and in his first letter to me he mentioned with respect Tolstoy.

As you can see by the above, I feel more at home with you now for these two reasons: (1) that you want to continue to develop as a poet, and (2) that you are "left-wing" by nature. One of my difficulties with Eliot, whom I knew fairly well for nearly 15 years, was his intellectual snobbery. (And the same, or worse, could be said of Yeats, about whom such a fuss has been made.) I can endure almost anything; but a snob I cannot endure for long.

You ask me in your letter (the date is the 20th–25th—our letters seem to be always crossing, and you may have written a later one) about *Conrad Aiken. From 1915 to about 1933 we were very close friends.* I have only seen him once since then, and we have drifted completely apart. His poetry I have always defended (perhaps because he was influenced much by my first style in *Irradiations* and *Symphonies*), but it has a certain monotony of effect that I fight against. His aesthetic taste is very good—and *his psychological Freudianism is at least interesting.* When he first met me, in the spring of 1915, he was very full of *Anna Hempstead Branch,* whom he had already read—and persuaded me to read. *Except for a purple sort of rhetoric, I don't think her worth reading.* Also he is a great admirer of Wallace Stevens—whom I also admire in a way, not for what he has to say, but for the way he says it. *And he never could stand Sandburg, whom I respect.* He gave up reading all poets about 1923, since "The Waste Land," and I feel pretty sure he has never looked at my latest work.

You will therefore find his anthology not only pre-Audenite but a reflection of his own personal taste, which is largely to the good. But he is, or was, *a devotee of "pure poetry"*—poetry detached from any social context. And I stopped being that, after World War Number One. My "ivory tower" was then shot from under me—Aiken's seems to have lasted, for whatever it is worth.

I must admit that for the past two or three years, I have found it difficult to read the poems printed in *Poetry.* And I feel just as you do: sometimes they now print an interesting critical article, but a good poem *never.* Healey's article I missed, and I must read it. I liked James Daly's, being done by a man I have met, and about a poet I admire—I have read the book that provoked it, too, and I agree with Daly's judgment.

Muriel Rukeyser's *Gibbs* was given me for a Christmas present. I have only had time to dip into it here and there. Concerning her *poetry, it seems to me to have a tremendous lot of energy* but also a wild disorder in it—a sort of disorderly Crane. Where Crane, however, *lived* his Bridge and his water-front saloon, and his subway, *Miss Rukeyser just fills up notebooks* about them. I find the same disorder rampant in *Gibbs*—she fails to relate Melville (a very great artist) and Adams (pretty good for a historian) and others to the *man* Gibbs—though she tries to equate his science to their striving. Her book is full, however, of flashes of insight—which mark the poet. I am going to read her more carefully, this summer, going back possibly to *Theory of Flight* (still unread by me) and some—not all—of her later work.

Incidentally, I may mention here that I have persuaded Scott Greer to take an interest in Lola Ridge, the only really good "proletarian" poet I have seen. Her work, especially *Firehead* (written after Sacco and Vanzetti were done to death) is very extraordinary; and I have spent years wondering why she is so neglected. *As she, like Miss Rukeyser, was a Jewess,* there is a similar intensity to her work—and her themes, of suffering and martyrdom and rebellion, are more humanly handled than Miss Rukeyser's generally are.

Your comparison of yourself to Byron and to Robinson is very just (though Robinson, unlike you, did not write at white heat, did a great deal of thinking beforehand, and seemed to be able to go on while his mental blood-pressure was very low). I sense the same sardonic devaluation of accepted values in your work as in Byron's and in Robinson's. Byron of course is a difficult case. No one can deny *him* the title of "great poet." But no one has caught just the same reckless devil-may-care, plus keenness of wit, and variety *despite* the academic form he used—for it is a matter of record that he personally preferred Pope (a formalist if there ever was one) to Wordsworth and Shelley! He seems to have admired Shelley the man but not the poet Shelley. I feel that maybe no one will *ever* succeed in quite reproducing Byron—I mean spiritually, for there were so many paradoxes and contradictions in the man, so much mockery and hope and despair mixed up in one bundle. I can well understand what he meant to his age and why a great man like Goethe was tremendously impressed—yet also shocked and appalled—by him. Personally, his life was far crazier than Hart Crane's—and some of that craziness got itself bedded into his work inescapably.

In your case, I cannot help feeling (though I may be mistaken about this) that it is now time for you to mitigate some of your intensity and to seek for Wordsworth's strongest trait, the "emotion recollected in tranquility." I quite agree with you that *English* poetry should avoid the *Latin* quality; and since the Imagists *did* follow certain Latin qualities, they were probably on the wrong track. *Be as Saxon as possible (as Hopkins splendidly was)*. Study Beowulf and Middle English and *that powerful, proletarian masterpiece "Piers Plowman."* But don't forget: the Latins (French, Italian, Spanish) were great masters of *form*—whatever their language. Don't forget that John Milton (though he should never be imitated, as Keats discovered) constructed two great poems *(Paradise Lost* and *Samson)* on the *Latin* model. And don't forget (though I don't see any danger of your forgetting) that the rules that apply to English poets *cannot* be made to apply to American ones. Our greatest poet, Walt Whitman, splendidly disregarded all the rules.

Your remark that I ought to scheme out a new series of poems containing the lush sensuousness of the *Irradiations* and the *Symphonies* plus the better thought-structure of the *Elegies* is perfectly true. I am going to try for that in the next two or three years. *Irradiations* and the *Symphonies* were written in 1913-15—published in 1915 and 1916. The *Elegies* were all (with one exception) written after 1918—published in 1935. The time has now arrived when I approach the problem—to construct symphonic order out of a whole host of ideas and fugitive impressions. I shall try it.

In one of your recent letters you asked me whether I minded your sending to Scott Greer the confidential letter I wrote you criticizing your work. Of course, I don't mind. Greer has, for a youth, a great deal in him. *And poetry is, by its very nature, a matter of such an individual approach, that it always takes a poet to criticize or to appreciate another poet*—my criticism was in any case, tentative, for you surely have been different—in many respects—to any other poet who came my way. I shall follow your career with interest, at Kansas City I hope, or wherever you are, from now on.

You also asked me once about *Masters*—what else he had written besides *Spoon River.* I did read *Domesday Book,* which he thinks is better; it is a novel in verse form (a difficult form to handle) and I am not sure his approach was correct. *The New Spoon River* is just as good as the old. *Poems of People* and *More People* have many of those vigorous, sharply-etched portraits which he does so well. Recently he has sent me *Invisible Landscapes,* a series which has less realism, more imaginative sweep. It contains in "The Lost Orchard" and in "The Seven Cities of America" two very powerful and strikingly original poems; and the poem "Beethoven and the King Cobra!" is a magnificent idea, maybe not so well written (his detail is sometimes weak), but infinitely greater and more overwhelming as an idea than anything attempted by Eliot, for instance. Someday this man will be done justice, when he is in his grave, probably. I long to see that day.

Yours,
John Gould Fletcher

[J. V. Healy's "Contemporary Criticism" appeared in Poetry *LXI (March 1943): 672–80, and James Daly's review of Hugh I'Anson Fausset's* Walt Whitman: Poet of Democracy *followed in the same issue on pages 687–90. "One of the best books on Shelley" was Carl Grabo's* A Newton Among Poets: Shelley's Use of Science in Prometheus Unbound *(1930).]*

TO GERALD SANDERS

Johnswood
Route 5, Box 435
Little Rock, Ark.
April 16, 1943

Dear Sanders,

Thanks for your letter. I quite appreciate the blessings of my present position, so different from yours (Dos Passos gives a very harrowing picture of the sort of thing you are up against). My chief danger here is just the opposite: I see so few people, and vegetate so much—dreaming rather than creating, planning rather than resisting—that it is quite likely I shall grow "out of date" not to say extinct like the dodo and the Tasmanian [wolf], before this war is even over. We are thinking of trying to rent this house and of going East this summer just because we have already lost so many contacts, by living here.

I quite agree with you that a long war is in prospect. We probably won't get Germany down before 1945. And then it remains to be seen whether the powers that be (U.S.S.R. and England) will help *us* to lick Japan—provided that China can keep up some sort of resistance that long. There are ominous signs that they (Russia and England) may just walk out at that point, leaving us to hold the bag of an unfinished war with Japan. I have no optimism left concerning the present situation.

I am very sorry that the Eliot difficulty has cropped up—and that the copies of C.M.P. already out, have to be recalled. Of course, I feel in that responsible, though I merely passed on to you just *what* Gregory had assured me was the fact. Your information, as you point out, came from Auden. Everybody who knew Eliot in London (and I knew him quite well from 1916–17 to 1932—when he came over here and lectured at Harvard) knew, for a fact, that the first Mrs. Eliot was a "mental case"—I don't know *why* he married her; she did not seem to me either very bright, or even physically attractive, the very first time I saw her (in 1916 or 1917). Several of his friends wondered why he went on living with her; but it was not possible, under English law, to divorce on the grounds of insanity till 1937—I think that was the date. Gregory was over there in August 1939—came back because of the war, as you did—and when I asked him (in 1940) whether he had met Eliot's wife, assured me *most positively* that he had been introduced to a young, attractive American girl, as Mrs. Eliot. Eliot himself (as an Anglo-Catholic) presumably does not want the fact known, if it is a fact; or he may simply be living with someone, not having legalized the position. I don't know, and I could not—without giving offense—write him about it. I suppose it is all right for Macmillan to withdraw the statement; but I am sorry if you were misled. And I don't think much of Eliot's attempt to fog the situation further, if the facts *are* as you stated them. Being an Anglo-Catholic (or a Roman-Catholic) is all right—I make no objections—but a marriage such as he had (it was far worse than my own earlier marriage) was simply no marriage at all. His effort to cover up a primal incompatibility went on too long, in my honest opinion—and if he *did* marry again in the end, I respect him for it, and would not care to conceal the fact, at all.

Of course, the withdrawal of a statement already printed (it is in the copy you sent me, which I mean to keep) could do you some injury—and I shan't *ever under any circumstances,* tell anyone else about *why* the edition was changed. It was partly my own fault, anyway. I am sure that Gregory did not deliberately lie to me in making his statement. He might be able, even, to find future means of verification (he has friends there in England, with whom he keeps in touch). But I agree with you, that, under the circumstances, Macmillan is *perhaps* justified. Not that I think that any publisher is ever *fully* justified!

Well, this is an unfortunate business. I hope that your speech went well. As for "saving the humanities," it seems more than ever doubtful if they can be saved. This is a civilization for robots, and those who try to modify it in the direction of humanity, or the humanities, do so at their own peril.

John Gould Fletcher

[In the third edition of Chief Modern Poets, *Sanders and Nelson had concluded the headnote to the Eliot selections with a one-sentence paragraph to the effect that Eliot had been divorced and remarried. Fletcher's copy in Special Collections at the University of Arkansas Library bears his marginal notation "Not true!" Wartime paper shortages made the withdrawal of the early copies a serious problem.]*

TO JAMES FRANKLIN LEWIS

Johnswood
Route 5, Box 435
Little Rock, Arkansas
May 14, 1943

Dear Lewis,

Your letter of May 7th has been here several days. And this morning the two books (very carefully wrapped) came back, along with *The Long March.*

I shall have to delay reading this last work till I have finished some more of my play, which now absorbs practically all my time and attention. But thank you for sending it.

Your remarks about what is to be done with the present poetry situation are interesting—they are on a topic which interests me particularly. Up to less than a year ago, I felt that the only thing to be done with those you call "the pipsqueak authorities" was just to ignore them; that poetry would probably revive, in despite of them, when the time came. This point of view was largely expressed in the article I finally did for Greer. I am not so certain, at the moment. With the coming on of the depression, some twelve years ago, most of the publishing houses frankly were not willing to take any risks in bringing out poetry—and the art ceased to be cultivated anywhere except on University campuses, and through the medium of such publishing ventures as James Decker, a New Directions, or the like. The result was (and is) a new academicism, which is now triumphant. People like John Crowe Ransom (a man I once knew, did not altogether dislike despite his dryness, but now consider hopelessly obscurantist) and Allen Tate (ditto, ditto), and Robert Penn Warren, and of course the ineffable Winters—all, from their college chairs, do their damndest to show how (1) *all* romantic poetry was wrong; (2) that without "metaphysical" rules and formulae of all sorts poetry should not be written at all. Now these people, sitting in the seats of the mighty, control what once promised to be a flood (I hope, by the way, you haven't been drowned out by the other, the actual flood, of the White River). And the results, as you see, are such things as Howard Moss's essay on Crane—in *Poetry* last month. And such people are not likely to loose their hold very easily.

Personally, I am beginning to think there may be infiltration—gradually the abused romantics may come back, gradually people may come to realize that poetry can't be done with "microcalipers," to quote your letter again, but only with spirit, courage, and resource. I believe another five years of obscure effort may bring back American poetry into a renewal of favor. Perhaps by that time, Auden (I regret, for his sake, that he actually took the course he did) will get back to his native country—and the situation will then clear up! At least I hope so. For Auden belongs to "the enemy"!

At present—I agree with you—a real frontal attack on the embattled ranks of the critics (each with his pet "classicist," whether it is Donne or Dryden or Rochester—whom I see New Directions is now reviving) is quite impossible. One would have to do so much spade-work, also one would have to get the Universities won over, and one would have to discover two or three fairly new major poets who had the same analytic faculty you speak of as being in Auden, and yet at the same time an even greater facility in form—and all that is quite out of the question. I can't do it at my age; and I don't think you can. The utmost, at the moment, one can do is to recognize that fact that the really good poets (and there are still a decent number) are always "classic" in the final and human sense of being freshly readable, full of sap. This, no doubt, applies to Ruth Lechlitner—whom you mention—but whom I have not read at all. It also applies to Rukeyser at her best, whom you did mention earlier. Talent isn't by any means altogether destroyed, even though all the Winterses in the world do their damndest to destroy it.

I have recently read through Eliot's latest: *The Four Quartets*. Pretty dreary and pretty narrow—and yet—from the present-day English point of view—as good as can be expected from one who (according to Matthiessen) is the only great poet of this age! For the life of me, it seems that all this modern version of "classicism" works by sheer exclusion of everything important—Eliot literally writes about nothing now except theology, as if that were everything in life! An awful narrowing down of the field, till it seems there is no more fresh air to breathe than there is under a glass bell-jar. I certainly expect nothing more from Eliot for the rest of his days.

The dramatic *opus* on which I am working is by no means my first. *I have already written (but not published) some five or six full length plays*—all with some kinship to poetry—for it seems to me that a thorough grounding in poetry should lead somewhere to dramatic work—though under present day conditions, the dramatic problem is acute. This present attempt is a one-act affair, not overlong, and I am hoping—by hook or crook—to get what I have never yet had—a real stage production, even if only by amateurs. I resolved many years ago never to publish a play (though I have wanted to write them) unless I had an actual stage performance to my credit. This vow has been kept religiously.

As I suppose you will be pushing off the end of this month for K.C., I enclose the letter for Benton. I hope you find him at home—I understand he has (with characteristic energy) been doing a lot of traveling recently, painting life in the Army camps.

Yours
Fletcher

P.S. I am very glad that your reading of "The Shadow," an early—1913 or 1914—Amy Lowell poem gave you what is undoubtedly the real clue to her personality. As you say, she struggled for unattainable perfection of beauty—(those strange watches in the poem!), struggled against the barriers of her physical person (if she had not been unfortunately too fat from young womanhood on, she would undoubtedly have attracted *many* men, for her *face* was regally handsome and her manner charming), struggled *against* all the social conventions that were all her position in Boston gave her. The famous "black cigars" (really a light brown) which are all most people remember of her, were *one* aspect of her determination to be as different as possible from the Society Matron her parents and brothers and sisters expected a female Lowell to be! I am very glad you see this—it casts a flood of light on what she really was—and makes her amazing craftsmanship, which you also note, all the more extraordinary—as a part of the same *personal protest* against the cheap and the commonplace.

J. G. F.

TO FREDERIC EUGENE HAUN

Johnswood
Route 5, Box 435
Little Rock, Ark.
November 20, 1943

Dear Gene Haun,

    I arrived back here on Thursday, the 18th; and this is to let you know that I am here, and that if there is anything you want very much, please let me know. Also I hope that you may be able to visit us, soon.

    Your last letter—which I have unfortunately lost—contained a long critique of T. S. Eliot. To me, Eliot's meaning is quite plain; I happen to have studied some of his sources, in both the Upanishads and the Christian mystics (St. John of the Cross and St. Theresa, as well as St. Augustine). Briefly, the position is this. All that we know of God is *negative* knowledge. Therefore we can only approach God by depriving ourselves of everything (life even). This is the negative path of salvation. Thereby we come closer to the absolute zero which is in heaven (I don't mean this as a joke). Eliot has chosen to revive this particular creed, which means and says that life itself is bad, but can only be transcended by its opposite (by complete acceptance of death). His "Four Quartets," which you criticized, means just that.

    My feeling about Eliot is not the same as yours—I don't feel he is deliberately confusing, or otherwise than clear. My feeling is that such a creed is unhuman. It is not even Christian, so far as I can discover. The only God I have ever honestly found is in human life and is the only God I know; it is a God we see only in glimpses, but one whose complete revelation is in human love (if I speak with the tongue of men and angels and have not charity, I am become as sounding brass and tinkling cymbal). [I Corinthians 13:1] Because all the churches seem to me to presume upon possessing more knowledge of God than my poor self, I prefer not to be associated with any church—I am an agnostic as regards all theological systems. But if there is a God beyond my human (and natural) insight, I don't expect to know anything about it (or him) as long as I live here on this planet. If I go on living after I die here, I may know more. But no absolute zero, no negative paths for me! I want to be *positive* in my loves and hates, my creativity. This world as I see it suffices, both for its bad and its good. The Kingdom of Heaven is here, or nowhere at all.

This is surely a lovely fall season—after a hot and dry summer. I hope sincerely you are feeling much better now. And please drop me a line, and forgive me for not answering your good letters.

Yours,
John Gould Fletcher

TO SCOTT GREER

Route 5, Box 435
Little Rock, Ark.
January 17, 1944

Dear Scott,

Your last letter, dated January 3, is still here on my desk waiting to be answered. I am sorry I did not answer it but could not do so. This year got off to a tough start for me.

I wrote you some time ago mentioning the fact that my water-supply here at the house was failing. Over a month ago I finally decided to get my well redrilled, and since then life has been a nightmare. To get anyone to do this job was a Herculean task; and when the drilling actually started, Christmas had already come and gone—we had been hauling in water in iron containers in the back of our car every day for about a solid month. The drilling was then held up by one of the biggest snowfalls I ever saw, on the 7th–9th of January, which was really a foot deep—and left us without fuel, water, or much food for a couple of days. I finally was reduced to moving into town. Finally three days ago the well was finished and now provides us with plenty of water.

During that time—in fact, ever since we got back here in November—my life has been so upset and uncertain that it has been very difficult for me to concentrate on any work. Hence my delay in writing you. I also have neglected Frank Lewis during that period—and only yesterday got around to answering a letter from him which he sent to me on New Year's Day.

I hope things will now go on with better breaks for me, at least till spring arrives. I want to get started revising that "1939" poem when I can get some other things out of the way. About the books you ask for, the only copy I have of Louis Ferdinand Céline's *Journey to the End of the Night* is the French text *(Voyage au Bout de la Nuit)*, which I picked up in Santa Fé, New Mexico, in the summer of 1933. His French is difficult, being full of Parisian *argot* (slang) expressions, and probably you could not read it. The English translation I saw and owned once, but gave it away to a friend.

Incidentally, I understand that Céline (a doctor in the Paris slums) wrote a furious book about the Jews around 1936 or 7—very anti-Semitic; and this fact has now resulted in his being one of the few French authors, probably the only good one, who was taken up by the Nazis when France collapsed. I understand that his books are still to be found on sale in Paris—which must be a ghost town by now.

I do not own, and I can't remember having read, anything by Randolph Bourne, though his mind (strongly pacifistic up to 1917, and later on violently ironic) was undoubtedly a very deep influence on Van Wyck Brooks, Waldo Frank (whom I never could bring myself to like), Paul Rosenfeld—and many of the Socialist intellectuals of the generation of 1912–1917. I believe that recently a biography of Bourne has appeared—I think I saw a review of it in a recent issue of the Book Supplement of *The N.Y. Sunday Times*.

As for James Oppenheim, I must admit that I have read quite a number of his poems during the period 1910–1925. He died sometime around then, being, as I understand, utterly disillusioned by his reception at the hands of critics and public generally. Louis Untermeyer, whom I particularly despise, trumpeted him as the greatest American poet and then completely let him down—and I understand that Oppenheim died heartbroken, practically abandoned by all his old friends. I never knew him—but I must admit that the only poem he wrote that I can recall as being good was the Randolph Bourne elegy. All the others seem to me too full of Whitman optimism, which can't be recovered any longer. Horace Gregory wrote (on p. 114 of his *Collected Poems*, which I have) the best memorial poem on Oppenheim. (It is also in his *Chorus for Survival* book, published previously).

Aiken *is* a difficult person to take—though I believe he is at bottom a real poet and one better worth survival than Eliot. His life has been one long and unceasing fight between the desire for suicide and the determination to go on living. I like his poetry—though sometimes his command over sheer melody of words gets tiresome; and one wishes for something harder and tougher.

As regards my own books. The best work I've done in my lifetime is in *Preludes and Symphonies*, in *The Black Rock*, and in *XXIV Elegies*. These are the three books I am most proud of having written. *Breakers and Granite* also has some good work in it, but suffers from the fact that it is uneven, having been worked on at two distinct periods of development. *The Tree of Life*, which Aiken, when I knew him (I haven't seen him since 1936) swore was one of my best books, has in it a fault that is also common to Aiken's poetry—

monotony of effect—too many poems on one type of theme. The best of it is in Part II of my *Selected Poems*.

I'd like you to read *The Black Rock*, which Frank Lewis discovered in Kansas City a few months ago, and wrote me very enthusiastically about. Unfortunately, the only copy I possess is a very worn-out one, marked up, and in poor shape. The book is out of print, and I don't know where I could get you a good copy. If I sent you my worn-out copy to read, would you please take good care of it, and return it to me?

Life Is My Song is also out of print, and I simply can't come by a copy (though there are copies in the Public Library here, which I might borrow for a short time, and send on to you). *Japanese Prints* wasn't an important book at all; just little scraps. *The Two Frontiers* is a book of which I happen to have an extra copy. It isn't a good book, being written under the most utterly impossible conditions, mentally and physically—but its main thesis is at least interesting. I'm sending you the extra copy I have, for you to read.

I'm also sending you (as the present to keep) a copy of the limited edn. of *Branches of Adam* published in 1926 in England. I've had two books published over there (the earlier one was *Parables* published in 1925) which never have been published in this country. Both were written under a strong Blake influence. But *Branches of Adam* is my first attempt to write a long poem—and maybe it might interest you as such.

This is about all, and covers the ground of your letter. Sometime ago, you promised me two copies of the *Crescendo* issue that contained my article on American poetry since 1912. These haven't come. Frank Lewis wrote me that he'd sent you the MSS for the next *Crescendo*—mentioning one Thomas Howells, enthusiastically. I haven't read Howells at all. Best of luck.

Yours
John Gould Fletcher

[Loius Filler's Randolph Bourne: With an Introduction by Max Lerner *appeared in 1943.]*

TO JAMES FRANKLIN LEWIS

Johnswood
Route 5, Box 435
Little Rock, Ark.
April 26, 1944

Dear Frank,

Your letter of April 20 arrived here day before yesterday. It was good to get some news of you and to learn about your position in regard to K.C.

University. You are fortunate, indeed, to have a job that will enable you to get by. Those of us who have not and whose income is fixed (mine is shrinking) are being steadily forced to more and more desperate expedients to keep themselves from being pinned to the wall and starving to death.

Yes, I know the news about Greer. *He wrote me a whole set of letters around the first to the tenth of this month,* and sent me besides a long poem, "Homage to Huitzliopochtli," *which is a masterpiece of very strange and disturbing genius.* I wrote him what I could, as I realized that he was in very deep waters and needed sympathy. As regards his conscientious objection, my own sympathy is entire on his side. However, I happen to know (I knew a few conscientious objectors from the last war) that his attitude requires supreme courage, and endurance of others' disapproval, and indifference concerning one's personal fate, to sustain. I advised him to go into the army, but under a clear objection to *combat* service—there are some who have taken this way out—they are used for hospital duty, etc. He has apparently taken a harder course—and one that will inevitably affect him in the future. Incidentally *(please don't tell him this),* in the midst of the anguish I could read from his personal letters, I received an appeal from his father begging me to "Stop him from doing what he is planning to do." I had to write to the father, asking him *please* not to disapprove too much of his son. In truth, I was tempted to quote the greatest of Jesus' parables: that of the Prodigal Son.

In the last letter I wrote Scott—except for a poem which I wrote for him and sent him about the 14th—I asked him to return my poem, "The Builders of the Bridge"—but he has not done so. Of course, I can quite well understand how his personal suffering being what it was, everything else went by the board. *The girl he lives with, Delia Kinzinger,* should, however, have tried to fulfill my request. I don't quite understand their relationship—he wanted to try and raise the cash to come here with her and spend Easter (a very dismal one it was) with us in this house, but Mrs. Fletcher's parents were visiting us at the time, and I had to refuse him. I hope to see him some day—but he may break down under the strain he has been subjected to—and *I don't think he is likely to live very long in any case.* I would like to see him, though, *because I believe he has in him more possibilities than any poet I know of since the deaths by suicide of Lindsay and Hart Crane. He is far greater than Eliot,* or *any of the Eliot following.*

If "The Builders of the Bridge" can be obtained from him, I should like to have it appear in *The University Review,* by way of acknowledgment for the poem you wrote about me. If you can't pry it loose from him, please don't bother. He will have to go his own course, now, whatever it may lead to—insanity, death, the madhouse, I don't know. Perhaps he may win through to a still greater and finer integration. I hope and pray that he does.

As regards your *founding your own magazine:* you may be somewhat surprised at my *opposing* this idea. But I do oppose it for what seems to me to be a sound reason. Unless you can get the already existing magazines up to a higher standard, one more venturesome effort in this field seems to me rather a waste of time. There are already in the field, *The Maryland Quarterly*, *The Quarterly Review* at Chapel Hill, *The New Mexico Quarterly* (possibly Swallow runs this, I don't know), Ransom's *Kenyon Review* (though that seems to have gone under at last), as well as several others you probably already have heard about. Any editor adding to this group runs up against the difficulty of assembling a list of subscribers, and the even greater difficulty of *finding paper—all the book publishers are now postponing everything but immediate best-sellers*—not to mention capable printers. And magazines such as *Crescendo* which do not meet their regular publication dates, which do not continue to publish except irregularly, are of no use to anyone at all. The road to Hell is paved with their good intentions.

I feel deeply that what is wanted is not new magazines developing fresh talent but some attempt to give the talent that undoubtedly exists some sort of reading public. Either the existing writers are going to have to find a public demand for their work somehow (and where that is going to come from, I cannot tell you) or they are going to have to walk the road sketched out by Henry Miller (whom Scott introduced me to—and who is honest—and even a great writer in spots—but who has posed the problem of the naked, moneyless individual at war with his age in an extreme form). I just don't know the answer to *that* question as I happen to be a writer without a public (or in any case, only a very limited one) myself in these days; but I feel that the thing to do is to try to build up the exciting "little reviews," not add to their number.

The trend in American literature today is away from regionalism and towards a wider internationalism promoted by the discovering of the Latin-Americas, the activities of the refugees from Hitler, etc. This leaves out in the cold the poets of the Northwest, whom you mention in connection with *Interim* as being late-comers on the stage of American regional culture—which, heaven knows, *I believe in* and tried my best to promote. But I think the counter-current towards the internationalism is going to be too strong for them! For the rest, the cry that was raised some five years ago by MacLeish in his notorious "Irresponsibles" and backed up by Brooks, that all the writers of the 'twenties were bad, has now at last overreached itself. Its latest convert, Bernard De Voto, whose *Literary Fallacy* I have just read—there is a good review of it in the current *New York Times Book Review*—simply indulges in sheer irresponsible fury leading to nonsense—there is nothing whatever in his thesis to *deny* that the best writers of America are *not* Elinor Porter, author of *Pollyanna*, and Harold Bell Wright!

I myself hope that all the alarums and excursions in American writing that I have seen come and go since 1912–13 will eventually lead to a frame of mind that will contain the best of the Oriental Buddhistic quality of self-contained calm, and *also* the best of the Occidental striving for perfections—but I see very little to justify such a hope now. Man *(homo sapiens or homo stultus)* is going to have to come to terms first with *the scientific development* that has gone on since *Newton (whom Blake hated,* and with reason) and also learn the bitter lesson that certain moral generalizations concerning our duty to our neighbors—however vague they be—are things that are *not* going to be got over in any stage of society. The only other alternative I see just now is a universal descent into anarchistic barbarism, of the super-Hitler sort. The threat of *this* seems to me so acute just now—and it is a threat that is just as terribly common in America as anywhere else—that I cannot, if I am to preserve any honesty, *help feeling* and saying to any who may happen to be interested, that it behooves us all to do everything possible to avoid this descent into chaos and to rebuild *this vast, blundering, floundering and dubious experiment we call the United States* into something resembling common decency and respect *not* for "individual enterprise" *(there is no such thing in the first place)* but for human personality and human cultural achievement.

Yours
John

TO FREDERIC EUGENE HAUN

Johnswood
Route 5, Box 435
Little Rock, Ark.
January 18, 1945

Dear Gene Haun,

You must be wondering when—if ever—you are going to hear from me. I heard through Charlie May—as well as through Elsie Freund—that you were here around Christmas, when I was in a Memphis sanitarium trying my damndest to get cured of a nervous breakdown which came on in full force in New York. I am now perfectly all right again, and I hope you discounted the letter I wrote you, and which must have been absurd, that I would rather have you write about Ransom.

I am extremely glad and proud that you decided to do your thesis on J. G. F. rather than on Imagism in general. And I can lend you all sorts of material on J. G. F. I have run to earth—after a long, fruitless search—a copy of *Japanese Prints,* which I am sending on in a day or so. I also have a lot of other published work dealing with the Imagist movement and my own association with it. In sending these to you, I shall state what books I want returned. Have you Hughes' book, as well as Hulme's?

As regards early drafts and poems worked out in manuscript, I do *not* lend private notebooks. They probably would not be legible, anyway, and I do not possess any early notebooks. You will have to formulate your conclusions concerning me from *printed* material, solely.

Taupin's thesis that I borrowed right and left from Fontaine is *all wrong*. I never read *one word* of Fontaine's till around 1918—I first heard of him through an enthusiastic notice *he* gave *me* in *The New Republic* about that time, and the pamphlet I did on him (I have a copy of this and will send it) was written *after that*. The chief French poets who influenced me in the direction of Imagism were Baudelaire, Mallarmé, Rimbaud, Verlaine, and Verhaeren. By the way, I believe that Taupin is now at Duke or maybe that strange place, Black Mountain College. Anyway, he is wrong about me.

The principal dates to recall in regard to my poetic career are these:
1901–1913—the five early volumes
1913. Spring. *Irradiations*
1913. Fall. *Sand and Spray*
1914–1915. *The Symphonies*
1913 Fall–Spring 1916. *The Tree of Life*
I have an extra copy of this to give you.

1914 Fall–1920. *Breakers and Granite*—I believe the pieces in the original book are all dated.

1922–1923. *Parables*

1923–1924. *Branches of Adam* A failure, because of too much Blake.

1914–1934. *XXIV Elegies* Can send you a copy with dates to every poem added on, if you want it.

1934–1935. "The Story of Arkansas" in *South Star*. "My Father's Watch" in this book must have been written in England, in 1924. "In Mount Holly" was written in 1926–1927, on a return to Arkansas. Ditto "Magnolia," a sort of answer to Amy Lowell's "Lilacs." "The Christmas Tree," "The Scythe," "The Journey," "By Old River" all came from that period. So does "An Unfamiliar House" which refers to the Pike Mansion. "The Pioneers" was written at Batesville early in 1927. "Lost Corner" was written in London in 1930—"On My Father's Birthday" also. "Grandfather's Grave" comes from 1933—the fall of that year, when I had definitely returned. "Conversation with an Important Ghost" (Pike himself) and "Arkansas Red Haw" come from 1934–1935, as does "The Three Oaks," but "The Farewell" was written as early as 1927, when I thought I was going to return.

This covers the whole ground, except for *The Black Rock*. I am sending you my private copy, and if you fail to return it, I shall skin you alive. It contains the dates of these poems. All these books are out of print.

My new book, probably not out till 1946, consists of poems written since 1933. The last section of *Selected Poems* was written to Charlie May in 1935–1936.

Today is the ninth anniversary of our wedding—and I hope the 18th—if I live that long, will be as happy as this is.

I am sorry if my nervous breakdown has made it hard for you to go on with your thesis. I heard weeks ago from Howard Stebbins that enough money had been raised for you. He asked you to thank the donors—I hope you did. Am quite broke at present—thanks to the doctors' bills.

Regards to Donald Davidson—if you see him—and to Frederick Cloud.
Yours,
John Gould Fletcher

P.S. Am sending you, not only *Japanese Prints*, but *Parables, Black Rock, Breakers and Granite*. They *must be returned to me by Easter. The Tree of Life* and *XXIV Elegies* I can send. If you don't want to keep *them*, please give them to Vanderbilt.

[*In 1929 René Taupin, in* L'Influence du symbolism français sur la poésie américaine de 1910 à 1920, *had suggested that Verhaeren was the most consistent model, with Rimbaud, Corbiere, and Laforgue also influential.*]

TO SCOTT GREER

Johnswood
Route 5, Box 435
Little Rock, Ark.
March 5, 1945

Dear Scott Greer,

You must be wondering when you will hear again from me. I want to warn you that I may be unable to write to you as often as I like. Not only has this last spell of sanitarium life (sheer hell it was) reduced my strength, but the modern shock treatments they give for psychoneurotics (I am a manic-depressive, along with Michaelangelo, Blake, Dr. Samuel Johnson, Coleridge, D. H. Lawrence, and many others) have got my nerves steady only at the expense of making the arthritis I have suffered from in my back ever since that attempt at suicide back in 1932 acute. My back hurts so that I have to lie down and rest most of the time. But whatever happens, believe me I am glad I met you—and if I can be of any help to you, I will try and help.

Financially, too, we are nearly broken—Charlie May and I. And no doubt the tale of my being insane has got around so that literary jobs or any chances to earn a penny that might come my way are now withheld. This also limits me in every way. But I don't want to think about the past—but only the future. I shall be 60 next January—and shall fight on, be my time long or short.

I have managed to go through the bound typescript *The Wet Season* which you sent me. The finest poems in it are "Murals in Clay," "Desert Son," "From a Vienna Wood," "Romance Triste," "The Cathedral" (by far the best), "Commencement 1943" and some of the smaller things, like "Street Song." I have just re-read practically everything in it—to be sure that I was right. And I have compared it with Eliot (I won't read Auden—his brand of slick cleverness just sickens me). Eliot is dull, colorless, cold by comparison. As you say, he is all self-disgust, nostalgia. I knew him well for many years, and I never knew whether to dislike him or to like him. His mind is infernally good; but he is fundamentally cold as an iceberg. I now prefer Tate—whom I also knew and quarreled with. Tate has got a temperament—he is irritating, but he has got his feelings. He doesn't altogether conceal them under a cold superiority, either.

I am going to send you some books which I don't want any more and which are not likely to be in the Portland Library. This in celebration of the fact that it was about a year ago we first got in touch with each other.

I will also send you *The Wet Season* marked up in pencil if you want that. It may make *you* as mad at *me* as I was—(at the age of 27!) with Ezra Pound when I first met *him*. However, *I didn't continue* quarreling with Pound—who is probably dead by now, physically, just as he died spiritually with the *Cantos*—which nevertheless have some fine poetry in them. Pound, despite his devil, which got the better of him in the end, was yet a human being and he believed in poetry. Even the Ransoms, Tates, Eliots, Blackmurs, etc. who once believed in him will now swear off him—because he damned himself in the end. Horace Gregory (whom I like) told me in New York that he couldn't find out from anyone anything at all about Pound.

I hope you won't feel, if I criticize any of your poems, that I am trying to be superior. The events of my life have taught me to be humble. I believe you will leave your mark, with reasonable luck and some care for your health. And though you couldn't publish *The Wet Season* now (God knows, the publishing trade has now hit *absolute bottom* with this war on), someday you will bring out a book—I am sure of that. Don't despair. Hold on.

Your chief faults *are*—so far—vague rhetoric, a monotony of effect, and—at times—oversentimentalism. These faults are also in my own poetry. What you have *got*—is an ability to weave themes together, to knit the whole thing into one, and a wonderful sense of rhythm and of color that is your own. You are a real poet—not just a juggler with words. And your day will come. If you can cut clear off Tom Wolfe repetitions (a friend of his once told me that the chief fault of Wolfe was that he boasted of having written twenty thousand words in two hours and at the same time was sorry he couldn't write them in two minutes) you will go far.

I am returning herewith "For the Pines" and "Ice Stopped the Child's Mouth." Also "Apology for My Poetry," which is lots better—it is a real affirmation and it shows you are not done for. These I have scribbled on, but you can rub the scribbling off. Also "Stallion in Storm" which struck me as being more like Wolfe or Jeffers than Dean Swift. "Nocturne" struck me as largely a failure, but "Song of the Sad Hamlet" seemed to me largely a success but not so good as "Huitziopochtli" which is the greatest poem you have done.

As for "To John in His Garden"—we resumed work on this garden today after the worst and most ruinous ice-storm in 7 years, and after all wires were down over the entire Ozarks for several days—it is a poem I shall never criticize. It means too much to me that you wanted to write it and did. Coming to me when it did, it meant a great deal.

Now I must quit and lie down to rest my back. If you want anything, let me know what it is. I will send "To John in His Garden" back to you if you haven't another copy. I have forgotten what the prose book you are doing is about—my memory is now full of gaps and holes thanks to the horrors I have been through. Please write and tell me the subject again. I am afraid I destroyed some of your early letters—but I am keeping them now.

And the best of luck in the worst of times.
John

TO SCOTT GREER

657 20th Avenue
San Francisco, California
Aug. 20—(August 21, 1945) between
8 and 9:30 P.M. to be mailed on the 21st.

Dear Scott,

Your letter of the 16th has just arrived, forwarded across the Bay from Oakland. *This* is now my address—and I will be here up to Sept. 6th with the *rent paid up to then*. Charlie May (she is now in Los Angeles, expected back by the end of this month) managed to find it through her friends in San Fran. while I was lecturing at Seattle. (I enclose a program so you can see what I had to do there.)

I am glad that you saw Kenneth Gordon just after the Conference was over. I met him (also Stevens) for the first time while there. I liked very much his honest, solid Americanism, not the show-off sort but the real thing. He is a very valuable person—I do not know whether he amounts to much as a writer, but he is *good*, sound to the core. Stevens (whom I saw and talked with from 6 in the evening to 1:30 in the morning of Tuesday, August 7th), is still young, far more brittle (friends on the campus told me about *his* war experiences), but he has a nice wife in Dodie's sister, and he *should* be encouraged. I am writing *a special poem* for his next number to take the place of any part of "1939." I don't feel I can break up *that* poem—it must be published as a whole or not at all.

On Monday (the first day is my hardest at these conferences) I did not hear of the *atomic bomb* till *after* my lecture—in fact I did not see a newspaper or listen to the radio. I learned only about it early Tuesday—and I started my second lecture with a *protest against this bomb and its use* (whether used against Japanese or Germans or Russians or Americans or English or French—is quite immaterial). I delivered *my protest* with no response at all from the audience.

Gordon and I, whom I met for the first time that night, *agreed* that the secret of its manufacture could not be kept; that in another war, if one comes, there will be *no* place for the human race (just about what you have said in your letter now). The Conference (I put in hours on them) kept me running ragged, so I did not hear any other speeches; but on the evening (Wednesday) following the Press Club meeting, my host, Prof. Griffith, and I went to a novelists' Round Table discussion at which Sophus Winther, who is a Dane teaching there, and who also has written some novels, said (I quote from memory):

> Perhaps we had better stop discussing the novel and discuss the atom bomb. Science has brought humanity now to this pass, that in a few years' time we will either all wipe each other out, or learn to do without wars. Maybe humanity will now decide to turn to the artists, *not* the scientists, because artists have all along known what was in store for man if he followed materialism. If humanity won't turn to the artists for help, perhaps it is just as well that the atom bomb exists; mankind might *then* just as well be blown to pieces and commit suicide en masse.

Winther's statement simply electrified the audience. *They gave him an ovation.* At Friday's banquet he was next to me at the speaker's table, and I was immensely proud of sitting by such a man. His "moment" had been the *greatest* of all the Conference.

The next day the Seattle papers revealed that many of the Seattle churches (including Catholic and Baptist, but not the Jewish rabbi) had signed a solemn protest *against* the use of the atom bomb.

I got back to San Francisco in time for the peace-day celebrations—which started on Monday, went through Tuesday (when Japan surrendered) continued into Wednesday night, when a regular riot occurred. As I live uptown, in a very quiet section, I did not see any of them—thank goodness.

Dear Scott, the only reason I write all this to you is because I sense a very deep depression in your letter. It is something I cannot help you to shake off—you must shake it off yourself. But you are not *alone* in your feeling that maybe the jig *is* up with humanity—after World War I H. G. Wells (his early "scientific fantasy" novels are his best; containing startling predictions of the present horror; *The War of the Worlds, The Sleeper Wakes, The First Man on the Moon,* etc.) said that *history* was now "a race between Education and Catastrophe." The *Catastrophe* has come—but only in such a way that Japan *has* speedily given up; and every *responsible person* should and must know that *now or never* is our last chance. In twenty years' time there may come another war, with *both sides* using atom bombs *against each other!* Meantime, the lesson of your Cathedral (I haven't a copy, but I know it is still your greatest poem, the one I most envy you for having written) *still stands!!!*

Scott, I don't feel you have a right to feel depressed. True, you are younger in years than I am, but the spirit is truly ageless, and in a body growing more and more worn out I know I have hold of something ageless—I have lost it for periods in my life, but *this* is a period when I have found it again in full measure, heaped and running over.

You are the real heir to my own spirit, if any man ever was; and I want you to live and complete as much of my own work, as well as yours, as you can (Dodie can and *will* help; her sister showed me a photo; she is a fine-looking person). When I die, I would like you to do a final biography of me—I really believe you could almost re-live my life. Also I want you to finish your prose book, get out a book of poems, become active—*you are needed.* If you have 20 years before you, that is enough for you to show the stuff you are made of. Remember "The Song of the Swiss Guard," which you once quoted in one of your letters.

I still hope somehow to see you (maybe I can rake up enough money to get to Klamath Falls next month). I'll be sure to let you know. Don't, for goodness sake, *don't* give way to that side of your character that is unworthy of you, and of your genius (you have that gift which always torments its possessor, so that the person who has it tries to rid himself of it continually). Gordon, when I saw him, spoke of your revolutionary pacifism. *That's it! A fight, a real fight for revolutionary pacifism is what the world needs.* You are the best fighter—and though you have no money and no prospects—maybe you are the best equipped of any that I know of among the younger generation for the fight that needs a superman to wage—the fight to keep the world from committing suicide.

Yours, humbly, but with deep hope.
John

I'll send the Nietzsche poem back to you when I've read it.

TO SCOTT GREER

Johnswood
Route 5, Box 435
Little Rock, Ark.
January 11, 1946

Dear Scott,

In the last letter I wrote you I said that your Van Gogh print had arrived. As the letter I wrote you was already sealed, I noted the arrival on the back flap of the envelope; I do not know whether you ever saw it or not. I want to write to you again and thank you and Dodie for your very beautiful gift.

This portrait of Madame Roulin (the wife of the Arles postman, whom Van Gogh painted several times, and at whose house he apparently lived for a time before acquiring the famous bedroom over the corner cafe on the square, which he also painted) is one of Van Gogh's best pictures: a very beautiful thing, revealing that love and respect he always showed for simple, honest, plain people, and also a touch of his own fantasy and aspiration and idealism, especially in the handling of the background, which I suppose is wallpaper—but such wallpaper as was never seen or dreamed of by any other artist! In this picture, there is a triumphant demonstration of what an artist with a real mission to fulfill and an imagination big enough to enable him to fulfill it can do with the most ordinary things. I am having it framed and I hope to keep it always.

As regards Charlie May, to whom the picture was also sent, she asked me to tell you that she thanked you. But—*please, this is confidential*—Charlie May has not been satisfied with our marriage for the past two years. When I saw you here in Little Rock in 1944, trouble was already brewing—largely because I have never been able to learn to drive a car, while we live in the country; and she has to take time out from her work to drive one; but also we took different positions in regard to the war. I have hung on to our marriage (though my nervous breakdown in 1944 was partly due to the trouble that developed) because I have sincerely loved her; but I feel very deeply that it is at times difficult to go on. As Robert Louis Stevenson (of all people) somewhere said: "Marriage is no bed of roses; it is more frequently a battlefield"—and surely mine has been, just as D. H. Lawrence's was (I have heard all sorts of stories about how he and Frieda even threw things at each other in the violence of their quarrels). I simply don't know the remedy, or if there is one, for what seems at times to be irreconcilable differences which sometimes develop, perhaps *because* of or *in spite of the fact,* that two people love each other. Gauguin's idea of getting away from his wife's bourgeois background, and running off to Tahiti—which used rather to appeal to me during my first marriage, which was far worse than this one is—doesn't seem to me really valid.

I don't know why I write you all this. You haven't met Charlie May; and there isn't anything you *can* do about it. Besides, you are about to embark on matrimony yourself—*and I don't want to persuade you not to.* Apart from what you owe to Dodie for standing by you so bravely at a difficult time, you two seem to me very much suited to each other. And I surely wish you luck. As for me, I am past sixty—and whatever I do, the main effort of my life has already been made. So don't waste any pity on me—I don't deserve it. And don't talk about this business to anyone outside.

Both your letters of December 28 and of December 31st arrived together four days ago. I am glad you have been working towards your Baylor degree, not that it matters so much: but if you had to teach (D. H. Lawrence supported himself that way for some years; and his school book on European history—written under a pseudonym—made more money for him than his novels) you would find a degree necessary. I am glad you have read Niebuhr, whom I have also read—and who is the kind of theologian socialist—the radical kind—I can respect. And I am glad he helped you to clarify your ideas.

Both your letters were *very* interesting, Scott, and especially the last one, in which you have a truly superparagraph on art as experience—and *the experience,* rather than the formal structure of art, being really the only valid basis for criticism. I feel exactly the same way as you do about all this. I believe firmly that the only real criticism that mattered came out of appreciation (self-identification) with what the artist aimed at and did, up to the time I met Eliot in 1917–18. Then he, with his negative, ironic skeptical attitude towards all romanticism—his better command over the technique than almost anybody—and his cold, dry, analytical mind, knocked me off my perch until about 1928. As you say, the reason he developed as a critic (and his criticism is formal, verbal, logical rather than instinctive; and also it is obscenely exact) was largely because his type of mind—lacking in warmth and very conscious of its own purposes—did not permit him to be anything else. And I too have found exactly the same thing in Ransom (a college professor with a deadly sense of logic and *no* really creative drive), in Tate (who got himself mixed up and *could* have been better but posed as an American Eliot because he thought that the thing to do), in Robt. Penn Warren (really vicious at bottom). Compared to these three, a person like MacLeish—bad as he often is—seems to me to be fairly respectable; and Malcolm Cowley (he is stone-deaf and hard to talk to besides being a drunkard and a chaser after women) is fairly decent—within his limitations.

Eliot's formalism, his insistence that only *form* matters, is completely revealed by the fact that he rates *Dryden* above all English poets except Shakespeare, and possibly Milton. And Dryden was another skillful formalist, with little to say but a great deal of facility in saying it—ready to serve the side—(he switched from Cromwell to Charles II quite easily) which kept him and supported him. A bad poet—inferior in my opinion to Blake at his best, or Keats or Shelley or even Browning or Byron or Wordsworth. Eliot's influence had a great deal to do with the drying-up of American poetry after 1928—and it was because *form* was set above substance, tricks of the technique were taken for the real thing, criticism of the formal sort was set above the effort of creation.

All this is mentioned here because you are now reading Shapiro's *Essay on Rime*, which I sent you. I liked myself Shapiro's *Person, Place, and Thing*, which seemed to me one of the best first books of poetry I had seen in many years. I haven't read *V-Letter*, but was told it was not so good; but it is obvious that Shapiro, because of his Guggenheim Fellowship, his Pulitzer Prize, has been induced to feel that he is the logical successor to Auden. I found *Essay on Rime* frankly very superficial. It doesn't really and fundamentally come to grips with the subject. I note that the critics are of two minds concerning it. Matthiessen (who teaches at Harvard and is a strong Eliotite) praised it highly; Theodore Spencer (another Harvard teacher) denounced it as being forced out of Shapiro by his publishers and backers. I haven't seen the review by Aiken—but Aiken's chief weakness is that he wants to belong to the right gang, and he often placates the powers that be by truckling to them. Now you tell me that Delmore Schwartz blew up about the book and that Shapiro was goaded into answering him. Whenever two Jews quarrel, they really do quarrel masterly.

I want you to read the book—bad as it is. It is a sample of our time— and also glance through the file of back numbers of *Poetry* I sent you so you can see what wins prizes today. (I marked the prizewinners on the cover). I don't know if anything can be done to take poetry (which is a combination of unconscious striving after harmony of spirit plus conscious observation of contradictory fact) out of the hands of the slick, opportunist-minded brittle intellectuals (with their "iron turds in lavender water" to quote Patchen from your letter), and bring it back to the really heroic, the really important struggle for some sort of decency in this obscene chaos of today. Auden, with intellectual handsprings, his smart Oxford background, his verbal facility, seems to me to have been as bad an influence as Eliot. I prefer Day Lewis, who sweated out the war in England—and whose last book seems to me worth reading. Or even Spender, whom Frank Lewis preferred, though he is at times tough going. (MacNeice is mainly drivel). Altogether, these are bad times for poetry—I feel that the war just about drained me of the last of my strength in my effort to keep sane and functioning. And without tough strength, poetry is not important at all.

As for the prevailing fashionable school of Wallace Stevens, Marianne Moore, William Carlos Williams—I prefer Stevens (though he is terribly limited as regards theme, and he gets more so: he is an aesthete of aesthetes as regards his subjects, but his work does give me some pleasure). Marianne Moore is a half-crazy old maid who should never have been a poet at all. Williams has a good mind, but he got just so far and then stuck fast—at best half-a-poet, and half a hard-working and devoted doctor in the industrial slums of Paterson, New Jersey (his prose is often better than his poetry). The younger generation seem to me to be mostly badly confused in all this: I don't know what they are heading towards, but it is obvious that Hart Crane (despite his faults) had a bigger conception of poetry than any of them!

I am better now (physically at least) since I wrote you my last letter. I really would like—since I believed in it for many years, and studied so hard—to go back to poetry again and write some more (have written so very little since 1941 that seems to me any good). But as I wrote you in my last, I have now received a letter asking me to lecture at Mills College in Oakland, California, next summer; and these lectures have to be prepared—besides I have reviews to write, also, which bring me in some money. Our debts are still very much with us as I write this letter. I am taking time out from hard prose slogging to write this—because I believe you have it in you to do something better than the Shapiros or the Schwartzes or the rest of the bunch.

Gregory (whom you don't like; but the poor devil—he is not at all a well man and has had to become a galley-slave, with a wife and two children to support) did write a very poor and cheap book on Lawrence, probably because he needed the cash desperately! But all the same, Gregory is—*or was when I last saw him* at least aware that poetry exists, and is on the whole ready to do something about it. I wrote you last month that I was asking someone else to look over your *Pilgrimage* and write MacLeish about it; *the person I mentioned was not Gregory, and the person I mentioned did not even answer my letter!* Now I feel very much like putting your manuscript into an envelope and shipping it off to Gregory, asking him to use his influence with MacLeish. Or I may write to MacLeish myself stating that I have admired your work—*though this might destroy all your chances.* I do want you so much to win that prize, Scott. Apart from the fact that your work owes something to mine, I believe you are on the right track—I wish there were more like you. Would you object if I send your MS off to Gregory? He is harassed with a college job, hardly has the strength to sustain it, and may not be able even to read your work. But I want it to be published in some way.

Again, all the best, Scott. And don't forget that I have faith—strong faith—in you.

John

TO CONRAD AIKEN

Route 5, Box 435
Little Rock, Arkansas
Jan. 29, 1946

Dear Conrad,

I am writing you because I happen to have just seen (I live in the country and rarely go into town) your review of Karl Shapiro's *Essay on Rime* in *The New Republic* of last month. I do not take the paper, but read it—usually several back issues at a time—in the Little Rock Public Library. Shapiro's book I first heard discussed by your old friend Houston Peterson, who was acting as one of the chairmen to introduce the speakers at the Book Fair in Dallas, Texas, last November. I immediately obtained the book and read it at a sitting after his eulogistic recommendation of it.

In many ways I agree with your review; and in some ways I do not. The paragraphs in which you wrote concerning the Poetry Renaissance of 1912–1930, and of your own part in it, moved me to deep nostalgia. You were right in hinting, too, that Eliot—and I admire his perfection of technique as much as anyone—finished off the American poetry movement—because he has (as a young American poet, a kid of 23 or so, who had a hard time in the war, recently wrote me) really got "the mind of a ghoul." *The Four Quartets* are all wastelands all over again: and their mysticism is dreary, dead stuff.

I don't entirely agree with you about Shapiro. I have read some of his work before this *Essay* came out—and I concluded that he has a lot of talent but suffers from one bad complex: in a world as materialistic and morally rotten as this, he can't see any real place for the poet, and he "takes it out" by attacking the poet as such (one of the poems of his you used in your Random House anthology has this as theme). It is the poets who have been to blame for everything that is poor in the modern world, in *his* view; whereas, *you have only to think of what this age would have been like had there been no poets in it* to learn how squalid and horrible the last thirty years have really been.

Shapiro seems to me in many ways—though I admire his courage, his determination, and his real range of talent—rather clinical in his approach to the question of what the poet really aims at: rather like Max Nordau, whose *Degeneration* I read at Harvard, and who thought he was getting rid of modern literature by labeling it as degenerate. Or rather like W. H. Auden, who happens to be the one modern poet I now *completely mistrust*—all that so-called science, all the Freudianism masquerading as a real diagnosis of humanity's ills—all that clever and false homosexual religionism, seems to me bad. I regret that Shapiro published this *Essay* because it seems to me superficial to a degree and not really at bottom a good grapple with the subject. It is, at best, good poetic journalism. But I wonder whether you really liked it as well as you said you did?

I have been told that you have recently gone back to England. If so, I hope this letter will be forwarded to you; for among other things, I want to write and thank you, in behalf of American poetry in general, for your brave attempt to keep Pound in your Random House anthology. Now that Pound is adjudged insane and has no one at all to defend him, I feel sure that you did the right thing (and you deserve to be honored for it). He probably was insane on politics (everybody is insane on something), and I don't suppose he will ever get out and be able to run loose again. But he wasn't insane on poetry; he was sane, and we all owe him something. The comments made on his imprisonment by such harlot papers as *The Saturday Review* were too nauseating to be worth notice. All that Pound did was no worse than what is done inside the country every day. The only difference is that he did it openly (and was paid for it). It does *not* affect his position as poet one bit. If you condemn it, you must condemn us all.

The war left me horribly depressed, but now I am coming to life again. This year, sometime, I am going to have a new book out (the last poem in it was written around 1942; but I simply could not obtain a publisher) entitled *Burning Mountain*. I have scarcely written a dozen poems (most of my time is spent in reviewing, lecturing, running this place) in the last six years—my last long effort, a thing called "1939" written then and revised in 1944, is still unpublished as I write. But in the last month, for some reason too obscure for me to trace, I wrote three poems, all of them around 40 lines long! Not bad for a man now past sixty. I'm even beginning to think it might not be a bad idea to send out to various magazines. It's been ages since I last did send anything at all.

It would be nice to hear from you, and to know what you are doing. If

I can help in any way (with books or such) just let me know. And forgive me for not writing to you over so many years.

All the best, as always,
John Gould

P.S. This summer I am going out to Mills College, Oakland, California, to teach two courses in summer school: one on 20th Century American Literature and the other on 20th Century American Culture in general. I shall have ten hours of work every week, and it is a pretty stiff assignment, but it pays rather well. Think of me, my dear Conrad, as a schoolteacher in my old age!!!

J. G. F.

TO FREDERIC EUGENE HAUN

Route 5, Box 435
Little Rock, Ark.
April 3, 1946

Dear Gene Haun,

This is a letter I should have written you—in view of your interest in my work—some weeks ago. But I have been using all my energy daily in pushing on with my Mills College course of lectures. I want you to get this before you receive your degree, in any case, so I am writing in the afternoon, after working all morning.

You have asked me now several times about the "Elements" series of poems. These, as I told you, were conceived as a series in 1916 (immediately after my return to England) and I worked on them, on and off, up to 1919. In that summer, as you know, I wrote the "Gateways" series, now the first book of my *Black Rock* volume. The "Elements" were written concurrently with the war poems—title of which was "Red Harvest," but they did not refer to the war except indirectly.

The book was divided into four sections and the first group was called "Sea"—this term was used to suggest poems conceived in *exile* (I had come back to England after a year and a half of fruitful effort in the U.S.), separation, and loss. The first poem in this group was my "Black Rock" itself, written in the summer of 1917 but not published till 1920 in a magazine. The group led on to two poems, entitled "The Oarsman" and "Jason at Corinth"—both of them connected with an idea I also tried to work in:— an idea to use Greek myths or heroic legends in each section of the book.

These poems dealt with the Argonaut story—which interested me very much at the time, and which I discussed with H. D., who was also interested. I have copies of both of these poems here, and can send them to you, if you will return them.

The second group was called "Earth." The title poem here has been published. Edd Winfield Parks in his *Southern Poets*—American Book Company—1936—put it in his anthology on p. 259. It appeared in *The Yale Review* around 1920. I can send you Parks' book. The book went on with poems in which the mood of various earth-aspects was caught—such as "Rain" and "Snow" (I have copies of these), as well as "Blackberry Harvest" (which appeared in *Some Imagist Poets*, 1917) and a poem—also Greek in inspiration—about "The Sorrows of Demeter"—Demeter seeking for her daughter, Persephone. "Moonlight" and "Dawn" are here too (both in *Some Imagist Poets*, 1917).

The third section was called "Air"—and here was a poem called "Wind"—portraying the furious autumn equinox gales so common in England. I can't find a copy of this, and I am sorry. As this section dealt with even wilder manifestations of determination and revolt that the first two, somewhere along here was a long poem in four parts, called "Heroic Symphony" which I recall but cannot find a copy of. I don't know just what Greek myth was used here—probably Orpheus.

The last section dealt with "Fire"—and the background was, of course, Prometheus. I don't know whether I ever finished this group to my liking. As I told you when I last saw you, I had planned a book to contain a hundred poems—but the final manuscript had no more than around fifty. In this last section was a poem called "In the Valley of Vision"—a post-war poem, one of my very best. I am glad to say I have found a copy of this. I will send it to you, if you wish, as a sample.

One of the *war-poems*, entitled "Armies" appeared in *Some Imagist Poets*, 1917—and another, and better one, is in Untermeyer's *Modern American Poetry* to this day: "A New Heaven." In these war-poems, as in the "Elements" series, I aimed at a style which was more direct in statement (less "allusive") than in the *Symphonies* (consequently more Anglo-Saxon). I made several attempts to get the "Elements" series published—finally gave up. The last copy of my manuscript was given to the American artist, John J. A. Murphy, often mentioned in my autobiography. I gave it to him in 1926—I haven't heard from him now since 1935, and I do not know where he is.

I still think this series of poems was one of my most ambitious (and because it was less topical that the war-poems, it might have been published), but I couldn't find a publisher—and lost interest. Your interest has made me recall these details.

Please let me know whether you want to see the poems I have mentioned. As regards letters: my correspondence with Amy Lowell, covering years 1913–1923 is now in the Harvard College Library; my correspondence with Harriet Monroe covering 1914 to 1936 is in the Library of the University of Chicago. Both might perhaps be made accessible. Other manuscripts of mine are at Yale College, and in the Allbright Memorial Library, University of Buffalo.

Hoping this will help you in some way.

John Gould Fletcher

P.S. I had never read Hardy before 1916. Then I went through *The Dynasts* also all the other books. These helped to form the style used in *Elements*.

[Elements was a projected book that was not published.]

TO RAYMOND AND SARA HENDERSON HAY HOLDEN

788 South Grand Avenue
Pasadena 2, California
January 2, 1947

Dear Raymond and Sara Henderson Hay Holden,

Your letter of December 6 written on behalf of the Women's National Book Association, and addressed to Little Rock, arrived here—where I am staying up to next spring—in time for the annual Christmas rush. It is only now that I can find time to answer it as it deserves to be answered. I take up your points in order.

1. I do not believe that local organizations, such as Poetry Societies, Scribblers' Groups, etc. have any real value in furthering creative ability. There may be one or two exceptions, but for the most part these Societies are purely a waste of time. Those who belong are not actually interested in poetry as an art at all.

2. As an established poet, I feel that my association with the Imagist group was of considerably benefit to my own work. This group, you may recall, had very simple and flexible principles but was composed of a half-dozen people all interested in doing creative work. The idea that inspired the Imagists (to have a simple set of general rules, and a wide application of them) seems to have motivated the Fugitive group in Nashville; under it they did their best work. The same idea has undoubtedly inspired various college groups. It, of course, cannot be of much help to the mature artist; but it is of help to the young.

3. The serious working poet is essentially a solitary, but he should be very much aware of what other serious poets have done and are doing.

4. I do not think college courses in writing poetry are of any use. I never took any, and I do not know of a single good poet who did. At the best, they only give a certain facility in handling well-known forms. They cannot tackle the primary poetic problem, which is the fitting of the form to the substance to be expressed, a problem implicit in every good modern poet's work. The difference between work in the modern vein and in the vein of the Early Romantics or the nineteenth-century Americans or Victorians is a difference in toughness of substance. A new substance has to have a new form in order to grow into art.

Thanking you for permitting me to express my opinion of these vital and interesting questions.

I remain
Yours sincerely
John Gould Fletcher

TO CONRAD AIKEN

788 South Grand Avenue
Pasadena 2, California
February 3, 1947

Dear Conrad,

Your letter of December 6th and the copy of *The Soldier* you sent to me have been on my desk for over a month—but that month has been hectic. In the first place, I have had to correct galley and page proofs on a four-hundred-page prose book on Arkansas, which the University of North Carolina Press is publishing next May. *Second,* I have had to do a three-thousand-word essay on Poetry, 1937–1946 for a publication planned by *The Encyclopedia Britannica,* to be called "The Eventful Years." *Third,* I've done a dozen new poems in the last six months, the longest of them over two hundred lines long, entitled "Christmas at Sixty" and done around that season. They have served to break an almost continuous silence which I kept throughout the War. Altogether, I've started the New Year not with a whimper, but a bang—and I am now sixty-one, with a considerable number of age-handicaps to fight against. In the midst of all this, your very interesting letter and book were not even acknowledged, though they were read.

I've now read *The Soldier* three times; and I like it so much, that I've gone back and started to read *Brownstone Eclogues,* which I neglected previously. I think you did very wisely in seeking for a stronger "objectivism" in these poems. *The Preludes for Memnon,* [and] *Time in the Rock* were a little too vague, too dissolved in their own music. I find a virtue in hardness, which is necessary to meet this hard age.

I don't know whether you have got back to America or not, but all the news I get from England is very disquieting. It seems like the British Empire, like Jonathan Swift, is now "dying at the top" (the top being England). As this letter might go astray, I am sending it in care of Duell, Sloane and Pearce despite the fact that, as you tell me, you've had a run-in with them over your latest poem, *The Kid*. Personally, I would be glad to see *The Kid* and to tell you what I think of it. I may add that Tate (whom you mention in your letter) has no judgment worth considering (he, like all his gang, thinks Eliot the *only* good poet of the century).

As for your being out of fashion, I am in somewhat worse case than you. My last book, *The Burning Mountain*, published last July, received two reviews in New York; and about three or four scattered over the rest of the country. One of the New York reviews was quite unfavorable; and the book so far has not brought me in two hundred dollars. I still have enough money to live on, and I don't think I have any right to complain: but I know that anything I do from now on, will only exist on sufferance. Unlike you, I haven't gone into the theater (though I might try a shot at the movies, a hard choice) though I would like to take up that medium. Most of my literary earning comes now from lectures, and from prose reviewing and criticism.

What a world! Incidentally, if you are still in England, I would like to know whether my former wife is still living. As she has been drawing alimony out of my funds ever since I left in 1933, I'd like to ascertain whether the sums sent her are really being used by someone else. Her name is Florence Emily Fletcher and the last address (during the blitz) she lived at was "Arwenack," Tootswood Road, Bromley, London. Could you find out, through someone, if she is still listed in the London telephone book? I really would like to know.

I owe you a book of my own in exchange for *The Soldier* and I'll send it on to you as soon as I know your address. Meanwhile, good luck to you—and thanks very much. Your account of Paul Nash's death was extremely moving.

Yours,
John Gould

P.S. After April 14, I go back to my old address: Route 5, Box 435, Little Rock, Arkansas.

[The survey of poetry was apparently that published as "Poetry, 1937–1947," Georgia Review 1 (Summer, 1947): 153–62, a sweeping but not particularly incisive critical assessment of the poetry of the decade.]

TO JAMES SCHEVILL

788 South Grand Avenue
Pasadena 2, California
February 13, 1947

Dear James Schevill,

Your letter has come. Yes, I agree with you about Franklin Lewis. His ambition, to tackle the biggest problems of poetry in our time, in a day when most poets have resigned themselves to existing on sufferance (and not attempting the big problems) was undoubtedly his most important trait. As you say, he wrote few poems that are complete as structures throughout: but very many that have in them vivid flashes of genius. And I think he grew and developed to the end.

It may interest you to know that I am the "well-known American poet" referred to in the column conducted by J. Donald Adams, in the *New York Times Book Review* of February 9th, as having said recently that I was on the point of giving up writing all poetry. Ever since 1942 (when I first heard of Frank Lewis) this has been largely the case. The war—and its utterly unsolvable aftermath—have worked on me up to the point that I don't suppose I'll do much more for the rest of my lifetime. This, I admit, is a confession of weakness; however, I am now past sixty, and perhaps I should retire for good and all.

I am now—at last, not finding hitherto time for it—reading the Blake book by Mark Schorer. It is a very interesting, and wholly sound, argument. I quite agree with him that Blake was not a Christian mystic in the orthodox sense (as Eliot, for example, is; or Auden—in his last, and perfectly *bad*, phase—tries to be). It is good to see that Schorer has grasped the essence of William Blake, the "Liberty Boy," the rebel who—as Schorer says—had to stand trial for high treason (p. 172: I don't doubt that Blake said exactly what the two soldiers, Schofield and Cox, swore that he did), and who remained a friend to the rebels all his life. The main difference between Blake and a deist like Tom Paine was that Blake acknowledged Jesus to have been superhuman; to Blake (the visionary) the Deists were all mistaken in supposing Jesus to have been purely and solely a moral teacher: "If religion is morality, Socrates was the Savior." Blake was like D. H. Lawrence in his insistence that there was an element in life itself (he was not so explicit as Lawrence in naming that element as sex: to him it was rather, "imagination") which defies all laws of reasoning and morality. This element he pursued relentlessly. Schorer is especially good in the numerous parallels and contrasts he draws between Blake and Yeats (another mystagogue).

His book suggests other books which might be written along the same lines. It would be interesting for some critic to take up the three writers whom Schorer calls "the great primitives": in other words, Blake, Whitman, and D. H. Lawrence, and point out the kinship and the contrast between them. Schorer rarely writes a page that is not suggestive—and he has, so far (I have only read the first two hundred pages,) completely demolished the perfectly unreal figure set up by Foster Damon as the actual flesh-and-blood Blake. Whether he is as good in analyzing the Prophetic Books remains to be seen: I have myself read "Vala" (or "The Four Zoas") at least twice through, if not three times; and am fairly familiar with all the others.

Yes, I know of Bern Porter—I believe he is a great friend of Henry Miller, but I have never seen any of his publications. I shall, of course, be glad to get your book. By the way, I am wondering whether you have actually met Miller. I have, so far, failed to do so: I am wondering what are your impressions, if you did.

John Gould Fletcher

P.S. Please tell Schorer that I like his book very much.

TO SCOTT GREER

788 South Grand Avenue
Pasadena 2, California
March 14, 1947

Dear Scott,

Your very good letter of March 9 arrived here yesterday—along with the photographs which I was glad to have. Eve certainly looks like a good and contented baby. I am sure she should give you both a lot of pride and happiness.

I am sending you two photos of myself (taken in Pasadena this year) in exchange for the excellent ones you sent.

Your fine summation of Nietzsche is very good. He, or rather his ghost, controlled very much of my own thinking from the time I was at college in 1903–04 (when I first read him) up to the time of World War I; and after that, though it seemed hard, the ghost marched on; even the Soviet determination to keep and expand in power (though done for the anonymous mob rather than for the super-individual) has today a Nietzschean ring about it. The fury of repression in this minister's son accounted for a good deal that has happened in this world since he was born just over a century ago (in 1844). He was kept down in the army, in the Franco-Prussian War of 1870, because of his bad health; kept out of the job (as professor) in that insignificant little University of Basle, by his own repressed temper with the faculty, probably; kept away from women because he couldn't give away anything; kept back by Wagner (who used *everyone* for Wagner's own supreme egotism); and so he finally exploded in *Zarathustra, Antichrist, Ecce Homo*, all written at white heat and all full of the most wonderful fury of poetry—but as you say, except to saints and dancers and philosophers, all leading to the pit into which he fell headlong. However, I still am not sorry I read him; but the contrast between him and another minister's son, a very great artist like Van Gogh, is terrific. Van Gogh knew his own value as an artist—but still remained humble before his brother. Nietzsche would certainly have paid no attention to his own kin. He broke with his sister, Elizabeth (who later on created the cult in Germany which caught Hitler in the end), because she chose to marry an anti-Semite. Yet his attack on Christianity is, fundamentally, an attack on Semitism (as Pius XII has said, "We are all of us spiritually Semites"). The contradictions in his own philosophy (true chaos within him out of which *this* dancing star was born) are the most amazing things about the man!

I agree with you about Robert Lowell. I've read quite a lot of *Lord Weary's Castle* and I saw this poem "The Holy Innocent" you sent me. Quite recently, I saw still another, also in *The Nation*, entitled "Her Dead Brother," which was quite hard to read; it didn't say much more than that, in New England, family relationships get so close (witness the *Lowell* family!) that they go over into incest: which is quite true. My feeling is that Lowell's mind in this "Holy Innocents" poem attempts to jump from the oxen he saw drawing a cart in some backwoods New England town to the killing of the children by Herod—and as the connection is really arbitrary, it *remains* arbitrary. This fault spoils most of his poems for me: I fail to see the link between two very different things (his Catholicism and his pacifism, for instance. Catholicism has always been militant.) I can't see the connection between an ox and a human child in this poem. As for the "undefiled with women" business, the whole trouble with the Catholic Church today in America, since it is now run by priests—who really *are not* allowed any contacts with women (in the Middle Ages and the Renaissance, *all* priests—not the monks but the priests—had women as mistresses or as common-law wives) is that it has become so insane on the subject of *sexual purity* and *abstinence* that it is raising a brood of bullies and perverts. For example, see the conditions described—with deadly accuracy—by James T. Farrell in his best, the "Studs Lonigan" trilogy. Or just look for a moment into the Heirens case— where this son of a Catholic marriage was told by his mother that "all sex is dirty, and will give you a disease" while his father said nothing. He wound up by killing and dismembering the body of a six-year old girl (also Catholic!) in order to get an orgasm.

Incidentally, Lowell is now married, as I have learned recently, to a

Boston girl, Jean Stafford, a novelist. I feel rather sorry for her; I am sure he is likely to give any woman a bad time.

By the way, while I am on this subject, I heard the other day (from a college professor who was in the East last fall) that W. H. Auden has now turned Catholic, one of the converts made by Fulton Sheen (who seems to me as good—I have heard him on the broadcast—as *any* Catholic priest today). I wish the "Holy Roman and Apostolic Church" joy of roping in this particular cheapskate—it ends his poetry stunt, which is a good thing. At least, I hope so!

I did read Frank Waters' very fine novel, *The Man Who Killed the Deer*. His Colorado book, which I am just finishing, has some excellent and indeed, brilliant ideas in it about the influence of the environment on the men who first went there.

I want to keep the copy of *Pilgrimage Toward the Rains* you sent me. If you made a new try to get a commercial publisher, I think the symbolic *landscape* poems might have better success than the love poems. It is the subject of a constant complaint by English and Irish critics that American poetry is *not* rich in love poems. Apparently, love between man and woman (though it exists here) is a topic our own Puritan heritage doesn't let us expound upon too freely in poetry. You may do it better than most, but I believe your "landscape as symbol" idea has richer possibilities.

As I wrote you, I am planning to go East in August and September and will sound out various publishers, if I can, about the prospects.

(I had gotten this far in this letter when your MS arrived for the *Georgia Review* people. I will look these over, and send on).

Meanwhile, I enclose a sheet from a letter I have just received. You might consider *The Southwest Review* as an outlet for both poetry and prose. They pay small sums.

John

TO JAMES SCHEVILL

Johnswood
Route 5, Box 435
Little Rock, Arkansas
October 13, 1947

Dear Jim Schevill,

The first number of *Berkeley* has come, and it is remarkably good. The Anderson letters might serve to draw attention again to a man who was one of the most interesting, most generous, and most completely American writers we ever had—a Dreiser without Dreiser's acid bitterness, or Dreiser's submerged lust for power (witness *The Financier* and *The Titan*). Anderson had a soul greater than Dreiser (I still cherish the copy of *Winesburg* he gave me in London, where I first met him) and a childlike yet sublime urge to be an artist in every sense of the word. He was one of the last who were really touched and exalted by the Whitman spirit. "There was a child went forth," that marvelous poem of old Walt's, could have been spoken of Anderson. I did not know that he and your father were friends before these letters came out.

The Robert Edmond Jones article is excellent—and perfectly true. Unfortunately, neither Broadway nor Hollywood are in the least likely to help produce the Jones type of drama—combined screen-and-stage play. It is a lovely incredible dream.

Frank Lloyd Wright is—as ever—part right and part wrong. But I admire his courage, his dogged, cross-grained opposition, his obstinate devil-may-care.

Now that the first number is out, I hope I'll have the others. The five dollars I sent to Porter were for a subscription, not a donation. Although copies may be scarce, please see that I get mine.

I find I am in more agreement than I thought with you on the subject of poetry. As regards fixed forms, I understand from a friend that Allen Tate boasted that he wrote his "To Our Young Proconsuls of the Air" (and no doubt also his "Seasons of the Soul") on a pattern already established. To me, that sort of thing is horrible. I believe (contrary to such ideas of classicism) that form should be variable, shifting, controlled largely by the emotion, not the thought. The thought-element should on the contrary be fixed. (Eliot, whom I still like, seems to me excellent for development of the thought—and controls his thought element in the *Quartets* extremely well. His form varies.) As regards the degree of classical restraint to be shown, I must say that I am a romantic—though not quite so romantic as Scott Greer, whose poetry bears traces of Hart Crane, D. H. Lawrence, and Thomas Wolfe. I long ago passed my most romantic, lush phase—and try nowadays to be clear (but with a lot of interplay of sound, at least, if not sense) and flexible in form as much as I can be. My chief fault as a poet (as the critics have pointed out in my case for years) is descent into the banal commonplace (I seem unable to recognize the fault, when I get caught up in the business of putting poetry to paper) and sometimes sheer awkwardness of rhythm—I still keep a certain amount of unfortunate improvisation in my work—I can't revise, rethink, rework poems.

I could send you the first draft of "Room on the Highway," the poem you are printing (I hope) as proof of my lack of revising powers. I don't suppose anything I've ever done has been revised more than 3 times. After that, I lose interest.— "Room on the Highway" was revised very little from its first draft.

One of the reasons I like Stevens' poetry (apart from its ideas) is his remarkable power of inventing form, fitting form to the content. Williams (William Carlos, not Oscar) on the contrary, is far less resourceful in form. One reads his poetry for the sheer vividness of its language, the remarkable clarity and honesty of the man who made it: his attempt to see, taste, touch everything afresh.

The trouble with Auden (I dislike him the most of all the recent ones) is that with all his dazzling brilliance of surface, there are really *no* ideas, *no* thoughts underneath: and I fear also, not much feeling, either. He is like the story of the king's new clothes, which were actually nothing but nakedness— though everyone thought them splendid. As you say, Robert Lowell is the best of the formalist type of poet. That is because he really understands rhetoric, and its place in poetry. His style (modeled on Melville and the Bible plus Rimbaud) is superbly rhetorical. It goes Tate one better.

(Greer also is far more rhetorical than I—but you need not, should not, tell him this. It is all right—the Imagism of H. D. and the early Pound drove me away from developing in this direction.)

I liked "Five American Fantasies" because I believe that in all good art, there is a play-element (Auden overdoes this element by exhibiting his playfulness at all times). I frequently fail at this element by being too didactic, just as Jeffers fails at it by being too intensely absorbed in violence (he still apparently thinks "The Women at Point Sur" his finest poem). I think the play-element did not altogether lack a certain fundamental and compensating seriousness in the "Fantasies."

These random observations are put down as they came. An old man's garrulities, as he sits before his unlit fire, with slippers on, on a very warm October night.

Yours,
John Gould Fletcher

TO KARL SHAPIRO

Johnswood
Route 5, Box 435
Little Rock, Arkansas
November 10, 1948

Dear Karl Shapiro,

About a month ago (I have been back here from my far-Western trip since the middle of September) I noticed you had some sort of publication out about meter—I saw a review of it in *Poetry* magazine. I do not know whether the publication in question embodied your Moody lecture, which struck me as being so extraordinarily good when I read it in the columns of the same magazine. If so, I would like to have a copy. Perhaps you could tell me the price—I think Johns Hopkins must have brought it out.

I hope your summer teaching was successful. Mine was rather hard, as I am beginning to get too old to take long trips across country and to tackle such enormous classes as there are at the University of California at Los Angeles. Since I have been back here, I have been struggling to get revised and shaped up less than a dozen poems, all I have written so far this year. When one gets past sixty, it becomes an increasing burden to attempt to carry a little further along the weight of what one has already said. At least it is so, in my own case. And now that I have most of this material to my liking, I realize—more than ever before—just how little it seems to fit in with the background (as I understand it) of any of the various periodicals—either high, low, or middle-brow—in this country.

One of the few things that have pleased me in the last few months has been the award of the Nobel Prize to Eliot. I thought the Swedish Academy took the correct ground in giving him the prize on the grounds of "his remarkable pioneering in the field of modern verse," to quote my own local newspaper. That—I think you will agree—does not say that his social, political, or even religions views are the correct ones. It does say that he has done vital and abiding work in the development of new forms, and in a new type of expression. In other terms, he has discovered a new (non-Victorian) way of creating the "not-word" to use your Moody lecture terminology. And that is true though others have also done so: for example, William Carlos Williams, whose latest book, *The Clouds, Aigeltinger, Russian*, seems to me to be more convincing than much in his *Paterson*—or Wallace Stevens, though I think he suffers from limitation of subject; or Robert Lowell, who has certainly created an idiom of his own; or E. E. Cummings—though there is much in Cummings that seems to me a vast waste of time.

I regret that, while he was here, I did not get a chance of meeting Stephen Spender. He was in New Mexico, I learned, while I was at Los Angeles—but I missed meeting him. He also has his own magic, his own direction as regards language—and I thought his poem issued as a sort of farewell in *Poetry* was a very fine one. Meanwhile we have still with us Auden, whom, I am sorry to say, I simply cannot stand. Also we have the Sitwells with us this fall—and though Edith has elements of genius, there is much in that background that I do not find pleasant, either.

Eliot, however—or so the Library of Congress has informed me—is to be here, and to speak on "Edgar Poe and His Influence in France" on the 19th of November. Unfortunately, I am unable to leave my jackrabbit-hole in the Ozarks and come to Washington to hear him—though his topic has considerable interest to me. If you do attend, I would appreciate it if you could write me a letter and tell me what he said.

With every good wish, I am
Yours sincerely
John Gould Fletcher

[Karl Shapiro gave the William Vaughn Moody lecture at the University of Chicago on November 13, 1947. The lecture was published as "A Farewell to Criticism" in Poetry *LXXI (January 1948): 196–217. The poem of Stephen Spender which Fletcher regarded as a valedictory was "Tom's A-Cold," published in* Poetry *LXXIII (October 1948): 1–6.]*

TO ROBERT W. STALLMAN

Monterey Apartments
615 Ida Avenue, Fayetteville
April 4, 1949

Dear R. W. Stallman,

I've been too busy with my teaching and lecturing and coaching of students to answer your postcard of March 22. All that you sent me was some offset reprints of your articles. I wrote you very briefly on your "Note on Intentions" *(if you have another copy, I wish you would send it to me).* I believe I said that I agreed with Robert Penn Warren, that the intentions of any poem are not known till the poem is finished; but I disagree sharply with the critic (was it Wellek?) who said that a work of art is independent of its intentions. I cannot believe that is so, for the writer; it may be so for a critic (but the critic who cannot read the intentions of a work of art, in reading the work, cannot really read at all, and should not be a critic). For instance: Eliot's *Four Quartets,* considered a single work, has as its intention the relationship of time to the eternal. This relationship is stated first in terms of childhood ("Burnt Norton"), continues through early maturity ("East Coker"), to exile in early middle age ("The Dry Salvages"), to end on the purgation through pity and terror, and the vision of the future, expressed in "Little Giddings." Four aspects of the same theme seen sometimes as past, at other times as present. The main intent is thus to link the philosophy of the Bhagavad-Gita or St. John of the Cross with the temporal affairs of Eliot himself (numerous biographical references in each poem preserve the link with temporal experience) in order to portray the spiritual pilgrimage of what we might call a typical modern poet. Eliot himself may deny this intention and say that all he wished to do was to produce a set of musical variations on given themes—but the critic *must* deny this. For apart from the skillfulness with which Eliot introduces ideas *in variation,* he is obviously *not doing this alone.* Nor did he intend solely to do this.

I will try to get the University library to order your *Critiques and Essays in Criticism.* But I am only here as a guest lecturer, not as a member of the regular faculty; and am not in a position to say what the library should buy.

Dr. Carter, head of the English Dept., is quite young—not more than 35. Graduated University of Chicago, won a Folger Library Fellowship for two years afterward, then joined the War Dept. in Washington in Dept. of Cryptography; and this is actually his first teaching job! He is first-rate on Shakespeare and Milton, but has not yet made up his mind about the moderns. He also is a great enthusiast on Flaubert, as I wrote you; and has quite a knowledge of 19th century French literature to his credit.

I am just now tackling Stanley Edgar Hyman's *The Armed Vision.* I suppose you have read it already. I wonder what you think of it. I believe it is used as a textbook in some advanced courses here.

Yours,
John Gould Fletcher

TO SCOTT GREER

Monterey Apartments
615 Ida Street
Fayetteville, Arkansas
April 26, 1949

Dear Scott,

Yours of April 9 has been here for some time. Here, at this University, the academic year is already moving into its home stretch—to be at an end, thank goodness, by June. Although I have now conditioned (I hate that word) myself to bear teaching, I shall feel grateful to God when June comes, and I no longer have to do it. Though it enables me to live without going bankrupt, I look forward to the day when I won't have to do it any longer. I took it up too late in life to enjoy it; and I would far rather live the life of a beggar, and have more time to write.

I have to turn the MS of that *Anthology of Southern Poets* in by July, (and will have to postpone the delivery of the MS). I simply can't concentrate on anything beyond the grind of teaching. Because I do not have papers to mark, or grades to give out, I have been—in the intervals—doing a little more tinkering on my *King's Country* book—which has hung fire ever since the end of the war. I do hope, sometime this year, to get down to it again and to give it a good going-over. It won't bring me in any money, but it *might* be good.

As I wrote you before, I am accepting "Breughel on the Brazos" for the prospective *Anthology*—I have a copy of "The Landscape Has Voices" here. I want another, longer, and less obviously Southern and regional, poem of yours—and I think I will take "Homage to Huitzliopochtli." I will send you a check—as soon as I can. It probably won't be much—around fifty dollars, I expect. I have to get all my selections, from works that are still in copyright, in on a total expense account of three hundred dollars. Not much—seeing that I intend to quote the moderns extensively. I have seen Roethke's book—was loaned a copy by the President of this University [Lewis Webster Jones], who has met Roethke. As you say, Roethke's poems are extraordinarily moving (though one doesn't know, finally, just what they do mean). I read this book, along with *Mrs. Whittier and Other Poems* by Winfield Townley Scott (whom Gregory has mentioned to me before, as a very promising New Englander). In view of that title (John Greenleaf Whittier is one of my *abominations* among American poets) one can only say that Scott is a *professional* New Englander, in the same way as Tate is a professional Southerner. But between him and Allen Tate, I prefer *him*—for all his Yankee quality. He has caught something of the iron-and-acid method of *old* Robinson: and produces damn good poems on Woodrow *Wilson*, for instance, also *Columbus*—has an intellectual backbone to his stuff, as well as a good technical quality.

Poetry Magazine—I am still on their free list—is so utterly bad that I simply cannot read it at all. Every poem in it seems to me timid, feeble, and dead—and the "portraits of the poets" they print do not encourage anyone to believe in poetry. It is just as bad as *Partisan Review* and for the same reason. I really wish the magazine had folded up and quit in 1945—since then it has just become a morgue of half-dead nobodies.

The Library of Congress records of the readings by poets from their own works (this was Robert Lowell's project last year, when he held that job) are now out—and since I got into it, I have heard one album, sent to me free. I don't suppose these records will do much (if anything) to make people realize that poetry is still alive—but I think the project was not a bad one, and I am glad I met Robert Lowell last year, and I wish him well.

I have received *Gale*, published at Arroyo Hondo, with some of my 1939 poems in it. I was glad to get it—must send in a sub. Have been reading a good deal of Edith Sitwell's "Song of the Cold" and others of her recent things. Although I do not belong to the English country-house aristocracy at all (maybe where I do belong is just as bad), I must say that—to anyone who has read Blake and Rimbaud and Verlaine—Edith Sitwell seems to me the finest of English poets: and I sincerely hope they make her Poet Laureate of England when that driveling, slobbering old fool of a Masefield is dead.

It was really fine for her brother, Sir Osbert, to say at the end of their lectures and readings in New York, that *he would henceforth consider anyone who ran down Americans to be* his own personal enemy. That (coming from an Englishman) was grand.

Incidentally, speaking of women poets, I understand that Marya Zaturenska (Horace Gregory's wife) nearly died this last winter in New York, of pneumonia. But apparently she has finished her book on Christina Rossetti (*The Tiger's Eye* had a good chapter from it). That whole crowd around Dante Gabriel Rossetti—William Morris, whose early poems have some of the same quality in them as Rossetti's—Christina herself ("Goblin Market" is very good)—as well as the later "decadents" of the Rhymers' Club: Dowson, Lionel Johnson, etc.—are so much more poets than that hollow idol of all the college professors, *Lawn* Tennyson! I tried to knock Tennyson in my first lecture here and, of course, was slapped down for it by a professor!

There has been no witch-hunt for supposed "Communists" here at this University—as already at so many. We are very lucky to be able to escape—for a time. I am afraid that next year someone in this legislature of this State will try to tear this University apart. I don't know whether a witch-hunt is in progress in Los Angeles—but no doubt you saw what happened at the University of Washington—and I see that Robt. Hutchins, of the University of Chicago, was forced to defend himself the other day before the Illinois legislature on the usual charge of "UnAmerican activities." As if the American Legion and so-forth were the only American things that ever existed!

I do hope, Scott, that you will soon escape from the smog—as well as from the blatant and outrageous lies—of Los Angeles. You might find New Mexico not bad—although food is expensive there (not much can be raised in the desert). I believe I have been in Arroyo Hondo—those backwoods villages are all right.

John

[Neither the Anthology of Southern Poets, *which Fletcher had agreed to edit for Rinehart & Company's paperback series of Rinehart Editions, nor the* King's Country *was completed.]*

TO CHARLIE MAY FLETCHER

Saturday 28 May–
Sunday 29 May [1949]

Dearest,

I am now a member of the National Institute [of Arts and Letters]. I nearly missed getting there—way uptown—as the taxi I took was caught in a jam of traffic (everybody going out of town for Decoration Day weekend).

I arrived 15 minutes late—but was able to slip on to the platform. I received a program, but not the sash I hoped for.

I haven't much time to give you a detailed account. I sat at the back, on the left side of the stage. Bill Benét was already on his feet, giving out the list of new artists elected. A short biography of each was given in turn, and each had to rise and be applauded by the audience. I was sitting at the back, just behind Van Wyck Brooks (he turned around and gave me a handshake just before my name was called. They say he is quite deaf now) and I noticed, on my side of the stage, Marianne Moore (I sat beside her), John Marin (looking terribly old and tired), Georgia O'Keeffe (a new member), Robert Hillyer. Over on the other side were Carl Sandburg, Malcolm Cowley (he now wears a hearing aid and looks much older), Archibald MacLeish (the best looking of all), Louis Untermeyer (he sat next to Cowley, who talked to him all through. I avoided him all afternoon, and did not speak to him) and many others, including Leon Kroll (the ugliest of all) and the visiting English novelist, E. M. Forster (one of the lions).

We all sat in rows of chairs, arranged in a semi-circle around the speaker's stand—which was equipped with microphones, as the acoustics in the hall are poor—and I think some of the program was broadcast. Just close to the speaker's stand, on my side, sat Mrs. MacDowell. She had Padraic Colum (looking more of the stage Irishman than ever) and that poor, weak, feeble sap of Ridgely Torrence, on the other side of her, and Nina Maud in attendance at the back.

When Benét began calling the roll of authors, the first name he came to was that of Cowley. Cowley arose and bowed, and was applauded. Then followed Cummings. He was not there. When it came to my name, Benét referred to me as "one of the original Imagists, writer of poetry and criticism, author of a history of his native State, Arkansas"—he paused just for a moment. Probably he hadn't even seen me slip in—the last on the platform. Then he mentioned "Mr. Fletcher," and I received my diploma. I was followed by Frances Hackett (now on the Atlantic, crossing) followed by Kreymborg (to whom he referred in much more friendly terms), by Isherwood (not there), by Tate (also absent).

Igor Stravinsky was also not present—and the large audience began to show signs of restlessness. MacLeish then took over from Benét, and named the new members of the Academy (none present except Kroll). The proceedings began to seem dull to me—and Marianne Moore lamented that so few turned up.

The Institute of Arts and Letters grants proceedings followed next (Glenway Wescott was not there, and MacLeish did this job) and it was nice to see such good looking young people come up to the stage (I believe these grants are for a thousand dollars). Almost all were present to receive their awards, and the atmosphere of boredom brightened.

Then Padraic Colum (he told me later he was sailing again for Ireland—what he does *not* know about America would fill a large volume) got up, and in a thick Irish brogue, extolled Mrs. MacDowell. I simply could not hear a word he said. Mrs. MacD was then *helped to her feet* by her acolytes, Torrence and Colum, and *led* to the speaker's stand. As she spoke, she grasped the microphone mouthpiece, and though I strained my ears, I could scarcely hear anything. I *did* hear her mention the sacred name of Edwin Arlington Robinson. It was like a ghost saluting a ghost. (The audience rose when she got to the stand, as they did later for Forster, but, personally, I feel sure that Mrs. MacD is now speaking from the grave). I shook her hand after, and she couldn't say anything. Nina Maud had to ask after you.

There followed another gold medal presentation to Frederick Olmsted, an architect. He was pleasant, and I did hear what he said.

Thomas Mann's presentation came next, and MacLeish, who made it, had to get in some of his left-wing propaganda, as usual. I thought it was in poor taste. Mann was not there (Klaus Mann died a week ago in the South of France) but sent in reply a fairly dignified letter, referring to Klaus' death keeping him away.

José Ferrer, the actor, came next, and made the best speech of all—he has very fine diction. He spoke of being born in Puerto Rico, of poor parents—and of his struggles to get on the stage. He said the gold medal was an honor, not only to him, but to all the people of Puerto Rico—all of whom would celebrate because one of their countrymen had been honored under the *American flag*. He received great applause for this (thank God).

E. M. Forster's talk on "Art for Art's Sake" which followed was very good. I could hear some of it. After that, we broke up and went upstairs to the outdoor terrace (rather chilly—New York today is quite cold). On the way, a woman in glasses (I did not recognize her) paused to shake my hand, and congratulate me. It was Esther Bates. She rushed away to catch a train—but she asked after you.

On the terrace (I had given my guest tickets away to Jim Putnam, and he was the only soul there I thought I would know) a very small woman in black hat, neatly dressed, grasped my hand. I did not recognize her either. Bill Benét, rushing past like a hippopotamus in advance, had just yelled to her "Hello, Baby!" It was Frances Frost! She really was looking quite neat, and almost pretty. She asked after you, too. I talked with her for about ten minutes. She said that the children (by that first marriage) were now growing up, and after she had finished a "kid's book" (for Whittlesey House) she expected to be more free to do what she liked. I told her I still felt her poetry *was* worth while, and I could see she was pleased. She has not been in Peterborough since the disgrace, and does not hear any more from Mrs. Langley.

Jean Starr Untermeyer came next—looking very chic, quite youthful, and expensively dressed. She is now off to Paris—I suspect she may have another man in tow, though she spoke of having gall-bladder trouble, and needing an operation. I only had a few words with her, and she spoke of you (but in an insincere sort of way, as an afterthought).

Then I sighted, hobbling along, Norman Holmes Pearson. I hadn't even told him I was coming up—and he was delighted. We went off to the Yale Club, and he gave me a fine dinner—catching the 9 p.m. train back to New Haven. We just talked and talked. I am glad Norman is still on my side.

I also met (since Pearson had not met her) Georgia O'Keeffe, surrounded by her admirers—and we had a short talk. Some people I did not even know, came up and shook my hand. Jim Putnam (looking very pompous) was there, but I rather tended to snub him. And I am sure the Gregorys (they are moving back into town) are never going to forgive me for not having seen them. Horace is now dabbling with *The Tiger's Eye* crowd, which has millions of money—and I think it time to break with him, and that cat, Marya, at this point.

I think I'll stay over through the 31st—and come back on June 1st. I already have reserved plane [reservations] for tomorrow, but I believe I'd better postpone, and try and find Linscott at Random House—he is an editor there. I have now gotten over my fears of New York—and I believe I really *can* play my cards better by seeing Linscott. I don't have to be back before the 2nd, and my money *is* holding out (I drew out four hundred dollars).

Marguerite Vance and I had a telephone conversation. She was quite nice, but rather patronizing in tone. She told me that the firm is not publishing any more poetry *(nobody is)*. But she added, in the next breath, that Louise Townsend Nicholl (poetry editor there) is getting out another book of poetry next year! I am sick of these firms, where all the editors write books—and hold their jobs, just so they can. She said you need not worry, that both she and Elliott had written you. They were waiting for a report on production costs from Recca (who has been ill). The costs of producing books are still rising. And the printers promise another strike next month. But you have Dutton's still, if you want them.

I went to the Museum of Modern Art yesterday, and saw the Braque show. Today, I'll tackle the Metropolitan. This will be the last letter I write. I am really beginning to enjoy New York again (after the bad times of 1943 and 1944): I think I may even ring up the Shaflens. Robert has now a new book out (left wing, of course) about American and the Far East. I must close now, as I have a lot more to do. It has taken me more time to adjust myself again to this city, but I believe I am all right again. I certainly have been left with fears I must overcome.

Don't forget to bring along with you the *typewriter*—and *please put into the car* about three or four copies of my book, *XXIV Elegies*—I mean to give them to friends, including David Durst and Miss Parler and John Poindexter—and possibly Mrs. Lewis Webster Jones. Better give the extra key to the Temples, and tell them to look after the place. You might even work out an arrangement, whereby they can pay Buchanan while you are away.

My love to you.
John

TO KARL SHAPIRO

Johnswood
Route 5 Box 435
Little Rock, Ark.
August 17, 1949

Dear Karl Shapiro,
I have been intending to write you for several months, but have delayed doing so till all the blasting and counter-blasting of Hillyer's attack (in *SRL*) on Pound, Eliot, and the Fellows of the Congressional Library died away. You no doubt saw my letter on the subject (*SRL* July 9) which mentioned your first, and quite dignified, attitude towards the First Bollingen Award. However I noted that towards the end of the controversy, you signed the letter that the Fellows put out, protesting that you were right and that Hillyer was wrong—a judgment which I cannot accept fully. I suppose you simply did it because of the envenomed scurrility of Hillyer's mode of attack. Personally, I thought he made out his case, in the main (though I really have no use for the man) but spoilt it by revealing—completely—his own fury of embittered jealousy, that no one had thought of *him* as a possible Fellow of the Congressional Library.

I also have read your postscript to "A Farewell to Criticism," that piece you had in *Poetry* in the spring of last year. The postscript was good, a complete reply but was not so brilliant as the original Moody lecture.

As for myself, I spent the months of February, March, April, and May very actively in giving lectures on Modern American Painting (since Homer, Eakins, and Ryder) and Modern American Literature (since Dreiser and Robinson) at the University of Arkansas. I was in New York briefly at the end of May—my first visit since 1944. I returned to the University of Arkansas to start and promote an Ozark Folklore Society and to give a brief folk-festival in June on the campus of the University.

The reason why I am writing you—I recall our pleasant correspondence last year—is that I am eager to know whether you are working again, and at what. Also any news of poetry activities that may come your way might be of interest. I heard, in New York, that Robert Lowell had suffered a complete mental breakdown this last spring and was in a sanitarium. I wonder if he is any better now—since his name appeared on the final letter of the Fellows.

I am now busy with an *Anthology of Southern Poets*—from John Smith down to the present day—including both Negro and Caucasian poets—for Rinehart. As I believe you were born in Baltimore and attended the University of Virginia, I wonder whether you would not like to be in this volume. The Southern States, for my purposes, are to be Maryland, Virginia, North and South Carolina, Georgia, Florida, Alabama, Tennessee, Kentucky, Mississippi, Louisiana, Texas (at least the Eastern part) and Arkansas.

I would appreciate it if you would send me your birth-date and place, and also the chief events of your life. I have all of your books published here. Of course if you would rather *not* be listed as a Southern poet, it is up to you to say so. I will send you, later on, my selection—hoping that your fees will be low, as Rinehart is giving me very little for them.

My work on the Southern poets has led me to undertake a long essay on Sidney Lanier which is going to come out in *University of Kansas City Review* this coming fall. The essay owes a good deal to your fine *Bibliography of Modern Prosody*. My feeling is the same as yours—that Lanier went very much further into the field of "temporal" prosody, as opposed to "stress" prosody that anyone—further even than Hopkins, who unfortunately tried to reconcile the two systems. As for Lanier the poet, one has to discount his frequent lapses into sentimentality, and also his tendency to use abstractions—and possibly he may be judged as being equally sentimental by some later age than ours.

In selecting poems from Lanier for my anthology, I have begun to wonder how much of the most recent edition (the Johns Hopkins Centenary Edition) is still under copyright, apart from the Introductions and Notes. I suppose I had better either write to the Press, or to Scribner's (who published Lanier before the Press did), though maybe you could tell me something about it. I want to quote, for example, a fine poem from *Poem-Outlines* (p. 118) which was copyrighted by Scribner's in 1908. I do hope I don't have to pay a fee for it—as well as for "The Marshes of Glynn," "Sunrise," "Corn," "The Revenge of Hamish," etc.

Excuse this rather rambling letter—which I nevertheless hope you will answer. I often feel that Stephen Spender was perfectly right when he said that all American authors suffer from acute isolation—from total absence of contact with other American authors. I certainly have tended to be more solitary and detached than most since I seem to be nearly the only author active in Arkansas. And this has certainly colored (or perhaps discolored) my mind over the past sixteen years.

Please be sure in any case to send me the biographical information I want—also whatever you would care to have appear in my *Anthology of Southern Poets.*

Yours,
John Gould Fletcher

P.S. I am sorry to say that I disagreed with you about the high poetical quality of *The Pisan Cantos.* After a careful reading, I found several passages full of fine poetry, but so embedded in cloacal rubbish that I cannot (finally) do anything else but deplore Pound, or Pound's present satellites. I recall that long ages ago (according to Harriet Monroe's *Seventy Years*) he wrote to Harriet that "Fletcher was sputter, bright flash, sputter." I can honestly say that my sputter, bad as it has been, has not been quite so bad as the really outrageous filth that Pound has permitted to pass under his name. Unquestionably, he is insane.

J. G. F.

[Fletcher had discussed the Moody lecture in his letter of November 10, 1948. The anthology of Southern poets proposed by Rinehart & Company was part of a publishing boom that followed World War II: the paperback Armed Forces Editions that had been distributed during the war prepared American readers for paperbacks like the Penguin and Tauchnitz Editions long known to European readers. Sidney Lanier's Poem-Outlines *(1908) is a collection of verses, notes, and proposed subjects for poems. Fletcher's copy is now in Special Collections at the University of Arkansas. The first volume of the Centennial Edition of Lanier's works, which contained* Poem-Outlines, *appeared in 1945, so Fletcher's query about copyright shows a lack of familiarity with the subject. Fletcher's analysis of Lanier's poetry was published sooner than Fletcher anticipated: "Sidney Lanier" appeared that fall in the University of Kansas Review 16 (Winter 1949): 97–102. In 1948 Pound was awarded the first Bollingen Prize for* The Pisan Cantos, *which had been written while he awaited trial for treason in Pisa. The committee awarding the prize included Aiken, Auden, Eliot, Shapiro, Allen Tate, Robert Penn Warren, and others of like literary reputation. Robert Hillyer attacked the award on the grounds of Pound's political views in the* Saturday Review of Literature, *and was countered by a riposte in* Poetry, *"The Case Against the SRL." Pound was released in 1958 as being incompetent to stand trial.]*

TO CONRAD AIKEN

Johnswood
Route 5 Box 435
Little Rock, Ark.
August 23, 1949

Dear Conrad,

I have been intending to write you ever since the University of Georgia Press sent me a copy of *The Divine Pilgrim*—which was earlier this summer. I have been more than usually busy, and more than usually concerned with the number of things I have to do (at 63 years and 7 months!) to keep my head above water (living is now more and more difficult). We both—Charlie May and I—have taken to teaching and lecturing more and more in the last four years to keep this household of ours going—I was at the University of Arkansas from February to the end of May nearly—then flew to New York for a few days to get installed in the National Institute (I made it at last) and to see publishers, extending to the first of June. It was my first trip East in five years. I came back to the University of Arkansas, and stayed there while Charlie May taught, up to a month ago—or a little over.

In New York, I saw briefly Bob Linscott, who seems to me far less interesting than he ever was—and also saw several others. I now have a contract to do a college text-book of Southern poets from John Smith down to the present day. I am not being allowed by Rinehart much money for permissions but have listed a lot of your poems to be included in it. I enclose this list (may probably have to shorten it). I am wondering—since your books are under your own copyright—just what fees you are likely to ask. So far, Rinehart has only promised me three hundred dollars in all.

I do not include any poem later than *Preludes for Memnon* [1931] because I do not own any book of yours later than that—but I believe the Little Rock Public Library has a copy of *Brownstone Eclogues* [1941]. Owing to my financial position, I haven't bought much poetry over the last eight or nine years. I recall that many poems in *Brownstone Eclogues* seemed to me very good—and I also liked parts of *The Soldier*, of which you sent me a copy (now it seems to have been mislaid) of the English Edition.

I should appreciate it, if the enclosed list has to be cut down, if you will designate, yourself, by putting a cross (+) against them, the six or seven pieces you prefer to be represented by. Meantime, I'll see if I can run down a copy of *Brownstone Eclogues*.

The Pound-Eliot-Hillyer fiasco finally proves to me (if nothing else previously did) that poetry, and Art for Art's Sake (which E. M. Forster spoke so eloquently for, at the Institute meeting—his remarks were later in *Harper's*) has simply *no place* in this world. Personally, I think Pound would have done better to steer clear of politics altogether—and the most interesting parts of the Cantos are the least historical, the most romantic and personally legendary. I now see the Library of Congress has abolished all prizes, for all time to come. The bread line of the poets is getting large, and longer, in these days. Maybe, after all, Pound *is* better off in his insane asylum than either you or I.

I hope that you did not follow the hosts of Americans rediscovering Europe (or rather what little *is* left) this summer. It would be good to hear from you—and again, thanks for *The Divine Pilgrim*. I will read it—whenever I can find the time—right through.

Hoping you had a good summer,
Yours,
John Gould Fletcher

TO EARL MINER

> Permanent address: Route 5, Box 435
> Little Rock, Ark.
> Temporary address to Feb. 28
> Tamarack Ranch
> Tucson, Arizona
> Jan. 27, 1950

Dear Mr. Miner,

Your letter of Jan. 19 was forwarded to me here at this spot, where I am stopping for about a month.

The interest that the Imagists, back in 1910–1912, took in *haiku* did not continue since the movement itself broke up in 1916–1917, and has not since continued, except as a general influence on much modern poetry. As regards myself, I recall reading *haiku* in Lafcadio Hearn's translations (not very exact) also in Basil Hall Chamberlain's book on Japanese Poetry; also in Hans Bettege's *Die Japanische Flöte* and some other German translations; also in French (I have forgotten the name of the translator). I was also influenced at that time by the works of the Japanese poet, now dead (he died at the close of the war) Yone Noguchi, who wrote in English. (*Seen and Unseen* and *Selected Poems* are some of his works). Flint, whom you mention, had picked up the Japanese form from some French poet or other. Ezra Pound was more influenced by the Chinese than the Japanese, though his "In a Station of the Metro" has strong Japanese implications:

> The apparition of these faces in the crowd;
> Petals on a wet, black bough.

This was written, I think, early in 1913. Aldington was not influenced by haiku at all, nor was H. D. Amy Lowell, who only came in in 1914, produced "Twenty-Four Hokku as a Modern Theme" around 1920. Pound did some fine Nō play translations, based on Fenellosa, around 1920.

I do not know if you have ever seen my *Japanese Prints* (1918) volume—long since out of print. It contained several poems which attempt something close to the haiku idea. These were written from 1914 to 1916, during the time I was most close to the Imagists.

I had certainly read the Busōn haiku at the time I wrote *Irradiations*.

I do not know if you have seen *A Pepper Pod* by Kenneth Yasuda, published in 1946 by Knopf—with an introduction by me. The title refers to another poem by Busōn; and I think Mr. Yasuda (he is a Japanese-American knowing both languages) has been the one poet who has caught most of the quality of haiku. There was an earlier, around 1939, American attempt made in a book called *A Bamboo Broom* by some translator whose name [Harold Gould Henderson] I do not recall. (I am here without my books.) Mr. Yasuda's book is still in print. Also he has done some very fine *tanka* translations, published in post-war Japan. He went there after the conclusion of the war with the American occupation army.

I hope this answers your question. If there is anything else you might want to ask, let me know. I have never been in the Far East, and I am almost impelled to envy you that experience.

John Gould Fletcher

TO EARL MINER

Tamarack Ranch
411 East Lee
Tucson, Arizona
February 24 [1950]

Dear Mr. Miner,

Thank you for your letter of February 2. I am sorry, but I cannot give you the address of Frank Flint. I do not know if he is still living. But Professor Stanley Coffman, of the English Dept., University of Oklahoma, Norman, Oklahoma, has written a book on the Imagists (which I read in typescript last fall, and which the University of Oklahoma Press is publishing this year) and I gather from that book that Professor Coffman has recently been in correspondence with Flint. He may be able to furnish you the address.

It seems strange to think that of the Imagist group, Ezra Pound is now in an insane asylum; Richard Aldington, having published last year his *Collected Poems*, has now retired to somewhere in France, I think; H. D., who was knocked to pieces in the last war, spends her summers in Lugano, Italy—and her winters in Lausanne, Switzerland—and I have wandered restlessly over this whole country for the past seventeen years (since 1933—March) and have no home except in Arkansas, and am generally forgotten as a poet, in favor of W. H. Auden or someone like that! It is really a strange business.

Kenneth Yasuda (his real name is Kenichiro but he Anglicized it) happens to be a specially dear friend of mine, and I don't want to criticize him. Up to the time his—and Henderson's *Bamboo Broom* translations (I understand the Henderson book did not sell and went out of print) I was convinced that rhymeless translations of haiku were the best ones, as in Amy

Lowell's "Twenty-Four Hokku on a Modern Theme" (in one of her books). I think now that rhymed translations are the best. Yasuda has now undertaken to translate the entire Manyōshu, the first great anthology of old Japanese poetry, and the first volume of it (there are to be twelve) appeared last year in Japan. He was over there, at the end of the war, for the period of 1947–1949, as interpreter and writer, with the American Army. Did not get into the War before because as a "relocated" California-born Japanese-American, he resented the way he had been treated. Is now back in California, and I correspond with him frequently.

I should say that the influence of haiku on the Imagists was much more considerable than almost anyone has suspected. It helped them make their poems short, concise, full of direct feeling for nature. At that time, there were very few Chinese translations—James Legge (very prosaic), Herbert Giles were about all. I don't know whether you ever saw "Scented Leaves from a Chinese Jar," a series of Chinese adaptations which Pound published in his first *Des Imagistes* anthology, 1914. I believe they are also in Harriet Monroe's anthology *The New Poetry*. These adaptations, done by a middle-aged former barrister in England, Allen Upward (he later took his own life, aged past seventy), who had become an obscure author, had a great influence on both Pound and me at that time. I still think Chinese poetry has more to say than Japanese, partly because of form. I don't think haiku or the Nō plays (which both Pound and Arthur Waley, whom I also know, translated) had any influence outside the Imagist group although some of Yeats' later plays are deliberately modeled upon the Nō.

I shall be going back to Arkansas on March 12. My address will be Route 5, Box 435, Little Rock, Arkansas

John Gould Fletcher

[Coffman's book, Imagism, *did not appear until 1951.]*

CHARLIE MAY FLETCHER TO JERRY WALLACE

Rt. 5, Box 435
Little Rock, Ark.
May 17, 1950

Dear Mr. Wallace,

I know how grieved and shocked you were at the news of John's death. He was fond of you, too, as you were of him.

We were planning to go back to Tucson next winter. In fact, we had made arrangements to rent our house for a year and go first to New York and New England, and then turn West. The Arizona sun had helped him so much that he was free of pain except for brief spells. And we felt one whole winter there would make the cure permanent.

John's illness was mental—it was a recurrent malady, and few knew of it, for, while it came over him in about five-year cycles, and doctors said nothing in particular brought it on, and nothing could prevent it—but when he recovered his mind was unimpaired and as brilliant as ever. It was manic depressive. He dreaded those suicide impulses that always came with those periods. He even told the doctor, this time, to be sure his sleeping tablets were the harmless kind. And often, in sane moments he spoke with horror of these impulses. He had tried it before.

His doctor wanted to try treating him with drugs and hormones instead of putting him in a sanitarium for the shock treatments that he has formerly had. He felt John could recover better and be happier in his own home. He wanted ten days to experiment, then he would know whether John should be in a sanitarium or whether I should have someone here to help me watch over him. The tenth day was the day of his funeral.

He seemed so much better on Tuesday evening and Tuesday night. His last words before he went to sleep were "I believe the doctor is going to put me on an even keel at last." And for the first time in weeks, I felt relaxed. His sleeping tablets put him in a sound sleep. I awoke at six o'clock and looked over to see how he was. He was asleep then, and I went on back to sleep until seven-fifteen. He was seen on the highway, walking toward the lake, at six-thirty.

Whatever it was, happened in that brief half hour.

There might be some consolation if John were driven to this by pain or sorrow or worry, for we would feel at least that he had found release. But there is no consolation. John, as you know, had a way of getting these things out of his system and he never brooded. I am convinced he started out for the morning paper in the box on the highway, and some impulse stronger than himself, one he dreaded and fought against, drove him on to the lake.

We received the Holy Communion together here at Christ Church after he returned, and before his illness became apparent. I know that you will be comforted to know that.

Sincerely,
Charlie May Fletcher

CORRESPONDENTS

AIKEN, CONRAD POTTER

Took lodgings next door and regarded Fletcher as his guru when Fletcher came to Boston in 1915 to wait for Daisy to get a divorce. They began a friendship that lasted until Fletcher's death in 1950. During the thirty-five years, Fletcher was a frequent visitor to Aiken's home in Rye, and a voluminous correspondent. They shared literary problems and personality imbalances that neither felt himself capable of solving permanently.

BERGEN, HENRY

A Hoosier of Dutch descent who graduated from Yale, earned a doctorate at Munich, and then went to London to live on an independent income and edit the works of John Lydgate for the Early English Text Society. His scholarly pursuits were diluted somewhat by the distractions of Marxism and Oriental art. He helped Fletcher escape from Bedlam, but the friendship seems to have faded after Fletcher's return to America, and he is not mentioned in *Life Is My Song*.

BROOKS, VAN WYCK

Treated the Puritan isolated idealism in conflict with frontier materialism and the crippling effect of Puritan dualism in *The Ordeal of Mark Twain*. His major work was the five-volume Finders and Makers Series in which he applied his thesis to American literature down to the First World War.

CANBY, HENRY SEIDEL

Professor of English at Yale for two decades, literary editor of the *New York Post*, first editor of the *Saturday Review of Literature*, chairman of the board of the Book-of-the-Month Club, biographer of Walt Whitman and others. His several volumes of autobiography are interwoven with extensive reflections on American education, literature, and culture. He was a prominent opponent of censorship.

COURNOS, JOHN

Odessa-born, Philadelphia reared, American expatriate in England during World War II and later employed by British intelligence. He was a novelist, critic, poet, and translator. Fletcher much admired his early novels.

Damon, Samuel Foster

Poet, professor at Brown, and biographer of Blake, Chivers, and Amy Lowell.

Davidson, Donald Grady

Critic and poet of the Fugitive group to whom Fletcher felt closest because of his admiration for the leaders of the Confederacy and his opposition to centralized industrialization.

Eliot, Thomas Stearns

British poet and critic. Although Fletcher knew Eliot's poetry earlier, he first met Eliot in London in 1917 and for a decade was on friendly terms with him, contributing both money and literary works to *The Criterion*. Later, Fletcher admired Eliot's critical works but regarded his poetry as an almost satanic influence on modern writers.

Ellis, (Henry) Havelock

Editor of the Mermaid Series of early plays, and essayist and critic before the sensational or notorious *Studies in the Psychology of Sex* replaced his reputation as interpreter of Whitman, Ibsen, and Tolstoy.

Fletcher, Charlie May Hogue Loewenstein Simon

Artist, biographer, author of children's books. She became Fletcher's second wife in 1936.

Fletcher, Florence Emily (Daisy) Goold Arbuthnot

Fletcher's first wife, who divorced Malcolm Arbuthnot to marry the poet, taking two children with her.

Flint, Frank Stewart

An English member of the original Imagist group, who abandoned poetry for translation.

Greer, Scott A.

Published *Crescendo* while an undergraduate at Baylor. He was a conscientious objector and forest ranger during World War II. He later took graduate degrees at UCLA and became a distinguished sociologist and urbanologist.

GREGORY, HORACE

Poet, critic, biographer, and anthologist. His *A History of American Poetry, 1900–1940,* done in collaboration with his wife, Marya Zaturenska, did not please Fletcher.

HAUN, FREDERIC EUGENE

Planned to write a biography of Fletcher when an undergraduate at Hendrix. For his master's thesis at Vanderbilt, he began his research and collected many of Fletcher's letters. Later Fletcher withdrew his support and Haun's Fletcher papers were acquired by the University of Arkansas after four decades.

HAY, SARA HENDERSON (HOLDEN)

Pittsburgh poet best known for *Story Hour,* a satiric treatment of fairy tales.

HOLDEN, RAYMOND

Novelist, poet, writer of mystery stories. At one time he was the husband of Sara Henderson Hay.

HUGHES, GLENN ARTHUR

Rhodes scholar, professor of English at the University of Washington, historian of the American theater whose *Imagism and the Imagists* (1931) is one of the first major studies of the movement.

LEWIS, JAMES FRANKLIN

Professor of chemistry at Arkansas College at Batesville. Fletcher advised, encouraged, and praised him. He died at the age of forty shortly after moving to the University of Kansas City.

LINSCOTT, ROBERT NEWTON

Houghton Mifflin editor and early enthusiastic publisher of Fletcher's poetry. His esteem lessened as less poetry was published.

Lowell, Amy

Leading member of the Imagist school. Fletcher was introduced to Lowell by Pound in 1913 and became her ally in the Imagist movement after Pound became a Vorticist. In 1917 Fletcher felt that Lowell had not supported his submission of a manuscript to Robert Linscott, and there was a gradual estrangement that lasted until her death.

Miner, Earl Roy

A graduate student at Minnesota. Later he was a distinguished professor at UCLA, Princeton, Columbia, and elsewhere.

Monroe, Harriet

Poet, playwright, and biographer. She founded *Poetry: A Magazine of Verse* in October 1912. A landmark in the poetic renaissance, *Poetry* printed Pound, Yeats, HD, Amy Lowell, Lindsay, Aldington, and William Carlos Williams its first year. Subsequently, *Poetry* became the arbiter of American poetry. In 1917 with Alice Corbin Henderson, she published *The New Poetry*, another landmark. Her own poetry is less interesting than her autobiography, *A Poet's Life*.

Mumford, Lewis

Futurologist disciple of Patrick Geddes and founding member of the Regional Planning Association of America. His thesis, which Fletcher found congenial, was that man should realize his obligation in a technical and scientific world to utilize his infinite resources in creating a better life.

Owsley, Frank Lawrence

Vanderbilt historian known chiefly for *King Cotton Diplomacy* (1934). He was one of the most determined apologists for the old South.

Pearce, Thomas Matthews

Chairman of the department of English at the University of New Mexico, biographer of Mary Austin, and editor of *The New Mexico Quarterly*.

Sanders, Gerald DeWitt

Head of the English department at Michigan State Normal College at Ypsilanti and coeditor with John Herbert Nelson of the popular *Chief Modern Poets of England and America*.

Schevill, James Erwin

After Harvard and military service wrote poetry and took part in the literary scene in San Francisco before he began teaching at San Francisco State. He later moved to Brown.

Shapiro, Karl

Won the Pulitzer prize in 1945 for *Essay on Rime*. Fletcher then regarded him highly, but when Shapiro became editor of *Poetry* and rejected some of his poetry, Fletcher was less impressed.

Stallman, Robert Wooster

Professor of English at the University of Connecticut. He was primarily interested in the fiction of James, Crane, and Conrad.

Stringham, Edwin John

Composer, teacher, author, and editor at Juilliard and Queen's College, who set many literary works to music.

Teasdale, Sara

Neurotic poet whose *Love Songs* (1917) received the Pulitzer prize. In her relations with her parents and persons of the opposite sex she shared some of Fletcher's tensions.

Terry, Adolphine Fletcher

John Gould Fletcher's older sister. Adolphine Terry was a graduate of Vassar who was a long and tireless advocate of public education, literacy, human rights, and racial equality. She was a leader of the open-school forces in Little Rock in 1957.

Untermeyer, Louis

Poet, translator, novelist, parodist, biographer, and anthologist. His *Modern American Poetry* (1919) molded the taste of the American public for almost half a century.

Wallace, Jerry

Native of Clarksville who had published a volume of love lyrics while a sophomore at the University of Arkansas. He was rector of Grace Episcopal Church in Tucson, Arizona.

PEOPLE MENTIONED

Aldington, Richard
Imagist poet and husband of Imagist H. D. (Hilda Doolittle), novelist, biographer of Wellington, prolific translator, and in his autobiography, *Life for Life's Sake* (1941), a lively reporter of the literary scene from 1912 to 1940.

Anderson, Margaret
Founded *Little Review* in Chicago in 1914, espoused radical and experimental literature, and in 1920 fined for printing parts of *Ulysses*. She moved to New York and then Paris.

Austin, Mary Hunter
Poet, novelist, playwright, and critic. Austin moved from Carmel to Santa Fe in 1924 to become, for the last decade of her life, a proponent of regional and folk arts and champion of the Indian and Hispanic culture.

Babbitt, Irving
Longtime professor of Romance languages at Harvard. He was a leader of the New Humanism, along with Paul Elmer More and Norman Foerster. His best known work was *Rousseau and Romanticism* (1919).

Barr, Stringfellow
Editor of *The Virginia Quarterly* and critic of the Nashville group, later famous for his great books program at St. John's College at Annapolis.

Bourne, Randolph
Radical journalist, uncompromising in his support of liberty and human welfare, subject of his friend Van Wyck Brooks' *The History of a Literary Radical* (1920).

Braithwaite, William Stanley Beaumont
Poetry editor of *The Boston Evening Transcript* and editor of an annual (1913–29) *Anthology of Magazine Verse and Year Book*. His own poetry, like his anthologies, is not especially distinguished.

Brett, Lady Ashley
Deaf and eccentric English painter, a friend of Mabel Dodge Luhan and D. H. Lawrence in Taos.

Brodzky, Horace
Artist and art critic who accompanied Fletcher on a trip to Europe and broke with him after a quarrel. His work on Gaudier-Brzeska is an early study.

Brown, Edmund R.
Editor of *The Poetry Journal* and owner of the Four Seas Press and Bookstore in Boston.

Cannéll, Skipwith
Expatriate American poet who introduced Fletcher to Pound in Paris in 1913.

Charques, Richard Denis
Novelist, essayist, and historian whose *Contemporary Literature and Social Revolution* contained comments on Russia that Fletcher found interesting.

Clarissa
Clarissa M. Lorenz, Conrad Aiken's second wife.

Collins, Seward
Edited *The American Review* (1933–37). Although he did not print poetry initially, in May, 1934 he included a poetry supplement edited by Allen Tate which published Fletcher's verse.

Constable
Constable and Company, published *The Book of Nature* (1913) and *Some Imagist Poets* (1915, 1916, 1917).

Corbin, Alice
See Henderson.

Crookshank, F. S.
Wimpole Street psychiatrist who cared for Fletcher for several years before and during his confinement to Bedlam from 1932 to 1933.

Cross, Wilbur Lucius
Professor of English and dean of the graduate school at Yale, editor of *The Yale Review* (1911–39), and governor of Connecticut.

Decker, James A.
The owner of The Press of James A. Decker, Prairie City, Illinois, which published young, unknown, and nontraditional poets.

De Voto, Bernard Augustine
Novelist, historian, and critic. He edited the *Saturday Review of Literature* from 1936 to 1938, and from 1935 to 1955 conducted "The Editor's Chair" in *Harper's Magazine*.

Dodie
Delia Kinzinger Greer (Mrs. Scott Greer).

Dole, Nathaniel Haskell
Poet, translator, editor of *Bartlett's Familiar Quotations* (tenth edition), and poetry editor of the *Boston Evening Transcript* after Braithwaite.

Doolittle, Hilda
An early Imagist, married Richard Aldington. Her poetry and fiction were influenced by the classics. She disliked her name and was known as H. D.

Drennan, Mary Fletcher (Mrs. Leonard)
Girlie, Fletcher's favorite sister, graduated from Little Rock High School and attended Vassar a year. She married a professional army officer in 1914 and after his retirement lived on a dairy farm, Verdant Valley, at Monkton, Maryland, where Fletcher visited after his return from England. Before her marriage she was an active suffragette and president of the Little Rock Political Equality League.

Duckworth
London publishing firm.

Dudley, Dorothy
Mrs. Henry B. Harvey, Chicago poet who contributed poetry and reviews to *Poetry*.

Durst, David

Chair of the art department of the University Arkansas. Although he cosponsored Fletcher's visiting professorship in 1949, the two were of differing views on modern art.

Ella

Sister of Daisy.

Ellis, Clough William

English urbanologist and environmentalist who founded the District Improvement Association.

Firuski, Maurice

Owner of the Dunster House Bookshop in Cambridge, Massachusetts.

Foerster, Norman

Professor, critic, and editor at the University of North Carolina and then at Iowa. Foerster was a leader in the New Humanist Movement. As director of the School of Letters at Iowa, he sponsored a program that opened the Ph.D. to candidates publishing a novel or a volume of poems, in lieu of the usual academic dissertation.

Fort, Paul

French poet credited by Amy Lowell with the invention of polyphonic prose, the label a coinage of Fletcher.

Frank, Waldo David

Editor, writer, translator, and interpreter of contemporary civilization, especially that of Latin America. Both his novels and nonfiction earned great critical esteem.

Frost, Frances

Novelist, poet, and journalist whose work usually dealt with New England.

Golding, Douglas

An editor of the *English Review*, founder and editor of *The Tramp*, and founder of the Georgian Group, a branch of the Society for the Protection of Ancient Buildings. His major poetic work was *In the Town: A Book of London Verses* (1916).

Hackett, Frances Goodrich
Actress and scriptwriter for such movies as *The Thin Man, Easter Parade, Father of the Bride,* and *The Diary of Anne Frank.*

Head, Cloyd
Experimental dramatist whose "Grotesques" appeared in *Poetry* IX (October 1916): 1–30.

Henderson, Alice Corbin
Associate editor and co-founder of *Poetry: a Magazine of Verse* until 1916, when she moved to New Mexico and edited *The Turquoise Trail* (1926), an anthology of New Mexican poetry. Her husband was an artist.

Hindus, Maurice
Author of novels and books on Russia.

Hodgson, Ralph
One-legged Yorkshire hobo poet, famous for broadsides and booklets illustrated by Lovat Fraser, known for his love of nature and animal life.

Hook, Sidney
Philosopher, essayist, and apostle of John Dewey's pragmatism.

Hoover, Mary
Third wife of Conrad Aiken.

Hughes-Stanton, Blair
London printmaker and illustrator.

Hulme, Thomas Ernest
Founder of the Poets' Club in London in 1909. Hulme is often considered the founder of the Imagist movement.

Hyde, Lawrence
One-world activist in New Europe Group in London, husband of Lorna.

Hyde, Lorna (Mrs. Lawrence Hyde)
One-world activist in the New Europe Group and religious eccentric who was a friend of Fletcher from 1932 to 1933, during the dissolution of his marriage to Daisy.

Johnson, Charles D.

Head of English department at Ouachita Baptist College, 1916–22; head of Baylor University department of journalism, 1922–29; president Ouachita Baptist College, 1929–33; dean of Blue Mountain College, 1936–38; head of department of sociology at Baylor University from 1939.

Jones, Barbara

Mrs. Lewis Webster Jones.

Jones, Lewis Webster

After coming to the University of Arkansas as president in 1947, built a fine arts center and strongly supported the humanities programs and folklore research.

Kinzinger, Delia ("Dodie")

Mrs. Scott Greer.

Knickerbocker, William S.

Editor of *The Sewanee Review*.

Leach, Bernard

A potter Fletcher described as "an admirable artist and a skilled craftsman," who lived in Devonshire.

Leibowitz, Samuel S.

Famous defense attorney for the defendants in the Scottsboro case. His strong Democratic support of Roosevelt partially blunted allegations of Communist connections by the Alabama establishment.

Lowry, Malcolm

English novelist who traveled to China and Canada before going to Oxford. His most famous work, *Under the Volcano* (1947), is a portrayal of a man's disintegration.

Luhan, Mabel Dodge

Art patron and memoirist whose salons in Italy and New York entertained Gertrude Stein, Bernard Berenson, John Reed, Carl Van Vechten, and a host of others. Later at Taos she was best known for her acquaintance with D. H. Lawrence and her love of the culture of the Pueblo Indians.

Luhan, Tony
Mabel Dodge Luhan's Indian husband.

Mew, Charlotte
Considered by Thomas Hardy the best woman poet of her day. She lived as a recluse in the heart of Bloomsbury.

Monro, Harold
Poet whose verse attempted to merge reality and fancy, founder of The Poetry Bookshop as a London center for poets to meet and read their poetry. He founded *Poetry and Drama*, a quarterly which became *The Chapbook* in 1919.

More, Paul Elmer
After teaching at Bryn Mawr and Harvard, retired to Shelburne, New Hampshire, produced fourteen volumes (Shelburne Essays), and with other works became the leader of the New Humanists. Among the writers he provoked into attack were Mencken, Van Wyck Brooks, Edmund Wilson, Kenneth Burke, and Lewis Mumford.

Morley, Sylvanus Griswold
Harvard friend with whom Fletcher went on an archeological expedition to Mesa Verde in 1907. He was later a distinguished Mayan scholar.

Murry, John Middleton
Editor of *Rhythm*, *The Athenaeum*, and the *Adelphi*. He made critical studies of, among others, Dostoevsky, Keats, Shakespeare, and D. H. Lawrence.

Nash, Paul
Landscape painter and art critic for *The Nation* and *The New Statesman*.

Nicholl, Louise Townsend
An editor at Dutton's.

Nixon, Herman Clarence
Reactionary historian at Tulane and Vanderbilt whose ideas attracted Fletcher and some of the other Agrarians.

Nordau, Max

Hungarian physician whose *Degeneration* (1905) equated the degeneration of contemporary art and literature with the moral imperfections of anarchists, criminals, and lunatics.

O'Brien, Edward Joseph

Wrote a volume of poetry and several plays. He is best known for the annual collections of short stories published from 1915 to 1940 as *The Best Short Stories of 1915*, etc. His religious fanaticism and eccentricities fascinated and sometimes angered Fletcher.

Oppenheim, James

Poet, novelist, essayist, and welfare worker. Oppenheim was described by Untermeyer, the grand arbiter, as producing songs as if translations from the Bible by Whitman in collaboration with Freud. In 1916 he founded *The Seven Arts*, a magazine which printed some of the best poetry of the day before it died of pacifism.

Orage, Alfred Richard

A Fabian friend of Shaw, edited *The New Age* and later *The New English Weekly*.

Parler, Mary Celestia

Folklorist and professor of English at the University of Arkansas, later Mrs. Vance Randolph.

Pearson, Norman Holmes

Anthologist, professor of English, Hawthorne scholar, and collector of manuscripts for the Beinicke Library at Yale.

Pipkin, Charles Wooten

Sociologist, dean of the graduate school at Louisiana State University, and editor of *The Southern Review*.

Poindexter, John

Instructor in English at the University of Arkansas.

Porter, Bern

Research physicist at Berkeley who had a small press, prepared a bibliography, and otherwise befriended Henry Miller. He supported contemporary poets and was editor of *Experiment*.

Pound, Ezra

American poet, critic, editor, and leader of the Imagist movement. Fletcher was introduced to Pound by Skipwith Cannéll in Paris in the summer of 1913. Pound reviewed Fletcher's first volumes in *Poetry*. Fletcher fell under the spell of Amy Lowell, but Pound became a Vorticist so that by the summer of 1917 they had no common interests.

Putnam, James M.

Editor at Macmillan's.

Read, Herbert Edward

Poet, editor, critic, and anthologist.

Reed, John

Harvard-educated radical journalist famous for his description of the Russian revolution, *Ten Days that Shook the World*.

Ridge, Lola

Irish-born poet, painter, model, follower of Whitman and the Imagists.

Riding, Laura

Poet, biographer, and novelist with a politically radical bent. Sometimes compared to Gertrude Stein, Riding claimed that hers was "a jokeless modern mind." She was married to Robert Graves.

Russell, Ada Dwyer (Mrs. Harold)

Companion of Amy Lowell from 1914 to 1925 and publisher of her posthumous *Ballads for Sale* (1927).

Sadleir, Michael

Biographer of Sheridan, bibliographer of Trollope, director of Constable & Co. His name did not appear on the title page of *Gauguin*.

Schorer, Mark

Poet, professor, and author of *William Blake* (1946) and *Sinclair Lewis* (1961).

Skinner, Constance Lindsay

Born in British Columbia, wrote extensively of the Indians of the Northwest and edited the Rivers of America Series.

Speyer, Leonora
Violinist and poet whose *Fiddler's Farewell* won the Pulitzer Prize for poetry in 1926.

Stallman, Robert Wooster
Crane and Conrad scholar, poet and critic.

Stevens, A. Wilbur (Wil)
Professor of English at the University of Washington and coeditor with Edith Dewey Stevens of *Interim*.

Stevens, Wallace
Usually listed among the important poets of the day by Fletcher, although Fletcher had nothing adulatory to say of "Three Travelers Watch a Sunrise," a play which appeared in *Poetry* VIII (July 1916): 163–69.

Storer, Edward
Member of Hulme's dinner club which was sometimes described as the cradle of Imagism, a contributor to *The Egoist*, and apologist for the Imagists.

Syrian, Ajam
Syrian-born New York rug dealer and poet.

Tagore, Rabindranath
Calcutta-born author of prose and poetry who wrote in both Bengali and English. He was awarded the Nobel Prize in 1913.

Taupin, René
French critic whose *L'Influence du symbolisme Français sur la poésie américaine (de 1910 à 1920)* analyzed the influence of the French Symbolists on the poetry of Fletcher.

Temple, Latane
Oil mill owner, poet, painter, and neighbor at Johnswood.

Thompson, William Hale (Big Bill)
Colorful and corrupt Republican mayor of Chicago in the Prohibition era.

Tomlinson, Henry Major
Novelist, critic, and travel writer known for *Galleon's Reach* (1927), a romance of the Orient, as well as for *All our Yesterdays* (1930), an indictment of civilization, and *The Snows of Helicon* (1933).

Underwood, Leon
Sculptor and director of an art school with whom Fletcher took refuge before his hospitalization at Bedlam.

Untermeyer, Louis
Poet, translator, parodist, and influential anthologist for whom Fletcher expressed little admiration.

Wade, John Donald
Fugitive contributor to *I'll Take My Stand*, biographer of Augustus Baldwin Longstreet, editor of *Georgia Review*, and professor of English at the University of Georgia.

Warren, Robert Penn
Writer and poet, first poet laureate of the United States. Fletcher met Warren during the Fugitive period when both contributed to *I'll Take My Stand*. Fletcher broke with Warren over the editorial policies of *The Southern Review*, which Warren edited from 1935 to 1942.

Weaver, Harriet Shaw
With Dora Marsden, founder and editor of *The New Freewoman*, a feminist journal, which broadened its interests to the arts and poetry as *The Egoist*.

Weber, Max
German sociologist and political economist whose *Protestant Ethic and the Spirit of Capitalism* contained religious and ethical ideas which opposed the economic determinism of Marx.

Wheelwright, John Brooks
Rebel Brahmin, heretical Christian, and Trotskyite Marxist, called the best American socialist poet of the 1930s.

Winters, (Arthur) Yvor
Poet and critic, advocated classicism and moral judgment while attacking obscurantism and romanticism. He is best known for *Maule's Curse* (1938).

Winther, Sophus Keith
Novelist, critic, O'Neill scholar, and professor of English at the University of Washington.

Wolf, John Quincy, Jr.
With major interests in the Romantic poets and American folk music, taught at Arkansas College, Batesville, Arkansas, from 1923 to 1937 and at Southwestern (now Rhodes) in Memphis thereafter.

Wolfe, Humbert
A poet skilled in the Swinburnian treatment of old themes. Wolfe is at his best in satirical verse. *Requiem* (1927), his most popular volume, deals with losers and winners in the world.

Yasuda, Kenneth
Japanese-American poet interested in Imagism, relocated at Rohwer.

Zabel, Morton Dauwen
Critic, associate editor of *Poetry*, a director of Yaddo, and professor of English at the University of Chicago.

Zaturenska, Marya (Mrs. Horace Gregory)
Poet, biographer of Christina Rossetti, and, with Horace Gregory, the author of *A History of American Poetry, 1900–1940*.

INDEX

academicism, in literature, 206
Accent, 193
Adams, Henry, 102
Agrarians, 150, 177, 185, 187, 189–90. *See also* Fugitives
Aiken, Clarissa, 124
Aiken, Conrad, 31, 55, 58, 62, 64, 81, 91, 92, 108, 121–25, 128, 146, 171, 180–84, 201, 210, 225, 230, 248; "Illusory Freedom" by, 56; *King Coal* by, 180; *The Preludes* by, 124; *The Soldier* by, 230
Aldington, Richard, 3, 4, 5, 10, 15, 23, 26, 27, 31, 35, 36, 42, 48, 49, 50, 250, 251
American literature, 146, 206
American Monthly, 137
American reading public, 54, 145, 172, 178, 213
American Review, 164
Anderson, Margaret, 17, 29
Anderson, Sherwood, 88, 101, 235–36
anthologies, 15, 178
anthology for children, proposed, 87
Anthology of Southern Poets [unfinished], 240, 241, 247
anticommunism, in American universities, 242
antiindustrialism, 141, 150, 164, 174
antisemitism, JGF and, 155
Apollinaire, Guillaume, 85
Arbuthnot, Malcolm, 16, 21, 22, 23
Arkansas, 163; JGF returns to, 133–34
Armory Show, 85
art and artists, modern, 143
"Athanaeum bunch" (Huxley, Murry, Pound, et al.), 81
Atlantic Monthly, 11, 13, 14, 146
atomic bomb, 219
Auden, Wystan Hugh, 193, 206, 217, 224, 226, 235, 237
Austin, Mary Hunter, 168

Babbitt, George F., 101
Babbitt, Irving, 100
Baker, Howard, 187
Bamboo Broom, tr. H. S. Henderson, 251
Barr, Stringfellow, 177
Bates, Esther, 244

Beard, Charles A., 106–7
Beaumont, 28, 39, 44, 57, 58, 60, 62
Bedlam (sanitarium), 128
Belloc, Hilaire, 44, 171
Benét, Stephen Vincent, 141
Benét, William Rose, 13, 243
Bergen, Henry, 110, 111, 120, 133, 142, 144, 151–61, 166–70
Berkeley (journal), 235
Bettege, Hans, 250
Blake, William, 39, 92, 115, 155, 166, 194, 232–33
Boar's Hill, Oxford, 81
de Bosschère, Jean, 69, 82
Botkin, Benjamin, 138
Bourne, Randolph, 210
Braithwaite, William Stanley, 39, 57, 60
Branch, Anna Hempstead, 201
Brett, Lady Ashley, 169
Brodzky, Harold, 3
Brooks, Van Wyck, 86, 93, 98, 174, 179, 210, 243; influence on JGF, 175
Brown, Albert Gallatin, 136
Brown, Edmund R., 56, 57, 59
Bryant, William Cullen, 30
Buck, Pearl, 146
Byron, George Gordon, Lord, 202

Caldwell, Erskine, 146
Calhoun, John C., 102
Canby, Henry Seidel, 172, 188
Cannéll, Skipwith, 3
capitalism and community, 80
Caravan, 98, 99, 118, 142
Carroll, Gladys Hasty, 146
Carter, Albert Howard, 240
Cash, W. J., 192
Catholicism, 107; in America, 234
Céline, Louis Ferdinand, 209–10
Century Magazine, 40, 93
Charques, Richard Denis, 144–46
Chase, Stuart, 164
Chatto & Windus, 83
Chekhov, Anton, 70
Chesterton, Gilbert Keith, 67
Chicago, 17–18
Civil War, 135–36

Clay, Henry, 102
Cleburne, Patrick R., 154
Coffman, Stanley, *Imagism* by, 251
Collins, Seward, 140, 176
Colum, Padraic, 243, 244
Commonwealth College, 176
Communism, 160, 166–67, 181
Conrad, Joseph, 88
Constable and Company, 11, 42
Contemporaneos, 115
Corbin, Alice. *See* Henderson, Alice Corbin
Coughlin, Father Charles, 192
Cournos, John, 71, 82, 88,
Cowley, Malcolm, 181, 243
craft tradition, 143
Crane, Hart, 117, 141, 196, 202, 224
Crescendo, 211
Criterion, 116
Crookshank, F. S., 127
Cros, Guy Charles, 6
Cross, Wilbur Lucius, 93
Cummings, E. E., 197, 238, 243

Dada, 84–85
Daily Worker, 166
Damon, S. Foster, 112
Dante, Alighieri, 100, 115
Davidson, Donald, 96, 99, 104, 118, 139, 177, 185, 186, 189; and *I'll Take My Stand*, 119; *The Tall Men* by, 99, 190
Day Lewis, Cecil, 224
democracy: JGF's opposition to, 98
De Voto, Bernard, 188–89, 213
Dewey, John, 151
Dial, 89–90
District Improvement Association, 117
Dole, Nathaniel Haskell, 60
Doolittle, Hilda (H. D.), 3, 23, 27, 29, 30, 32, 48, 49, 228, 251
Dos Passos, John, 141, 146, 204
Dostoevsky, Fyodor, 70
Douglas, Helen Gahagan, 157
drama, modern, critique of, 52–53
Dreiser, Theodore, 101, 151, 236
Dryden, John, 223
Duchamp, Marcel, 85
Durst, David, 246

Eastman, Max, 162
Eberhart, Richard, 117
Eddington, Arthur Stanley, 154
Egoist, 10, 12, 25, 71; JGF's history of, 108–10

Ehrenberg, Ilya, 166
Eliot, T. S., 19, 29, 56, 57, 63, 71, 81, 83, 86, 88, 103, 105, 114, 116, 135, 138, 157, 160, 175, 196, 201, 204–5, 207, 208, 217, 225, 236, 239, 246; Nobel prize, 238; religious views, JGF critique of, 161–62, 208, 222–23. WORKS: *Four Quartets*, 207, 225, 239; "The Love Song of J. Alfred Prufrock," 19; *The Sacred Wood*, 105; *The Use of Poetry*, 157; "The Waste Land," 92
Ellis, Clough William, 117
Ellis, Havelock, 105, 153
Emerson, Ralph Waldo, 101
Encyclopedia Britannica, 230
English Review, 9
Epigrams, 9

Faber & Gwyer, 103
Fabian Society, 158
Farrell, James T., 234
Faulkner, William, 117, 141, 146; *Sanctuary* by, 122
Faure, Elie, 88
Fenollosa, Ernest, 250
Ferrer, José, 244
Fêtes Quotidiennes, 6
Ficke, Arthur Davison, 29
Firuski, Maurice, 93
Fletcher, Charlie May Simon. *See* Simon, Charlie May
Fletcher, Florence (Daisy) Emily Arbuthnot, 15, 20, 26, 33, 123, 124, 125, 126, 184; alimony, 231; divorce from Malcolm Arbuthnot, 20–23, 27; JGF describes marriage to, 123–27; JGF describes relationship with, 20; takes JGF's money, 181; wedding to JGF postponed, 43
Fletcher, John Gould, affair with Lorna Hyde, 182–84; aim of his writing, 78, 174; artifice and emotion in poetry, 37–39, 61, 76, 84; assessment of his own work, 198–99, 210–11, 236; autobiographical sketch, 45–48; breakdown, in 1932, 128–32, in 1944, 214, 216; chronology of his works, 215; death of, 252; depression, 62, 154; development as poet, 194; dream, 36–37; economic theories, 80–81; embraces regionalism, 174–75; finances, 18, 20, 25, 26, 28–29, 42, 69, 117, 118, 142, 158, 167, 175, 178, 212, 214, 217, 231; God, 106, 208; idea of

a "better world," 79–81; Imagist, 47, 108, 194; influences, 6, 215; isolation in Arkansas, 174, 247; loves his country, 16; marriage, views on, 222; method of writing, 5; misgivings about marriage to Daisy, 20–23; music and poetry, 6; Negroes, 150, 164–65; poetry reflects personality, 78; primitivism, 61; religious note in writing, 94–95; religious views, 94, 106, 159, 208, 234; repudiates Imagism, 50; return to Arkansas, 133; sectionalism, 154; Southerner, 154; subconscious, 76; teaching, 133, 151, 155, 185, 186, 189–90, 200, 224, 227, 238, 240, 242, 246. WORKS: "Apology for Solitude," 117; *Arkansas*, 192, 230; "Armies," 61–62; "August 1940," 194–95; *Black Rock*, 141, 210, 211; "Blue Symphony," 10, 13, 198; *Branches of Adam*, 97, 99, 211; *Breakers and Granite*, 210; "Builders of the Bridge," 212; *Burning Mountain*, 226, 231; "Caged Eagle," 198; "Chicago," 31; "Christmas at Sixty," 230; "Clipper-Ships," 31; "Contemporary English Poets," 62; "Divine Tragedy," 13; *Dominant City*, 1, 2; "Down the Mississippi," 199; "Ebb-Tide," 198–99; "Echoes from Arkansas," 141; "Elegy on Tintern Abbey," 199; Elements, 65, 76, 77, 227–28; "Faith," 198; "Gateways," 227; "Ghosts," 31; *Goblins and Pagodas*, 32, 34, 42, 59, 76; "The Grand Canyon of the Colorado," 198, 199; "In the Open Air," 198; *Irradiations*, 2, 3, 5, 6, 10, 11, 13, 18, 34, 59, 61, 76, 108, 114 194, 203; *Japanese Prints*, 78, 198, 211, 250; *King's Country*, 240; *Life Is My Song*, 186, 211; "Lincoln," 61, 108, 199; "The Lofty House," 178; "Lost Corner," 199; "Mexican Quarter," 199; "A New Heaven," 228; "1939," 209, 219, 226; "The Old South," 31; *Parables*, 91, 211; plays, unnamed, 207; "Poppies," 31; *Preludes and Symphonies*, 210; "Red Harvest," 227; "Red Poppies," 28; "Room on the Highway," 236; "Sea Symphony," 9, 10, 11, 13; *Selected Poems*, 191, 194, 211; "Skyscrapers," 199; *South Star*, 194; *Symphonies*, 61, 91, 194, 198; *The Tree of Life*, 76, 77, 78, 108, 198, 210; *XXIV Elegies*, 178, 210, 245; *The Two Frontiers*, 174, 211; "Unwinged Victory," 141; "The Wedding Ring," 198, 199;

"Western Dawn," 141; "White Symphony," 198; *Winged Victory*, 137
Flint, F. S., 48, 49, 82, 84, 89, 251; and Poetry Club, 23
Foerster, Norman, 187
form in art, 138
Forrest, Nathan Bedford, 136
Forster, E. M., 243, 244
Fort, Paul, 8, 12, 13
France, Anatole, 69
Frank, Waldo David, 210
Freeman, 93
French as language for poetry, 89
Frost, Frances, 244
Frost, Robert, 56, 97, 178, 188–89
Fugitives anthology, 97, 104, 139

Gannet, Lewis, 186
Gauguin, Paul: JGF's book on, 69
Gibson, Wilfred, 65
Gide, André, 141
Gill, Eric, 143
Gleizes, 85
Goethe, Johann Wolfgang von, 202
Golding, Douglas, 82
Gordon, Kenneth, 219
de Gourmont, Remy, 89
Goya, Francisco de, 193
Graves, Robert, 95–96
graves opened (Napoleon, Edward I, Charles I), 43
Gray, Thomas, 141
Gray Jackets, 150–51
Great Depression, 134
Greenslet, Ferris, 18, 31, 93
Greer, Scott A., 201–3, 209, 212, 216, 217, 218, 221, 233, 236 240; JGF's heir, 220; poems, 218
Gregory, Horace, 192, 196, 204–5, 210, 224, 245
Guenon, René, 103
Guest, Edgar, 188

Hackett, Frances Goodrich, 243
haiku, 250
Hardy, Thomas, 88, 136, 194, 229
Haun, Frederic Eugene, 208, 214, 227; as JGF's literary biographer, 214–15
Hay, Sara Henderson. *See* Holden
Head, Cloyd S., 52,
Hearn, Lafcadio, 250
Hegel, Georg W. F., 162
Heine, Heinrich, 179

Hemingway, Ernest, 110, 141, 146
Henderson, Alice Corbin, 17, 19, 29, 31, 59, 78
Hicks, Granville, 152, 158
Hillyer, Robert 243, 246
Hindus, Maurice, 152
Hitler, Adolf, 144–45
Hodgson, Ralph, 199
Holden, Raymond and Sara Henderson Hay, 229
Hook, Sidney, 151
Houghton Mifflin, 24
Hound and Horn, 137
Hueffer, Ford Maddox, 14, 88, 89
Hughes, Glenn, 107, 108
Hughes-Stanton, Blair, 135
Hulme, Thomas Ernest, 23, 24
Humanism, 118
Hyde, Lorna, 122–23, 126, 128, 182–85

I'll Take My Stand 118–19
Imagism and the Imagists, 2–5, 30, 35, 50, 51, 88, 108, 215, 249, 250, 251–52
Imagist Anthology, 7, 10, 14, 23, 35–36, 49, 63
Inge, William Ralph, 154
Isherwood, Christopher, 243

Jackson, T. J., 136
James, Henry, 67, 70, 88
Jammes, François, 8, 13
Jarrell, Randall, 187
Jeffers, Robinson, 103, 188, 237
Jefferson, Thomas, 102
Johnson, Charles D., 186
Johnson, Hugh, 157
Jones, Barbara, 246
Jones, Lewis Webster, 241
Jones, Robert Demond, 236
Joyce, James, 88, 91, 107, 175; *Ulysses* by, 91

Kansas City, Missouri, University of, 186–90
Kenyon Review, 213
Kinzinger, Delia (Dodie), 212
Kitchener, Lord, 41
Kreymborg, Alfred, 98, 243
Kroll, Leon, 243

LaFollette, Robert, 171
Lanier, Sidney, 247
Lawrence, D. H., 19, 26, 65, 82, 120–21, 141, 162, 168, 171, 222, 232–33; *Lady Chatterley's Lover* by, 111
Lawrence, Frieda, 169, 170

Leach, Bernard, 135
Lechlitner, Ruth, 207
Lee, Robert E., 136
Leibowitz, Samuel S., 148, 151
Lewis, James Franklin, 200, 205, 211, 232; science and, 200–201
Library of Congress, 238, 241, 246, 249
Lindsay, Vachel, 29, 32, 38, 44, 81, 82
Linscott, Robert Newton, 60, 66–70, 74–77, 78, 90, 245, 249
literary "schools," 42
literary societies, 229
Little Review, 17
London, literary scene, 4, 81, 83
London Mercury, clique, 81
Louis XVI, 44
Lowell, Amy, 2, 5, 7, 10–14, 17, 18, 23, 27, 28–32, 37, 38, 40–51, 63, 64, 69, 75, 82, 86, 112–14, 207–8, 228, 250, 252; article by JGF on, 64; Imagist intrigue, 3, 33; JGF account of relationship with, 33, 112–14; JGF assessment of her personality, 207. WORKS: critique by JGF, 6–9, 12–14, 208; "The Shadow," 207; *Six French Poets*, 108; *Violin Poems*, 31
Lowell, Robert, 234, 237, 238, 241, 247
Lowry, Malcolm, 124
Luhan, Mabel Dodge, 168–70
Luhan, Tony, 168

McColl, D. S., 38
MacDowell, Mrs. Edward, 243, 244
MacDowell Colony, 184, 194
MacLeish, Archibald, 117, 213, 224, 243
MacLeod, Fiona, 13
MacNiece, Frederick Lewis, 224
magazines, literary, American, 137, 213. *See also* specific titles
Mann, Thomas, 141, 180, 244
Marin, John, 243
Marsden, Dora, 109
Marxism, 151–52, 162
Masefield, John, 81, 241
Masters, Edgar Lee, 17, 56, 146; JGF critique of works by, 203
Matthiessen, F. O., 223
Maury, Matthew Fontaine, 102
Melville, Herman, 101, 102
Mencken, H. L., 98, 146, 176, 192
Metzinger, Jean, 85
Mew, Charlotte, 87
Millay, Edna St. Vincent, 100, 196; recipient of Pulitzer Prize, 92–93

Millburn, George, 146
Milton, John, 203
Miner, Earl, 250, 251
modern art, critique of, 143, 157
Modern Monthly, 137
Monro, Harold, 42, 87, 126
Monroe, Harriet, 3, 5, 6, 9, 11, 17, 18, 19, 24, 28, 30, 32, 37, 52, 63, 72, 78, 95, 229, 248, 252; editor of *Poetry*, 1
Moore, Marianne, 31, 224, 243
Moore, Merrill, 104, 197, 243
More, Paul Elmer, 118
Morley, Silvanus Griswold, 135, 168
Moss, Howard, 206
Mumford, Lewis, 98, 100, 116, 136, 140, 164; *The Golden Day* by, 101; *Sticks and Stones* by, 102
Murphy, John J. A., 228
Murry, John Middleton, 120–21, 156

Nash, Paul, 122, 231
Nation, 137, 147, 164–65
National Institute of Arts and Letters: JGF induction, 242
Negroes, 147–51, 165
New Age, dawning of, 81
New Age, The, 23
"New America" proposal, 51
New Deal, 144, 146–47, 157, 163, 166–68, 171, 175
New Directions, 206
New Europe, 128
New Freewoman, 3, 4, 5. See also *Egoist*
New Masses, 166, 168
New Poetry, 40, 59, 252
New Republic, 18, 28, 98
New Mexico Quarterly, 175, 213
New York City, 16, 153
Nicholl, Louise Townsend, 245
Nichols, Robert M. B., 81
Niebuhr, Reinhold, 222
Nietzsche, Friedrich, 106, 233–34
Nixon, Herman Clarence, 185
Nobel prize nominee, 180
Noguchi, Yone, 250
Nordau Max, 172, 226
Norris, George, 171

O'Brien, Edward Joseph, 124
O'Keeffe, Georgia, 243, 245
Olmstead, Frederick, 244
O'Neill, Eugene, 141, 146
Oppenheim, James, 56, 210

Orage, Alfred Richard, 171
Others, 44
Owsley, Frank, 135, 139, 149, 154, 176, 177, 185; "The Five Pillars of Agrarianism" by, 176
Ozark Folklore Society, 246

Paine, Thomas, 232
Parler, Mary Celestia, 246
Pearce, Thomas Matthews, 191
Pearson, Norman Holmes, 193, 245
Pender, R. Herdman, 109
Perkins, Frances, 157
Perkins, Max, 180
Petrarch, Francesco, 39
Picabia, Francis, 84
Picasso, Pablo, 85
Pipkin, Charles Wooten, 176
Poe, Edgar Allan, 67
poetry, publishing, 206
poetry, his own product, 215, 236
Poetry: A Magazine of Verse, 1, 12, 13, 14, 19, 25, 32, 54–55, 73, 201, 241; prizes, 29, 32, 73, 223
Poetry and Drama, 9, 14, 26
Poetry Club (London), 23–24
poetry societies, 229–30
Poets by the Poets, 114–15
Poindexter, John, 246
"polyphonic" poetry, 25, 37–39
Pope, Alexander, 202
Porter, Bern, 232, 236
Pound, Ezra, 1, 5, 7, 9, 12, 13, 15, 19, 24, 25–26, 27, 29, 30, 44, 57, 71, 81, 88, 89, 171, 217, 226, 246, 248, 249, 250, 251; and "Imagisme," 2, 3, 4, 33; JGF compares to boa constrictor, 71; as mentor, 162; as translator, 89; *Pisan Cantos* by, 248; *Ripostes* by, 24, 30
Proust, Marcel, 141
Pulitzer Prize, 93, 191
Putnam, James M., 244, 245

Quinn, Kerker, 193

Ransom, John Crowe, 99–100, 104, 177, 187, 196, 206, 214
Rawlings, Marjorie Kinnan, 146, 191
Read, Herbert Edward, 142, 171; *Art Now* by, 156
reading in America, 172–73, 213
Regional Art Show, 165
regionalism, 122, 138, 165, 174, 176

Regionalism, Virginia Conference on, 122, 174
Richards, I. A., 171
Richardson, Dorothy, 88
Richardson, Henry Hobson, 102
Ridge, Lola, 202
Riding, Laura, 104
Robinson, Edward Arlington, 97, 146, 178, 202, 214, 244
Roethke, Theodore, 241
Romanticism and Realism, 141–42
Rosenfeld, Paul, 98, 210
Rukeyser, Muriel, 202, 207
Russell, Ada Dwyer, 31
Russell, George (AE), 179

Sacco and Vanzetti, 98, 147, 202
Sadleir, Michael, 11
Sandburg, Carl, 17, 29, 146, 189, 243
Sanders, Gerald DeWitt, 183, 185, 195, 198, 204
Santa Fe, 139
Saturday Review, 172, 226
Saturday Evening Post, 146
Schevill, James, 232, 235
Schorer, Mark, 232–33
Schwartz, Delmore, 223
Scott, Winfield Townley, 241
Scottsboro Trials: JGF reaction to, 147–54, 165
Scribners', 146
sectionalism, 101
Seldes, Gilbert, 189
Shafer, Robert, 118
Shaflen, Robert, 245
Shakespeare, William, 141
Shaler, Nathaniel Southgate, 102
Shanafelt, Clarice, 31, 44
Shapiro, Karl, 223, 225–26, 237, 246; *Bibliography of Modern Prosody* by, 247
Shelley, Percy B., 200
Simon, Charlie May, 242, 252; marital difficulties, 221; marries JGF, 182; teaching, 249
Sinclair, May, 88
Sinclair, Upton, 171
Sitwell, Edith, 241
Skinner, Constance Lindsay, 29, 32
Smith, Joseph, 192
socialism, 201
Some Imagist Poets, 26. See also *Imagist Anthology*
sonnet, 39

South, 96–97, 192
Southern Poets, 228
Southern Review, 185, 187, 189–90
Southern Tenant Farmers Union, 185
Southwest Review, 175, 190
Space, 175
Spectrist School, 41
Spencer, Theodore, 223
Spender, Stephen, 144, 224, 238, 247
Speyer, Leonora, 86
Squire, J. C.: center of "Squire Bunch" at *London Mercury*, 82
Stafford, Jean, 235
Stallman, Robert W., 239
Stein, Gertrude, 98, 160 n., 171
Stephens, Alexander, 136
Stevens, A. Wilbur, 219
Stevens, Wallace, 53, 201, 224, 237, 238; "Peter Quince" by, 29
Stieglitz, Alfred, 85
Stravinsky, Igor, 243
Stringham, Edwin John, 194
Syrian, Ajam, 32

Tagore, Rabindranath, 37, 38
Tate, Allen, 104, 139, 177, 206, 236, 241, 243
Taupin, René, 215
Teasdale, Sara, 86, 93
technique *vs* innovation in poetry, 88–89
Temple, Latané, 246
Tennyson, Alfred, 105, 242
Terry, Adolphine Fletcher (sister of JGF), 24, 126, 155
Thompson, William Hale (Big Bill), 101
Thoreau, Henry David, 101
Torrence, Ridgely, 243, 244
291 (magazine), 85

Underwood, Leon, 129–33
University Review, 212
Untermeyer, Jean Starr, 244–45
Untermeyer, Louis, 56, 178, 210, 243
Upward, Allen, "Scented Leaves from a Chinese Jar" by, 252

Vance, Margaret, 245
Van Doren, Carl, 93
van Gogh, Vincent, 221
vers libre, 1
Virginia Conference on Regionalism, 122
Virginia Quarterly Review, 176, 177
visionary artists, 70–71

Wade, John Donald, 177
Waley, Arthur, 252
Wallace, Henry A., 157
Wallace, Jerry, 252
Waln, Nora, 146
Walpole, Horace, 141
war poems, 19, 59, 69, 77
Warren, Robert Penn, 104, 176, 177, 206, 239
Wasserman, Jakop, 88, 141
Waters, Frank, 235
Weaver, Harriet Shaw, 109
Wells, Herbert George, 220
Wescott, Glenway, 243
Westminster Quarterly, 175
Whitman, Walt, 67, 101, 105, 203, 233
Whitworth, Geoffrey, 83
Williams, William Carlos, 44, 45, 197, 224, 237, 238
Wilson, Woodrow, 67, 102

Winters, Yvor, 206
Winther, Sophus Keith, 219
Wolfe, Thomas, 118, 218
women in politics, 74
Woodin, William H., 157
Wordsworth, William, 200, 202
World War I, 26, 40–41, 42–43, 57, 60–61, 62–64, 65–68, 74, 77, 79, 158–59
World War II, 204; end of, 219–20; in Arkansas, 197
Wright, Frank Lloyd, 138, 236
Wylie, Elinor, 196

Yaddo, 178
Yasuda, Kenneth, 250, 251
Yeats, William Butler, 180, 201, 232

Zabel, Morton, 192
Zaturenska, Marya, 242, 245
Zeppelins, 40